STUDY COMMENTARY
ON THE OLD TESTAMENT

STUDY COMMENTARY
ON THE OLD TESTAMENT

RICHARD J. ALLEN

Covenant Communications, Inc.

The Lord Fulfilleth All His Words by Clark Kelley Price © Intellectual Reserve, Inc. Courtesy of the Museum of Church History and Art.

Cover design copyright © 2013 by Covenant Communications, Inc.

Published by Covenant Communications, Inc.
American Fork, Utah

Copyright © 2013 by Richard J. Allen
All rights reserved. No part of this book may be reproduced in any format or in any medium without the written permission of the publisher, Covenant Communications, Inc., P.O. Box 416, American Fork, UT 84003. This work is not an official publication of The Church of Jesus Christ of Latter-day Saints. The views expressed within this work are the sole responsibility of the author and do not necessarily reflect the position of The Church of Jesus Christ of Latter-day Saints, Covenant Communications, Inc., or any other entity.

Printed in the United States of America
First Printing: October 2013

19 18 17 16 15 14 13   10 9 8 7 6 5 4 3 2 1

ISBN 978-1-62108-538-6

CONTENTS

GETTING STARTED

Thou shalt also be a crown of glory in the hand of the LORD, and a royal diadem in the hand of thy God. (Isaiah 62:3)

WHAT WOULD YOU SAY IF a friend asked you, "Why should we focus on the Old Testament? Hasn't that ancient text been supplanted by the later word of God?"

Perhaps you would think of the Savior's words given at the beginning of His earthly ministry: "It is written, Man shall not live by bread alone, but by every word that proceedeth out of the mouth of God" (Matthew 4:4, quoting Deuteronomy 8:3). Perhaps you would consider with your friend the implication of the word "every"—which signifies a blessing of truth flowing to us from God by means of an enduring process, a continuous unfolding and renewing.

You and your friend see eye to eye about the meaning of the word *testament*. It means "covenant"—a sacred agreement between God and His children, empowered by the principles and promises of His plan of salvation and redemption. But is that an old plan? Or is it a new plan? Or is the plan of God eternal, applied across the various dispensations of time according to the love of God and the needs of His people? If your answer is "eternal," then you have confirmed that the sacred gospel covenant clearly encompasses every word of God, throughout all generations: the Old Testament, the New Testament, the Book of Mormon, and the Doctrine and Covenants—plus the words of the living prophets. No wonder the Savior reminded us that we are to live "by every word that proceedeth out of the mouth of God."

We have been blessed, in our day, with a restoration of His word as it was originally given to the first generations of His children—before it was partially lost in the process of compilation over the years. The books of Moses and Abraham in the Pearl of Great Price—brought forth through the inspired ministry of the Prophet Joseph Smith—have shed new light on the Old Testament, showing that it was indeed the beginning of the "Eternal Testament" of God. The Old Testament thus continues to have powerful relevance for our time, being renewed and restored as a confirmation of the eternal nature of the holy covenant.

In continuing your dialogue with your friend, you can agree that every individual has an opportunity to find in the Old Testament a source of daily strength and inspiration for honoring and keeping our personal covenants with God. After all, the eternal covenant is also our *personal* covenant, our individual agreement to live daily in obedience to His gospel plan.

Some years ago a young man, shortly after his marriage to a lovely young bride, requested that his widower father give him a special father's blessing. Let us turn to his account of what happened next—and to a consideration of how the outcome suggests a simple but appealing formula for how to learn from the Old Testament in new and inspiring ways:

My father was honored to respond to my request. He prepared himself during a long period of fasting and prayer and then bestowed upon my head a wonderful blessing containing many words of personal encouragement and counsel, somewhat in the spirit of Lehi's famous dream. At the conclusion of the blessing, he stated something that can be readily shared with others because of its universal application: "And now, my beloved son, as you journey forth into the uncertain world, reach up your hands to the lap of God. And if you will do this He will lead you, He will guide you, save and exalt you in the eternal worlds."

This touching image of reaching up one's hands to the lap of God came to my father in a special way. He told me that my request to receive this blessing had caused him much concern and effort, for he wanted to be in tune with the Spirit in order to carry out this task well. In praying about it one night, he received into his mind the image of a child kneeling before God and reaching his hands up to the lap of God in humility and devotion, as if to seek guidance and support. This image was then carried into the blessing as the seal of counsel. I have pondered countless times over the years how well this image reflects a true spirit of meekness and humility so essential to devoted discipleship and spiritual learning.

To reach one's hands up to the lap of a loving God is a manifestation of thanks given, humility expressed, unity sought, and blessings requested. In return, the Lord reaches down with His loving hand to grasp our own and begin the process of fatherly guidance. What did the resurrected Lord say to his humble disciple Thomas? "Reach hither thy finger, and behold my hands; and reach hither thy hand, and thrust it into my side: and be not faithless, but believing" (John 20:27). What did the Lord of the Restoration say to His disciple Thomas B. Marsh? "Be thou humble; and the Lord thy God shall lead thee by the hand, and give thee answer to thy prayers" (D&C 112:10).

The image of the hand in motion is a lively tool for organizing our process of learning in new ways. The action of reaching up our hand to the Lord and receiving His extended hand in return is the emblem of bonding love between Father and child, between Guide and learner, between Redeemer and the redeemed. Michelangelo made magnificent use of such an image in his *Creation of Adam* panel preserved on the ceiling of the Sistine Chapel in Rome. The observer is inspired in viewing the divine hand of the Creator reaching down to touch the upward-reaching hand of Adam, endowing him with life and vitality as a son of God.

In our current application, the outreaching hand is a reminder of how all of us can take steps to live by every word of God—including the truths served to us on the tablets of the Old Testament, enriched by the savory delights of the restored wisdom provided to us in the Pearl of Great Price. After all, the hand is an instrument of action. We can reach into the pages of the Old Testament and discover the elements of the eternal plan of salvation and redemption as they apply currently to ourselves, our family members, and our fellow Saints. We can reach up our hands to the Lord in prayer, asking for the guidance of the Spirit to unfold to our minds and hearts the key lessons of truth contained in the word of God. We can reach into our own souls and find there the intensity of purpose to apply those lessons in productive ways. And we can reach out to others with our refreshing witness of good things of the gospel of Jesus Christ, thus planting in their hearts the seeds of encouragement and joy.

Through sincere outreach, the Old Testament flows unto us as a healing balm from the Almighty. By study and faith, we can drink from the refreshing well of truth that awaits us in this priceless source of insight and wisdom:

> Yea, even the wonders of eternity shall they know, and things to come will I show them, even the things of many generations.
>
> And their wisdom shall be great, and their understanding reach to heaven; . . .
>
> For by my Spirit will I enlighten them, and by my power will I make known unto them the secrets of my will—yea, even those things which eye has not seen, nor ear heard, nor yet entered into the heart of man. (D&C 76:8–10)

In support of this promise, the present book aspires to build upon the foundation of the scriptures, foster unique ways to apply the lessons of the Old Testament, and spark creative thought leading to righteous covenant action. I sincerely hope that this approach will strengthen faith, bolster testimonies, and bring us all closer to meriting the promise of heaven: "Thou shalt also be a crown of glory in the hand of the Lord, and a royal diadem in the hand of thy God" (Isaiah 62:3).

The book does not attempt to cover the Old Testament in its entirety but rather focuses on select scriptural passages in accord with the reading assignments of the Gospel Doctrine curriculum of the Church. The flow of the book unfolds in forty-eight chapters designed to enhance the readers' understanding of the passages emphasized by Church leaders for study. Provided in the book is an abundant inventory of real-life illustrations about how the word of God enriches and empowers our lives. Also included is a panorama of creative scenes about how Old Testament personalities and their modern followers might well have thought, reasoned, and acted during scripture-based events. The objective of using this approach is to encourage readers to ponder, organize, and share their own personal stories and illustrations that confirm the everlasting truths of the gospel of Jesus Christ.

Sincere thanks is expressed to my wife, Carol Lynn, for her devoted support throughout the preparation of the book and to the staff at Covenant Communications for their expert involvement in bringing the finished book into the marketplace.

The Author

CHAPTER ONE

MOSES ON THE MOUNT:
WHAT WE LEARN AT THE SUMMIT

GOSPEL DOCTRINE READING ASSIGNMENT: MOSES 1

The words of God, which he spake unto Moses at a time when Moses was
caught up into an exceedingly high mountain. (Moses 1:1)

THE MISSING PREFACE

MOSES 1 IS THE LORD's preface to the Old Testament. It was restored to the biblical account by the Prophet Joseph Smith as part of his inspired translation of the Bible. In June 1830, the Prophet wrote: "Amid all the trials and tribulations we had to wade through, the Lord who well knew our infantile and delicate situation, vouchsafed for us a supply of strength, and granted us 'line upon line of knowledge—here a little and there a little,' of which the following [Moses 1] was a precious morsel" (*History of the Church* 1:98).

This "precious morsel" of divine truth is the introduction to the account of the wonders of the Creation and the unfolding of the history of God's children upon the earth. The word "preface" derives from a Latin source meaning, "a saying beforehand." It is thus the Lord's initial word of enlightenment for the scriptural treasure that lies before us as we read the inspired words of the prophets down through the ages. We can thank the Lord for restoring these priceless truths in the latter days for our enrichment and joy.

WHAT ARE THE LESSONS WE CAN LEARN FROM MOSES 1?

1. You are a child of God, created in His image.

> And God spake unto Moses, saying: Behold, I am the Lord God Almighty, and Endless is my name;
> for I am without beginning of days or end of years; and is not this endless?

And, behold, thou art my son; . . .
Thou art after the similitude of mine Only Begotten.
(Moses 1:3–4, 16)

This eternal truth about man's divine origin is central to the plan of happiness and exaltation. However, at times, world thinkers will deny the reality of the Creator. Ponder the following account about a question presented to an institute instructor:

> "Hey, Dan. How are things going?" asked the friendly teacher.
>
> The student hesitated for a moment and then spoke in concerned tones. "Well, in the reading assignment for my college physics class, I learned that the world-famous physicist Stephen Hawking said something like it's not necessary to believe in God, and that science takes care of everything."
>
> The teacher smiled and put his hand on Dan's shoulder. "Yes, Stephen Hawking did come to that conclusion at the end of his book *The Grand Design*, but many other noted scientists like Israeli physicist Gerald L. Schroeder are strong believers in God as Creator of the universe."

> **When and where did the events in Moses 1 occur?**
>
> The first chapter of Moses begins after Moses fled to the land of Midian (see Exodus 2:11–15; Exodus 3), but prior to the Exodus from Egypt—"for thou shalt deliver my people from bondage" (Moses 1:26). The name of the mountain in Moses 1 "shall not be known among the children of men" (Moses 1:42). According to traditional dating, Moses was born around 1627 BC; the Exodus took place around 1547 BC, when Moses was 80 years old; Moses died (was translated) around 1507 BC.

> Dan smiled with relief. His teacher continued, "When you want to have confirmation about the Lord as Creator, read the scriptures and then pray, asking Heavenly Father for the answer—and He will put your mind and heart at ease through His Spirit. My mission president was a noted scientist. I remember he sometimes reminded his listeners at Church about his high academic stature—not to boast, mind you—to assure them that if the Church and its teachings were in any way suspect, he would have long ago detected that and exposed it. However, such was not the case, he would emphasize, testifying that the gospel was not only logically true but confirmed through the power of the Holy Ghost. Dan, remember what the Lord said to Moses on the mount: 'Thou art my son' [Moses 1:4]. 'And worlds without number have I created' [Moses 1:33]. I can tell you that I know you are also a son of God and that He will guide you every day if you follow His word."
>
> With that, the teacher bid Dan farewell and watched the young man walk briskly away with a confident smile.

Pondering: How does the knowledge that you are a son or daughter of God inspire you to move forward with courage and conviction to live up to your destiny? (See Romans 8:16–17 on our being "children of God" and "joint-heirs with Christ"; see also Psalm 82:6; John 10:34; D&C 76:20–24, 58.)

2. It is the glory of the Lord and the power of His Spirit that will lift you up.

> And the presence of God withdrew from Moses, that his glory was not upon Moses; and Moses was left unto himself. And as he was left unto himself, he fell unto the earth.
>
> And it came to pass that it was for the space of many hours before Moses did again receive his natural strength like unto man; and he said unto himself: Now, for this cause I know that man is nothing, which thing I never had supposed. (Moses 1:9–10; see also verse 11)

Moses had been raised as a prince in Egypt. He understood the power of worldly thrones. But now, away from his privileged roots, he was in dialogue with the Supreme Being, the most powerful force of all. When the Lord removed His glory from Moses, He was teaching the newly called prophet an unforgettable lesson. Moses realized that man, on his own, "is nothing," which thing he "never had supposed." He was learning what King Benjamin would teach his people many centuries later: "Always retain in remembrance, the greatness of God, and your own nothingness, and his goodness and long-suffering towards you" (Mosiah 4:11).

Pondering: How do the assurance of the glory and the love of the Lord help offset a sense of your own inadequacy, your own infancy as a child of God aspiring to become like your Father in Heaven? (See also D&C 76:69–70)

3. The most inspiring and motivating truth available is to learn that the Lord's purpose includes your immortality and eternal life.

"For behold, this is my work and my glory—to bring to pass the immortality and eternal life of man" (Moses 1:39).

You are not an accident in the course of human history. You are not a flash in the pan of existence. You are not a statistic among the generations of human kind. Instead, you are at the heart of God's plan for mankind. You are God's work and glory. You are the reason for the Creation and the focus of the Creator's outreach and love. His mercy and light are extended to you—personally. You and your brothers and sisters—all the sons and daughters of God—are the essence of the universe. The purpose for mortal life is to prepare you to return to your heavenly home through obedience and the power of the Atonement of Jesus Christ.

Pondering: How does the knowledge that the Lord's work and glory are centered on your personal salvation and exaltation help you to rise in faith and obedience to His gospel plan? (See also D&C 18:10–13)

4. It is through the power of the Lord that you can withstand the temptations of Satan.

And it came to pass that Moses looked upon Satan and said: Who art thou? For behold, I am a son of God, in the similitude of his Only Begotten; and where is thy glory, that I should worship thee?

Calling upon God, he received strength, and he commanded, saying: Depart from me, Satan, for this one God only will I worship, which is the God of glory. (Moses 1:13, 20)

Contemplate the words of inspiration given by the Lord to the Prophet Joseph Smith on January 2, 1831, just six months after Moses 1 had been revealed: "For I have a great work laid up in store, for Israel shall be saved, and I will lead them whithersoever I will, and no power shall stay my hand" (D&C 38:33). Satan cannot prevail over the faithful Saints of the Lord as they go forward in the strength of the Lord to complete their errand of service.

> ### What is the significance of mountains in the scriptures?
>
> - Enoch beheld the Lord on "mount Simeon" (Moses 7:2–3).
> - Moses was taught by the Lord on the mountain (see Moses 1) and later on Sinai (see Exodus 19–20; 24–27).
> - Isaiah beheld the gathering of the Saints to "the mountain of the Lord's house" in the latter days (Isaiah 2:2–3).
> - Jesus Christ was drawn by the Spirit "into an exceeding high mountain" (JST, Matthew 4:8) where He repelled the temptations of Satan (see Matthew 4). Jesus later "went up into a mountain" (Matthew 5:1) to deliver the Sermon on the Mount. He brought Peter, James, and John to "an high mountain" of transfiguration (Matthew 17:1). The resurrected Lord commissioned His disciples on "a mountain" in Galilee to carry the gospel to all nations of the earth (Matthew 28:16, 19–20).
> - Joseph Smith likened the kingdom of God unto "a great mountain" that will "fill the whole earth" (D&C 109:72; compare Daniel 2:35, 45; D&C 65:2).

Pondering: How does the courageous action of Moses encourage you to pray humbly to God, asking that His strength and glory will give you the power to dispel the influences of evil in your life? (Compare also Numbers 11:29; Matthew 4:4, 10; Alma 20:4; 26:12; Helaman 5:12)

5. Like Moses, you have a calling from the Lord—multiple callings to grow and to bless the lives of others as part of your divine destiny.

What is the connection between Moses and Joseph Smith?

On the mount, the Lord promised Moses: "And in a day when the children of men shall esteem my words as naught and take many of them from the book which thou shalt write, behold, I will raise up another like unto thee [i.e., Joseph Smith]; and they shall be had again among the children of men—among as many as shall believe" (Moses 1:41). What was spoken to Moses was thus also spoken to Joseph Smith (see Moses 1:42). Moses appeared in the Kirtland Temple on April 3, 1836, to bestow upon Joseph Smith and Oliver Cowdery "the keys of the gathering of Israel from the four parts of the earth, and the leading of the ten tribes from the land of the north" (D&C 110:11).

The promise of the Lord is that "if ye have desires to serve God ye are called to the work" (D&C 4:3). That is *your* mountain to climb! Reflect on the words of the following true account and see if you can identify what is occurring:

Looming above him was an ice-encrusted rock tower rising forty ominous feet toward the summit. Would the ridges of ice and rock support his weight without collapsing? Should he go forward? He remembered the encouragement of his fiancée, whose warmth and cheerful personality, calmness, and common sense had empowered him in his challenging pursuits. "If you really want to go, then I think you should go," was her ongoing theme. At this moment of crucial challenge, he nodded and started upward—one tense handhold after another, one careful jam of his boot spikes after another—until he finally reached the top of the rock tower in safety. His confidence erupted! He could now see ahead the snowy dome of the summit. Breathlessly trodding forward, he reached a spot where he could see nothing but space in all directions. He had reached the top of the world!

As you may have surmised, these words summarize the final moments of the heroic achievement of Sir Edmund Hillary (1919–2008), the first person to conquer Mount Everest, an event accomplished at 11:30 a.m. on May 29, 1953.[1] The New Zealand explorer and philanthropist was no prophet, as Moses was, but he demonstrated with heroic courage that mortals can indeed conquer mountains—including the world's giants such as Everest.

Pondering: You too have mountains to climb. You too have callings from the Lord. You can rise in faith through His power, guided by His Spirit and assisted by loved ones. How does this insight strengthen the way you pray, read the scriptures, bear your testimony, do temple work, and look forward one day to returning home to the glory of the Father and the Son? (See also Isaiah 40:31; Obadiah 1:21)

AGENDA FOR ACTION

Moses 1, this precious morsel of truth, is part of the bread of life promised to the faithful (see John 6:35, 48, 51). Like Moses, we too can ascend the mountain of the Lord where divine truth is expounded and where the Saints can gather in safety. We can study with devotion the word of God and be lifted by the Spirit to a higher grasp of eternal truth. We can rise above life's tribulations "with wings as eagles" (Isaiah 40:31), pressing onward toward our destiny as chosen sons and daughters of God. We can visit the house of the Lord regularly and thus ascend as "saviours . . . on mount Zion" (Obadiah 1:21) to sustain the cause of salvation for our loved ones. Through the strength of the Lord, we enrich our daily lives and savor a wider view of eternal things. We sense fulfillment in having ascended with great devotion to a higher plane of existence. We feel the warmth of coming closer to the highest throne, the throne of God. All of this renders sublime our here and now.

LOOKING FORWARD: We learn much from Moses on the summit—but what did we learn *before* coming to this earth?

---

1   See *View from the Summit: The Remarkable Memoir by the First Person to Conquer Everest* (Random House eBooks, 1999),14–16, 29, 32, 36, 118, 126, 236.

CHAPTER TWO

THE GRAND COUNCIL OF HEAVEN: WHAT WE LEARNED BEFORE COMING HERE

GOSPEL DOCTRINE READING ASSIGNMENT: ABRAHAM 3; MOSES 4:1–4

Thou wast chosen before thou wast born. (Abraham 3:23)

OUR FIRST LESSONS

ON SUNDAY, MAY 12, 1844, just a month prior to his martyrdom, the Prophet Joseph Smith gave a sermon in Nauvoo in which he confirmed the principle of foreordination: "Every man who has a calling to minister to the inhabitants of the world was ordained to that very purpose in the Grand Council of heaven before this world was. I suppose that I was ordained to this very office in that Grand Council. It is the testimony that I want that I am God's servant, and this people His people" (*History of the Church* 6:364).

In his 1918 revelation concerning the spirit world, President Joseph F. Smith stated that he was permitted to see in vision Joseph Smith and his loyal associates of the Restoration "among the noble and great ones who were chosen in the beginning to be rulers in the Church of God. Even before they were born, they, with many others, received their first lessons in the world of spirits and were prepared to come forth in the due time of the Lord to labor in his vineyard for the salvation of the souls of men" (D&C 138:55–56).

Do those "many others" not also include all the faithful sons and daughters of God who serve Him in this mortal realm by honoring their premortal callings?

WHAT ARE THE LESSONS WE CAN LEARN FROM THE ACCOUNT OF ABRAHAM?

1. This earth was created for us as a transitional abode for proving our worthiness to return home someday to the realms of glory.

We will go down, for there is space there, and we will take of these materials, and we will make an earth whereon these may dwell;

And we will prove them herewith, to see if they will do all things whatsoever the Lord their God shall command them. (Abraham 3:24–25)

From the record of Abraham we learn that "there is nothing that the Lord thy God shall take in his heart to do but what he will do it" (Abraham 3:17). Similarly, we can use our mortal time of probation to commit with unshakeable fervor to do the will of the Lord and thus be among those who "shall have glory added upon their heads for ever and ever" (Abraham 3:26).

> **How were we blessed to receive the book of Abraham?**
>
> The book of Abraham was derived from Egyptian papyri that came into the hands of Joseph Smith in 1835. When he began the inspired process of translation and extraction in July of that year, he discovered that one of the rolls of papyrus contained the writings of Abraham and thus declared with joy, "Truly we can say, the Lord is beginning to reveal the abundance of peace and truth" (*History of the Church* 2:236). The book of Abraham was published segmentally in the *Times and Seasons* beginning on March 1, 1842 (vol. 3, no. 9).

The Lord has a way of tenderly reminding us how we have come here from the premortal world to follow in His footsteps and to learn how to return home again. This theme flowed into the mind of a joyful grandfather during the homecoming speech given by his missionary granddaughter:

You are a noble messenger of the Lord, dear granddaughter. Like your mother and father and many others in your extended family, you have honored the Abrahamic covenant to bring the truths of the restored gospel to the world. The light in your eyes and the warmth in your voice remind me of the promise of the Lord to Abraham that through his seed "shall all the families of the earth be blessed, even with the blessings of the Gospel, which are the blessings of salvation, even of life eternal" (Abraham 2:11).

I will never forget the day your grandmother and I welcomed you in the hospital as a new child born from the heavens on Grandparents' Day! What a beautiful soul you were and still are. There I was with my lovely wife, looking down upon you, a newborn babe, only a few hours old. I thought of a scripture about those precious souls who "received their first lessons in the world of spirits and were prepared to come forth in the due time of the Lord to labor in his vineyard for the salvation of the souls of men" (D&C 138:56). I knew there was a treasure of wisdom already invested in your heart and mind through the lessons you received firsthand in the premortal realm from the Creator Himself. Over the years, those truths have unfolded within you and blossomed as a light of charity in the service of the Lord. He loves you—and your grandparents love you, and your parents and siblings love you. We are all blessed to belong to the family of God.

Pondering: How does the assurance that we are all spirit children of our Father in Heaven—eternally belonging to Him—help us to live faithful and obedient lives as we prepare ourselves to return to our celestial home one day?

2. Christ, the Creator under the direction of the Father, was chosen in the premortal realm as Redeemer of all mankind.

And the Lord said: Whom shall I send? And one answered like unto the Son of Man: Here am I, send me. And another answered and said: Here am I, send me. And the Lord said: I will send the first. (Abraham 3:27)

Jesus Christ was and is the model of obedience, willing from the beginning to carry out the Father's plan of redemption and exaltation. He said, "Father, thy will be done, and the glory be thine forever" (Moses 4:2). The resurrected Lord declared to the ancient American Saints, "And behold, I am the light and the life of the world; and I have drunk out of that bitter cup which the Father hath given me, and have glorified the Father in taking upon me the sins of the world, in the which I have suffered the will of the Father in all things from the beginning" (3 Nephi 11:11). To the Saints in our day He confirmed, "Nevertheless, glory be to the Father, and I partook and finished my preparations unto the children of men" (D&C 19:19).

Pondering: How does the vibrant assurance that the Savior is our Redeemer—from the beginning and forever—inspire us to do the will of the Father, as He did? How can we become more like the Lord each day and follow His example of doing the will of the Father in all things?

3. The faithful do the will of the Father, whereas the prideful rebel.

And I, the Lord God, spake unto Moses, saying: That Satan, whom thou hast commanded in the name of mine Only Begotten, is the same which was from the beginning, and he came before me, saying—Behold, here am I, send me, I will be thy son, and I will redeem all mankind, that one soul shall not be lost, and surely I will do it; wherefore give me thine honor.

Abraham—A Brief Bio

Abraham (meaning "father of a multitude") was born over two millennia before Christ's earthly ministry. His original home was in Ur of the Chaldees, located possibly in what is now northwestern Syria or south central Turkey (see Paul Y. Hoskisson, "Where Was Ur of the Chaldees?" in *The Pearl of Great Price: Revelations from God*, ed. H. Donl Peterson and Charles D. Tate Jr. [Provo, UT: Religious Studies Center, Brigham Young University, 1989], 119–136). The Lord rescued Abraham from execution at the hands of idolatrous priests. Abraham fled at the command of the Lord to Haran and then to Canaan, with a subsequent stay in Egypt during the days of famine (see Genesis 11–13). Abraham was given a new name by the Lord: "Neither shall thy name any more be called Abram ['exalted father'], but thy name shall be Abraham; for a father of many nations have I made thee" (Genesis 17:5). Through the blessings of the Lord, Abraham accomplished his greatest desire: "To be a father of many nations, a prince of peace . . . a High Priest, holding the right belonging to the fathers" (Abraham 1:2; see also Abraham 1:18–19). He is regarded as the father of the covenant peoples of the Lord, including those who are adopted into the house of Israel through the gospel pathway.

But, behold, my Beloved Son, which was my Beloved and Chosen from the beginning, said unto me—Father, thy will be done, and the glory be thine forever.

Wherefore, because that Satan rebelled against me, and sought to destroy the agency of man, which I, the Lord God, had given him, and also, that I should give unto him mine own power; by the power of mine Only Begotten, I caused that he should be cast down." (Moses 4:1–3)

What is a "merism," and how did the Lord use this figure of speech to convey His eternal calling as Redeemer?

A merism (from the Greek word *meros*, meaning "part") is an expression in which an entire range of things is implied by mentioning only parts of that range. The Lord frequently spoke of Himself as "Alpha and Omega"—the first and last letters of the Greek alphabet. But He is also everything in between: the beginning and the end, the infinite and eternal Redeemer. "I am Alpha and Omega, Christ the Lord; yea, even I am he, the beginning and the end, the Redeemer of the world" (D&C 19:1 and frequently throughout the Doctrine and Covenants; see also Revelation 22:13 and 3 Nephi 9:18). We also use merisms in everyday expressions such as "searching high and low" (implying also everything in between). Perhaps we should search high and low in our lives to find and follow our Alpha and Omega!

Pride was the source of Satan's downfall: "And the second was angry [after being rejected], and kept not his first estate; and, at that day, many followed after him" (Abraham 3:28). By contrast, we followed the example of the Savior in the premortal realm and showed humility and obedience, keeping our first estate. Our Father in Heaven thus granted us the opportunity to show our faithfulness in our second estate (mortal probation). How great are the blessings that await us as we rise to our destiny of everlasting joy and glory by defeating the forces of pride and by manifesting unshakeable faith and enduring obedience.

How long is our mortal life?

From the record of Abraham, we learn about the Lord's celestial time scale: "A day unto the Lord, after his manner of reckoning, it being one thousand years according to the time appointed unto that whereon thou standest" (Abraham 3:4; see also Abraham Facsimile 2, figure 1; 2 Peter 3:8). If our average life span is around eighty years, we live on earth slightly less than two hours in the eyes of the Lord. Can we not be faithful to Him for two hours? Each moment of our life is precious. Our life revolves around the Lord. Let us give Him our all!

The following historical account displays the stark contrast between valiant obedience and destructive pride:

Joseph Smith, Hyrum Smith, Sidney Rigdon, and several other Church leaders, having been through a senseless trial for treason against the state of Missouri were, on November 30, 1838, consigned to Liberty Jail to await further legal consequences (*History of the Church* 3:215).

During the time of the trial, William E. McLellin, one of the original Twelve Apostles, now excommunicated, displayed prideful rebellion by plundering the houses of several of the prisoners, and actually sought permission from the sheriff to flog the Prophet. As the record reads: "Permission was granted on condition that Joseph would fight. The sheriff [informed Joseph of] McLellin's request, to which Joseph consented, if his irons were taken off. McLellin then refused to fight unless he could have a club, to which Joseph was perfectly willing; but the sheriff would not allow them to fight on such unequal terms" (3:215).

Earlier, McLellin had come to Parley P. Pratt during the trial and had said, "'Well, Parley, you have now got where you are certain never to escape; how do you feel as to the course you have taken in religion?' I answered, that I had taken the course which I should take if I had my life to live over again" (3:215). In the contrasting portraits of these early figures of the Restoration, we view the ongoing saga of how the followers of Christ continually encounter and overcome onslaughts from the followers of Satan.

Pondering: How can we use the valiant example of the Savior and His righteous followers to do the will of the Father and overcome the disease of selfish pride? In what ways can we showcase more humility in our lives?

AGENDA FOR ACTION

The purpose for our earthly existence is to prove ourselves worthy to return to our Heavenly Father. The highest exemplar of godly obedience is the Savior, who, in perfect and humble submission, offered Himself as Redeemer. To follow the Lord valiantly, we too can submit humbly to God's will throughout our mortal probation, just as we chose to do in the premortal realm (see Alma 13:3–5). The governing questions for each of the Lord's children to consider every day are the following: "How faithful am I in remaining on the pathway leading back to my heavenly home?" and "What goals do I need to set in order to be more in tune with the Spirit as I aspire to follow with greater devotion the example of my Redeemer?"

The darkest example of prideful rebellion is Lucifer, who manifests the destructive pattern of behavior that leads to a fall from the grace of God (see Isaiah 14:12–16; Revelation 12:7–9; D&C 29:36–39). It is that pattern of harmful pride that we can overcome through the guidance of the Spirit and the blessings of the Atonement. Our eternal Exemplar is Jesus Christ. By following Him we can return to our celestial home once again in honor. In this context, meaningful questions might be: "Do I have any personal, specific struggles with pride in my life?" and "What can I do to ensure that pride has no place in my life?"

LOOKING FORWARD: We learn through the account of Abraham about our experiences in the premortal realm prior to the Creation—but how do we personally participate in the ongoing process of creation?

CHAPTER THREE

THE CREATION:
A DIVINE WITNESS OF GOD'S GOODNESS

GOSPEL DOCTRINE READING ASSIGNMENT: MOSES 1:27–42; 2–3

All things which I had made were finished, and I, God, saw that they were good. (Moses 3:2)

THE GOODNESS OF THE CREATION

WHEN GOD LOOKED UPON THE outcome of the Creation of this world, He affirmed its goodness: "And God saw every thing that he had made, and, behold, it was very good" (Genesis 1:31). The word *good*, as applied to the Creation, is used seven times in both Genesis 1 and Moses 2—plus once more in the summary declaration given in Moses 3:2. These expressions establish a pattern for how we can view the Creation here and now. In a world of doubt and conflict, we too can look upon the divine creative process as "good."

A TOUCH OF REALITY

Every day our minds and hearts are enriched with uplifting scenes all around us—mountains rising in noble majesty, oceans and rivers of dynamic vitality, fields and forests of living beauty, captivating views of the starry heavens—all bearing the touch of the Creator's loving hand. But even the manifestations of the Creation often overlooked in the shadows of our everyday life resound with the goodness flowing from the hands of God.

Consider the testimony shared by a father about a walk with his five-year-old daughter:

There we were, hand in hand, walking along a pathway near our home in the warmth of the springtime sun. I was captivated by the majesty of the mountain peaks along the horizon, flashing into view through the shading branches of the trees passing us by.

The melodic melody of a mourning dove echoed from somewhere in the distance. "Hear that?" I asked. When she stopped in her tracks without responding, I looked down and found her staring at a lone dandelion peeking up through the grass along the edge of the pathway. She knelt down and tenderly grasped the simple blossom in the cup of her hand. I thought I heard it say something like, "Hi. Thank you for noticing me. I know I'm not much of a favorite with the landscape crowd—but God created me."

I knelt down beside my daughter and asked, "What do you see in this dandelion?"

"I don't know," she said. "Maybe it's just pretty."

"Sort of like *you*?" I asked.

She giggled and responded directly to the blossom, "I'm big and pretty, but you are—little and pretty. Where did you get your name—from a lion?"

Since the dandelion did not immediately respond, I tossed in a little boring dictionary talk. "Sweet daughter, the name came from a French expression meaning 'tooth of a lion'—'dent de lion.'"

She fingered the pointed leaves gently as if they were a lion's teeth. "There—you didn't even scratch me," she said. "You're my friend."

"Do you want to pick this flower and take it home?" I asked.

"Uh-uh," she replied directly to the flower. "You are going to stay here and grow." At that point I recognized that a little miracle was going on—in her mind and in mine as well.

My thoughts raced as I confirmed silently that there is indeed a bit of glory captured in the simple golden crown of a dandelion. In its own modest way, it testifies plainly and clearly about the Creation and the abundance of life. It has nothing of the grandeur of the orchid or the smell of the rose. But the Lord created it nevertheless. And it speaks a quiet lesson. Its aliveness is a thing of no little beauty to those—like my lovely daughter—who can perceive therein the invisible hand of God at work. It is, in its own humble way, a tender reminder that "without him was not any thing made that was made" (John 1:3) and that all aspects of the Creation are a witness of God at work.

My daughter and I continued on down the pathway. But she looked back one last time toward her dandelion and smiled. I thought to myself, "Sweet daughter, you are young—but in the eyes of God I am just as

---

What are the "days" or successive periods of the Creation as portrayed in the accounts of Moses and Abraham?

First Day—Earth and light: formation of the empty earth and introduction of light in cycles of night and day (see Moses 2:1–5; Genesis 1:1–5; Abraham 4:1–5)

Second Day—Waters: interrelationship set up between the waters of the atmospheric heavens ("firmament" or "expanse") and the waters of the surface of the earth (see Moses 2:6–8; Genesis 1:6–8; Abraham 4:6–8)

Third Day—Land: dry land separated from the seas and made ready to receive seeds of various kinds; Vegetation: plant life unfolds (see Moses 2:9–13; Genesis 1:9–13; Abraham 4:9–13)

Fourth Day—Sun, moon, and stars: seasons are established (see Moses 2:14–19; Genesis 1:14–19; Abraham 4:14–19)

Fifth Day—Animals: animal life unfolds in waters and sky (see Moses 2:20–23; Genesis 1:20–23; Abraham 4:20–23)

Sixth Day—Mankind: man and woman are organized in the image of God; Land animals: each type after its own kind (see Moses 2:24–31; Genesis 1:24–31; Abraham 4:24–31)

Seventh Day—Day of rest (see Moses 3:1–3; Genesis 2:1–3; Abraham 5:1–3)

young as you are." Somehow that little dandelion, disappearing behind us, seemed to whisper a message worth remembering: Perhaps all of us in our own spiritual infancy, in our own nothingness before the perfection of God, seem as dandelions from the higher perspective. We too have a little of the crown of glory upon our heads. He created us. And as sons and daughters of God, we have within us the potential of flight, of rising to a higher level of spirituality where we will see ourselves truly to be in His image.

WHAT ARE THE LESSONS WE CAN LEARN ABOUT THE CONTINUING GOODNESS OF THE CREATION?

1. For all of us, the Creation bears the everlasting signature of the Creator and Redeemer.

And worlds without number have I created; and I also created them for mine own purpose; and by the Son I created them, which is mine Only Begotten. . . .

And as one earth shall pass away, and the heavens thereof even so shall another come; and there is no end to my works, neither to my words. (Moses 1:33, 38; see also John 1:1–3)

"All things which I had made were finished, and I, God, saw that they were good" (Moses 3:2). "Spiritually were they created and made according to my word" (Moses 3:7).

Why is the Creation "good"? Because it reveals directly to our senses—our sight, our hearing, our touch, our smell, our taste, our feelings—a compelling witness of the reality of Deity, the Father of all goodness who chose His Son Jehovah to be the Creator and Redeemer of all mankind (see Moses 6:63; Alma 30:44).

Is Jesus Christ also the Savior of all the other worlds?

The magnificent vision of the realms of glory (see section 76 of the Doctrine and Covenants) presents an inspiring view of the purpose for the Creation: to enable God's children to receive the highest degree of glory in the eternal world. In an excerpt from the poetic version of these truths called "A Vision"—published in the *Times and Seasons* (vol. 4, no. 6, February 1, 1843)—Joseph Smith confirms that Jesus Christ is the Savior of *all* the worlds:

Whose inhabitants too from the first to the last,
Are sav'd by the very same Saviour of ours;
And, of course, are begotten God's daughters and sons,
By the very same truths, and the very same pow'rs.

Pondering: The work of the Creator is dynamic and endless, imbued with His perfect goodness and His enduring love for the salvation and exaltation of His children. How can we ensure that our own work of creativity and obedience also radiates enduring goodness and love? How can we become more skilled at creating noble plans and carrying them out with the guidance of the Spirit? How can we do better at encouraging others to use their creative minds for their own improvement and for the well-being of others?

2. All of us have been created in the image of God with the enduring capacity to follow in His footsteps as active students of creativity.

Within the soul of every son and daughter of God is the seed of creativity, the aspiration to engage in the continuing process of bringing new life into being. The nurturing essence of motherhood and fatherhood is a quality of the divine nature planted within us:

And I, God, created man in mine own image, in the image of mine Only Begotten created I him; male and female created I them.

And I, God, blessed them, and said unto them: Be fruitful, and multiply, and replenish the earth, and subdue it, and have dominion over . . . every living thing that moveth upon the earth. (Moses 2:27–28; see also Abraham 4:26–28; 5:7; Genesis 1:26–28; 1 Nephi 17:36)

Why is the Creation "good"? It is good because it confirms that we also participate in the creative process unfolding before us. Man and woman are created in the image of God to become companions to each other and parents to their own children, thus serving as active participants in the ongoing creative process through which the eternal purposes of God are realized.

Pondering: Being created in the image of God, we are given the divine attributes of creativity and leadership. How can we seize new opportunities each week to express and develop that creativity?

3. Our God-given agency empowers our spiritual rebirth.

> And we will make an earth whereon these may dwell;
> And we will prove them herewith, to see if they will do all things whatsoever the Lord their God shall command them. (Abraham 3:24–25)

> Nevertheless, thou mayest choose for thyself, for it is given unto thee. (Moses 3:17)

Why is the Creation "good"? It is good because we are also involved in the dynamic process of achieving spiritual rebirth through the gospel of redemption. We all have the gift of agency, enabling us to choose the divine pathway of spiritual creativity leading to immortality and eternal life. This earth was organized as a proving ground for our obedience: "For behold, this life is the time for men to prepare to meet God; yea, behold the day of this life is the day for men to perform their labors" (Alma 34:32).

Pondering: In what ways can we remind ourselves each day that *we* are the purpose of the Creation? How can we make the spirit of love the energizing force of spiritual renewal for ourselves and for others?

4. Our ultimate goal is the attainment of the glory of God's rest.

> God rested on the seventh day, His holy Sabbath:
> And I, God, blessed the seventh day, and sanctified it; because that in it I had rested from all my work which I, God, had created and made. (Moses 3:3; see also Genesis 2:2–3; Abraham 5:2–3)

Why is the Creation "good"? It is good because it is an all-encompassing reminder of the state of "rest" that lies ahead of us. We are all striving to return once again, through obedience and the grace of God, into His eternal rest—"which rest is the fulness of his glory" (D&C 84:24)—to dwell with our families forever.

Pondering: How can we maintain our focus each Sabbath day on the goodness of God as Creator? How can we strengthen our commitment to endure to the end as worthy sons and daughters of God, prepared one day to enter into His eternal rest and glory?

AGENDA FOR ACTION

We can discern in the Creation the signature of the Creators—both Father and Son—who radiate dynamic goodness and eternal love. The earth, in all its splendor and beauty, has a singular purpose—to be a preparatory place for us to cultivate our worthiness to reside one day in the celestial kingdom. Having been created in the image of God, we can assist with full diligence in accomplishing His eternal plan of salvation and exaltation.

We can be active participants in the creative process. Through the strength of the Lord, we can bring splendid new things into existence: our expanding

---

How does the Lord instruct us to "use" His Creation?

"And it pleaseth God that he hath given all these things unto man; for unto this end were they made to be used, with judgment, not to excess, neither by extortion.

And in nothing doth man offend God, or against none is his wrath kindled, save those who confess not his hand in all things, and obey not his commandments" (D&C 59:20–21; compare also D&C 89).

family circles, our homes of harmony and peace, the cultivation of our gifts from the Lord, our original songs and journals and works of art, our abundant gardens, our unfolding relationships, and myriad other miracles of the creative process that bless lives.

Above all, we can create a new heart within us through the blessings of the Spirit. We can use our agency wisely in the achievement of spiritual rebirth through the gospel of the Atonement. We can honor the Sabbath day each week as we prepare one day to return to our heavenly home of rest. We prepare for the sacrament through deeds of love: fulfilling our callings with devotion, visiting with those who need encouragement and comfort, writing letters of support to the missionaries, providing referrals to our ward leaders, and following the guidance of the Lord in many similar ways. Then, when we humbly partake of the emblems of the sacrament, we can feel the blessings of the Spirit assuring us that we are doing our best to honor our covenants and prepare for the future transition into the rest of the Lord, "which rest is the fulness of his glory" (D&C 84:24).

The creative process continues unabated. We observe it in gratitude. We engage in it with passion. We rise as agents of the Creator toward the goal of eternal glory. Each day is a day of creation. Each day is a step closer to exaltation.

LOOKING FORWARD: This earth was created as a blessing for us all, but how is the Fall also an essential blessing?

CHAPTER FOUR

THE FALL OF MANKIND: GATEWAY TO THE BLESSINGS OF THE ATONEMENT

GOSPEL DOCTRINE READING ASSIGNMENT: MOSES 4, 5:1–15, 6:48–62

I am the Only Begotten of the Father from the beginning, henceforth and forever, that as thou hast fallen thou mayest be redeemed, and all mankind, even as many as will. (Moses 5:9)

HOW IS THE FALL A BLESSING?

THE FALL IS THE GATEWAY to acquiring wisdom, generating families, and receiving the blessings of redemption. The Creation established the platform for the Fall, the Fall legitimized the need for the Atonement, and the Atonement became the empowering force for the renewal of life—physically through the universal resurrection and spiritually through the deliverance of the faithful.

Thus the Fall is a brief though essential interlude in the history of God's children. The shadows of the Fall—including the sorrows, trials, and challenges of mortality—are dispelled by the glories of the everlasting gospel of Jesus Christ and His Atonement (see Articles of Faith 1:2, 3, 4). These key factors—the Creation, the Fall, and the Atonement—are the three pillars of eternity, forming the foundation of our destiny.[2]

Lehi confirmed, "Adam fell that men might be; and men are, that they might have joy" (2 Nephi 2:25). And Paul declared, "For as in Adam all die, even so in Christ shall all be made alive" (1 Corinthians 15:22).

A TOUCH OF REALITY

How do we know that we are part of the "Fall"? That very question was posed by a young boy to his older brother one Sunday afternoon:

---

2   See Bruce R. McConkie, "Christ and the Creation," *Tambuli*, September 1983, 22.

"What did you learn in Sunday School today?" asked the older brother.

"Oh, we talked about the Savior. And then a lot about the Fall. Our teacher said we're all part of it, and I wanted to ask her how we know that for sure, but the bell rang too soon."

"Well, let's talk about it right now. Who are you?"

"What?" responded the boy. "I'm your brother."

"Are you sure you're here?"

"Of course!" he replied.

"You're sure you exist?" the older brother asked.

"What's going on?"

"Well," the older brother responded with a twinkle in his eye, "if you're here, the Fall worked—otherwise you wouldn't be here."

"What do you mean?" was the startled response.

"Because of the Fall," the older boy answered, "the human family came into this world. You said you talked also about the Savior in your Sunday School class. When was the last time you saw Him in person?"

The young boy had a perplexed look on his face. "We don't get to see Him in person!"

"That's true. At least not for now. Because of the Fall, we were separated from our Father in Heaven and His Son so we can make good choices on our own and show Them that we want to be like Them. Are you being good?"

The younger brother shrugged his shoulders.

"Of course you are!" came the encouraging words. "You set a good example for our whole family! You're going to be a great missionary one day and teach the gospel just like I have done. Are you getting hungry?"

"Always."

"Then you must be part of the Fall," he replied with a wink. "All of us in this mortal life get hungry and thirsty and have to work to make ends meet."

The boy rubbed his stomach and nodded. "Guess I'm part of the Fall."

"Right! We all are. That's why we're looking forward to the time when—thanks to our Savior and His sacrifice—we can all be together in our heavenly home."

"Even Grandpa?" the boy asked.

"Sure," his older brother added. "I know you miss him a lot. We all do. Because of the Fall, life's a mixture of sorrow and joy, pain and happiness. It's all part of the plan—but so is the Atonement. The Atonement can bring us all back together again. I know that for sure."

"I think I'm catching on," said the younger brother with a cheerful grin.

"Think about it tonight. Read your scriptures, and ask Heavenly Father for more understanding. Let me know what you learn about all these things—even weeding the garden."

"Weeding the garden? What do you mean?" asked the younger brother.

"Just like I saw you doing yesterday," the older brother replied. "You did a great job out there in the garden. Weeds are part of life's challenges. That's life. And that's part of the Fall. But we can succeed in the strength of the Lord."

The younger brother rubbed his stomach again. "Do you smell something tasty? I think Mom's fixing some of those vegetables from the garden for our supper."

How does modern scripture shed greater light on the Fall?

The word *fall* (or a variant such as *falling*, *fallen*, *fell*, etc.)—referring specifically to the Fall of mankind—occurs 42 times in modern scripture within 25 key passages:

Book of Mormon—eighteen passages: 1 Nephi 10:5–6; 2 Nephi 2:4–8; 2:17–26; 9:6–8; Mosiah 3:11; 3:16–19; 3:26; 4:5–7; 16:3–6; Alma 12:22–30; 18:36; 22:12–14; 30:25–27; 42:1–15; Helaman 14:16–19; Mormon 9:11–14; Ether 3:2; 3:13

D&C—four passages: D&C 20:17–28; 29:42–44; 93:38; 138:18–19

Pearl of Great Price—three passages: Moses 5:7–9; 6:47–50; 6:55–62

The Bible provides several key passages concerning the Fall, but without specifically using that word—see for example Genesis 2:17; 3:6–19, 22–24; Romans 5:12; 1 Corinthians 15:22. It is clear that modern scripture provides a far more complete and vivid road map of the Fall.

"Thanks to you!" was the reply. "This year we have the best garden ever!"

The young boy accepted the compliment with a smile of satisfaction and started walking toward the steps leading up to the back door of the house, his brother following. Suddenly, the boy tripped on the first step. His brother caught hold of him before he hit the ground. They both looked at each other.

"You saved me from the fall!" said the boy.

His older brother smiled. "Maybe that's a reminder of how our Lord saves us from the big Fall. You might even say that through His love we can fall into heaven!"

With that, the two of them slipped arm and arm into the house—taking a few more safe steps forward in life.

WHAT ARE THE LESSONS WE WANT TO LEARN ABOUT THE FALL?

1. The Fall came by choice—just as we have the choice in mortal life to live by gospel principles.

In the Garden of Eden, Adam and Eve received instructions about the plan of redemption. They were also given a specific choice about the next phase of life:

Of every tree of the garden thou mayest freely eat,

But of the tree of the knowledge of good and evil, thou shalt not eat of it, nevertheless, thou mayest choose for thyself, for it is given unto thee; but, remember that I forbid it, for in the day thou eatest thereof thou shalt surely die. (Moses 3:16–17; also Genesis 2:16–17; Abraham 5:12–13)

In due time, Satan beguiled Eve to partake of the forbidden fruit, but she refused, quoting the commandment of God: "Ye shall not eat of it, neither shall ye touch it, lest ye die" (Moses 4:9; also Genesis 3:3). With subtlety, Satan countered, "Ye shall not surely die; For God doth know that in the day ye eat thereof, then your eyes shall be opened, and ye shall be as gods, knowing good and evil" (Moses 4:10–11; also Genesis 3:4–5).

What is the meaning of "Eden"?

The word may be related to an Aramaic source meaning "fruitful" or "well watered" (*Oxford Dictionary of the Jewish Religion* [2011], 288–289). Certainly the implication is that the Garden of Eden was a place of delight.

Eve considered carefully then partook, as did Adam. The Fall was thus triggered and the transition to the mortal state activated. In the testimonies of both Adam and Eve following their expulsion from the Garden of Eden, we have the extraordinary witness of the good that ensued:

And in that day Adam blessed God and was filled, and began to prophesy concerning all the families of the earth, saying: Blessed be the name of God, for because of my transgression my eyes are opened, and in this life I shall have joy, and again in the flesh I shall see God.

And Eve, his wife, heard all these things and was glad, saying: Were it not for our transgression we never should have had seed, and never should have known good and evil, and the joy of our redemption, and the eternal life which God giveth unto all the obedient. (Moses 5:10–11)

Pondering: How can we transform life's adversities into learning tools in our textbook of wisdom? In what ways can we confirm that the goodness in our mortal experience far outshines our tribulations?

2. The Fall brought us down into the valley of mortality just as the Atonement lifts us up upon the mountain of the Lord.

Through the Atonement we can all experience the renewing light of hope and comfort in our mortal years of tribulation, as the following true account confirms:

He was a brilliant attorney with a successful practice and a wonderful young family. I distinctly recall hearing him say that things seemed almost too easy, too effortless, and that he was so grateful to the Lord for all of his blessings. It was not long thereafter that he unexpectedly contracted a serious illness and was suddenly called home. His family was devastated. We all reeled at the sudden loss. Even so, at the funeral, Elder

Mark E. Peterson, an Apostle of the Lord, beholding the inconsolable sorrow of the widow and her children, counseled them in a loving way that they should withhold their tears. Some wondered at these words until he made the reason clear: Look at things from a higher perspective. Find comfort and joy in the gospel of Jesus Christ that will eventually unite the family once again. They listened and obeyed. Through courage and faith, the widow carried on her motherly mission, guiding her children by the comfort of the Spirit. Adversity had brought them the means to know the joy of personal triumph over suffering, the bliss of rising over sorrow, and the peace of victory over life's shadows.

Pondering: In what ways can we be assured that suffering enhances our testimony of the truthfulness of the gospel of Jesus Christ? What is the source of comfort and hope in mortality?

3. When we lift others, we help the Lord lift all mankind.

It was in the days of Adam and Eve that the gospel of Jesus Christ was first proclaimed on the earth. Adam and Eve set the pattern for how we should teach our families the saving truths of the gospel (see Moses 5:1–4, 12; D&C 138:38–39).

Let us try to imagine the thoughts and feelings of Eve—the glorious "mother of all living" (Moses 4:26; Genesis 3:20)—in those first days of mortality:

Her eyes glistened with the touch of the light from the unfolding glow along the horizon. Slowly, silently, the features of the natural world began to emerge around her from the shadows of night, reborn again in the emerging radiance of the coming day: a wilderness of wild brush and knotty trees, a vast enclave of open fields struggling to foster growth in the dry breezes of the climate, a few lonely creatures wandering grasslands and hidden valleys, looking for survival.

How long had it been since she and her husband had taken leave of the Garden? Soothing memories of that glorious abode kindled a flame within her soul: luxuriant and vibrant vegetation, welcome shelter protecting against winds, absence of care and anxiety of how to sustain life, and, above all, the inspiring visits of the Father and the Son, who brought nurturing truth and wisdom in grand abundance. The warmth of those memories flowed outwardly into the morning landscape, transforming the bleakness of this new world into a realm not devoid of promise and hope. It was promise and hope that confirmed the wisdom of her choice to partake of the fruit and embark with her husband on the journey of life to raise families that could one day return to the celestial garden of immortality and eternal life in a future world of glory and joy.

She remembered hearing the words of the Lord emanating from the distant garden, counseling the couple in a loving way that they should worship the Lord their God and make offerings unto Him of the firstlings of their flock—this being a similitude of the sacrifice of the Only Begotten of the Father (see Moses 5:5–8). She remembered how she and her husband joyfully taught their children to repent and call upon the name of the Son forevermore.

> **Why did God forbid Adam and Eve to partake of the fruit of the tree of knowledge of good and evil when He knew that this act would bring about the Fall—an essential pathway to joy and salvation?**
>
> Joseph Fielding Smith explains: "It is that the Lord said to Adam that if he wished to remain as he was in the garden, then he was not to eat the fruit, but if he desired to eat it and partake of death he was at liberty to do so. So really it was not in the true sense a transgression of a divine commandment. Adam made the wise decision, in fact the only decision that he could make" (Joseph Fielding Smith, *Answers to Gospel Questions*, Vol. 4 [Salt Lake City: Deseret Book, 1963], 81). We see that Adam and Eve needed to make the choice to enter the mortal pathway. They needed to take responsibility for their action. Since they were to become subject to mortal forces of suffering, pain, agony, and death, they could never blame God for this state. It was their choice, just as it would be their choice to live according to principles of faith and obedience and thus learn to achieve a counterbalancing state of joy and happiness through the power of the Atonement.

Yes, this new world required sacrifice and continual effort: motherly sorrow and anguish accompanying the bringing forth of new souls; husband and wife laboring together by the sweat of their brow to sustain and nurture their family; constant commitment and perseverance to gather their children and teach them to follow after the Lord.

Suddenly, she felt a hand on her shoulder. She looked up and saw her husband smiling at her in the emerging light. He put his arm around her in loving affection and then pointed toward the horizon, nodding in confirmation that a new day was about to begin. In that moment, she felt a renewed spirit of calm and serenity come over her. Their lives were truly blessed by the Almighty; their hope was being regenerated; their vision of the eternities was being unfolded; their wise choice was being confirmed. They had peace in their hearts as the sun rose silently over the horizon: the dawning of a perfect day.

Pondering: How can we help others discover joy in understanding the purpose for the Creation, the Fall, and the Atonement? How can we strengthen our vision of a future realm in which our joy will be eternal and our happiness everlasting?

AGENDA FOR ACTION

The choices made by Adam and Eve opened our own gateway to wisdom, family growth, and everlasting life through the Atonement of Jesus Christ. We can choose to take every step forward with the conviction of honoring our covenants. We can look upon our challenges and tribulations not as walls of confinement but as steps toward eternal life. We can reach out and guide our children and all those around us to view this life as a blessing, a miraculous opportunity to honor our premortal commission to "do all things whatsoever the Lord their God shall command [us]" that we may "have glory added upon [our] heads for ever and ever" (Abraham 3:25–26).

Our choices have a profound impact on our progress toward the fulfillment of our destiny. What blessings have you experienced from choosing to rise above tribulation through the strength of the Lord? How can you preserve a witness of these blessings in your personal journal to be shared with loved ones? What forks in the road have you encountered that have required you to make choices in accordance with righteous principles and the whisperings of the Spirit? How was the correctness of such choices later confirmed? What major choices are you facing right now, and how can you approach the decision-making process with wisdom and a firm commitment to act in such a way that blessings will flow to all who might be affected by your choices?

LOOKING FORWARD: How can we be certain that we are accepted of the Lord?

CHAPTER FIVE

HOW TO BE FAVORED OF THE LORD

Gospel Doctrine Reading Assignment: Moses 5–7

If thou doest well, thou shalt be accepted. (Moses 5:23)

THE THREE PILLARS OF ETERNITY

THE CREATION, THE FALL, AND the Atonement—upon these three pillars of eternity rests our destiny. Through the gospel of Jesus Christ we have the sacred opportunity to please God and receive His blessings. "O all ye that are pure in heart, lift up your heads and receive the pleasing word of God, and feast upon his love; for ye may, if your minds are firm, forever" (Jacob 3:2).

A TOUCH OF REALITY

Imagine that you have been born as an early participant in the unfolding family of Adam and Eve. You find yourself in a boundless landscape that stretches before you in all directions. How do you survive? At first, you feel alone. But you learn that you're not alone. You're surrounded by family members who support and encourage you. You have light flowing to you from heaven in the form of prophetic teachings and guidance. You have choices that can lift and propel you forward. You have the opportunity to work closely with the Lord by entering into covenants. And as you move forward in faith and obedience, you're overwhelmed with comfort and joy. The vast new world becomes a land of promise and happiness as you look forward to the time when you will again come into the presence of the Lord.

The pattern for survival is clear. It is centered in the plan of eternal life—the gospel of Jesus Christ. You learn it. You choose it. You covenant to keep it. And you do it. These four steps serve as your Liahona to guide you across the landscape of your new world. Your survival is certain. Your acceptance before the Lord is assured. Your life is filled with joy.

You—and all of us—have been born into a vast new world in our own day. It is the same for us now as it was for those early pioneers in the days of Adam and Eve. How do we survive? In the very same way—through the gospel of Jesus Christ. We learn it. We choose it. We covenant to keep it. And we do it.

WHAT LESSONS CAN WE LEARN FROM THE EARLY STORIES ABOUT GOD'S CHILDREN?

1. We are favored of the Lord when we follow His counsel.

We learn through the account of Cain and Abel how to become accepted of the Lord. At the beginning of their mortality, Adam and Eve were instructed to worship the Lord and offer sacrifices of the firstlings of their flocks in similitude of the sacrifice of Jesus Christ (see Moses 5:5–8). As loving parents, Adam and Eve "made all things known unto their sons and their daughters" (Moses 5:12). Prompted by Satan, Cain, a tiller of the ground, offered unto the Lord the fruit of his labors, whereas Abel, a keeper of sheep, was obedient in offering the firstlings of his flocks. The outcome is highly revealing:

> And the Lord had respect unto Abel, and to his offering;
>
> But unto Cain, and to his offering, he had not respect. Now Satan knew this, and it pleased him. And Cain was very wroth, and his countenance fell.
>
> And the Lord said unto Cain: Why art thou wroth? Why is thy countenance fallen?
>
> If thou doest well, thou shalt be accepted. And if thou doest not well, sin lieth at the door. (Moses 5:20–23; see also Genesis 4:4–7)

What was Cain's response to the Lord's solemn injunction to repent? "Cain was wroth, and listened not any more to the voice of the Lord, neither to Abel, his brother, who walked in holiness before the Lord" (Moses 5:26). Because he loved Satan more than God, Cain entered into a secret conspiracy to murder his brother Abel in order to take over his property. When the Lord later asked, "Where is Abel, thy brother?" Cain gave the lying response: "I know not. Am I my brother's keeper?" (Moses 5:34). Cain, thereafter known as "Master Mahan" (Moses 5:31), became the exemplar of a rebel not accepted of the Lord (see 1 John 3:11–12; Helaman 6:26–27).

Pondering: How can we follow Abel's example of obeying the Lord so that He will be pleased with us and accept our offering? How can we continually walk "in holiness before the Lord" (Moses 5:26; see also 2 Nephi 2:25–27)? How can we be our brother's keeper (see Matthew 22:37–40; 1 John 3:11–18)?

2. The gospel of Jesus Christ, declared from the beginning of the world, dispels darkness and illuminates the pathway to salvation.

Joseph Smith clarifies why Cain's offering fell short:

"Cain offered of the fruit of the ground, and was not accepted, because he could not do it in faith. . . . It must be shedding the blood of the Only Begotten to atone for man; for this was the plan of redemption; and without the shedding of blood was no remission; . . . the sacrifice was instituted for a type, by which man was to discern the great Sacrifice which God had prepared; to offer a sacrifice contrary to that, no faith could be exercised, because redemption was not purchased in that way . . . consequently Cain could have no faith; and whatsoever is not of faith, is sin. But Abel offered an acceptable sacrifice, by which he obtained witness that he was righteous, God Himself testifying of his gifts." (*Teachings of the Prophet Joseph Smith*, 58; see also Hebrews 11:4)

What is the meaning of "Master Mahan"?

Hugh Nibley suggests that the title "Master Mahan" applied to Cain may derive from ancient words meaning "great secret keeper"—in this case conspiring by secret covenant to take someone's life in order to gain worldly power and wealth (see Hugh Nibley, *Ancient Documents and the Pearl of Great Price* [Salt Lake City: Deseret Book, 1986], Lecture 19, p. 12). The enduring sequence of "great secret keepers" down through the ages—such as Lamech (see Moses 5:49) and the Gadianton robbers (see Helaman 6:25–30)—have brought great havoc against the Lord's people. Who are the "great secret keepers" of today?

Who was Enoch?

Enoch was the great high priest, seventh from Adam in priesthood lineage, who talked with the Lord "face to face" (Moses 7:4) and who, along with his righteous city of Zion, was taken up, as the Savior said, "into mine own bosom" (D&C 38:4; also Moses 7:23). From the biblical account we learn few details of the life and ministry of Enoch (see Genesis 5:18–24; Luke 3:37; Hebrews 11:5; Jude 1:14). However, modern-day revelation provides a fuller vista of Enoch's extraordinary accomplishments—in Moses 6 and 7, plus this statement from the Doctrine and Covenants: "Enoch was twenty-five years old when he was ordained under the hand of Adam; and he was sixty-five and Adam blessed him. And he saw the Lord, and he walked with him, and was before his face continually; and he walked with God three hundred and sixty-five years, making him four hundred and thirty years old when he was translated" (D&C 107:48–49).

Eternal truth is essential to our salvation. If we are to learn it, choose it, covenant to keep it, and do it, then we need to stay close to the Lord at all times and allow His light to shine continually within our being. That light has been radiating to all the world from the days of Adam and Eve:

> And thus the Gospel began to be preached, from the beginning, being declared by holy angels sent forth from the presence of God, and by his own voice, and by the gift of the Holy Ghost.
>
> And thus all things were confirmed unto Adam, by an holy ordinance, and the Gospel preached, and a decree sent forth, that it should be in the world, until the end thereof. (Moses 5:58–59; see also Moses 6:1)

In subsequent years, the prophet Enoch was called to spread the gospel truth: "And he heard a voice from heaven, saying: Enoch, my son, prophesy unto this people, and say unto them—Repent, . . . Say unto this people: Choose ye this day, to serve the Lord God who made you" (Moses 6:27, 33).

The Lord taught Enoch the same truths that He had revealed unto Adam concerning spiritual renewal: Just as we are born into this mortal world "by water, and blood, and the spirit" (Moses 6:59), we are likewise to be reborn spiritually into the kingdom of heaven through faith and covenant baptism, being redeemed through the blood of the Lamb and quickened by His Holy Spirit (see Moses 6:59–62; also Mosiah 3:19; John 3:3–7, 16).

Pondering: In what ways have we been blessed with a fulness of truth to light up our lives and guide us forward along the pathway of salvation and exaltation? How can we use that truth more faithfully?

3. Unity and purity are the qualities of a Zion people.

Enoch fulfilled his commission with such might that "all nations feared greatly, so powerful was the word of Enoch, and so great was the power of the language which God had given him" (Moses 7:13). The blessings of the Lord were poured out upon His people: "And the Lord called his people ZION, because they were of one heart and one mind, and dwelt in righteousness; and there was no poor among them" (Moses 7:18). Zion was subsequently taken up into heaven (see Moses 7:21, 69), and Enoch was shown in a vision the unfolding of wickedness among the people remaining on the earth, causing the heavens to weep over them because of the consequences of their unrighteousness (see Moses 7:37).

How can the Saints of today live more fully in accordance with the spirit of unity and righteousness and thus be a Zion people? How can we cultivate harmony in our relationships with those whose views differ from our own?

Contemplate the following true account from a professor who served as the director of a BYU semester abroad program many years ago:

> We were behind the Iron Curtain. We were in the hands of the leadership of the Communist Youth Movement. Would we be subjected to heartless propaganda and find ourselves locked in a hard-nosed debate with our political foes? It didn't turn out that way at all. Our BYU semester abroad group was on tour to learn about Eastern European mores and culture, and the consensus among our students—as well as the members of our young welcoming delegation—was that we should have a party and a dance. So that's what we did. As I

looked on peacefully with my wife and other faculty members, the young people from both sides simply related to each other as human beings, as young people seeking new friendships and new dialogue, as energetic, fun-loving citizens of one grand human family. They danced and laughed and shared insights about life and the hope of the future. For an hour or two, all potential acrimony about important differences in principles of government was suspended—replaced by a dance. Hope flourished. Peace abounded. Friendship took root. It was like a modest anticipation of the millennial era when borders will dissolve and the government will be in the hands of the divine King of Zion.

Pondering: In what areas of our lives do we need to work toward a greater spirit of unity and purity? How can we more fully reflect the qualities of a Zion people?

AGENDA FOR ACTION

Adam, Enoch, and all of the Lord's chosen prophets have projected the patterns of truth and righteousness radiating from the gospel. Truth redeems. We learn it. We choose it. We covenant to keep it. And we do it. Our life becomes a record of faith and obedience. We too can write our own "book of remembrance" (Moses 6:5; D&C 107:57) according to the practice established in the days of Adam. We can become righteous examples. We can help to spread the gospel of Jesus Christ in many ways: sharing our witness in the spirit of friendship, passing out copies of the Book of Mormon inscribed with our testimony, contributing referrals to the full-time missionaries and ward missionaries, volunteering for and participating in missionary lessons, and using social media to open channels of learning for those seeking the truth. Through our faithfulness and devotion in living the gospel and sharing it with others, we will find our lives filled with peace and joy through the blessings of a loving and gracious Lord.

LOOKING FORWARD: Like Noah, are we sometimes called upon to "build an ark" of rescue for our own family?

What is the meaning of the word *Zion*?

Originally, the name Zion (from a Hebrew source) applied to a hill near Jerusalem used by the Canaanites as a fortress location prior to its capture by David (see 2 Samuel 5:7). Today, the term Zion evokes a variety of meanings in the hearts of the followers of Christ: Zion is a place, an institution, a state of mind, a noble destination, a people, a vision of perfection, and an abode of God. "Therefore, verily, thus saith the Lord, let Zion rejoice, for this is Zion—THE PURE IN HEART" (D&C 97:21; see also Articles of Faith 1:10). Moses 7, with sixteen occurrences of the word *Zion*, might be considered the "Great Hymn of Zion in the Former Days," while Doctrine and Covenants 133 (with ten occurrences) might be considered the "Great Hymn of Zion in the Latter Days."

CHAPTER SIX

THE SAVING HAND OF THE LORD

GOSPEL DOCTRINE READING ASSIGNMENT: MOSES 8:19–30; GENESIS 6–9, 11:1–9

But with thee will I establish my covenant; and thou shalt come into the ark, thou, and thy sons, and thy wife, and thy sons' wives with thee. (Genesis 6:18)

THE GATHERING

THE LORD GATHERS HIS PEOPLE to safety in miraculous ways. In the days of Enoch, the Lord lifted the city of Zion out of the grasp of the spreading evil of worldly nations. In the days of Noah, the Lord cleansed the earth by removing all of His wayward children from the mortal sphere—leaving only the eight souls preserved in the ark. In the days of the tower of Babel, the Lord directed a righteous clan to safety in a new world. The merciful love of the Lord is manifested in all generations for the preservation of the faithful, as He confirmed: "That the work of the gathering together of my saints may continue, that I may build them up unto my name upon holy places; for the time of harvest is come, and my word must needs be fulfilled" (D&C 101:64).

How does the saving hand of the Lord reach out to us in our day and age?

A TOUCH OF REALITY

The events described below took place in June 1834:

The Lord has promised, "I will fight your battles" (D&C 105:14). When Zion's Camp was sent to defend the persecuted Saints in Missouri during the early days of the Restoration, the Lord fulfilled this promise in a miraculous way. A mob of nearly four hundred men had vowed "to kill Joe Smith and his army" (*History of the Church* 2:104) and were converging upon the Saints' location at Fishing River in Clay County, Missouri. Five scouts from the mob visited the camp, threatening that the Mormons would "see hell before morning" (*HC* 2:103). Some of the brethren wanted to load their weapons and fight, but Joseph Smith dissuaded them, saying, "Stand still, and see the salvation of God."[3] Wilford Woodruff recorded what appeared in the previously clear skies moments after the scouts' departure: "A small cloud like a black spot appeared in the northwest, and it began to unroll itself like a scroll, and in a few minutes the whole heavens were covered with a pall as black as ink" (*HC* 2:104). The ensuing storm of unprecedented violence entirely frustrated the schemes of the scattering mob. Joseph declared, "God is in this storm." The surviving mobocrats decided that "when Jehovah fights they would rather be absent" (*HC* 2:104).

How can we conduct ourselves in order to "see the salvation of God" as it brings safety to our families in times of tribulation? What is our modern-day ark of rescue? Let us consider some key strategies.

WHAT LESSONS CAN WE LEARN FROM THE ACCOUNT OF NOAH AND THE ARK?

1. The Lord always warns of impending danger and calamity. We should listen and obey.

During the days of Noah, wickedness flourished to such an extent that the Lord called upon His prophet to forewarn the people of the disaster rushing upon them. But they did not listen, since "every man was lifted up in the imagination of the thoughts of his heart, being only evil continually" (Moses 8:22; see also Genesis 6:5). The word of the Lord continued with power through the voice of Noah:

> Hearken, and give heed unto my words;
>
> Believe and repent of your sins and be baptized in the name of Jesus Christ, the Son of God, even as our fathers, and ye shall receive the Holy Ghost, that ye may have all things made manifest; and if ye do not this, the floods will come in upon you; nevertheless they hearkened not. (Moses 8:23–24)

Noah served as a beacon of light in a dark and sinking world: "And thus Noah found grace in the eyes of the Lord; for Noah was a just man, and perfect in his generation; and he walked with God, as did also his three sons, Shem, Ham, and Japheth" (Moses 8:27; see also Genesis 6:9). But Noah was virtually alone in his world, having as supporters only his wife, his three sons, and their wives—a small party of but eight souls heeding the warning of the Lord (see 1 Peter 3:18–20; 2 Peter 2:5).

Was Noah fearful in his calling? Are we fearful today as we face a flood of eroding values in a wicked world?

What does it mean to be a "just man"?

Noah (meaning "rest") was the great patriarch of the Old Testament who preserved the lineage of the righteous during the global cleansing of the world in the flood. In the words of Joseph Smith, the priesthood of God was given "to Noah, who is Gabriel; he stands next in authority to Adam in the priesthood; he was called of God to this office, and was the father of all living in his day, and to him was given the dominion" (*HC*, 3:385; see also D&C 84:14–15; 107:51–52). Noah was a "just man" (Moses 8:27; Genesis 6:9). How was this quality applied to other prophets and leaders in the scriptures? Jacob was a "just man" because he taught his son Enos "in the nurture and admonition of the Lord" (Enos 1:1; see also Proverbs 20:7). Shiblon, son of Alma, was a "just man" because "he did walk uprightly before God; and he did observe to do good continually, to keep the commandments of the Lord his God" (Alma 63:2). The centurion Cornelius was a "just man" because he "fear[ed] God, and [was] of good report" (Acts 10:22; see also Acts 10:2). Those worthy of a celestial glory are "just men made perfect" because they accept and obey Jesus, "the mediator of the new covenant, who wrought out this perfect atonement through the shedding of his own blood" (D&C 76:69; see also D&C 129:6). In the same way, Noah was a "just man"— obedient and devoted to the Lord, serving the people with sincere love, and nurturing his family without ceasing.

---

3   *Church History in the Fulness of Times*, 148; compare Exodus 14:13.

The celebrated British psychologist John Bowlby (1907–1990) developed a series of pioneering studies about the causes of fear in children. Research about the experiences of children—including the traumatic impact of the blitz of London during the Second World War—caused him to conclude that the source of their fear generally went back to a condition of their being alone in dark places, suddenly separated from the support of loved ones, surrounded by strange noises, and accompanied by confusing and unfamiliar figures and shapes.

If that is the source of basic fear, then it is reasonable to conclude that the source of basic joy would be the opposite: being in familiar and comforting circumstances with loved ones, being in an atmosphere of healing light and uplifting sounds. In a spiritual sense, fear arises when one is separated from the glory of God and left alone in darkness, while joy arises when one is rendered worthy through obedience to the gospel.

Noah was not fearful for himself but only fearful and grieving over the inevitable suffering of the wicked (see Hebrews 11:7), for "the earth was corrupt before God, and it was filled with violence" (Moses 8:28). Because the people rejected the warnings, a total cleansing of the earth took place. The Lord always gives plain and unmistakable warnings about the destructive effects of sin (see 2 Nephi 25:9; Amos 3:7). Now the moment had come.

Pondering: In what ways can we receive strength from the Lord in order to overcome fear and doubt? How can we better recognize the warnings of the Lord? What influences in modern-day culture are akin to the destructive influences that made it necessary for the Lord to send the cleansing flood upon the world? How can we overcome such influences? How can we act in the spirit of Noah—a "just man"—to guide our families in the pathway of the Lord?

2. Noah's ark was an ideal model of rescue. Many modern "arks" are available for us in our day.

Tragically, Noah's world had become willfully and irreversibly corrupt. The Lord devised a plan to save Noah and his family from the impending global flood by directing them to build an immense ark—300 cubits long, 50 cubits wide, and 30 cubits high (see Genesis 6:15). Since a cubit was equivalent to the length of a man's arm from elbow to fingertips, such a vessel would be around 450 feet long, 75 feet wide, and 45 feet high—a three-story ship with a horizontal profile equal to around one-and-a-half football fields! Though only half as big as modern cruise liners or aircraft carriers, the ark was large enough for Noah's family and all of the creatures the Lord wanted to save.

The Lord caused an immense rainstorm and water surge to bury the earth in water for 150 days (see Genesis 7:24). All life was destroyed except on the ark. Noah knew that the flood had abated when a dove he sent forth returned with an olive leaf. When the dove flew out again seven days later and did not return, that was good news (see Genesis 8:11, 12). Soon thereafter, the Lord directed Noah and his entourage to exit the ark and return to their mortal work. Noah obeyed and built an altar for sacrifices in gratitude to the Lord (see Genesis 8:20). The Lord set the rainbow in the heavens as a reminder of His covenant to protect and guide His faithful children forever (see Genesis 9:8–17; especially the expanded passage in JST, Genesis 9:21–25).

The divine covenant made by the Lord with Noah and his descendants remains in force to this day. In His own due time, the Lord will return to the earth as millennial King. Meanwhile, we have the opportunity to prepare for the Second Coming by seeking shelter in the rescue arks of our day—the holy homes, stakes, and temples of the kingdom of God preserved as a blessing "for a place of refuge, and for a covert from storm and from rain" (Isaiah 4:6).

How is the family an ark of rescue? The following story is one example:

Where did the descendants of Noah settle?

In order of their birth, Noah's sons were Japheth, Shem, and Ham (see Moses 8:27). The descendants of Japheth settled in a region extending from the eastern Mediterranean coasts to the areas around the Black Sea and the Caspian Sea. Shem is traditionally considered to be the ancestor of the Semitic language family of nations—Hebrews, Phoenicians, Arabs, Aramaeans (or Syrians), Babylonians, and Assyrians. Abraham and Christ came through the lineage of Shem (see Luke 3:23, 36). The descendants of Ham settled in eastern Africa (Egypt and Ethiopia), southern Arabia, Libya (originally Put or Phut), and Palestine (before the arrival of the Semitic peoples). (See the Bible Dictionary entries for "Ham," "Japheth," and "Shem.")

A guard at the international boundary peered into the car. "Who is that boy you have with you?" he asked.

"He's my nephew," the young driver explained. "He's coming with me for a few days while I visit my father."

The guard was not impressed. "How do I know you have permission from the boy's parents to take him out of the country?" he inquired.

The student didn't have an answer because it had not occurred to him that it would be a problem to have his young nephew as a companion. "This boy is my sister's son," he said. "Should I try to get her on the phone?"

"Wait a minute," said the guard. "Did you say you were going to visit your father?"

"Yes," the student replied.

"Who is your father?" the guard asked. The student then stated the name of his father. A smile crept across the guard's face. "We know him. He's a good and honest man. If you are his son, then it will be all right." And he waved the car through the border.

There is power in a noble and righteous reputation. At an even higher level, there is power in being the son or daughter of our Heavenly Father and a faithful follower of His Only Begotten Son.

Pondering: How can we be assured that we are accessing all of the "rescue arks" made available to us by the Lord in these trying times? How can we make our own eyes, ears, and feelings more sensitive to the invitation of the Lord to "stand in holy places" (D&C 45:32; 101:22)?

AGENDA FOR ACTION

The pattern is clear: The Lord protects His faithful sons and daughters in all generations. Enoch and his city of Zion were taken upward—away from the wicked culture of the times. Noah and his family—the only faithful souls in a world of total iniquity—were rescued from the flood. Several generations later the Jaredites of the Book of Mormon (see the book of Ether) were led away to a promised land when the Lord confounded the language of the builders of the Tower of Babel and scattered the people because of their vain and prideful purposes (see Genesis 11:1–9).

By what steps will the Lord bring about our own rescue from the darkness and evil abounding in modern times? How can we become more like Noah—a "just man"—in order to merit the blessings of deliverance? We can lift our level of obedience. We can follow the counsel of living prophets. We can serve others with more love. We can honor more fully our covenants with the Lord. We can bring our families aboard the "rescue arks" of our day—homes of unity and caring, sacred congregations, holy temples. All children of God have the opportunity to make wise judgments and honorable choices that will lift them above the flood of evil in the world to a higher place of joy where they can see the salvation of God.

Moreover, how could this process of building our own "arks of rescue" be enlivened for each family through fun activities that foster togetherness and joy? Here are some ideas that can be adapted and applied:

- Make and apply a family plan for growing foods that can be enjoyed now and stored for future emergency use.
- Use family home evening gatherings to study the First Presidency message for the month and decide what the Lord is telling us to do now in preparing our own family ark of rescue.
- Organize activities where children or grandchildren make little paper boats as a backdrop for discussing the story of Noah and grasping the principle of how the Lord gives us tools to build our own arks of rescue.
- Take steps as a family to reduce indebtedness and increase savings for a rainy day.
- Look around and find those who are adrift and need encouragement and support.

All of these ideas and many more from your own inventory of inspired thoughts can increase preparation and contribute to family comfort and safety, for "if ye are prepared ye shall not fear" (D&C 38:30).

Looking Forward: What are the blessings that flow to us as participants in the Abrahamic covenant?

CHAPTER SEVEN

THE BLESSINGS OF THE ABRAHAMIC COVENANT

GOSPEL DOCTRINE READING ASSIGNMENT: ABRAHAM 1:1–4, 2:1–11; GENESIS 12:1–8, 17:1–9

And in thy seed after thee . . . shall all the families of the earth be blessed, even with the blessings of the Gospel, which are the blessings of salvation, even of life eternal. (Abraham 2:11)

THE TIME LINE OF EXALTATION

IMAGINE A TIME LINE FOR Abraham, beginning with the premortal realm—where he is identified as one of the "noble and great ones" (Abraham 3:22–23)—and extending to the postmortal realm of glory—where, through obedience, he enters into his exaltation and sits upon a throne. That is Abraham's time line or path of exaltation. In the middle of the line, representing Abraham's mortal years, we see his steps of honor, including his obedience to the Lord in journeying from his homeland, Ur of Chaldees, to Haran, and then on to Canaan (see Abraham 2:1–6; Genesis 12–13)—and his receiving the extraordinary promise known as the Abrahamic covenant:

And I will make of thee a great nation, and I will bless thee above measure, and make thy name great among all nations, and thou shalt be a blessing unto thy seed after thee, that in their hands they shall bear this ministry and Priesthood unto all nations;

And I will bless them through thy name; for as many as receive this Gospel shall be called after thy name, and shall be accounted thy seed, and shall rise up and bless thee, as their father;

And I will bless them that bless thee, and curse them that curse thee; and in thee (that is, in thy Priesthood) and in thy seed (that is, thy Priesthood), for I give unto thee a promise that this right shall continue in thee, and in thy seed after thee (that is to say, the literal seed, or the seed of the body) shall all the families of the earth be blessed, even with the blessings of the Gospel, which are the blessings of salvation, even of life eternal. (Abraham 2:9–11; see also Genesis 12:2–3, 7; 17:1–8)

The Abrahamic covenant continued through the lineage of Isaac (see Genesis 26:1–5, 24) and Jacob (see Genesis 28:10–15; 35:9–15; 48:3–4) and is still in effect today. All of the Lord's sons and daughters share in the blessings and duties of that sacred covenant. How is the Abrahamic covenant related to our personal covenants with the Lord? As sons and daughters of God, we can all participate in the global expansion of the kingdom of God through family growth and missionary service—and thus honor our personal covenants while helping fulfill the commission of the Abrahamic covenant to bring the blessings of the gospel and the priesthood to all nations of the earth. In doing so, we are drawing our own time line of exaltation that began in the premortal realm, continues day by day in our mortal experience, and extends to the hour when we will return again to our heavenly home of glory.

WHAT LESSONS CAN WE LEARN FROM ABRAHAM AND HIS COVENANT WITH THE LORD?

1. The Abrahamic covenant blesses us with a home of safety and refuge.

Said the Lord unto Abraham, "And I will give unto thee, and to thy seed after thee, the land wherein thou art a stranger, all the land of Canaan, for an everlasting possession; and I will be their God" (Genesis 17:8; see also Genesis 12:7; 15:7, 18). Isaac and his seed received the continuing promise (see Genesis 26:3), as did also Jacob and his seed (see Genesis 28:10–13; Genesis 35:12; 48:3–4).

The peoples of the Book of Mormon were blessed with access to the promised land across the expanse of the sea (see 1 Nephi 14:1–2; 17:13–14; 18:22–23; Alma 37:44–45; Ether 6:5–12). During the Restoration, the Lord established a place of refuge and gathering for His Saints: "And it shall come to pass that the righteous shall be gathered out from among all nations, and shall come to Zion, singing with songs of everlasting joy" (D&C 45:71; see also D&C 115:6; Articles of Faith 1:10). The blessings of a covenant home continue beyond the veil in the "city of the living God, the heavenly place, the holiest of all" (D&C 76:66; see also D&C 132:19). As the Savior said, "Ye are the children of the prophets; and ye are of the house of Israel; and ye are of the covenant which the Father made with your fathers, saying unto Abraham: And in thy seed shall all the kindreds of the earth be blessed" (3 Nephi 20:25).

One missionary recounts how he came to learn the reality of our divine potential:

Often limited in their resources—even poor—humble German families often took in missionaries, serving the best food they could afford. One family was excited to offer us baked rabbit the day after they had caught the animal nearby in a thicket. They had nothing else to offer but that rabbit—and their loving kindness. I met them unexpectedly at the Swiss temple many months later, and after all of these decades, I can still see that family in my mind's eye. They looked resplendent in their temple clothing, complete with the glow of happiness in their faces. In the house of the Lord—this holy place of gathering—they had set aside the homely and simple everyday clothing of their poverty for the robes of spiritual abundance. They had the appearance of what they were all along—royalty in disguise, sons and daughters of God endowed with the capacity to be enduring servants of the Almighty.

Pondering: In what ways do the gathering places of Zion—our homes, our stakes, and our temples—remind us of the fulfillment of the promises of the Abrahamic covenant? How can we more fully show our gratitude to our Heavenly Father for such blessings?

2. The Abrahamic covenant blesses us with an eternal family.

The Lord promised Abraham, "And I will make of thee a great nation" (Abraham 2:9; see also Genesis 12:2–3; 17:1–8). How great? See the Lord's measure: "Look now toward heaven, and tell the stars, if thou be able to number them: and he said unto him, So shall thy seed be" (Genesis 15:5). Isaac received the same promise (see Genesis 26:4). To Jacob the Lord said: "And thy seed shall be as the dust of the earth, and thou shalt spread abroad to the west, and to the east, and to the north, and to the south" (Genesis 28:14; see also Genesis 35:11; 48:4).

How do the blessings of a great posterity continue beyond the veil? (See D&C 132:19–22, 30–32)

Pondering: How can we do our part to ensure that our family will be an eternal family? How can we find ways to express our thanks unto the Lord for this sacred blessing?

3. The Abrahamic covenant blesses us with the gospel and with the power of the priesthood.

The Abrahamic covenant includes the promise that all worthy participants shall have the full blessings of the gospel and the priesthood—"which are the blessings of salvation, even of life eternal" (Abraham 2:11; see also Genesis 12:2–3). The blessings of the Abrahamic covenant are available to all who come into the fold of Christ: "And they shall also be crowned with blessings from above, yea, and with commandments not a few, and with revelations in their time—they that are faithful and diligent before me" (D&C 59:4).

How do the blessings of the gospel continue beyond the veil? (See D&C 132:19–20; see also D&C 59:2; 66:12; 84:38; 103:13–18)

Pondering: What qualities demonstrate that we fully accept the gospel of Jesus Christ? How can we be more faithful in living according to the spirit of the Abrahamic covenant?

4. The Abrahamic covenant blesses us with the opportunity to spread the gospel to the world.

From the beginning, Abraham understood that his covenant with the Lord included global missionary work (see Abraham 2:9–10). As a crowning part of His earthly ministry, the Savior commissioned His disciples to carry on this sacred duty: "Go ye therefore, and teach all nations, baptizing them in the name of the Father, and of the Son, and of the Holy Ghost" (Matthew 28:19). In the Kirtland temple on April 3, 1836, the Lord renewed the commission: "After this, Elias appeared, and committed the dispensation of the gospel of Abraham, saying that in us and our seed all generations after us should be blessed" (D&C 110:12). Missionary work is a central focus of the restored gospel (see D&C 133:7–10; also D&C 39:13; 45:69, 71; 64:41–42; 66:11–12; 112:6; 132:31).

Pondering: How is our life changed when we share with others the truths of the gospel?

Joseph Smith on the Abrahamic Covenant

"If there is anything calculated to interest the mind of the Saints, to awaken in them the finest sensibilities, and arouse them to enterprise and exertion, surely it is the great and precious promises made by our Heavenly Father to the children of Abraham; and those engaged in seeking the outcasts of Israel, and the dispersed of Judah, cannot fail to enjoy the Spirit of the Lord and have the choicest blessings of Heaven rest upon them. . . . He who scattered Israel has promised to gather them; therefore inasmuch as you are to be instrumental in this great work, He will endow you with power, wisdom, might, and intelligence, and every qualification necessary; while your minds will expand wider and wider, until you can circumscribe the earth and the heavens, reach forth into eternity, and contemplate the mighty acts of Jehovah in all their variety and glory" (in a letter dated May 14, 1840, to Orson Hyde and John E. Page, called on a mission to the Jewish people in Europe and Palestine, *HC* 4:128).

AGENDA FOR ACTION

The Lord delights in blessing His children. He gives them places of refuge in this world. He gives them hope for eternal mansions on high. He makes them fruitful in their posterity and gives them the promise of eternal increase through the blessings of temple marriage. He provides the fulness of the everlasting gospel of Jesus Christ and the priesthood with its ennobling and redeeming power. For all of these extraordinary blessings, He asks only that we walk in righteousness and share our witness to the world.

How can we improve our effectiveness as participants in the Abrahamic covenant? Here is a short scriptural checklist:

- "If ye were Abraham's children, ye would do the works of Abraham" (John 8:39).

- "Know ye therefore that they which are of faith, the same are the children of Abraham" (Galatians 3:7).

- "And if ye be Christ's, then are ye Abraham's seed, and heirs according to the promise" (Galatians 3:29).
- "Go ye, therefore, and do the works of Abraham; enter ye into my law and ye shall be saved" (D&C 132:32).

Focus your scripture study this week on better understanding the Abrahamic covenant—both the Lord's promises and your responsibilities.

LOOKING FORWARD: Where is a safe place to "pitch your tent"?

CHAPTER EIGHT

THE WAY OF THE LORD

Gospel Doctrine Reading Assignment: Genesis 13–14, 18–19; JST, Genesis 14:25–40, 19:9–15
They shall keep the way of the Lord, to do justice and judgment. (Genesis 18:19)

SODOM OR SALEM—A VITAL CHOICE

THE ERA OF ABRAHAM IN Canaan—including his close relationship with Melchizedek, the high priest and king of Salem (Jerusalem)—provides a powerful vista concerning the importance of our choices in mortality. Through the strength of the Lord we can turn away from the allure of worldly evil (Sodom) and instead gather with the Saints of peace and eternal glory (Salem). The former is the plunge into destruction; the latter is the rise toward divine redemption and joy. The worthy examples of Abraham and Melchizedek provide compasses for our journey of life—a stark contrast with the rock-hard rebelliousness and wickedness of the people of Sodom and Gomorrah. King Lamoni in the Book of Mormon confirmed the right pathway: "I know, in the strength of the Lord thou canst do all things" (Alma 20:4).

WHAT LESSONS CAN WE LEARN FROM THE EXPERIENCES OF ABRAHAM?

1. There is wisdom in "pitching our tent" away from Sodom and toward the house of the Lord.

Abraham arrived in Canaan with his wife Sarai (later named Sarah—see Genesis 17:15) and his nephew Lot, who was the son of Haran, brother of Abraham (see Genesis 11:27, 31; 12:4–5; 13:5; Abraham 2:4–5, 14–15). The flocks and herds of Abraham and Lot were so abundant that a separation was necessary in order to find terrain of sufficient size for both families. When Abraham granted Lot the choice of where to reside, Lot favored the verdant plains, so "Abram dwelled in the land of Canaan, and Lot dwelled in the cities of the plain, and pitched his tent toward Sodom" (Genesis 13:12).

That location exposed Lot to a battle that rocked the area in due time. Chedorlaomer, king of Elam, in league with three princes of Babylon, defeated the kings of Sodom, Gomorrah, and several other cities who had revolted against Chedorlaomer (see Genesis 14:1–10). In the battle, the victors "took all the goods of Sodom and Gomorrah, and all their victuals, and went their way. And they took Lot, Abram's brother's son, who dwelt in Sodom, and his goods, and departed" (Genesis 14:11–12). Learning of this abduction, Abraham marched out with 318 of his own men and routed the forces of Chedorlaomer. "And he brought back all the goods, and also brought again his brother Lot, and his goods, and the women also, and the people" (Genesis 14:16)—but he refused to accept the material spoils of war offered to him by the king of the liberated Sodom (see Genesis 14:17–24).

However, Lot and his family were not liberated from danger, for they dwelt by choice in a wicked city. Messengers of the Lord were sent to warn Lot to remove his family from the midst of evil, lest they should be present when the impending destruction from heaven should take place. When Lot seemed to resist, the messengers took forceful action: "And while he lingered, the men laid hold upon his hand, and upon the hand of his wife, and upon the hand of his two daughters; the LORD being merciful unto him: and they brought him forth, and set him without the city. And it came to pass, when they had brought them forth abroad, that [they] said, Escape for thy life; look not behind thee, neither stay thou in all the plain; escape to the mountain, lest thou be consumed" (Genesis 19:16–17; see also JST, Genesis 19:24–25). "Then the LORD rained upon Sodom and upon Gomorrah brimstone and fire from the LORD out of heaven" (Genesis 19:24; compare JST, Genesis 19:31–32; Luke 17:28–29; 2 Peter 2:6–8).

> **Where was the location of Sodom and Gomorrah?**
>
> Historians and archaeologists cannot determine with precision the location of these cities. Certainly they were near the Dead Sea, most likely in an area near the south end of it (see "Bible Maps and Photographs," Map 10, area C8).

Lot's two sons, Moab and Ammon, became the ancestors of the Moabites and Ammonites (see Genesis 19:37–38; Deuteronomy 2:9, 19). We can look back on the experience of Lot and remember to avoid following his example when he "pitched his tent toward Sodom" (Genesis 13:12). Instead, we can do as the people of King Benjamin did: "And they pitched their tents round about the temple, every man having his tent with the door thereof towards the temple, that thereby they might remain in their tents and hear the words which king Benjamin should speak unto them" (Mosiah 2:6). We are counseled to focus our view on eternal things rather than on the enticements of the world, as the following true account illustrates:

The young mother and father did a courageous thing. As a way of assuring a wholesome environment for their growing family, they chose to forgo television in the home. Instead, they assembled a library of interesting and uplifting digital programs. With church activities, music lessons, gymnastics, sports, school lessons, and other active involvements occupying their time, they found that commercial television programs were not missed. It is an admirable thing for parents to take leadership in controlling what influences come into the home. Parents are wise to take a firm stand in rejecting that which draws minds and hearts away from God.

We can also remember to avoid the experience of Lot's wife when she disobeyed the counsel of the Lord and "looked back," thus perishing (see Genesis 19:26). "Remember Lot's wife," was the counsel of the Savior in warning the people to let go of all earthly things and focus on things of heaven (Luke 17:32). At the same time, we can garner from the story the mercy and compassion of the Lord in taking steps to save Lot and his family from the fiery destruction of Sodom and Gomorrah.

Pondering: What are the modern Sodoms of our time? What steps can we take to "pitch our tent" away from Sodom and toward the house of the Lord? What actions can we take to avoid looking back at the environment of evil from which we are fleeing?

2. Abraham and Melchizedek are models of the qualities we seek to emulate in our own lives.

Review the following historical summaries concerning Abraham and Melchizedek and note the noble quality or qualities displayed:

A. Abraham followed the directive of the Lord to journey to Canaan and establish his home in what would become the Holy Land. He paid tithes to Melchizedek in keeping with gospel principles (see Genesis 14:18–24; Alma 13:14–15; Hebrews 7:1–4). So great was Melchizedek's office and stature that he was placed in charge of the abundance of the Lord's kingdom: "And he lifted up his voice, and he blessed Abram, being the high priest, and the keeper of the storehouse of God; Him whom God had appointed to receive tithes for the poor. Wherefore, Abram paid unto him tithes of all that he had, of all the riches which he possessed, which God had given him more than that which he had need" (JST, Genesis 14:37–39). Abraham was "the father of the faithful" (D&C 138:41), for he "received all things, whatsoever he received, by revelation and commandment, by my word, saith the Lord, and hath entered into his exaltation and sitteth upon his throne" (D&C 132:29).

B. Abraham wisely settled a territorial dispute between his cattle workers and those of Lot: "Let there be no strife, I pray thee, between me and thee, and between my herdmen and thy herdmen; for we be brethren" (Genesis 13:8). The ministry of Melchizedek, king in Salem (later called Jerusalem), exhibited a similar quality, for he achieved harmony in a city that was under a veil of spiritual darkness and rebellion, "yea, they had all gone astray" (Alma 13:17). Through his leadership, the people returned to a state of unity and righteousness (see Alma 13:18). Abraham later displayed a similar yearning on behalf of the wayward people in Sodom and Gomorrah, obtaining an agreement from the Lord that the cities would be spared if at least ten people of righteous character could be found in them (see Genesis 18:23–33). But alas, not even ten could be found, and the cities were destroyed (see Genesis 19:24–25).

C. Of Abraham the Lord declared: "For I know him, that he will command his children and his household after him, and they shall keep the way of the Lord, to do justice and judgment" (Genesis 18:19). Of Melchizedek, Alma declared: "But Melchizedek having exercised mighty faith, and received the office of the high priesthood according to the holy order of God, did preach repentance unto his people. And behold, they did repent; and Melchizedek did establish peace in the land in his days; therefore he was called the prince of peace, for he was the king of Salem; and he did reign under his father. Now, there were many before him, and also there were many afterwards, but none were greater; therefore, of him they have more particularly made mention" (Alma 13:18–19; compare JST, Genesis 14:33, 36).

D. The Lord declared unto Abraham: "Behold, I will lead thee by my hand, and I will take thee, to put upon thee my name, even the Priesthood of thy father, and my power shall be over thee. As it was with Noah so shall it be with thee; but through thy ministry my name shall be known in the earth forever, for I am thy God" (Abraham 1:18–19). Paul declared concerning Melchizedek: "For this Melchizedek was ordained a priest after the order of the Son of God, which order was without father, without mother, without descent, having neither beginning of days, nor end of life. And all those who are ordained unto this priesthood are made like unto the Son of God, abiding a priest continually" (JST, Hebrews 7:3; compare also Alma 13:14, 19). Note how Abraham received the priesthood: "Abraham received the priesthood from Melchizedek, who received it through the lineage of his fathers, even till Noah" (D&C 84:14). In our day, the Lord

> **Take a Little Time to Improve**
>
> "When you get up in the morning, before you suffer yourselves to eat one mouthful of food, call your wife and children together, bow down before the Lord, ask him to forgive your sins, and protect you through the day, to preserve you from temptation and all evil, to guide your steps aright, that you may do something that day that shall be beneficial to the Kingdom of God on the earth. Have you time to do this? Elders, sisters, have you time to pray?"—Brigham Young (*Discourses of Brigham Young* [Salt Lake City: Deseret Book, 1954], 44.)

explained that Melchizedek was "such a great high priest" that the higher priesthood was named after him "to avoid the too frequent repetition of [the Lord's] name" (D&C 107:2–4).

Pondering: How can we obey the Lord more faithfully? How can we improve our ability to be peacemakers? How can we teach the gospel more effectively? How can we honor the priesthood with greater diligence and valor?

AGENDA FOR ACTION

The Lord has given us a road map of righteousness by preserving the record of the lives of His chosen prophets such as Abraham and Melchizedek. We can savor the goodness of God by studying the example of these individuals. At the same time, we can take to heart the destructive consequences of permitting the alluring enticements of the world to displace the solid anchor of righteousness. Lot looked with longing toward the decadent cities of the plain; he pitched his tent toward Sodom and came narrowly close to the precipice. Let us be watchful and prayerful, valiant and humble, devoted and grateful—ever willing to follow in the footsteps of the Lord by cultivating divine qualities. "Therefore I would that ye should be perfect even as I, or your Father who is in heaven is perfect" (3 Nephi 12:48).

That process of perfection often involves simple but profoundly important actions. For example, our choices for seeking entertainment and relaxation can have a significant impact on the spiritual quality of our lives. Wise monitoring and filtering in the selection of television programs, movies, and websites can protect the family from degrading influences and pollution while opening up wholesome and uplifting channels of entertainment. As Church leaders confirmed in the worldwide leadership broadcast on June 23, 2013, social media and Internet applications, used with wisdom and high standards, can have a powerful and positive effect on missionary work and spreading the gospel.

LOOKING FORWARD: What is the nature of the sacrifice that the Lord expects us to offer?

CHAPTER NINE

"BEHOLD, I WILL LEAD THEE BY MY HAND"

Gospel Doctrine Reading Assignment: Abraham 1; Genesis 15–17, 21–22
God will provide himself a lamb. (Genesis 22:8)

A STAIRCASE OVER TRIBULATION

How do the Lord's prophets down through the ages of time rise above the intense persecution and tribulation that mark their journey through life? Let us look at the pattern followed by Abraham, one of the Lord's noble and great rulers. Even before he commenced his ministry, Abraham had a clear vision of his own destiny:

> Having been myself a follower of righteousness, desiring also to be one who possessed great knowledge, and to be a greater follower of righteousness, and to possess a greater knowledge, and to be a father of many nations, a prince of peace, and desiring to receive instructions, and to keep the commandments of God, I became a rightful heir, a High Priest, holding the right belonging to the fathers. (Abraham 1:2)

When the wayward priests in Ur of the Chaldees, the homeland of his fathers, raised their hands to take away his life on the sacrificial altar of the Egyptian gods, Abraham lifted up his voice to the Lord, who then "filled [him] with the vision of the Almighty" (Abraham 1:15) and snatched him away to safety, saying: "Behold, I will lead thee by my hand, and I will take thee, to put upon thee my name, even the Priesthood of thy father, and my power shall be over thee. As it was with Noah so shall it be with thee; but through thy ministry my name shall be known in the earth forever, for I am thy God" (Abraham 1:18–19).

Carried forth by the light of that vision, Abraham acted in faith to follow the directive of the Lord in journeying to a land of inheritance, where he could unfold his covenant destiny as the father of nations, called to carry the gospel and the priesthood to the ends of the earth (see Abraham 2:8–11). That mission was threatened by wars and contentions, evil forces in Sodom and Gomorrah, perils inflicted upon his family members, plus the inability of his wife Sarah to bear children. But through the strength of the Lord, Abraham prevailed, and the work of the Lord flourished.

The pattern of victory is clear: *Vision reveals the goal. Faith inspires action. Strength flows from God. Mission is accomplished.* What Abraham achieved is a manifestation of the same pattern of divine triumph that we see in the life of the Savior. We can recall the Lord's words of comfort to Joseph Smith in Liberty Jail after the Prophet and his family had suffered unbearable persecution at the hands of conspiring enemies:

> Know thou, my son, that all these things shall give thee experience, and shall be for thy good.
>
> The Son of Man hath descended below them all. Art thou greater than he?
>
> Therefore, hold on thy way, and the priesthood shall remain with thee; for their bounds are set, they cannot pass. Thy days are known, and thy years shall not be numbered less; therefore, fear not what man can do, for God shall be with you forever and ever. (D&C 122:7–9)

A TOUCH OF REALITY

How do these promises apply to each one of us in our daily endeavors to honor our covenants and overcome our trials? Consider the following account from a member of a branch presidency in the Missionary Training Center at Provo, Utah:

> At one of the weekly devotional services, Elder Richard G. Scott was the scheduled speaker. He approached his assignment in an unusual way by inviting questions from the audience of several thousand aspiring missionaries. A young elder seated not far from me rose to the nearest microphone and asked the Apostle what to do when one came upon walls in life that seemed to act as barriers to progress. I shall never forget Elder Scott's thoughtful response. He said, in effect, that walls, when viewed from the right perspective, are not walls at all, but the vertical part of a step upward. Thus our attitude toward opposition in life can influence how we respond to adversity, and what might at first glance seem to be a barrier can turn out to be an opportunity for advancement.

What positive and inspiring counsel! As we rise above adversity through the strength of the Lord, we advance another step upward: "For after much tribulation come the blessings. Wherefore the day cometh that ye shall be crowned with much glory" (D&C 58:4). A staircase of tribulation is one that we are able to climb through vision, faith, and the strength of the Lord, "For with God nothing shall be impossible" (Luke 1:37).

WHAT LESSONS CAN WE LEARN FROM THE EXPERIENCES OF ABRAHAM, SARAH, AND ISAAC?

1. Nothing is too hard for the Lord.

By virtue of his covenant with the Lord, Abraham was to be "a father of many nations" (Genesis 17:4, 5; see also Abraham 1:2), just as Sarah was to be "a mother of nations" (Genesis 17:16). The posterity of Abraham was to be as countless as the stars in the heavens (see Genesis 15:5; 22:17) or the dust of the earth (see Genesis 13:16). And yet Sarah was barren. How could the promise be fulfilled? It is true that Sarah gave her Egyptian handmaid, Hagar, to Abraham as a wife, according the law of the day, resulting in the birth of Ishmael (see Genesis 16:15). And it is true that the Lord was kind to Hagar and Ishmael—though they were sent forth by Sarah—and promised that Ishmael would become "a great nation" (Genesis 17:20). However, the Lord declared, "But my covenant will I establish with Isaac, which Sarah shall bear unto thee at this set time in the next year" (Genesis 17:21).

"Next year" would mean that Abraham would be a hundred years old and Sarah ninety—a condition that generated within the aging patriarch a state of skeptical mirth. Sarah laughed with disbelief. In response, the Lord encouraged them: "Is any thing too hard for the LORD?" (Genesis 18:14). And bless them He did, for Isaac (meaning "he laughs") was born into the world as the next divinely appointed representative of the Abrahamic covenant (Genesis 21:2–3).

Truly there is nothing too hard for the Lord. We can all make obedience a governing pattern in our lives, knowing that God will bless us with every needful thing.

Sarah (meaning "princess") became indeed "a mother of nations," just as all worthy sisters—whether mothers, aspiring mothers, or motherly guardians of the children of the Lord—can partake of the blessings of the Abrahamic covenant in helping to build the kingdom of God on earth. Contemplate the following account:

On Wednesday, October 8, 1845, Lucy Mack Smith, revered and aging mother of the Prophet Joseph, rose and spoke before some five thousand Saints assembled for the last conference of the Church in Nauvoo. She exhorted all to protect their children from idleness by giving them work to do and books to read. She counseled all "to be full of love, goodness and kindness, and never to do in secret what they would not do in the presence of millions" (HC 7:470–471). Then in a noble gesture, she wished to learn whether the congregation might consider her a "mother in Israel," whereupon Brigham Young responded, "All who consider Mother Smith as a mother in Israel, signify it by saying yes!" According to the minutes, "One universal 'yes' rang throughout" (HC 7: 471).

All the "faithful daughters who [have] lived through the ages and worshiped the true and living God" (D&C 138:39) can be ennobled by the title "mother in Israel" in blessing the lives of the Lord's sons and daughters according to the spirit of love and compassion.

Pondering: What burdens or challenges in your life might seem at times to be impossible to overcome? How can you apply the principle that nothing is too hard for the Lord?

What happened to Ishmael?

Upon the passing of Abraham, Isaac and Ishmael came together to bury their father "in the cave of Machpelah . . . which is before Mamre" (Genesis 25:9). Ishmael passed away at age 137 (see Genesis 25:17). His descendants seem to have become a wandering people who intermingled with the nations of Canaan. Thus Joseph was sold by his brethren into the hands of Ishmaelites who took him to Egypt (see Genesis 37:25, 27–28; 39:1). Gideon later dealt with the Ishmaelites (see Judges 8:24; see also Psalm 83:6). Paul refers to the situation with Isaac and Ishmael with these words: "But he who was of the bondwoman was born after the flesh; but he of the freewoman was by promise" (Galatians 4:23).

2. Willing sacrifice is the key to personal redemption and joy.

Abraham treasured his son Isaac. Through Isaac, the covenant promises of the Lord would be realized, and Abraham would become the father of many nations. Then the Lord gave unto Abraham an unexpected commandment: "Take now thy son, thine only son Isaac, whom thou lovest, and get thee into the land of Moriah; and offer him there for a burnt offering upon one of the mountains which I will tell thee of" (Genesis 22:2). Abraham "rose up early in the morning" (Genesis 22:3) and commenced the journey to Moriah in obedience to the Lord.

His heart must have been heavy and his soul weighed down with sorrow. Perhaps he remembered the painful time when his own father had conspired to take away his life as an offering upon the altars of the Egyptian gods (see Abraham 1:30). Abraham was commanded to offer up his own son as a sacrifice. When Isaac inquired about a lamb, his father responded, "My son, God will provide himself a lamb for a burnt offering" (Genesis 22:8). Then Abraham bound Isaac and placed him on the altar—apparently without resistance from the dutiful son. A moment of drama had arrived—unequaled for intensity in all of Old Testament writ:

> And Abraham stretched forth his hand, and took the knife to slay his son.
> And the angel of the LORD called unto him out of heaven, and said . . .
> Lay not thine hand upon the lad, neither do thou any thing unto him: for now I know that thou fearest God, seeing thou hast not withheld thy son, thine only son from me.
> And Abraham lifted up his eyes, and looked, and behold behind him a ram caught in a thicket by his horns: and Abraham went and took the ram, and offered him up for a burnt offering in the stead of his son. (Genesis 22:10–13)

What is the gospel meaning of "broken" and "contrite"?

The Savior was "broken" through the sufferings of the Crucifixion. He was "contrite" (from a source word meaning "ground to pieces") because He submitted to the will of the Father and sacrificed His life on the cross. The Lord requires of His sons and daughters "a broken heart and a contrite spirit" (3 Nephi 9:20)—meaning humble awareness of the need to do the will of the Father through faith and honor, having "godly sorrow" for sins (2 Corinthians 7:10), hence meriting supreme joy through repentance. President Spencer W. Kimball said we have to lay whatever is necessary upon the altar of sacrifice. The first step, he continues, is offering a broken heart and contrite spirit. Next, we must give our best efforts in our labors and callings. . . . No matter what the duty—father, mother, home teacher, bishop, neighbor, visiting teacher, or friend—he points out that there is always an opportunity to give our all to the Lord (see "Becoming the Pure in Heart," *Ensign*, May 1978).

A test of epic proportions had been surmounted. The Lord then declared, "Because thou hast done this thing, and hast not withheld thy son, thine only son: . . . in thy seed shall all the nations of the earth be blessed; because thou hast obeyed my voice" (Genesis 22:16, 18).

Abraham had demonstrated his unshakeable commitment to do the will of the Lord in all things and thus sealed his blessing to become the father of many nations. From the foundation of the world, the Father had ordained the atoning sacrifice of His Only Begotten Son, just as the Son would willingly comply with the will of the Father in giving His own life for the redemption of mankind (see 3 Nephi 11:11). Abraham's humble obedience to the will of the Father fully anticipated the nature of sacrifice to be instituted by the Savior following His Resurrection: "And ye shall offer for a sacrifice unto me a broken heart and a contrite spirit. And whoso cometh unto me with a broken heart and a contrite spirit, him will I baptize with fire and with the Holy Ghost" (3 Nephi 9:20; see also 2 Nephi 2:7; 3 Nephi 12:19; Ether 4:15; Moroni 6:2; D&C 20:37; 59:8).

Pondering: In what ways does the obedience of Abraham touch our hearts and inspire us to give our all unto the Lord? How does the broken bread of the sacrament remind us to have "broken hearts and contrite spirits" continually?

AGENDA FOR ACTION

The vision of our personal destiny flows unto us from the word of the Lord—bestowed through the scriptures, the counsel of the living prophets, blessings from patriarchs and other leaders, and personal revelation. By looking "unto Abraham, your father, and unto Sarah, she that bare you" (2 Nephi 8:2; compare Isaiah 51:2), we learn that *vision reveals the goal, faith inspires action*, and *strength flows from God*—all blending together to ensure that *our covenant mission is finally accomplished*. What steps can we take to see and share our vision more clearly? In what areas of our life can we seek and cultivate faith leading to righteous action? In which of our relationships and activities do we need the abundant strength of the Lord more fully—and how can we obtain that blessing?

We can ponder these questions with an open mind and a willing heart and devise a list of actions that apply to our lives at the present. Then we can go to the Lord for a confirmation of our choices and ask for guidance and strength to carry them out effectively according to His will and blessing—despite the challenges and obstacles that sometimes lie in our pathway.

We are told by the Lord that the Saints "must needs be chastened and tried, even as Abraham" (D&C 101:4). Through the blessings of heaven, we can perceive life's tribulations not as an impenetrable wall but rather as a staircase of steps leading upward toward the realization of our divine potential: "But learn that he who doeth the works of righteousness shall receive his reward, even peace in this world, and eternal life in the world to come" (D&C 59:23).

Looking Forward: Can you describe in a few sentences your own personal "birthright"?

CHAPTER TEN

BIRTHRIGHT BLESSINGS

GOSPEL DOCTRINE READING ASSIGNMENT: GENESIS 24–29

Fear not, for I am with thee, and will bless thee, and multiply thy seed. (Genesis 26:24)

BIRTHRIGHT AS A BADGE OF HONOR AND POWER

IN THE DAYS OF THE ancient patriarchs, it was customary for certain rights, powers, and privileges to be passed on from the father to the firstborn son (such as from Abraham to Isaac) or to the son designated by the Lord (such as Isaac to Jacob, Jacob to Joseph, or Lehi to Nephi). In later dispensations the "birthright" as a general blessing for the sons and daughters of God became available to all worthy individuals based on faithfulness and obedience.

What is the nature of this universal birthright? What opportunities and blessings flow from it unto the children of the Lord? Here are some:

- Birth. When we are born into mortality, we come forth in the image of our Father in Heaven: "So God created man in his own image, in the image of God created he him; male and female created he them" (Genesis 1:27; Moses 2:26). The Creation gives us an eternal birthright, for we are all imbued with the opportunity and destiny to become as the Father.
- Baptism. The gospel of Jesus Christ allows us to be "born again . . . of water and of the Spirit" (John 3:3, 5). Through that process of faith and repentance, our birthright blesses us with forgiveness and leads to salvation and eternal life. The word *baptism* is not used in the Old Testament, but modern revelation confirms that this ordinance was standard from the beginning of time (see Moses 6:59–61, 64; JST, Genesis 17:3–7;

Moses 7:11; 8:23–24; Isaiah 48:1 as rendered in 1 Nephi 20:1; D&C 20:25–27). Baptism of water and fire provides a birthright for the companionship of the Holy Ghost.

- Belong. Through the gospel plan we come into the fold of Christ and enjoy the birthright of belonging to the family of God: "Now therefore ye are no more strangers and foreigners, but fellowcitizens with the saints, and of the household of God" (Ephesians 2:19). We are gathered to the holy places of Zion—homes, congregations, and temples—to receive the blessing of glory in the kingdom of God (D&C 130:2).

- Beacon. As participants in the Abrahamic covenant, we have the opportunity to spread the gospel throughout the world as beacons of light and truth: "Thou shalt be a blessing unto thy seed after thee, that in their hands they shall bear this ministry and Priesthood unto all nations" (Abraham 2:9; see also Matthew 28:19–20; D&C 68:8–9). As Peter declared, "But ye are a chosen generation, a royal priesthood, an holy nation, a peculiar people; that ye should shew forth the praises of him who hath called you out of darkness into his marvellous light" (1 Peter 2:9).

- Be fruitful. The birthright allows us to establish abundant families in Zion. We participate in becoming a "great nation" (Genesis 12:2; 17:20; 46:3; Abraham 2:9). The sealing power of the temple endows our families with a birthright of eternal duration (see D&C 132:19–24).

- Be perfect. Our universal gospel birthright offers the ability to become perfect "through the merits, and mercy, and grace of the Holy Messiah" (2 Nephi 2:8). "And if ye shall deny yourselves of all ungodliness, and love God with all your might, mind and strength, then is his grace sufficient for you, that by his grace ye may be perfect in Christ" (Moroni 10:32).

Our sacred and universal birthright leads to such glorious blessings.

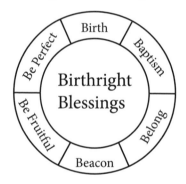

WHAT LESSONS CAN WE LEARN FROM THE BIRTHRIGHT EXPERIENCES OF ABRAHAM AND HIS POSTERITY?

1. The Abrahamic covenant is empowered through the spirit of revelation.

Brigham Young stated, "No person can receive a knowledge of this work except by the power of revelation. . . . The spirit of revelation, even the spirit of eternal life, is within that person who lives so as to bear properly the yoke of Jesus. The heavens are open to such persons, and they see and understand things that pertain to eternity."[4] The accounts of the marriages of Isaac and Jacob to their wives Rebekah and Rachel are remarkable stories of how revelation from the Lord directs the unfolding of His kingdom. Note the striking flow of events:

- Abraham is inspired to seek a wife for Isaac from within the family circle (see Genesis 24:4, 40).
- Abraham's chief servant is inspired to find Rebekah (see Genesis 24:12–14, 27, 42, 48).
- Laban and his father Bethuel are inspired to approve Rebekah as the wife of Isaac (see Genesis 24:50–51). "And they blessed Rebekah, and said unto her, Thou art our sister, be thou the mother of thousands of millions" (Genesis 24:60).
- Rebekah is inspired to accept the proposal without delay: "And they called Rebekah, and said unto her, Wilt thou go with this man? And she said, I will go" (Genesis 24:58).

---

4   *Discourses of Brigham Young* (Salt Lake City: Deseret Book, 1954), 35.

- Isaac is inspired to pray for the health of his new wife, who was barren (see Genesis 25:20–21).
- Rebekah is inspired to ensure that the blessings of the birthright would be conferred upon Jacob: "And she went to enquire of the LORD. And the LORD said unto her, Two nations are in thy womb, and two manner of people shall be separated from thy bowels; and the one people shall be stronger than the other people; and the elder shall serve the younger" (Genesis 25:22–23). The elder twin Esau (also called Edom—meaning "red") sold his birthright to Jacob for a mere serving of pottage (see Genesis 25:31–34).
- Jacob is inspired by a vision confirming his blessing: "And the LORD appeared unto him the same night, and said, I am the God of Abraham thy father: fear not, for I am with thee, and will bless thee, and multiply thy seed for my servant Abraham's sake" (Genesis 26:24). Jacob then received the birthright blessing from Isaac (see Genesis 27:13, 28–29).
- Isaac and Rebekah, grieved by the marriage of Esau to a noncovenant wife (see Genesis 26:34–35), are inspired to send Jacob to Haran to seek a wife from within the extended family circle (see Genesis 27:43–46; Genesis 28:1–4, 7).
- Jacob is inspired by the Lord during his journey to Haran (see Genesis 28:14–15, 20–22).
- Jacob is inspired to receive Rachel as his wife: "And Jacob kissed Rachel, and lifted up his voice, and wept" (Genesis 29:11). "And Jacob loved Rachel; . . . And Jacob served seven years for Rachel" (Genesis 29:18, 20). When Laban imposed Leah, his older daughter, upon him, Jacob agreed to serve seven more years and thus received Rachel as well (see Genesis 29:26–28).

The blessings of inspiration revealed in the account of Abraham and his posterity apply to our own service in the kingdom of God. President Thomas S. Monson has urgently counseled the young men of the Church to avoid procrastinating marriage (see "Priesthood Power," *Ensign*, May 2011). Perhaps the following true account by a young priesthood holder reflects how the spirit of inspiration can help to start the marriage years earlier:

> Wednesday and Thursday had been set aside as special fast days. I had prayed all along that I might learn of the Lord's approval for continuing my relationship with this wonderful girl. On Thursday morning as I was walking down a hillside, pondering about my situation, I was struck by the beauty of a small garden and pond that came into view. I stood near the pond to meditate. Should I ask her? Would she be happy with me? Factors came clearly and forcibly before my mind. Things became logical. I knew she was the one. No voice spoke and no light appeared—certainly no outward manifestation was given to me on that beautiful morning. But the inward calm and peace, the heartfelt conviction that all areas of importance had been explored and successfully answered—this was indeed overwhelming. I knew that the Lord would have it so; therefore, I committed to ask her and prayed that she would agree to be my wife. Seldom have I been blessed with so powerful an outpouring of truth. The light of heaven seemed to be reflected in that pond. I bowed my head and thanked the Lord for His mercy and inspiration.

Pondering: How have the examples of Abraham and Sarah, Isaac and Rebekah, Jacob and Rachel touched your life? How has inspiration from the Lord helped you to make important decisions?

2. Mothers of the covenant bring about the unfolding of the kingdom of God on the earth.

Sarah was to be "a mother of nations" (Genesis 17:16). Rebekah was to be "the mother of thousands of

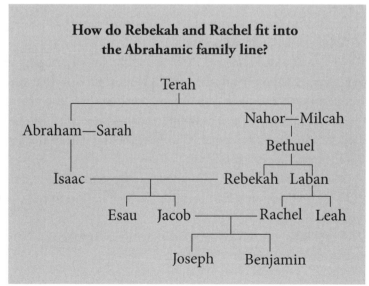

How do Rebekah and Rachel fit into the Abrahamic family line?

Terah

Abraham—Sarah

Nahor—Milcah

Bethuel

Isaac ——————— Rebekah   Laban

Esau   Jacob ———— Rachel   Leah

Joseph   Benjamin

millions" (Genesis 24:60). Rachel was to be a key factor in fulfilling the Lord's promise to Jacob (Israel) that "a nation and a company of nations shall be of thee" (Genesis 35:11). Each mother in Zion shares with Eve the honor of being "the mother of all living" (Genesis 3:20; Moses 4:26). Often that honor is achieved only through great sacrifice, even ultimate sacrifice.

How might the expectant Rachel have felt during her last hours on the earth? Here is a possibility based on details from the scriptural record:

A warm breeze caused the gentle fabric of the tent to billow in melodic rhythms. Young Joseph knelt beside his mother and held her hand as she rested on the portable divan, protected by a delicate, filmy canopy of white, green, and blue cloth held in place with fine linen cords. With his other hand, he gently wiped away the moisture from her forehead with a soft cloth.

"Are you feeling better, Mother?"

Rachel responded quietly. "Yes, thank you, son. So kind of you to ask. How is your father?"

"He will return soon. He's bringing some fresh water for you."

Just then the bleating of young lambs could be heard in the distance. "They are calling your name," said Joseph with a twinkle in his eyes. His mother smiled, remembering the time she had told him that the name given to her by her parents in Mesopotamia meant "ewe."

She reached over and stroked his face. "Your own name is a constant reminder to me of the blessings the Lord has given to our family. When we were passing through Bethel on our journey here, the Lord visited your father and confirmed that his new name would be Israel" (Genesis 35:10; 32:28).

"What does that name mean, Mother?"

"It means that he is bound to God with an eternal covenant of love and service. He is to follow in the footsteps of his father and grandfather to become 'a father of many nations'" (Genesis 17:4). She stroked the hair of the young lad. "When God remembered me and blessed me with a precious son in my homeland of Padan-aram, we gave you a name that means 'increase,' for you will carry on the promise of your father to become a multitude of nations" (Genesis 30:22–24).

Joseph took her hand again and held it closely. "This has been a long journey, Mother. But now we are so close to our destination of Bethlehem."

"A long journey, yes," she responded. "But also a journey of peace, a journey on which your father was able to bring harmony into our family once again. When the Lord commanded him to leave my homeland and take us to his kindred in the land of Canaan (see Genesis 31:3, 13; 32:9), my father, Laban, was troubled. But your father worked things out with him through the guidance of the Lord (see Genesis 31:44, 52–55). And on this journey, your father also reconciled the differences with his brother Esau (see Genesis 33:1–16). Your father is a man of peace—and you will also be a man of peace."

A shadow came over her face. "Ben-oni," she whispered (Genesis 35:18).

"Mother, what do you mean?"

She took a deep breath. "After I had the joy of bringing you into the world, I was promised from heaven that 'the LORD shall add to me another son' (Genesis 30:24). That time is approaching. Ben-oni means 'son of my sorrow,' for in my strength and pain, I shall bring your brother into the world" (Genesis 35:18).

At that moment, a stately figure parted the folds of the tent doorway and entered. He came over and knelt at Rachel's side to embrace her. Gently he held a cup to her lips and poured in drops of soothing water. She beamed a radiant smile back at him.

"You are my love," he whispered. He remembered the uplifting years he had served to earn her hand in marriage— and they seemed but a few days, for the love he had to her (see Genesis 29:20). *I would gladly do it again and again*, he thought to himself.

There was a moment of silence before he spoke up. "Joseph, my son. Please go and invite the midwife and the maidens to come in."

The hour had arrived. It was not long before a new life came into the world—a son now called Benjamin by his father, meaning "son of my right hand."

But sadly, Rachel, the noble daughter of destiny, the glorious example of motherhood, had passed on to a better world.

Pondering: How have the mothers in your life been a source of inspiration and guidance? How can we all improve in honoring our mothers as the fountainheads of the unfolding of the Abrahamic covenant? How can we have the strength to increase our own sacrifices in helping to build the kingdom of God on the earth?

AGENDA FOR ACTION

Let us find special ways this very week to honor a motherly figure in our lives—our own mother or grandmother, the mother of our children, or a charitable woman acting as a mother to others in our neighborhood or ward. We can honor such noble figures through kind words of gratitude or with simple gifts that reflect their qualities of charity. We can perform acts of service to make their lives easier.

To follow in the footsteps of Abraham and his faithful family posterity, we can don the badge of birthright honor and move forward in the strength of the Lord. Our birth in the image of God, our baptism by water and fire, our belonging to the family of God, our beacon of service, our being fruitful in the spirit of the Abrahamic covenant, and our being perfected in the grace of the Lord—all of these constitute an agenda for our life of honor. The family is to be eternal. The blessings of the temple ensure this divine destiny. Through obedience and humble prayer, we can receive the supreme gift of personal revelation to guide our lives. Let us not delay any action that will contribute to the forward motion along the pathway of salvation and exaltation—for ourselves and for all those we love and serve.

LOOKING FORWARD: What are the blessings of moral purity?

CHAPTER ELEVEN

THE HEALING POWER OF GOODNESS

GOSPEL DOCTRINE READING ASSIGNMENT: GENESIS 34, 37–39

The Lord was with [Joseph], and that which he did, the Lord made it to prosper. (Genesis 39:23)

THE ANCHOR OF MORAL STRENGTH

WE LEARN MUCH BY OBSERVING those who precede us down the pathway of life. Joseph, son of Jacob and Rachel, lived a life anchored in moral strength and valiant leadership. By contrast, his brothers were often slaves to a spirit of crushing envy, hateful greed, and (in the case of some) unchecked lust. These two opposing positions confirm that choices bring inescapable consequences—at one end of the spectrum joy and productivity, and at the other end, pain and destruction. From goodness flows joy; from vice flows sorrow.

Parents understand this reality all too well. Isaac and Rebekah rejoiced over the marriage of Jacob but were grieved when Esau married outside the covenant (see Genesis 26:34–35). Jacob (Israel) rejoiced over Joseph "because he was the son of his old age: and he made him a coat of many colours" (Genesis 37:3). But he wept inconsolably when the bloodstained coat was returned to him as evidence of Joseph's apparent death (see Genesis 37:33–35). Lehi and Sariah rejoiced over Nephi and Jacob but were grieved over Laman and Lemuel, to whom Lehi stated, "And I have none other object save it be the everlasting welfare of your souls" (2 Nephi 2:30). John confirmed the deep yearning of all parents: "I have no greater joy than to hear that my children walk in truth" (3 John 1:4).

The Father and Son grasp better than any of us how choice can lead to joy or sorrow. A third of the host of heaven was lost through the wayward leadership of Lucifer, thus causing the heavens to weep (see D&C 76:26).

The Lord likewise wept over the wickedness of mortals during the ministry of Enoch because they were destined to suffer for their choices (see Moses 7:37). Yet the resurrected Lord wept tears of joy over the faithfulness of the Nephites (see 3 Nephi 17:20–22). His desire is to gather His children into the fold as a hen gathers her chickens (see Luke 13:34; 3 Nephi 10:4–6; D&C 10:65; 29:2; 43:24). When they come home, He rejoices; when they do not, He is sorrowful. But the ultimate objective of the plan of salvation is eternal joy and happiness: "For behold, this is my work and my glory—to bring to pass the immortality and eternal life of man" (Moses 1:39).

What can we do to bring more joy to the Savior?

The scriptures give us a specific checklist, including the following examples:

- Accept and honor the Atonement (see Hebrews 12:1–2; 3 Nephi 27:30–31)
- Be obedient (see John 15:10–12)
- Bear our testimony (see D&C 62:2–3)
- Become the Lord's people (see Isaiah 62:4–5; 65:18–19; Jeremiah 32:40–41; Zephaniah 3:16–17)
- Gather together in the spirit of goodness (see Jacob 5:60, 71, 75)
- Offer the song of the heart (see D&C 25:12–13)
- Pray righteous prayers (see D&C 88:1–2)
- Repent (see Luke 15:7, 10; D&C 18:11–13; 90:34; 106:6)
- Show faith unto the Lord (see 3 Nephi 17:20)

Through the hope of the gospel we can indeed look forward to joy. The burdens of life—be they the result of a lapse of good judgment or because of mere happenchance—can serve a constructive purpose: "All these things shall give thee experience, and shall be for thy good" (D&C 122:7).

At times our courage can wane and our hope slacken. Those are the times when the Comforter can breathe new hope into our being. Truly the Lord can revive us on a daily basis—if we will allow Him to do so. Jeremiah expressed the healing function of the Redeemer, whose will it is to teach us the principles of righteousness and joy: "O the hope of Israel, the saviour thereof in time of trouble" (Jeremiah 14:8). Thank heaven for families and for loved ones who can serve together and make the pathway of life bearable.

WHAT LESSONS CAN WE LEARN FROM THE STORY OF JOSEPH AND HIS BROTHERS?

1. From sin flows sorrow.

The choices made by Joseph's brothers uncover the hurt and instability that come from envy, greed, and immorality. By taking a little time to focus on such negative happenings, we can perhaps learn better how to avoid that pathway and how to help loved ones do the same.

Here are a few examples that show how sorrow flows from poor choices:

- When Dinah, Jacob's daughter by Leah, is defiled by a man from the Canaanite race of Hivites living nearby, Dinah's brothers Simeon and Levi deceitfully establish a covenant of peace with the Hivites that authorizes them to retain Dinah. But the brothers instead invade the city, killing all the males and seizing all their wealth (see Genesis 34:25–29). Jacob is shocked, saying to his sons, "Ye have troubled me to make me to stink among the inhabitants of the land" (Genesis 34:30). He then is forced to move his family to another territory to avoid being destroyed by the Canaanites.
- Young Joseph, favored by his father, is hated by his jealous brothers, who are annoyed with Joseph's dreams about being a leader over them. When Jacob sends Joseph to visit with the brothers as they tend their flocks, tragedy takes place. The brothers conspire to slay Joseph. It is only the hesitation of Reuben that saves his life (see Genesis 37:21–22). Then, at the suggestion of Judah, they sell Joseph to a company of Ishmaelites en route to Egypt (see Genesis 37:26–28). To cover their conspiracy, the brothers stain Joseph's coat with the blood of a slain goat and return the coat to Jacob:

And Jacob rent his clothes, and put sackcloth upon his loins, and mourned for his son many days.

And all his sons and all his daughters rose up to comfort him; but he refused to be comforted; and he said, For I will go down into the grave unto my son mourning. Thus his father wept for him. (Genesis 37:34–35)

- Judah sinks to a base level of immorality with a Canaanite woman named Shuah and also with Tamar, the wife of one of his three sons by Shuah (see Genesis 38). In doing so, Judah chooses to follow the example of Reuben—Jacob's eldest son by Leah—who had an immoral relationship with Bilhah, one of Jacob's wives (see Genesis 35:22), and thus lost his birthright to Joseph (see Genesis 49:3–4; 1 Chronicles 5:1–2).

Such messages bring sorrow into our hearts, but they also remind us that repentance can bring correction into the lives of the wayward. The brothers of Joseph would repent for their sins against him and be forgiven (see Genesis 45:4–8). Does this not remind us of the parable of the prodigal son, told by the Savior (see Luke 15:11–32)? Here is a modern version of that parable:

It took courage to return. It took faith. But he returned. The young husband and father had slipped, and for his confessed moral indiscretion, he had lost his membership in the Church. He had been one of the most popular youth leaders of the ward. The young men thought highly of him. And now he was back, sitting with his family and participating each week in meetings. He was humble, but his head was held high. He was on the road back. People accepted him—even respected him for his courage in rebuilding what he had lost. Before long he was serving again with the young people. They loved him. They loved his family. They valued his testimony and his example. He was a living example of the gospel of repentance at work. "For with God nothing shall be impossible" (Luke 1:37). How grand it would be if all of us were as anxiously engaged in the process of daily repentance as he was. It would be a better world, and we would be closer to a Zion society.

Pondering: How do the stories of sorrow concerning Joseph's brothers help us find hope in the gospel of repentance? How can we avoid the pitfalls of life and stay on the pathway of joy and righteousness?

2. From goodness flows joy.

Joseph's example of integrity and morality in Egypt is among the most celebrated instances of strength of character in all of holy writ. Joseph was purchased from the Ishmaelites by Potiphar, "an officer of Pharaoh, captain of the guard, an Egyptian" (Genesis 39:1).

And the LORD was with Joseph, and he was a prosperous man; and he was in the house of his master the Egyptian.

And his master saw that the LORD was with him, and that the LORD made all that he did to prosper in his hand.

And Joseph found grace in his sight, and he served him: and he made him overseer over his house, and all that he had he put into his hand. (Genesis 39:2–4)

As the narrative unfolds, Joseph is approached and tempted by Potiphar's wife. In response, Joseph says, "How then can I do this great wickedness, and sin against God?" (Genesis 39:9). Being of sterling character, Joseph took immediate action "and fled, and got him out" (Genesis 39:12). Potiphar's wife accused him falsely and reported him to her husband. Consequently, Joseph was imprisoned.

But again, the hand of the Lord preserved him. He was appointed as a supervisor in the prison (see Genesis 39:21–23). Then, through the power of the Lord, Joseph was able to interpret the dreams of Pharaoh concerning the seven years of plenty followed by the seven years of famine (Genesis 41). Pharaoh was pleased and elevated Joseph to a position of leadership in Egypt, second only to Pharaoh (see Genesis 41:39–43), thus laying the groundwork for Joseph's future role as preserver of his family.

Joseph's integrity is a beacon of light that still shines today in our world where enduring principles of righteousness are being rapidly abandoned. The message for our time is clear: as we heed the Lord and His prophets, life will be sweet and full of joy. In our dealing with others, we can make integrity the power of personal progress and the central principle of spiritual growth and vitality. Joseph had the strength of character to flee the scene of temptation and rise up in leadership. We can follow his example and do the same.

Pondering: How can we follow the example of Joseph and defeat the allure of temptation in any aspect of our lives? How can we help our loved ones to do the same?

AGENDA FOR ACTION

With the story of Joseph and his brothers as a backdrop, consider the following statement by Brigham Young and ask yourself how you can apply this counsel and help your loved ones to do the same: "The sooner an individual resists temptation to do, say, or think wrong, while he has light to correct his judgment, the quicker he will gain strength and power to overcome every temptation to evil."[5] In our day, Gordon B. Hinckley reminded us that we are sons and daughters of God and that we should walk in faith and rise above the evils of the world in order to honor our divine birthright and destiny.[6]

LOOKING FORWARD: What is the key to forgiving those who have wronged you?

5   Brigham Young, *Discourses of Brigham Young* (Salt Lake City: Deseret Book, 1954), 266.
6   See Gordon B. Hinckley, *Teachings of Gordon B. Hinckley* (Salt Lake City: Deseret Book, 1997), 7.

CHAPTER TWELVE

THE VISION OF SERVICE

GOSPEL DOCTRINE READING ASSIGNMENT: GENESIS 40–45

For God hath caused me to be fruitful in the land of my affliction. (Genesis 41:52)

WITH AN EYE SINGLE TO THE GLORY OF GOD

JOSEPH WAS A MAN OF pure vision. As a youth he looked into the future and grasped the certainty of his calling to serve his people—though his brothers were annoyed by his dreams of leadership (see Genesis 37:5–11). While confined in an Egyptian prison, he was able to interpret the strange dreams of Pharaoh's chief butler and baker (see Genesis 40). When Pharaoh learned of Joseph's gift, he requested an interpretation of his own unusual dreams. Said Pharaoh to his servants, "Can we find such a one as this is, a man in whom the Spirit of God is?" (Genesis 41:38).

Joseph had a gift that enabled him to see things from a higher perspective. He was able to understand things through the Spirit of God. He looked forward "with an eye single to the glory of God" (see D&C 4:5). What is implied by that expression? It occurs only seven times in the scriptures—all of them in scripture revealed in our day:

Acting "with an eye single to the glory of God" means bringing forth the truth for "the welfare of the . . . covenant people of the Lord" (Mormon 8:15). It means acting with "faith, hope, charity and love" (D&C 4:5). It means "remembering unto the Father" the Lord's redeeming Atonement (D&C 27:2). It means becoming worthy for "a remission of your sins and a reception of the Holy Spirit" (D&C 55:1). It means gathering with the people of the Lord "according to my commandments" (D&C 59:1). It means improving on our talents—"Every man seeking the interest of his neighbor" (D&C 82:19). And it means to sanctify ourselves in order to "be filled with light" and thus comprehend "all things" (D&C 88:67, 68).

Joseph was an example of all those traits. He acted for the welfare of his people with genuine charity. He lived a life that opened the gateway for the redeeming blessings of the Lord. He brought his people together in safety and unity. He exercised his talents of service as the Lord directed. And he filled his soul with light in order to comprehend all things pertaining to the Lord's plan of temporal and spiritual salvation.

A TOUCH OF REALITY

The following account illustrates how we can learn to follow the example of Joseph in our daily lives and thus fill our souls with light:

A young boy—a mere fourteen years of age—was earnestly seeking for truth according to the counsel of James: "If any of you lack wisdom, let him ask of God, that giveth to all men liberally . . . and it shall be given him" (James 1:5). When he went into the woods to pray on a spring morning in 1820, a miracle awaited him. The First Vision opened the era of the Restoration. Like Joseph of Egypt, he was able to see "with an eye single to the glory of God." The unfolding of his commission took place that morning like a glorious dawning of blessings for the world.

What was the connection between this Joseph and the ancient Joseph? Nine years later, Joseph Smith was at work translating the Book of Mormon. He came upon a passage where Father Lehi shared with his last-born son, Joseph, the words of Joseph of Egypt, their distant ancestor. Said Lehi, "Joseph truly saw our day" (2 Nephi 3:5). That same Joseph who gathered his people to safety in times of dire famine also saw how the Lord would gather His people in the latter days and bring them "out of darkness unto light—yea, out of hidden darkness and out of captivity unto freedom. For Joseph truly testified, saying: A seer shall the Lord my God raise up, who shall be a choice seer unto the fruit of my loins" (2 Nephi 3:5–6).

Joseph of Egypt revealed who that future seer would be: "And his name shall be called after me; and it shall be after the name of his father. And he shall be like unto me; for the thing, which the Lord shall bring forth by his hand, by the power of the Lord shall bring my people unto salvation" (2 Nephi 3:15).

That future seer was Joseph Smith, whose father also bore the name Joseph. Thus Lehi's young son Joseph learned of three others called by that same name. He learned that he too, like his faithful brethren, would participate in the ongoing blessings of the Lord through the Abrahamic covenant. He learned that the Lord would bless all of humanity in the final dispensation of time with the Restoration of the gospel of peace, salvation, and exaltation—allowing the faithful to see "with an eye single to the glory of God."

WHAT LESSONS CAN WE LEARN FROM THE LEADERSHIP OF JOSEPH IN EGYPT?

1. The Lord reveals unto us our personal pathway of service.

Joseph of Egypt had remarkable gifts from the Lord. His gift of vision, combined with his gifts of charity and leadership, empowered him to rise up as a deliverer, as one who saves. Like the Redeemer, Joseph also redeemed. And he did so with humility. To the butler and baker, he said, "Do not interpretations belong to God?" (Genesis 40:8). To Pharaoh, he said, "It is not in me: God shall give Pharaoh an answer of peace" (Genesis 41:16). Pharaoh was deeply touched by Joseph's counsel to set food aside in preparation for seven years of coming famine:

> And Pharaoh said unto Joseph, Forasmuch as God hath shewed thee all this, there is none so discreet and wise as thou art:
> Thou shalt be over my house, and according unto thy word shall all my people be ruled: only in the throne will I be greater than thou.
> And Pharaoh said unto Joseph, See, I have set thee over all the land of Egypt. (Genesis 41:39–41)

Joseph acted to save the people of Egypt from famine. He saved his own family by bringing them to a new home where they could survive. He was their redeemer just as the Savior is the Redeemer for the whole family of God.

All of us are blessed with gifts and talents that plant seeds of redemption within us. All of us can help save others. The Lord counseled:

> Seek ye earnestly the best gifts, always remembering for what they are given;
>
> For verily I say unto you, they are given for the benefit of those who love me and keep all my commandments, and him that seeketh so to do; that all may be benefited that seek or that ask of me, . . .
>
> For there are many gifts, and to every man is given a gift by the Spirit of God.
>
> To some is given one, and to some is given another, that all may be profited thereby. (D&C 46:8–9, 11–12; see also 1 Corinthians 12:3–12; Moroni 10:8–18)

How can we identify our gifts and cultivate them for the good of others?

The young man was shy and reserved. He did not comfortably blend into the circle of his peers—who were often highly competitive and outspoken. But he had some unique qualities that were already shining through. He told his Young Men leader that he felt envious of the others who found it so easy to take initiative in social settings. That was the opportunity for the leader to remind him of the gifts and talents he had been given—different from those of his colleagues. There were things he could do that they could not so easily do, and these gifts would enable him to render valuable service to others. And, indeed, this young man did go on to earn his Eagle Scout award and accomplish much good through academic excellence and faith.

Another young deacon was also shy and reserved as he went about his duties. His leader often thought, "What will become of him over time? Will he realize that he is a giant in the Lord, endowed with all the strength and capacity of a noble son of God? Will he discover his unique talents and cultivate them for the good of others? Will they someday say of him, 'We expected a lamb and got a lion?'"

> **Who was Asenath, wife of Joseph?**
>
> Asenath (meaning "gift of the sun-god") is mentioned only three times in the scriptures:
> - "And Pharaoh . . . gave him to wife Asenath the daughter of Potipherah priest of On" (Genesis 41:45).
> - "And unto Joseph in the land of Egypt were born Manasseh [meaning 'forgetting one's toil'] and Ephraim [meaning 'fruitful'], which Asenath the daughter of Poti-pherah priest of On bare unto him" (Genesis 46:20; see also Genesis 41:50).

As it turned out, that young deacon did rise up in strength and leadership to become a choice missionary for the Lord and a faithful family man who loves and serves others. Such is the gospel plan: our Father in Heaven gradually illuminates our souls with the truth of who we are and how we can rise triumphant as servants of the Lord. As Isaiah reminded us, "But they that wait upon the Lord shall renew their strength; they shall mount up with wings as eagles" (Isaiah 40:31).

Pondering: How can we, like Joseph in Egypt, apply our gifts and talents for the good of our loved ones and fellow Saints? How do we learn more of our potential gifts? How can we rise up on wings as eagles to contribute to the salvation of all?

2. Forgiveness and service go hand in hand.

When Jacob sent his ten sons to Egypt to obtain food during the famine (keeping young Benjamin at home), Joseph received them as governor of the land—at first in disguise and with a pretended domineering attitude but later with an overpowering spirit of forgiveness and love. Joseph perceived that his brothers were burdened with feelings of remorse over what they had done to him. "And he turned himself about from them, and wept" (Genesis 42:24).

When Jacob later agreed to send Benjamin, Joseph was elated and prepared a feast for them all. After a brief game of trickery, the weeping Joseph revealed his identity and spoke words of redeeming forgiveness:

> And God sent me before you to preserve you a posterity in the earth, and to save your lives by a great deliverance.

So now it was not you that sent me hither, but God: and he hath made me a father to Pharaoh, and lord of all his house, and a ruler throughout all the land of Egypt.

Haste ye, and go up to my father, and say unto him, Thus saith thy son Joseph, God hath made me lord of all Egypt: come down unto me, tarry not. (Genesis 45:7–9)

Joseph then "fell upon his brother Benjamin's neck, and wept; and Benjamin wept upon his neck. Moreover he kissed all his brethren, and wept upon them" (Genesis 45:14–15). The work of deliverance then commenced with the entire family moving to Egypt, where they could be nurtured and develop according to the blessings of the Lord.

How can we likewise display a spirit of unconditional forgiveness and support for our loved ones? The following true account demonstrates this:

The Prophet Joseph Smith was repeatedly subjected to the most vile derision and persecution without cause or provocation. His response was consistent. He forgave. He fought for the truth and defended the Church and its doctrines in the face of the most outrageous lies and malicious attacks. But he forgave, knowing that the Lord would bless him in the face of all affliction (see D&C 122:7–8; also 2 Nephi 2:2).

On Saturday, March 24, 1832, he and his wife Emma and their children were staying at the home of John Johnson in Hiram, Ohio. Suddenly, a mob of some dozen drunken men broke into the house and tore Joseph from the side of his ailing son, eleven-month-old Joseph Murdock Smith (one of two adopted twins). They dragged him outside, stripped him of his clothes, beat him brutally, and tarred and feathered him. After they left, Joseph's friends spent the whole night tearing the skin-searing tar from his body. Sidney Rigdon had also been dragged from his home, sustaining a concussion as his head thumped along the frozen ground. He was left comatose in the snow. Young Joseph Murdock, the Smiths' adopted son, already suffering with measles, contracted pneumonia from the exposure that night and died a few days later.

The day after the brutal attack, Joseph delivered a Sunday sermon before the gathering of Saints. What was his theme? The gospel of love and redemption. He baptized three individuals that afternoon (see *HC* 1:261–265).

It was a remarkable instance of unconditional forgiveness on the part of the Prophet as he reflected the same spirit of charity as Joseph of old. The Savior said, "I, the Lord, will forgive whom I will forgive, but of you it is required to forgive all men" (D&C 64:10; see also Matthew 5:44–45; 3 Nephi 12:44–45).

Pondering: How can we forgive others in the spirit of unconditional love? How can we teach others to live according to that same spirit?

AGENDA FOR ACTION

Let us observe with gratitude the hand of God at work in all things to bless us and our families. Let us humbly seek after the best gifts and apply them continually in the service of our fellow beings. Let us apply one of our personal talents in special ways this week to bless the life of someone who needs our support and help. Let us learn to kindle more fully the Redeemer's love each day by forgiving others according to His example and the example of the Josephs in our lives. Let us seek to fulfill our destiny as "children of the covenant" (see 3 Nephi 20:26; Genesis 49:22–26). When we do this, we will begin to catch the fuller vision of the grand scope of God's covenant plan, and we will see "with an eye single to the glory of God."

LOOKING FORWARD: What does it mean to "see the salvation of the Lord" (Exodus 14:13)?

CHAPTER THIRTEEN

"SEE THE SALVATION OF THE LORD"

Gospel Doctrine Reading Assignment: Exodus 1–3, 5–6, 11–14
The LORD is my strength and song, and he is become my salvation. (Exodus 15:2)

THE EXODUS AS A LIVING SYMBOL OF REDEMPTION

THE STORY OF MOSES IS legendary. He was rescued from the bulrushes by a princess, nursed clandestinely by his Hebrew mother, grew up in the court of the pharaoh, cultivated a passion for protecting his people—as evidenced by his slaying the Egyptian who was smiting a Hebrew—and then fled for his life to Midian, where he helped the daughters of Reuel (Jethro) and was given Zipporah to be his wife (see Exodus 2).

Meanwhile, the Israelites in Goshen were praying for deliverance from the crushing burdens of slavery placed upon them by the Egyptians: "And God heard their groaning. . . . For I know their sorrows" (Exodus 2:24; 3:7). On Mount Horeb, Moses humbly received the divine calling to deliver the Israelites from bondage. The Lord promised him:

> Certainly I will be with thee. . . .
> And Moses said unto God, Behold, when I come unto the children of Israel, and shall say unto them, The God of your fathers hath sent me unto you; and they shall say to me, What is his name? what shall I say unto them?
> And God said unto Moses, I AM THAT I AM: and he said, Thus shalt thou say unto the children of Israel, I AM hath sent me unto you. (Exodus 3:12–14; compare also Moses 1)

Moses and Aaron then implored Pharaoh to obey the commandment of the Lord—"Let my people go, that they may serve me" (Exodus 7:16; 8:1, 20; 9:1,13; 10:3)—but he stubbornly refused, even in the face of destructive plagues and judgments. Only when the firstborn of his sons was slain by an act of heaven did the pharaoh yield and permit the Israelites to leave (see Exodus 12:31–32). However, still obsessed with retaining them as slaves, Pharaoh and his hosts pursued them, finding them stranded on the shores of the Red Sea:

What was the location of Goshen and Midian?

During their long sojourn in Egypt, the Israelites lived in Goshen, an area adjacent to the eastern side of the Nile Delta, north of present-day Cairo. Goshen was a pasture land in which the Israelites could thrive while living apart from the main body of the Egyptian people. Midian, the homeland of Jethro and his people, was located east of the present-day Gulf of Aqaba in northwestern Saudi Arabia, south of Jordan. Moses received the Melchizedek Priesthood from Jethro (see D&C 84:6).

> And Moses said unto the people, Fear ye not, stand still, and see the salvation of the LORD, which he will shew to you to day: for the Egyptians whom ye have seen to day, ye shall see them again no more for ever.
>
> The LORD shall fight for you, and ye shall hold your peace. (Exodus 14:13–14)

Then, Moses, endowed with the power of the Lord, parted the Red Sea, and the Israelites walked across on dry ground. The Egyptians followed, only to be swallowed by the resurging waters. The Exodus then proceeded, and the Israelites marched forth in freedom, singing a hymn of praise unto their God (see Exodus 15).

The Exodus, traditionally thought to commence around 1547 B.C., is an unforgettable story of how we can "see the salvation of the Lord" as He fights for His sons and daughters in mercy and love. The ultimate battle is for the salvation and exaltation of our souls through the Atonement of Jesus Christ. The chosen pathway of the gospel leads to that glorious victory. In our own lives there may be wonderful occasions where we "see the salvation of the Lord" in personal and unforgettable ways.

WHAT LESSONS CAN WE LEARN FROM THE EXODUS?

1. The Lord is in charge—He will fight our battles.

The Exodus is compelling proof that the Lord fights the battles of His people. In the early days of the Restoration, the Lord proclaimed, "Therefore it is expedient in me that mine elders should wait for a little season, for the redemption of Zion. For behold, I do not require at their hands to fight the battles of Zion; for . . . I will fight your battles" (D&C 105:13–14). Thus the pioneers survived years of persecution and a long, toilsome trek across the plains in fulfillment of Jacob's blessing upon the head of Joseph: "The blessings of thy father have prevailed above the blessings of my progenitors unto the utmost bound of the everlasting hills: they shall be on the head of Joseph" (Genesis 49:26).

The sons and daughters of the Lord triumph as they survive the daily battles to achieve and maintain temporal and spiritual well-being. The following words from a newly ordained young bishop confirm this truth:

> Who's in charge? It's an overwhelming assignment to be called as a bishop—especially in a large, diverse ward with many complex challenges, and especially when you are a twenty-seven-year-old graduate

How did Zipporah save the life of her husband, Moses?

Moses had failed to circumcise his son Gershom, thus causing the Lord to be angry with him. About to embark on his commission to confront Pharaoh, Moses was about to be destroyed. However, Zipporah promptly completed the ordinance, and the Lord spared Moses (see Exodus 4:24–26): "And Moses was ashamed, and hid his face from the Lord, and said, I have sinned before the Lord" (JST, Exodus 4:26). Circumcision was practiced in ancient times as an ordinance to remind the people about the true order of baptism: "That thou mayest know for ever that children are not accountable before me until they are eight years old" (JST, Genesis 17:11; also JST, Genesis 17:3–7 on how baptism had fallen into misuse).

student with a young family. But after sincere prayer, and with the support of a loving wife, I humbly accepted despite great feelings of inadequacy. It was an act of sheer faith.

Following the sustaining vote that Sunday, I was shaking hands with a line of well-wishers outside the chapel and came to one member known for his candid method of expression. He was a merchant seaman who had seen many a dangerous campaign in his career. Looking directly into my eyes, he said, in all seriousness, "I just cannot understand how they could put an ensign in charge of the ship." There was a moment of silence as I searched for any kind of satisfying response. Then a light suddenly came on, and the Spirit whispered the words (which I dutifully repeated): "An ensign is not in charge of the ship. The Lord is in charge of the ship." The brother listened and paused then nodded his approval and subsequently became one of my most stalwart supporters. It is always good to sail on a ship where the Lord is in charge.

When we act with faith and hope, we can discern the strength of the Lord in our lives. He is our strength. He fights our battles. He is there to help: "There I will be also, for I will go before your face. I will be on your right hand and on your left, and my Spirit shall be in your hearts, and mine angels round about you, to bear you up" (D&C 84:88). As we seek to do His will, He will give us the strength and guidance to achieve all worthy pursuits.

Pondering: How have you felt the presence of the Lord as He fights battles on your behalf? How can you share this testimony with others and help them to seek the Lord's help in all of their undertakings (see D&C 112:10)?

2. The Lord gives us the opportunity to remember His blessings.

When the Lord called all of the firstborn sons of Egypt home, He protected the Israelites by virtue of a special ordinance. They were to mark the side posts and upper lintels of their doors with the blood of unblemished lambs of sacrifice. The Lord would then pass them by, and their sons would be saved in symbolic anticipation of the future Atonement of Christ, the divine Redeemer. That night they were to consume the roasted flesh along with unleavened bread: "And ye shall eat it in haste: it is the LORD's passover" (Exodus 12:11). Thereafter the Israelites were to observe the annual Feast of the Passover in celebration of the saving mercy of the Lord.

During His ministry, the Lord replaced this ordinance with the sacrament of the Lord's Supper—a sacred memorial of His atoning sacrifice (see Matthew 26:19, 26–28; D&C 20:75–79). We are blessed each week to partake of the sacrament and renew our covenants. The following account by a member of a stake presidency gives a memorable example:

> I recall many years ago being assigned to visit a branch in an outlying area of our stake. Being seated on the stand during sacrament meeting, I had a clear view of the deacons along the front row waiting to pass the emblems to the congregation. That day, the sacrament hymn was the beautiful and tender song that begins "While of these emblems we partake, in Jesus' name and for his sake." We continued with the words, "Let us remember and be sure our hearts and hands are clean and pure." Just at that moment, I happened to look down at one of the young deacons. There he was, holding both of his open hands out in front of him, palms upward.

What is the meaning of the phrase "see the salvation of the Lord"?

In some cases, to "see the salvation of the Lord" means to behold His intervention in mortal affairs for the purpose of saving and liberating His people—as declared by Moses in Exodus 14:13. Jahaziel would speak the same words in prophesying the victory of Judah over their threatening enemies (see 2 Chronicles 20:17; see also Psalm 98:2–3; compare also the words of Joseph Smith when Zion's Camp was saved from angry mobs as reported in chapter 6 of this book). In general, however, the expression "see the salvation of the Lord" (as in 1 Nephi 19:17 and Mosiah 16:1) or "see the salvation of our God" (as in Isaiah 52:9–10; Luke 3:4–6; Mosiah 12:23–24; 15:30–31; 3 Nephi 16:19–20; D&C 123:16–17; 133:2–5) refers to the ultimate triumph and unfolding of glory at the Second Coming and the beginning of the Millennium.

He was gazing at them intently as if to find reassurance that he was, indeed, a worthy servant of the Lord about to participate in a sacred ordinance. I shall never forget that image of the young man and his extended hands. Our hands are a constant reminder that we should be continually engaged in the Lord's errand, ever intent on keeping His commandments, ever vigilant that our hearts and hands remain pure, ever committed to that which is ennobling and edifying. The Lord counseled, "Be ye clean, that bear the vessels of the LORD" (Isaiah 52:11).

Pondering: How does the sacrament help you remember the love and mercy of the Lord? In what other ways does the Lord remind you of the blessings of His gospel plan?

AGENDA FOR ACTION

From the scriptural account of the Exodus, we renew our acquaintance with the miraculous way the Lord delivered Israel from bondage. In no less miraculous a way, we can be delivered personally from the bondage of sin through the redemption of Jesus Christ. Through faith and prayer we can maintain our own spiritual exodus and endure to the end in faith and hope. Through love, we help others, in the spirit of Moses, to escape the bondage of wrongdoing and become reborn and liberated through the Atonement. What can we do to remember in gratitude the blessings of the Lord as Liberator and Redeemer in our own personal lives? Since the holy ordinance of the sacrament is an opportunity to renew our covenants and strengthen our commitment, perhaps we can use that quiet occasion to speak a prayer of thanksgiving in our hearts for the love and mercy of the Father and His Only Begotten Son. Perhaps we can share with loved ones our deep appreciation for the glory and promise of salvation and exaltation.

LOOKING FORWARD: What does it mean to partake of living bread?

CHAPTER FOURTEEN

"ON THE WAY TO THE PROMISED LAND"

GOSPEL DOCTRINE READING ASSIGNMENT: EXODUS 15–20, 32–34

Now therefore, if ye will obey my voice indeed, and keep my covenant, then ye shall be a peculiar treasure unto me above all people. (Exodus 19:5)

"AND IN THE MORNING . . . YE SHALL SEE THE GLORY OF THE LORD"

SHORTLY AFTER THEY HAD CROSSED the Red Sea and begun their journey through the vast wilderness of Sinai, the liberated Israelites discovered that they were not liberated from hunger and thirst. Moses responded with the counsel, "Come near before the LORD: for he hath heard your murmurings" (Exodus 16:9). The promise of the Lord was of a covenant nature: "Behold, I will rain bread from heaven for you; and the people shall go out and gather a certain rate every day, that I may prove them, whether they will walk in my law, or no. . . . And in the morning, then ye shall see the glory of the LORD" (Exodus 16:4, 7).

From the cloud of glory, the words of the Lord streamed forth: "At even ye shall eat flesh, and in the morning ye shall be filled with bread; and ye shall know that I am the LORD your God" (Exodus 16:12). Subsequently, flocks of quail covered the camp of the Israelites in the evening, and in the morning "upon the face of the wilderness there lay a small round thing, as small as the hoar frost on the ground" (Exodus 16:14). The people were puzzled until Moses informed them, "This is the bread which the LORD hath given you to eat" (Exodus 16:15). Called manna (meaning "what is that?"), "it was like coriander seed, white" (Exodus 16:31).

A TOUCH OF REALITY

Imagine how it might have been for the migrating Israelites to collect manna in the early morning hours. Contemplate the following possibility (based on details given in Exodus 16, Numbers 11, Deuteronomy 8, Nehemiah 9, and Psalm 78):

Young Jacob saw the scorpion perched on the rock ledge protruding from the mound of sand. His heart pounded as he quietly moved around the mound and slipped farther up the hill toward a small palm tree, where his father was kneeling in the predawn shadows. Jacob had come with his father to gather manna outside the camp. In his hands, he held a pouch that was already half full of the "bread from heaven" (Exodus 16:4), bread rained down by the Lord six days of each week.

Jacob stooped down near his father and reached out toward a flat spot on the plain where the small white seeds were nestled like an army of tiny pearls on the dew-moistened ground. He gathered the seeds carefully in his hands and then dropped them quietly into his pouch. He felt pangs of hunger as he thought of how his parents would soon prepare the food.

"Well, Jacob," said his father. "Will you help me grind this manna into flour so your mother can make cakes of it?"

Jacob nodded and whispered out a willing yes. He remembered how his younger sister always smiled at breakfast, saying that the cakes tasted like fresh oil and honey. True, the meals in the wilderness were not as rich and varied as they used to be in Goshen, when the people lived in that Egyptian farmland. But the Lord had delivered them from bondage weeks before, and He had answered their prayers by providing them quail in the evenings and manna in the mornings to preserve them for the long trek toward the promised land.

At that moment, a few streaks of light began to creep over the distant mountain ridge to the east. Jacob tied shut his brimming pouch of manna and stood up to watch the coming dawn. He felt the gentle hand of his father resting on his shoulder and heard the encouraging words, "Now we shall see the glory of the Lord."

Jacob smiled as the sun reached over the horizon and added a touch of warmth to the coolness of the wilderness. "Thank you, Lord," he whispered. Another day had come. Another answer to prayers had quietly rained down from heaven.

Manna from the Lord sustained the Israelites for forty years in their journey toward Canaan. How does this heavenly blessing have spiritual significance for us today?

WHAT LESSONS CAN WE LEARN FROM THE EXPERIENCES OF THE MIGRATING ISRAELITES?

1. Throughout our mortal journey, the Lord provides both the bread of life and living water.

The Lord's mercy in nurturing the house of Israel in the wilderness is a symbol of the Lord's mercy in providing spiritual nourishment. The scriptures give many symbolic references to the higher nurturing that comes from the gospel, including "the tree of life" (Revelation 2:7; 1 Nephi 11:25; 15:36); "a tree springing up unto everlasting life" (Alma 32:41); the Savior's references to Himself as "the bread of life" and "the living bread" (John 6:35, 51); as well as the "living water . . . springing up into everlasting life" (John 4:10, 14; see also D&C 63:23).

The living body, sustained by the food of the earth, and the living spirit, sustained by the food of the gospel, blend together as one soul. It pleases the Lord to provide the fruit of the earth to nurture His children; and it pleases the Lord when His children feast upon the words of truth for spiritual rebirth, thus receiving "peace in this world, and eternal life in the world to come" (D&C 59:23). A modern illustration of the "manna of life" follows:

> While serving in the mission home, I observed firsthand how the mission president was inspired to handle a challenging matter. There was a metal plaque on the building identifying it as a "Mission"—which, in that country, also implied services for

What quantity is an "omer"?

The Israelites were to collect an omer of manna each day for each person in the family (see Exodus 16:16)—and twice that amount on the day before the Sabbath, when no manna would appear (see Exodus 16:22–26). The specific measurement in modern terms in uncertain; however, scholars estimate that an ephah—ten times the amount of an omer (see Exodus 16:36)—was in dry measure equivalent to around eight gallons or thirty-two quarts (see Bible Dictionary, "Omer"). Thus an omer would be just over three quarts, certainly sufficient for "every man according to his eating" (Exodus 16:21).

those in need of temporal assistance. Therefore, we had a steady stream of impoverished and homeless persons knocking on the door for aid. The mission president came up with an inspired solution to this problem: Tell each such visitor that he was welcome to have a meal with us provided he would be willing to do some gardening and lawn care in the yard behind the building. This would seem to cause the hunger of virtually all such candidates to disappear, for most of them turned down the offer to serve—except for one.

I remember seeing the pleasant middle-aged man and his young son enthusiastically working for several hours in the yard and then joining us for dinner. This man felt that he was being treated with dignity, and he was prompted by the Spirit to find out what sort of people these were. Subsequently, he took the missionary discussions and, with his son, joined the Church. The manna they had received opened up the blessings of the spiritual bread of life and the living water available through the restored gospel. The mission president was inspired to see in people the potential for adoption into the family of Christ through obedience to covenant principles.

Pondering: How is the sacrament a spiritual manna of living bread and water that brings you closer to the Father and the Son? How can you recognize more opportunities to nourish others both temporally as well as spiritually?

2. Plain and precious are the commandments of the Lord.

The Ten Commandments are given in plain and direct language (see Exodus 20). They are the words of the Lord—precious counsel on how to conduct our thoughts and actions in mortality. They are covenant words of plainness, given along with specific consequences—including the granting of "mercy unto thousands of them that love me, and keep my commandments" (Exodus 20:6).

The prophets of God talk frequently about plainness. "Plainness of speech" is a function of hope (2 Corinthians 3:12). "Plainness of speech" prevents people from stumbling (1 Nephi 13:29). "Plainness of truth" penetrates sin (2 Nephi 9:47) and speaks harshly against it (2 Nephi 33:5). "Plainness" allows people to learn from the words of prophecy (2 Nephi 25:4) such that "no man can err" (2 Nephi 25:7). "Plainness" brings delight, "for after this manner doth the Lord God work among the children of men" (2 Nephi 31:3). "Plainness of the word of God" directs one to guide others into the pathway of truth (Jacob 2:11). "Exceedingly great plainness of speech" prevents people from "going down speedily to destruction" (Enos 1:23). In modern times, the Lord declared a great summary of this principle: "And for this cause, that men might be made partakers of the glories which were to be revealed, the Lord sent forth the fulness of his gospel, his everlasting covenant, reasoning in plainness and simplicity" (D&C 133:57).

One of the great aspects of plainness pertaining to the Ten Commandments is that these are not generalities but divine laws directed *personally* to every son and daughter of God. Nephi shows how personal the word of God truly is: "For Christ will show unto you, with power and great glory, that they are his words, at the last day; and you and I shall stand face to face before his bar; and ye shall know that I have been commanded of him to write these things, notwithstanding my weakness" (2 Nephi 33:11). Our role in pondering the word of God is to see ourselves as the object of the discourse—the main player on the stage of action.

Here is a little parable to put this principle into focus:

Pete is waiting in line to pay for an item in a department store, and he notices that there is a closed-circuit television monitor over the counter—one of the store's measures against shoplifters. As he watches the jostling crowd of people on the monitor, he realizes that the person over on the left side of the screen in the overcoat . . . is having his pocket picked by the person behind him. Then, as he raises his hand to his mouth in astonishment, he notices that the victim's hand is moving to his mouth in just the same way. Pete suddenly realizes that *he* is the person whose pocket is being picked! This dramatic shift is a discovery; Pete comes to know something he didn't know a moment before, and of course it is important. Without the capacity to entertain the sorts of thoughts that now galvanize him into defensive action, he would hardly be capable of action at all. But before the shift, he wasn't entirely ignorant, of course; he was thinking about "the person in the overcoat" and seeing that that person was being robbed, and since the person in the overcoat is himself, he was thinking *about himself*. But he wasn't thinking about himself *as himself*; he wasn't thinking about himself "in the right way."[7]

The lesson of the parable is clear. When we learn to see ourselves as ourselves—as sons and daughters of God, with a destiny to become as He is—then a miracle occurs: our choices relate directly to the fulfillment of this personal destiny, and our actions are tied inextricably to the goal of building a pure and enduring relationship with Him so that we can one day return to His presence in the realms of glory. That is the right way to view ourselves and the right way to proceed along the pathway of life.

Pondering: When we study the word of the Lord, how can we ensure that we see ourselves *as* ourselves—personally in a dialogue with the Lord, just like Moses? How can we bring our covenant relationship with the Lord into personal focus leading to greater obedience and joy?

3. To please and obey the Lord brings joy; to provoke and disobey the Lord brings sorrow.

When the Israelites reached the area near Mount Sinai, the Lord promised them, "If ye will obey my voice indeed, and keep my covenant, then ye shall be a peculiar treasure unto me above all people: for all the earth is mine: And ye shall be unto me a kingdom of priests, and an holy nation" (Exodus 19:5–6; compare 1 Peter 2:9). The quality of being "peculiar" means belonging to the Lord, being His people. On the third day thereafter, Moses "brought forth the people out of the camp to meet with God; and they stood at the nether part of the mount" (Exodus 19:17). As the Ten Commandments were proclaimed, the people were consumed with fear and hid themselves behind Moses as their shield: "And they said unto Moses, Speak thou with us, and we will hear: but let not God speak with us, lest we die" (Exodus 20:19). Moses responded, "Fear not: for God is come to prove you, and that his fear may be before your faces, that ye sin not" (Exodus 20:20).

But sin they did, for in the absence of Moses, they induced Aaron to make a golden calf to worship. When Moses returned to discover their revolt, he broke the tablets of laws given to him by the Lord, who was stirred up in anger over their iniquity and held back His wrath only through the appeal of Moses (see Exodus 22; also JST, Exodus 32:14; 33:20). Later, Moses was called up onto the mount for forty days and given a revision of the law on two new tablets. Because the people had provoked the Lord through disobedience, the higher priesthood was to be withheld, and "they shall not enter into my presence, into my rest, in the days of their pilgrimage" (JST, Exodus 34:2; see also JST, Deuteronomy 10:2).

From that time onward, the term "provocation" or "first provocation" became an emblem for the sorrow of those who do not live up to their covenants with the Lord (see Hebrews 3:7–19; Jacob 1:7–8; Alma 12:34–37). At the same time, in confirming His covenant with the people, the Lord manifested His infinite mercy: "The LORD, The LORD God, merciful and gracious, longsuffering, and abundant in goodness and truth, Keeping mercy for thousands, forgiving iniquity and transgression and sin" (Exodus 34:6–7). And what is the infinite joy of obedience? John gave us this answer: "Beloved, now are we the sons of God, and it doth not yet appear what we shall be: but we know that, when he shall appear, we shall be like him; for we shall see him as he is. And every man that hath this hope in him purifieth himself, even as he is pure" (1 John 3:2–3).

Reflect on the following true account:

> One of my earliest recollections as a young child was learning that the chapel was the house of God. There was a faithful and loyal older brother who served there as the custodian, and I would often see him on Sundays, silver haired and patriarchal, coming up and down the stairs and walking the halls as he went about his duties. Somehow, a few of us very young members got the impression that this grandfatherly brother was actually the Lord—and it took some gentle counsel from parents to convince us otherwise. Since then I have often thought

---

7   Douglas R. Hofstadter, *The Mind's I: Fantasies and Reflections on Self and Soul* (New York: Bantam Books, 1982), 20–21.

that the naive innocence of a child's perspective is perhaps the best preparation for later life, for the whole purpose of life is to seek the face of the Lord and to aspire to be worthy of His presence (see D&C 101:38). Perhaps it is not so naive after all to think of the Lord as the spiritual custodian of our eternal home.

Pondering: How do we cultivate and expand the ways in which we please the Lord? How do we ensure that we avoid provoking Him in our thoughts, words, and deeds? Since the law of Moses was fulfilled in Christ (see Galatians 3:23–24; Alma 25:15–16; 34:14–15; 3 Nephi 15:4–10), how can our offering of a "broken heart and a contrite spirit" (3 Nephi 9:19–22) lead to eternal joy? How does our vision of someday seeing the Lord inspire us to better honor our covenants?

AGENDA FOR ACTION

Here is a wonderful phrase to memorize: "For I am the Lord that healeth thee" (Exodus 15:26). On our daily checklist, we can remember that all vitality flows from the Lord as a blessing of His love and mercy. While enjoying the abundance of the earth's harvest, we can also enjoy the nurture of spiritual manna—the living bread and water of the gospel of Jesus Christ. We can find our covenant anchor in the plain and simple words of the Lord. We can explore and ponder a gospel topic each week that may have a particular application in our life. We can choose a favorite verse and commit it to memory as a passage to revisit over and over again as we go about our duties. We can think of the Lord always as our Friend and Companion. We can look forward with hope and faith to the time when we will come into the rest the Lord, "which rest is the fulness of his glory" (D&C 84:24). Zion is the garden of the Lord. May we live worthy to grow and develop within its secure walls.

LOOKING FORWARD: What is the key to eternal life?

CHAPTER FIFTEEN

"LOOK TO GOD AND LIVE"

GOSPEL DOCTRINE READING ASSIGNMENT: NUMBERS 11–14, 21:1–9

Would God that all the LORD's people were prophets, and that the LORD would put his spirit upon them! (Numbers 11:29)

CROSSING OUR OWN WILDERNESS EN ROUTE TO THE PROMISED LAND

THE ACCOUNT OF THE ISRAELITES' forty-year sojourn in the wilderness is a blend of opposites: leadership and cowardice, hope and fear, courage and murmuring, obedience and rebellion, glory and shadows. This account can be viewed as a symbol of our own journey through life toward the promised land. The Lord declared His ultimate mission to Moses: "For behold, this is my work and my glory—to bring to pass the immortality and eternal life of man" (Moses 1:39). To Hyrum Smith—and to each of us—the Lord declared *our* objective: "Behold, this is your work, to keep my commandments, yea, with all your might, mind and strength" (D&C 11:20).

On the journey through our own wilderness of challenges, temptations, and tribulations, we can choose the course of leadership, hope, courage, obedience, and glory. For us, the border between the wilderness and the promised land is marked by the transition from our era of probation into the celestial kingdom of eternal light as "just men [and women] made perfect through Jesus the mediator of the new covenant, who wrought out this perfect atonement through the shedding of his own blood" (D&C 76:69).

Our choices determine how we please the Lord. What can we do to ensure that we follow the whisperings of the Spirit and complete our transition "unto Mount Zion, and unto the city of the living God, the heavenly place, the holiest of all" (D&C 76:66)?

A TOUCH OF REALITY

On one occasion in June 1965, President David O. McKay was giving counsel to employees of the Physical Facilities Department of the Church and emphasizing the importance of their service. During his remarks, he reminded them that they would one day have a personal interview with the Savior and have the opportunity to account for their earthly duties and responsibilities. Specific questions from the Savior would address key issues such as the following: how the individuals have contributed to the happiness and care of their wives and each of their children, how they have applied their talents given to them from the Lord, how they have served their fellowmen in their Church assignments, how they have been honest in all their dealings, and how they have contributed in a positive way to their community as well as to their state, country, and the world.[8]

WHAT LESSONS CAN WE LEARN FROM THE ACCOUNT OF THE ISRAELITES IN THE WILDERNESS?

1. Those who are meek receive the Spirit.

From the word of the Lord we learn, "Now the man Moses was very meek, above all the men which were upon the face of the earth" (Numbers 12:3). He listened to the Lord, he followed the Lord, he obeyed the Lord, he was the Lord's servant and prophet. When the people murmured over the manna being given to them, Moses was discouraged at their revolt. The Lord told him to gather seventy of the elders of Israel unto the tabernacle: "And I will come down and talk with thee there: and I will take of the spirit which is upon thee, and will put it upon them; and they shall bear the burden of the people with thee, that thou bear it not thyself alone" (Numbers 11:17).

Moses had already welcomed a lesson in delegation from his father-in-law, Jethro (see Exodus 18:13–26), but now the Lord raised the bar of support for the anxious prophet by blessing the newly called elders so that they too could prophesy (see Numbers 11:25). When two of the Seventy (Eldad and Medad) did not go unto the tabernacle but remained in the camp and still were able to prophesy, young Joshua appealed to Moses to silence them. Then Moses proclaimed a sublime truth: "Enviest thou for my sake? would God that all the LORD's people were prophets, and that the LORD would put his spirit upon them!" (Numbers 11:29).

Those who are meek, receptive, and give support to their leaders will receive the Spirit as their companion. In his day, Paul confirmed the blessing of spiritual witnessing: "No man can say that Jesus is the Lord, but by the Holy Ghost" (1 Corinthians 12:3).

There is but one who holds the keys of authority over the Lord's kingdom, and that is the living prophet, but all who labor with him in meekness and loyalty are prophets in their own right because they can bear witness through the Spirit of the truths of the gospel. Miriam and Aaron had to learn that lesson, for when they found fault with Moses on one occasion and boasted of their own prophetic power, the Lord chastised them severely, reminding them that "with him will I speak mouth to mouth" (Numbers 12:8)—rather than just through visions and dreams. And when the murmuring Israelites continued to complain about the bread from heaven, the Lord corrected them through a devastating plague (see Numbers 11:33).

The following account illustrates how the Lord provides opportunities for each of us to learn the blessings of meekness and humility:

> On one occasion when I was serving in a stake presidency, a young man came to me to complain that various leaders in his ward were giving him conflicting advice when he asked them for help on a challenging marital situation. He felt that the Relief Society president had the most valuable counsel, and he was troubled that the bishop hadn't come up with any better solutions. I assured him, first of all, that it was the individual's responsibility to consider prayerfully all options and then make the decision based on correct principles and the whispering of the Spirit. Next, I reminded him that each one of his mentors would look at his situation with a different level of understanding, viewed from a unique set of personal experiences—and thus a range of opinions was likely.

---

8   See Randy L. Bott, *Home with Honor: Helps for Returning Missionaries* (Salt Lake City: Deseret Book, 1995), 168–169; based on notes by Fred A. Baker, Managing Director, Department of Physical Facilities.

But my main point was this: As a common judge in Israel and the presiding high priest in the ward, the bishop is typically a loving and concerned man, usually a radiant and warm individual, and most often an effective counselor. And yet he is almost *never* the only font of wisdom for *all* members of his ward in *all* matter and at *all* times, for the Lord intended his Church to be a community of mutual support and trust—a living network of resources where even the humblest and least visible member is of value and worth. The various gifts of the Spirit are given unto the Saints. Each is blessed with one or more gifts "that all may be profited thereby" (D&C 46:12). Thus we can depend on one another in meekness and love.

Pondering: How have you been able to confirm that meekness and spiritual strength go hand in hand? How can you recognize within yourself the gift of prophesy? How can you be more supportive of our Church leaders?

2. Those filled with hope receive power and authority to help build the kingdom of God.

The Lord will fight our battles, but He expects us to step forward and join His army of faithful warriors. When Moses sent a team of spies into Canaan to investigate the state of affairs, most of them returned with a discouraging report about the impossibility of Israel moving forward. However, Caleb and Joshua were firm in their conviction that the Lord and His people would triumph. Said Caleb, "Let us go up at once, and possess it; for we are well able to overcome it" (Numbers 13:30). Both Caleb and Joshua declared, "The land, which we passed through to search it, is an exceeding good land. If the LORD delight in us, then he will bring us into this land, and give it us; a land which floweth with milk and honey" (Numbers 14:7–8).

> **Who were Joshua and Caleb?**
>
> Joshua (meaning "God is help"), son of Nun from the tribe of Ephraim (see Exodus 33:11; Numbers 11:28; 1 Chronicles 7:23–27), was the one chosen to succeed Moses in leading the house of Israel (see Numbers 27:18–23; 34:17; Deuteronomy 1:38; 3:28; 31:3, 23). Of him it was said, "And Joshua the son of Nun was full of the spirit of wisdom; for Moses had laid his hands upon him: and the children of Israel hearkened unto him, and did as the LORD commanded Moses" (Deuteronomy 34:9).
>
> Caleb was one of the twelve princes or heads of the tribes of Israel (see Numbers 13:6). He was of the tribe of Judah and received Hebron as an inheritance in the promised land. At age eighty-five, he left his testimony as a legacy of faith and courage: "My brethren that went up with me [to spy on the land of Canaan] made the heart of the people melt: but I wholly followed the LORD my God" (Joshua 14:8).

But the host of Israel were dead set against entering into Canaan and even called for a drastic reversal: "And they said one to another, Let us make a captain, and let us return into Egypt" (Numbers 14:4). The anger of the Lord was kindled against the Israelites for their murmuring and lack of faith and hope. It took the earnest supplication of Moses to dissuade the Lord from sending destruction upon the people in that very hour. Though the murmurers were pardoned, all those twenty years of age and older were denied entrance into the promised land (see Numbers 14:29). By contrast, those of faith and courage—such as Caleb and Joshua—were deemed worthy to enter therein (see Numbers 14:24, 30).

Through all generations, those with hope and faith have risen to assist the Lord in building His kingdom on earth. Ponder the following account of stewardship in the days of Joseph Smith:

Among the 133 contemporaries of Joseph Smith referred to in the Doctrine and Covenants, most remained faithful; however, just over one-third of them fell away from the Church and did not return, some of them even fighting against the Church.[9] On Sunday, May 28, 1843, the Prophet Joseph made this poignant entry in his journal: "Of the Twelve Apostles chosen in Kirtland, and ordained under the hands of Oliver Cowdery, David Whitmer and myself, there have been but two but what have lifted their heel against me—namely, Brigham Young and Heber C. Kimball" (*HC* 5:412). All of the others, to a greater or lesser degree, at one time or another, had differences with the Prophet or the Church.

---

9   See Ed J. Pinegar and Richard J. Allen, *Doctrine and Covenants Who's Who* (American Fork, Utah: Covenant Communications, 2008), 193–196.

Even Parley P. Pratt went through a period of disaffection in May of 1837 because of the serious financial difficulties in Kirtland: "I went to Brother Joseph Smith in tears, and, with a broken heart and contrite spirit, confessed wherein I had erred in spirit, murmured, or done or said amiss. He frankly forgave me, prayed for me and blessed me. Thus, by experience, I learned more fully to discern and to contrast the two spirits, and to resist the one and cleave to the other" (*HC* 2:488).

Pondering: What experiences in your life confirm that strength comes from supporting the Lord fully in building up His kingdom on the earth?

3. Those who look to God receive eternal life.

The Israelites in the wilderness were chronic murmurers: "And our soul loatheth this light bread" (Numbers 21:5). In response, the Lord sent fiery serpents to chastise them. The people then sorrowfully begged Moses to pray for relief. Obeying the counsel of the Lord, "Moses made a serpent of brass, and put it upon a pole, and it came to pass, that if a serpent had bitten any man, when he beheld the serpent of brass, he lived" (Numbers 21:9).

The act of looking upon the brass image became a powerful and enduring emblem of looking unto the Lord for life. The Savior taught Nicodemus this principle: "And as Moses lifted up the serpent in the wilderness, even so must the Son of man be lifted up: That whosoever believeth in him should not perish, but have eternal life" (John 3:14–15).

It was the same message that Alma had declared to his son Helaman: "For so was it prepared for [our fathers], that if they would look they might live; even so it is with us. The way is prepared, and if we will look we may live forever" (Alma 37:46). It is the same message that has been preached by prophets of all dispensations: "See that ye look to God and live" (Alma 37:47; see also 1 Nephi 17:41; Alma 33:18–23; Helaman 8:13–16).

Though our mortal experience is often clouded with tribulation, we can always see beyond to a higher view. The following account by an LDS couple confirms this truth:

> We had a neighbor with a remarkable gift—the gift of looking into the future with hope. Though her physical frame was severely racked with the effects of a degenerative disease for many years, she persisted resolutely in staying the course, preserving her gracious smile, confirming her faith and trust in the Lord, and speaking nothing but uplifting and positive words at every turn. To see her walking the halls of the chapel or bearing her testimony from the podium was to see the embodiment of hope in all of its majesty. The physicians shook their heads in wonder at her resiliency. Her friends nodded their heads in admiration of her faith. When the time came for her to go back to her spiritual home, we knew that she would be well received, for she had endured to the end by looking to God to live.

Pondering: Our modern world of digital technology buries us in an infinite variety of things to look at. How can we do better at focusing our view on the things of God? How can we bless the lives of our loved ones by helping them look to God and live?

AGENDA FOR ACTION

From the ancient account about Israel in the wilderness, we can learn that hands of meekness and hope lighten the load in building the kingdom of God. Loyalty and positive service move the work forward through the blessings of the Spirit. We can make it a habit of cultivating a positive attitude day after day. We can dissipate feelings of glumness by feasting upon the hope and cheer harvested from our gospel garden. Above all, when we keep our vision focused obediently on Jesus Christ as our Savior, we are immunized against the fiery darts of temptation and the consequences of sin. Let us all look valiantly to God and live. That is the sacred key to eternal life.

Looking Forward: How can we ensure that we choose the rewards of heaven over the rewards of the world?

CHAPTER SIXTEEN

"THE WORD WHICH I SHALL SAY UNTO THEE, THAT SHALT THOU DO"

GOSPEL DOCTRINE READING ASSIGNMENT: NUMBERS 22–24, 31:1–16

There shall come a Star out of Jacob, and a Sceptre shall rise out of Israel. (Numbers 24:17)

TWO KINDS OF WAGES

PAUL PUT FORWARD A MEMORABLE statement about the consequences of how we choose to serve: "For the wages of sin is death; but the gift of God is eternal life through Jesus Christ our Lord" (Romans 6:23). In His Sermon on the Mount, the Savior put it this way: "No man can serve two masters: for either he will hate the one, and love the other; or else he will hold to the one, and despise the other. Ye cannot serve God and mammon" (Matthew 6:24; also Luke 16:13; 3 Nephi 13:24). Temporal service takes second place to spiritual service and the associated wages that flow from both: "But seek ye first the kingdom of God, and his righteousness; and all these things shall be added unto you" (Matthew 6:33; also Luke 12:31; Jacob 2:18; 3 Nephi 13:33; D&C 11:23).

The story of Balaam is a chilling confirmation of the principle of wages. He tried to blend together the two kinds, with worldly honor coming first—and he was destroyed in the process. Peter reminded us of Balaam's troubling habit of loving "the wages of unrighteousness" (2 Peter 2:15). Jude and John also pointed out the error of Balaam's actions (see Jude 1:11; Revelation 2:14).

Balaam was a prophet-figure who lived in Pethor, a city by the Euphrates (see Deuteronomy 23:4; Numbers 22:5). When the hosts of Israel were encamped on the plains of Moab, the king of the Moabites, Balak, took action to hire Balaam—who had a reputation of divine influence—for the purpose of cursing Israel. Israel was perceived as a distinct threat to the Moabites and their associates, the Midianites. Balak said to Balaam, "Come now therefore,

I pray thee, curse me this people; for they are too mighty for me: peradventure I shall prevail, that we may smite them, and that I may drive them out of the land: for I wot that he whom thou blessest is blessed, and he whom thou cursest is cursed" (Numbers 22:6).

Because Balak's representatives came "with the rewards of divination in their hand" (Numbers 22:7), Balaam agreed to approach the Lord on their behalf. But the message was not to their liking, for the Lord warned Balaam: "Thou shalt not go with them; thou shalt not curse the people: for they *are* blessed" (Numbers 22:12). Still, Balak insisted, so Balaam, intrigued with the promise to be promoted "unto very great honour" (Numbers 22:17), continued with his plan, even though "God's anger was kindled because he went" (Numbers 22:22).

It was then that the famous event took place in which it became clear that Balaam's means of transportation—his donkey—had more spiritual discernment than Balaam himself. Seeing the angel of the Lord blocking the way, the donkey repeatedly held back and suffered beatings by an impatient Balaam. Finally, when the Lord opened Balaam's eyes, he was shocked at his own blind actions and confessed: "I have sinned; for I knew not that thou stoodest in the way against me: now therefore, if it displease thee, I will get me back again" (Numbers 22:34). But the Lord gave him permission to go with the princes of Balak if he would speak "only the word that I shall speak unto thee" (Numbers 22:35).

Thereafter, Balak directed Balaam three times to view the hosts of Israel and perform the cursing that he had paid him for. But each time the answer came back that Israel was to be blessed rather than cursed.

Thereafter, Balak and Balaam went their separate ways. But the Israelites had intimate contact with the Moabites and the Midianites and began to assimilate their pagan practices and immoral ways—just the kinds of activities Balaam had encouraged Balak to promote (see Numbers 31:16; Revelation 2:14). Thus the Lord commanded Moses to strike back in order to eliminate the evil influence of the local tribes. The result was decisive: "And they slew the kings of Midian, beside the rest of them that were slain; . . . Balaam also the son of Beor they slew with the sword" (Numbers 31:8).

WHAT LESSON CAN WE LEARN FROM THE ACCOUNT OF BALAAM?

1. The work of the Lord will ultimately prevail.

Balaam was destroyed because he tried to serve God and mammon at the same time. Just as he failed to see the angel of the Lord blocking the pathway, he also failed to grasp the higher meaning of the words that the Lord planted in his heart. True, he spoke the words given to him—"the word that God putteth in my mouth, that shall I speak" (Numbers 22:38)—but he overlooked the application: "All that the LORD speaketh, that I must *do*" (Numbers 23:26; emphasis added).

The words given to Balaam by the Lord are segments of what the scriptural account calls a parable, meaning a symbolic comparison. Balaam failed to understand fully what the words were pointing to, and he fell short in acting decisively on their hidden meanings:

- "Who can count the dust of Jacob, . . . Behold, the people shall rise up as a great lion, and lift up himself as a young lion: he shall not lie down until he eat of the prey, and drink the blood of the slain" (Numbers 23:10, 24). Hidden meaning: the people of the Lord cannot be conquered.
- "How goodly are thy tents, O Jacob, and thy tabernacles, O Israel! . . . and his kingdom shall be exalted" (Numbers 24:5, 7). Hidden meaning: the people of the Lord shall be redeemed and lifted up.
- "I shall see him, but not now: I shall behold him, but not nigh: there shall come a Star out of Jacob, and a Sceptre shall rise out of Israel" (Numbers 24:17). Hidden meaning: Jesus Christ will come forth as the Savior and Redeemer of mankind.

In a similar way, many wayward leaders in the world have been blind to the divine course of affairs unfolding around them, as the Prophet Joseph Smith learned:

On Friday morning, 29th, we proceeded to the house of the president [Martin Van Buren]. We found a very large and splendid palace, surrounded with a splendid enclosure, decorated with all the fineries and elegancies of this world. We went to the door and requested to see the president, when we were immediately introduced into an upper apartment, where we met the president, and were introduced into his parlor, where we presented him with our letters of introduction. As soon as he had read one of them, he looked upon us with a half frown, and said, "What can I do? I can do nothing for you! If I do anything, I shall come in contact with the whole state of Missouri." (*HC* 4:40)

The Prophet later summarized his dialogue with the president:

During my stay I had an interview with Martin Van Buren, the president, who treated me very insolently, and it was with great reluctance he listened to our message, which, when he had heard, he said: "Gentlemen, your cause is just, but I can do nothing for you;" and "If I take up for you I shall lose the vote of Missouri." His whole course went to show that he was an office-seeker, that self-aggrandizement was his ruling passion, and that justice and righteousness were no part of his composition. I found him such a man as I could not conscientiously support at the head of our noble Republic. (*HC* 4:80)

The Prophet declared, "May he [Van Buren] never be elected again to any office of trust or power, by which he may abuse the innocent and let the guilty go free" (*HC* 4:89). Van Buren was soundly defeated in the next presidential election in 1840 (receiving only 60 of 294 electoral votes) and again in the election of 1848 (in which he did not receive a single electoral vote). The moral of the story is clear: those who seek to destroy out of self-interest will themselves be destroyed. Those who serve the interests of mammon rather than the interests of the Lord are destined to fail. By contrast, the Lord's people of the Restoration eventually triumphed over their persecutors and, according to the promises given to Joseph of old, found security in "the utmost bound of the everlasting hills" (Genesis 49:26).

Pondering: How have you found in your own experiences that temporal obligations are best fulfilled when you put the work of the Lord first? When the Spirit whispers directions to you, how can you ensure that you take action without delay? How can you help loved ones to do the same?

AGENDA FOR ACTION

Imagine that you overhear a young man asking the Savior, "Good Master, what good thing shall I do, that I may have eternal life?" (Matthew 19:16). After confirming that the man is obedient to the commandments, the Lord says: "If thou wilt be perfect, go and sell that thou hast, and give to the poor, and thou shalt have treasure in heaven: and come and follow me" (Matthew 19:21). Then you watch the young man walk away with sorrow in his face, "for he had great possessions" (19:22). As you watch him disappear into the shadows, you start to think about yourself and silently raise the question, "Am I putting the Lord and His children first in my list of priorities? How can I do better?"

Balaam placed worldly honors ahead of the honor of God. He put his own desires and longings before the will of God. It is the same for us all—for the eternal purposes of the Lord will all be fulfilled. The best choice is to bring our will in harmony with the principles of righteousness and salvation—thus the blessings of

What comes to pass when we unitedly do the will of the Lord?

Joseph F. Smith explained, "It is true that we are in a measure of the earth, earthy; we belong to the world. Our affections and our souls are here; our treasures are here, and where the treasure is there the heart is. But if we will lay up our treasures in heaven; if we will wean our affections from the things of this world, and say to the Lord our God, 'Father, not my will, but thine be done,' then may the will of God be done on earth as it is done in heaven, and the kingdom of God in its power and glory will be established upon the earth. Sin and Satan will be bound and banished from the earth, and not until we attain to this condition of mind and faith will this be done." (*Gospel Doctrine: Selections from the Sermons and Writings of Joseph F. Smith*, compiled by John A. Widtsoe [Salt Lake City: Deseret Book, 1939], 261) heaven will flow unto us forever through the love and mercy of the Father and the Son. Paul stated it with power: "For the wages of sin is death; but the gift of God is eternal life through Jesus Christ our Lord" (Romans 6:23).

It is that gift that comes into our lives in the form of a seed. The Savior's parable of the sower is a case in point. When the seed, meaning "the word of God" (Luke 8:11), is cast by the wayside and is lost, it shows what happens when we lack faith (see Luke 8:12). When the seed is cast upon a rock and withers away without moisture, it is a reminder of what happens when we allow temptation to stunt the growth of healthy and enduring roots (see Luke 8:13). When the seed is cast among thorns and choked off, it is a confirmation of how worldly cares and pleasures wipe out the growth of nourishing fruit (see Luke 8:14). Only when the seed falls on good ground does it produce fruit "an hundredfold" (Luke 8:8), for then we are among those "which in an honest and good heart, having heard the word, keep it, and bring forth fruit with patience" (Luke 8:15).

What can we do each week to ensure that our seed emerges as "a tree springing up unto everlasting life" (Alma 32:41)? Can we share with our families stories about how the Lord has blessed us or our ancestors to grow in faith and endurance? Can we invite our loved ones to share with us how they have been blessed when they have put the Lord first in their lives? Can we focus on which aspects of the gospel have especially contributed to our growth and well-being? Can we sing songs about faith and courage, write poems about our testimony, paint pictures or sketches about our tree of everlasting life, pen journal entries about the good that comes from obedience? There are dozens of active manifestations of our faith. The Lord will guide and direct all such activities, leading to a harvest of peace and fulfilled dreams.

LOOKING FORWARD: What does it mean to build upon the "Rock"?

CHAPTER SEVENTEEN

THE ROCK OF OUR SALVATION

GOSPEL DOCTRINE READING ASSIGNMENT: DEUTERONOMY 6, 8, 11, 32

And thou shalt love the LORD thy God with all thine heart, and with all thy soul, and with all thy might. And these words, which I command thee this day, shall be in thine heart: And thou shalt teach them diligently unto thy children. (Deuteronomy 6:5–7)

FAMOUS LAST WORDS

FINAL WORDS RESONATE WITH POWER. We treasure the final words of Lehi to his children, including unforgettable lines such as, "Adam fell that men might be; and men are, that they might have joy" (2 Nephi 2:25). We rejoice to learn the words that King Benjamin shared with his people in his last sermon—words about the eternal truths of the gospel: "And now, if you believe all these things see that ye do them" (Mosiah 4:10). We remember with enduring gratitude the final words of Alma to his sons, including this counsel to Helaman: "O, remember, my son, and learn wisdom in thy youth; yea, learn in thy youth to keep the commandments of God" (Alma 37:35).

Deuteronomy partakes of the same spirit, for it contains the final words of Moses to his people at the end of his ministry. "Deuteronomy" means "repetition of the law." Thus the book—the fifth and last book of the Pentateuch (Genesis, Exodus, Leviticus, Numbers, and Deuteronomy)—is a shining review of the law of God given through Moses during the wilderness period. Moses presents his message in three discourses. The first one (chapters 1–4) serves as an introduction. The second one (chapters 5–26) covers the Ten Commandments and the Israelite code of special laws and practices. The third one (chapters 27–30) calls for the people to remember their covenant with the Lord in order to receive the blessings of obedience. An appendix to the book (chapters 31–34) includes exhortations to Joshua.

Deuteronomy contains precious wisdom to help guide our lives each day. We can gratefully acknowledge the final words of Moses as inspired counsel.

A TOUCH OF REALITY

Imagine that you were giving your final message to your family. What would you say? A young priesthood holder shared the following account:

> I can recall the last words my aging father said to me. He had been growing increasingly feeble in his senior years, so to assist him in his personal care, I drove the long distance to his home and presented him with a gift—a new electric razor. He looked at it, smiled gratefully, and then, much to my surprise, handed it back and whispered, "Do this for me." He was asking me to show him how to use it. Thus I bent over and carefully shaved away his grey whiskers—emblems of a long and productive life. "Do this for me." Those were his final words to me. He passed away not long thereafter.
>
> The inner meaning of that phrase still echoes in my mind, for it also implies the fatherly counsel to be good and follow the Lord—just as my father had done throughout his life. What better way for children to honor their parents than to follow their example by aspiring to a "godly walk and conversation" (D&C 20:69), thus also leaving behind a legacy of faith and courage.
>
> According to the Gospels, the Savior's last words including the following: "It is finished" (John 19:30); "My God, my God, why have you forsaken me!" (Matthew 27:46; Mark 15:34); and "Father, into thy hands I commend my spirit" (Luke 23:46). His entire life can be summarized in the phrase "Come, follow me" (Luke 18:22), a glorious variant of the humble words, said in so many ways by parents as a last request to their children: "Do this for me."

> **How do we know for certain that Moses is the author of the Pentateuch?**
>
> Latter-day revelation confirms it (see 1 Nephi 5:10–11; Moses 1:40–41). The resurrected Lord said, "Behold, I am he of whom Moses spake, saying: A prophet shall the Lord your God raise up unto you of your brethren, like unto me; him shall ye hear in all things whatsoever he shall say unto you" (3 Nephi 20:23; compare Deuteronomy 18:15; see also 1 Nephi 22:20–21 and Acts 3:22–23; see also 3 Nephi 21:11).

WHAT LESSONS CAN WE LEARN FROM THE FINAL WORDS OF MOSES?

1. There is a strategy for remembering the Lord in obedience—easy to use and powerful.

Moses blessed us with the Lord's Ten Commandments. But he also gave us ten points of power on how to remember the Lord and keep His commandments.

The Ten Commandments of Remembering

1. Absorb the words of the Lord: "And these words, which I command thee this day, shall be in thine heart" (Deuteronomy 6:6); "Man doth not live by bread only, but by every word that proceedeth out of the mouth of the LORD doth man live" (Deuteronomy 8:3; compare Matthew 4:4); "Therefore shall ye lay up these my words in your heart and in your soul" (Deuteronomy 11:18).

2. Add holy reminders to your environment: "And thou shalt bind them [the words of the Lord] for a sign upon thine hand, and they shall be as frontlets [strips of parchment] between thine eyes. And thou shalt write them upon the posts of thy house, and on thy gates" (Deuteronomy 6:8–9; see also Deuteronomy 11:18, 20–21).

3. Teach your loved ones the truth: "And thou shalt teach them [the words of the Lord] diligently unto thy children, and shalt talk of them when thou sittest in thine house, and when thou walkest by the way, and when thou liest down, and when thou risest up" (Deuteronomy 6:7; see also Deuteronomy 11:19; 32:46–47).

4. Learn from the testimony of your parents and ancestors: "Remember the days of old, consider the years of many generations: ask thy father, and he will shew thee; thy elders, and they will tell thee" (Deuteronomy 32:7; see also Deuteronomy 4:36; 6:21).

5. Count your blessings: "For the LORD thy God bringeth thee into a good land, a land of brooks of water, of fountains and depths that spring out of valleys and hills; A land of wheat, and barley, and vines, and fig trees, and pomegranates; a land of oil olive, and honey" (Deuteronomy 8:7–8); "But your eyes have seen all the great acts of the LORD which he did" (Deuteronomy 11:7).

6. Seek always after the Lord and His mercy: "But if from thence thou shalt seek the LORD thy God, thou shalt find him, if thou seek him with all thy heart and with all thy soul. When thou art in tribulation, and all these things are come upon thee, even in the latter days, if thou turn to the LORD thy God, and shalt be obedient unto his voice; (For the LORD thy God is a merciful God;) he will not forsake thee" (Deuteronomy 4:29–31).

7. Dispel pride when your wealth increases: "Beware that thou forget not the LORD thy God, . . . And thou say in thine heart, My power and the might of mine hand hath gotten me this wealth. But thou shalt remember the LORD thy God: for it is he that giveth thee power to get wealth, that he may establish his covenant which he sware unto thy fathers, as it is this day" (Deuteronomy 8:11, 17–18).

> **What is the most important word in the dictionary?**
>
> In an address to religious educators at Brigham Young University on June 28, 1968, President Spencer W. Kimball shared his belief that the most important word in the dictionary is the word *remember*. We can surely follow his counsel to remember our covenant promises to the Lord in obedience and honor. ("Circles of Exaltation," [Address to religious educators, BYU, June 28, 1968], 8)

8. Reject false prophets: "If there arise among you a prophet, or a dreamer of dreams . . . saying, Let us go after other gods, . . . thou shalt not hearken unto the words of that prophet, or that dreamer of dreams: for the LORD your God proveth you, to know whether ye love the LORD your God with all your heart and with all your soul" (Deuteronomy 13:1–3).

9. Sing songs of praise to the Lord: "Rejoice, O ye nations, with his people: for he will . . . be merciful unto his land, and to his people. And Moses came and spake all the words of this song in the ears of the people" (Deuteronomy 32:43–44).

10. Observe how obedience enhances your well-being: "And thou shalt do that which is right and good in the sight of the LORD: that it may be well with thee" (Deuteronomy 6:18; see also Deuteronomy 4:1, 40).

Pondering: Which of these Ten Commandments of Remembering seem to be the most relevant in your own life at this time? How can you apply one or two of them more fully from week to week?

2. *Those who build upon the Rock will prevail.*

In his final words before his people, Moses pronounced a glorious hymn of praise unto the Lord:

> GIVE ear, O ye heavens, and I will speak; and hear, O earth, the words of my mouth.
>
> My doctrine shall drop as the rain, my speech shall distil as the dew, as the small rain upon the tender herb, and as the showers upon the grass:
>
> Because I will publish the name of the LORD: ascribe ye greatness unto our God.
>
> He is the Rock, his work is perfect: for all his ways are judgment: a God of truth and without iniquity, just and right is he. (Deuteronomy 32:1–4)

The hymn of Moses continues to honor the qualities of the Rock, declaring that He presides "as an eagle stirreth up her nest, fluttereth over her young, spreadeth abroad her wings, taketh them, beareth them on her wings" (Deuteronomy 32:11), thus rising up as "the Rock of [Israel's] salvation" (Deuteronomy 32:15; see also Deuteronomy 32:31, 39–40).

The Israelites of the Exodus were not strangers to the image of the rock, for the Lord caused water to spew out of the rock to quench their thirst (see Exodus 17:6; Numbers 20:8–11; Deuteronomy 8:15). What they were slow to grasp was the hidden light of truth, for the rock was a foreshadowing of the eternal Rock—the heavenly source of living water—just as the manna raining down from above pointed toward the Bread of Life.

The rock is a dynamic image in the scriptures. The Savior counseled His listeners to build their house upon a rock of stability rather than upon the eroding foundation of sand (see Matthew 7:24–27; compare 3 Nephi 18:12). Helaman taught his sons: "And now, my sons, remember, remember that it is upon the rock of our Redeemer, who is Christ, the Son of God, that ye must build your foundation; . . . which is a sure foundation, a foundation whereon if men build they cannot fall" (Helaman 5:12). In our day the Lord confirmed, "Wherefore, I am in your midst, and I am the good shepherd, and the stone of Israel. He that buildeth upon this rock shall never fall" (D&C 50:44; see also D&C 11:24).

Did the Israelites build upon the Rock with full faith and valor? Hardly. With but few exceptions—such as Joshua and Caleb—only those younger than twenty were to be admitted into the promised land (see Numbers 14:29). Can we build more faithfully upon the Rock and look forward to eternal joy in the promised land of our heavenly home? Contemplate the following account shared by a bishop:

> He was a bright young man with a lovely wife and a growing family—just the kind of individual you would want to have as one of your ward clerks. When the Spirit whispered a quiet confirmation, I went to visit him with the invitation.

He was honored by the calling but somewhat reserved in his response. "Bishop," he said, "I want to be of help. But you know, there is something I need to explain. Ever since I joined the Church a few years ago, I have tried to do my duty and attend my meetings. But I have always had season tickets to the Sunday games to see our NFL team play. That's why you sometimes don't see me at the meetings."

I thought about his situation for a moment then felt impressed to offer him a special arrangement. The Lord wanted him to be a part of our team. Therefore, if he would complete his church assignment to the best of his ability, we would work around his schedule. When the team was in town with a home game, he would be away, and we would understand. He accepted the assignment, but I could see that he had a struggle going on inside—and that is just as it should be when one is learning.

A few weeks later on a Sunday when there was a home game, I was surprised when he showed up at my chapel office. He was energized, with a kind of glow about him and a sparkle in the eyes. "Bishop," he said, "I have decided to give up my season tickets. The gospel is more important. I will always be here on the Sabbath."

I put my arm around his shoulder and bore witness to the strength and courage of his correct decision, and I thanked the Lord in my heart for the patient way the Spirit often works. The words of the Savior came to my mind: "If any man will do his will, he shall know of the doctrine, whether it be of God, or whether I speak of myself" (John 7:17). Then I thought: There is always a home game. It takes place within the heart of every individual as he or she engages in the choices of life, the choices that define character and devotion to building the kingdom of God. When we build upon the Rock of the Redeemer, we cannot fall.

Why did Moses not enter into the promised land with his people?

When the Lord commanded Moses to strike the rock at Meribah and bring forth water for the thirsting Israelites, Moses obeyed, but he fell short in giving full credit to the Lord (see Numbers 20:12) and was thus excluded from entering the promised land (see also Deuteronomy 4:20–23; 32:51–52). But there were two other purposes for keeping Moses back: First, the people failed to seek after the Lord—"Therefore, he took Moses out of their midst, and the Holy Priesthood also" (D&C 84:25). And second, Moses was being prepared for another calling. The Old Testament account says that Moses died in Moab and was buried there (see Deuteronomy 34:5–6). But modern scripture confirms that "the Lord took Moses unto himself" (Alma 45:19)—translated him—in anticipation of his joining with the Savior and Elijah on the Mount of Transfiguration to restore priesthood keys to Peter, James, and John (see Matthew 17:1–13; Mark 9:2–13; Luke 9:28–36).

Pondering: What steps do we take in life to build upon the Rock of the Redeemer? In what ways does the Lord reach out to help us build upon this Rock? How do we help others to do the same?

AGENDA FOR ACTION

We can learn much from the chronicles of how God dealt with His ancient covenant people—teaching them through the words of a living prophet, sustaining them with mercy and love, and, yes, correcting them along the journey to the promised land. We can learn the steps of how to remember our covenants with greater courage and faith. We can learn how to build upon the Rock of our Redeemer by following His word: "And thou shalt love the Lord thy God with all thine heart, and with all thy soul, and with all thy might. And these words, which I command thee this day, shall be in thine heart: And thou shalt teach them diligently unto thy children" (Deuteronomy 6:5–7; compare Matthew 22:37; Mark 12:30; Luke 10:27).

One interesting exercise for sharing your testimony with loved ones would be to write down a statement comprising your "last words"—the message you would want them to hear as your departing words of counsel and love. What would you say? What aspects of the gospel would you emphasize? What experiences would you share as the most life changing and rewarding? For what qualities and contributions would you most like to be remembered?

Looking Forward: What shapes the way we choose to serve the Lord?

CHAPTER EIGHTEEN

CHOOSE TO FOLLOW THE LORD

GOSPEL DOCTRINE READING ASSIGNMENT: JOSHUA 1–6, 23–24
Choose you this day whom ye will serve; . . . but as for me and my house, we will serve the LORD. (Joshua 24:15)

IN THE FOOTSTEPS OF A LION

HOW WOULD AN INDIVIDUAL FEEL being called to succeed a prophet of immense stature and nobility such as Moses? Joshua (meaning "God is help") was certainly humbled by his calling, yet he was prepared and authorized by the Lord: "Have not I commanded thee? Be strong and of a good courage; be not afraid, neither be thou dismayed: for the LORD thy God is with thee whithersoever thou goest" (Joshua 1:9).

The challenges lying before Joshua were immense: to guide the vast host of Israel across the Jordan into the land of their inheritance (see Joshua 3–4), to bring down the walls of Jericho and silence all the enemies confronting Israel (see Joshua 6–12), and to declare unto the people the words of truth (see Joshua 23–24). All of this Joshua accomplished with divine help.

Through the ministry of Joshua, we can discover the keys of how to magnify and be magnified. From him, we learn anew the formula for making life-saving decisions without delay. We learn, as did Joshua, to honor the law of the Lord as unfolded in the Pentateuch: "This book of the law shall not depart out of thy mouth," counseled the Lord, "but thou shalt meditate therein day and night, that thou mayest observe to do according to all that is written therein: for then thou shalt make thy way prosperous, and then thou shalt have good success" (Joshua 1:8).

In the Sermon on the Mount, the Lord summarized the essence of His gospel: "Therefore all things whatsoever ye would that men should do to you, do ye even so to them: for this is the law and the prophets" (Matthew 7:12).

Joshua's story is the continuation of the inspiring story of those who served as the Lord's prophets down to the time of Jesus of Nazareth. From the days of Joshua onward, the phrase "the law and the prophets" became a banner for the gospel of love, obedience, and salvation (see Matthew 22:40; Luke 16:16; John 1:45; Acts 13:15; Romans 3:21; 3 Nephi 14:12; 15:10; D&C 59:22).

A TOUCH OF REALITY

How can we emulate the example of Joshua in our own callings—even if they are of modest scope? Consider the following account shared by a priesthood holder who had served a mission in a faraway land:

> In one of my cities, the local branch met in a small rented hall at the back of a commercial building. One weekday afternoon, my companion and I stopped by during the Primary hour. We opened the door a crack and saw one of the local sisters presenting a lesson. Not wanting to disturb the class, we quietly snuck into the back of room to listen. As we entered, we were amazed to see that the room—except for the teacher—was completely empty. She was teaching out loud to an empty classroom, not even holding back any of the visual aids that she had prepared. Noting our surprise, she made a comment that has stuck with me all my life. She said, "I have been given this calling by the Lord, and I need to follow through if I am to be worthy of His blessings." This sister was truly a dedicated teacher. Like Joshua of old, she was having "good success," based on her devotion (see Joshua 1:8). Certainly we were uplifted by her words of wisdom and the unforgettable lesson of dedication. Who knows but what the angels of the Lord were nearby, edified by her faithful performance. Her rehearsal of faith was indeed a preparation for the coming months of service when young lives would be blessed.

WHAT LESSONS CAN WE LEARN FROM THE MINISTRY OF JOSHUA?

1. The scriptures serve as a magnifying glass of truth. To be magnified by the Lord as we magnify our callings is the source of great peace and joy.

When the hosts of Israel arrived at the banks of the Jordan River, "the LORD said unto Joshua, This day will I begin to magnify thee in the sight of all Israel, that they may know that, as I was with Moses, so I will be with thee" (Joshua 3:7). It was then that Joshua announced the miracle about to occur: The Lord would cut off the waters of the river and allow the priests bearing the ark of the covenant to cross over on dry land toward Jericho. That is precisely what took place (see Joshua 3:15–17): "On that day the LORD magnified Joshua in the sight of all Israel; and they feared him, as they feared Moses, all the days of his life" (Joshua 4:14).

> **What is the origin of the word "magnify"?**
>
> The word derives from the Latin verb *magnificare* (meaning "esteem greatly, extol"), from *magnificus* (meaning "great, elevated, noble," as in our words *magnificent* and *magnificence*). In more modern times, the meaning of the word *magnify* in relation to enlarging an image with a telescope or microscope came into usage.

The word *magnify*—meaning to make greater or more splendid and glorious—occurs fifty-one times in the scriptures in the following pattern:

The Person: The Lord in His mercy magnifies *us* over time—as He did in the case of Joshua: "This day will I begin to magnify thee" (Joshua 3:7), followed by, "On that day the LORD magnified Joshua" (Joshua 4:14; see also 1 Chronicles 29:25; 2 Chronicles 1:1; 32:22–23).

The Lord: Central to our service, we magnify the Lord and enlarge His holy name before the world, as Nephi confirmed: "Wherefore, my soul delighteth to prophesy concerning him, for I have seen his day, and my heart doth magnify his holy name" (2 Nephi 25:13). Mary, mother of Jesus, spoke similar words when she declared, "My soul doth magnify the Lord" (Luke 1:46; see also 2 Samuel 7:26; 1 Chronicles 17:24; Psalm 34:3; 35:27; 40:16; 69:30; 70:4; Ezekiel 38:23; Acts 10:45–46; 19:17–18; Philippians 1:20; D&C 132:64).

The Office: When the Lord magnifies us and then we, in turn, magnify Him through service, the result is that we magnify the office to which we are called. In this sense, note the words of Jacob: "And we did magnify our office unto the Lord, taking upon us the responsibility, answering the sins of the people upon our own heads if we did not teach them the word of God with all diligence" (Jacob 1:19; see also Romans 11:13; Jacob 2:1–2; D&C 24:3, 9; 66:11; 84:33–34; 88:78–80).

The Gospel: Finally, this process allows the Lord and His servants to magnify the gospel for His followers so that the pathway to salvation and exaltation is illuminated with the light of truth: "The LORD is well pleased for his righteousness' sake; he will magnify the law, and make it honourable" (Isaiah 42:21; see also Job 36:24–25; Psalm 138:2).

This fourfold process of enlargement or magnifying is a buoyant force, a lifting force that carries us ever upward through the blessings of the gospel of Jesus Christ. How does this process take root and blossom? Ponder the following incident recalled by a man who had lost his mother when he was only ten:

> As a young boy, I began to spend many evening hours outdoors observing the stars and planets with the telescope that my father had given to me. In a way, it was like searching the heavens for my departed mother. At the same time, it was a soothing relief to admire the rings of Saturn and the moons of Jupiter with this miraculous instrument that made visible the invisible. I papered the walls of my bedroom with homemade charts that depicted the constellations of the heavens. From the experience of those early years, I came to cultivate an appreciation of God's majestic creation, magnified all around me.
>
> Gradually, I started to understand that the invisible can also be rendered visible through another kind of lens—the lens of adversity. Through this stark lens of amplification, I came to recognize that we often take for granted that which is, in fact, a miracle. Looking back through this lens at precious memories from yesterday, I could behold the sublime and brilliant image of my mother illuminated against the darkened background of mortality. She was a heavenly light of the first magnitude. She was an angel on earth—then, now, and into the future. She was the bringer of life—the only authentic mother we children would ever have in this world. As the Lord magnified for me the wonders of His Creation—including my angel mother—He also magnified my soul to understand and accept the mortal experience as an essential part of His glorious plan of salvation and a wondrous opportunity to serve and love others.

The Prophet Joseph Smith was also able to magnify his office as the living prophet of the Lord. In his earlier years, the Prophet was just beginning to unfold his ability as an orator. But as he progressed, he was able, through the strength of the Lord, to magnify his gift as a bold and powerful spokesperson for the Lord. During a trip to Philadelphia in early 1840, he met with a large public audience of some three thousand people to explain the doctrines and blessings of the restored gospel. Parley P. Pratt was on hand to witness what happened:

> The entire congregation were astounded; electrified, as it were, and overwhelmed with the sense of the truth and power by which he spoke, and the wonders which he related; many souls were gathered unto the fold. And I bear witness, that he, by his faithful and powerful testimony, cleared his garments of their blood. Multitudes were baptized in Philadelphia and in the regions around.[10]

During that same visit, Parley had the opportunity to speak with the Prophet in private concerning the glories of the eternal family:

> It was from him that I learned the true dignity and destiny of a son of God, clothed with an eternal priesthood, as the patriarch and sovereign of his countless offspring. It was from him that I learned that the highest dignity of womanhood was, to stand as a queen and priestess to her husband, and to reign for ever and ever as the queen mother of her numerous and still increasing offspring. . . . Yet, at that time, my dearly beloved brother, Joseph Smith, had barely touched a single key; had merely lifted a corner of the veil and given me a single glance into eternity.[11]

---

10   Parley P. Pratt, *Autobiography of Parley P. Pratt* (Salt Lake City: Deseret Book, 1970), 299.
11   Ibid., 298.

Pondering: How have you been lifted and sustained (magnified) by the Lord in your lifetime? How have you magnified the Lord and His gospel plan in your thoughts and actions? How can you help your loved ones do the same?

2. The defining choice in life is to choose to serve the Lord.

The Lord fights our battles provided "we are all enlisted till the conflict is o'er" ("We Are All Enlisted," *Hymns*, no. 250). Leading up to the battle of Jericho, Joshua sent spies into the city to prepare the way. In exchange for the protection of her family, the woman Rahab provided cover for the spies, for she told them, "The LORD your God, he is God in heaven above, and in earth beneath" (Joshua 2:11). Joshua next received confirmation that the Lord was in command of the campaign, for he discovered and was taught by the "captain of the host of the Lord" waiting for him near the city (Joshua 5:14–15).

Holiness prevailed, for the Lord instructed Joshua precisely how to proceed with his army to lay siege around the city for a week and then bring down its walls (see Joshua 6:20). The conquest of the remaining segments of the promised land then proceeded as planned "because the LORD God of Israel fought for Israel" (Joshua 10:42). Joshua then assigned areas of inheritance for the tribes of Israel according to the direction of the Lord (see Joshua 13–22). The children of Israel had a new home, for they had chosen to follow the word of the Lord and stay enlisted in His cause.

Still, it was important for Joshua to remind the people to continue choosing the right. In his final counsel to his people, the aging prophet made a statement that has become an enduring formula for decisive action on the pathway to salvation: "Now therefore fear the LORD, and serve him in sincerity and in truth: . . . Choose you this day whom ye will serve; . . . but as for me and my house, we will serve the LORD" (Joshua 24:14–15; compare also Alma 30:8 and Moses 6:33).

This inspired counsel continues to resonate in the hearts of all the faithful to this day.

Pondering: How have your life experiences confirmed that grand blessings flow from choosing to serve the Lord? How can you best help loved ones avoid the patterns and behaviors of worldliness and choose instead the way of holiness, peace, harmony, and salvation?

AGENDA FOR ACTION

We can apply the word of the Lord—ancient and modern—for the blessing of our families each day. We can grow in stature and service, being magnified by the Lord as we strive faithfully to magnify Him and others through our gospel callings. We can make the same decision Joshua made: "As for me and my house, we will serve the LORD" (Joshua 24:15). Blessings await us as the Lord fights our battles, for we are all enlisted until the conflict is over. In fact, it would be a rewarding experience to memorize the first verse of the hymn "We Are All Enlisted" (*Hymns*, no. 250) and then sing those words with our loved ones, or silently within our soul, as a stimulus to help us serve the Lord with greater courage and faith.

LOOKING FORWARD: What is the key to true friendship?

CHAPTER NINETEEN

JUDGES IN ISRAEL—THE LORD'S DELIVERERS

GOSPEL DOCTRINE READING ASSIGNMENT: JUDGES 2, 4, 6–7, 13–16

Surely I will be with thee. (Judges 6:16)

THE PATHWAY UPWARD

HOW WOULD YOU LIKE THE thrill and chill of a roller coaster ride that went on for several hundred years? Read the book of Judges! This chronicle of scripture reveals over and over again—cycle after cycle—that obedience and faithfulness lead to blessings and peace, and wickedness and pride lead to destruction and misery. During the period between the ministries of Joshua and Samuel, the Israelites in Canaan went through up-and-down phases—at times joyfully honoring their covenants and at times forgetting and falling into a state of misery and suffering.

When the roller coaster plunged into the depths of spiritual decline, the scriptures use words like the following: "And the children of Israel again did evil in the sight of the LORD" (Judges 3:12; see also Judges 2:11; 3:7; 4:1; 6:1; 10:6; 13:1). The roller coaster would rise again when a valiant leader (usually also a military champion) was called by the Lord as a deliverer of the repentant people: "And when the LORD raised them up judges, then the LORD was with the judge, and delivered them out of the hand of their enemies all the days of the judge" (Judges 2:18). However, on the passing of the judge, the Israelites would again plunge downward along the murky paths of idolatry and sin until the Lord allowed their enemies to scourge and persecute them so that they became humble and penitent once more (see Judges 2:3).

Like the cycles of obedience and decline recorded in the Book of Mormon, Judges serves as a lens of warning and relief: warning to avoid the painful harvest of worldliness, and the relief of savoring the harvest of joy flowing from obedience. Of the dozen-plus judges who served during the post-Joshua period leading up the ministry of the prophet Samuel, the most cited are Deborah, Gideon, and Samson. From each we can learn powerful lessons that remind us to follow the pathway of the Savior and avoid the painful ups and downs of an aimless lifestyle.

A TOUCH OF REALITY

How does the up-and-down narrative stretching across the book of Judges relate in our day and age? Share the ponderings of an LDS couple called as stake institute instructors:

> We were privileged recently to study the scriptures with several dozen young singles enrolled in a stake institute course. They were choice young people with a spirit of sincere inquiry and a desire to serve the Lord. We focused on the Book of Mormon as an inspired road map to guide our footsteps in the latter days, in keeping with the counsel of President Ezra Taft Benson to make the Book of Mormon the center of our study since it was truly written for our day and age.[12]
>
> What does that mean—"written for our day"? That question was answered for us dramatically by an event that occurred shortly after the start of the institute class that year—the terror attack of September 11. Like everyone in the nation, we were shocked by the devastating upheaval wrought upon our way of life by evil forces. Could there be any security and peace after such a violent happening? We read together from the promise of Isaiah included in Nephi's record: "For upon all the glory of Zion shall be a defence. And there shall be a tabernacle for a shadow in the daytime from the heat, and for a place of refuge, and a covert from storm and from rain" (2 Nephi 14:5–6, citing Isaiah 4:5–6).
>
> One of the students later wrote to us expressing how the scriptures, and specifically that passage from Isaiah, had been a blessing and a guide at a time of challenge: "When I consider 2 Nephi 14:5–6, I can't help but think of our nation's recent events. In a time when evil is so apparent and terror so present . . . I can find refuge in many places, like institute. After a hectic day at work, where my attention is distracted by so many busy, yet less important things, I am glad to have institute as a refuge, a place to associate with other Saints, to feel the Spirit, and to study the word of God. It has truly been a blessing, 'a covert from storm and from rain.'"

The word of God—shining forth in holy places—is truly a spiritual road map for our day. It is the iron rod set up by the great Judge of eternity to guide us along the higher road leading to salvation.

WHAT LESSONS CAN WE LEARN FROM THE LORD'S JUDGES?

1. Leadership and friendship are inseparable partners in the work of the Lord.

Deborah (meaning "bee") was a celebrated leader and prophetess (see Judges 4:4) who served as judge over Israel and unified the people. She commissioned Barak (meaning "lightning") to wage battle against the threatening Canaanites, who were under command of Sisera. Barak agreed to gather the forces and attack provided Deborah would consent to a special request: "If thou wilt go with me, then I will go: but if thou wilt not go with me, then I will not go" (Judges 4:8). She responded, "I will surely go with thee" (Judges 4:9).

That pact of friendship sealed the campaign with Deborah declaring, "Up; for this is the day in which the LORD hath delivered Sisera into thine hand: is not the LORD gone out before thee?" (Judges 4:14). That very day the Canaanites, with their much larger force, were overcome (see Judges 4:23–24). Thereafter,

> ### Who wrote the book of Judges? Which judges are included?
>
> The book was compiled by an anonymous writer long after the events took place. Judges mentioned are Othniel, Ehud, Shamgar, Deborah (and Barak), Gideon, Abimelech, Tola, Jair, Jephthah, Ibzan, Elon, Abdon, and Samson. Subsequently, Eli served as judge and high priest, followed by Samuel as judge and prophet.

Deborah and Barak joined in singing a glorious anthem of praise to the Lord with the final lines of triumph resounding: "So let all thine enemies perish, O Lord: but let them that love him be as the sun when he goeth forth in his might. And the land had rest forty years" (Judges 5:31; compare Hebrews 11:32).

Clearly the sting of the "bee" and the strike of "lightning"—working together in cooperative friendship—accomplished the errand of the Lord. But how does this lesson echo in the challenges of today? An important possibility flows from the following story shared by a high priests group leader:

There we were—four strangers in the home of this dear elderly sister who had just moved into our ward. As the high priests group leadership, we wanted to ensure that our new arrival felt welcome, especially since she had just lost her husband before moving here. As she responded to our greeting, it was clear that her heart was shadowed with grief and mourning. Not knowing anyone in the community, she was fighting back tears of loneliness.

We asked her about her upbringing and background. As she recounted her life's experience, one of my assistants responded with enthusiasm that he had grown up in the same part of the state where she was raised and knew many of her relatives. Her eyes brightened with surprise. As she continued, the other assistant remarked that he had known of her family in a city where she later lived, and he had even known her husband and had high regard for him. Her countenance took on an air of recovery. Then, as she continued her story, I recognized that I knew her son-in-law from a ward I had lived in some years back. Before long, we were all having an energized discussion about how the gospel creates a network of friends so that all are included as "fellowcitizens with the saints, and of the household of God" (Ephesians 2:19).

We saw that day the glimmer of hope in the eyes of our elderly sister as she realized that she was among friends in the fold of Christ. Over the next weeks we rejoiced to observe her mingling closely with many new friends in the spirit of togetherness. Said the Lord, "Verily I say unto you my friends, fear not, let your hearts be comforted; yea, rejoice evermore, and in everything give thanks" (D&C 98:1).

Pondering: How have you found that friendship and leadership can bond people together at home, in the Church, and in the community? How can you do more to help your loved ones and friends cultivate this kind of partnership in their everyday lives?

2. The servants of the Lord rise up in obedience to help liberate His people.

Gideon (meaning "warrior") was called to deliver Israel from bondage under the Midianites: "And the Lord looked upon him, and said, Go in this thy might, and thou shalt save Israel from the hand of the Midianites: have not I sent thee? . . . Surely I will be with thee" (Judges 6:14, 16). When an angel confirmed Gideon's commission, he exclaimed: "Alas, O Lord God! for because I have seen an angel of the Lord face to face. And the Lord said unto him, Peace be unto thee; fear not" (Judges 6:22–23). Gideon obeyed the command of the Lord to destroy the altar of Baal (see Judges 6:28)—thus earning the added name Jerubbaal (meaning "he that striveth against Baal"—see Judges 6:32; 7:1; 1 Samuel 12:11). He then triumphed over the Midianites despite the smallness of his own army (see Judges 7:19–25). Gideon is remembered fondly as a victorious deliverer of his people—foreshadowing the work of the great Redeemer (see Isaiah 9:4–7; Hebrews 11:32).

A former bishop suggests,

In a sense, our local bishops are the modern-day Gideons—righteous judges who set the tone of obedience and act in the defense of the Saints. Each bishop serves as a "common judge" in Israel (see D&C 107:74). His gift of prophecy and discernment sustains his calling as the presiding high priest and father of the ward, sent to help us honor our covenants.

If you want an interesting exercise in counting your blessings, make a list of all the bishops in your life—it could be many or a few—and write down a quality that you remember about each one of them. For example, I recall one bishop, most kind and sensitive, who never failed to call each member of the ward—young or old—to wish him or her happy birthday on that special day. Another bishop with a medical condition found it difficult to stay awake at times on the stand and would often ask the ward's forgiveness for his weakness. His example as a humble leader made it easier for the rest of us to confess our weaknesses and make improvements in our lives. To the kindness and humility of these two bishops I would add the qualities of my other bishops: positive attitude, overcoming adversity, honorable and truthful, service-minded, wise, skilled leadership, articulate in the word of faith, gracious, prayerful, and having a sense of humor. No bishop is a perfect embodiment of all these qualities, but your current bishop has special gifts and abilities that can add great blessings to your life if you will sustain him as your loving judge and friend.

Pondering: Who are the special Gideons in your own life who have helped "deliver" you from the burdens you face? In what ways have you served as a Gideon for your loved ones and fellow Saints?

3. Those servants of the Lord who endure in faith until the end are blessed with safety and peace.

> **What is a Nazarite?**
>
> The title Nazarite (meaning "one separated unto the Lord, one consecrated") was applied to an individual under vow to abstain from strong drink, to avoid cutting the hair from the head, and to avoid any contact with persons deceased (see Numbers 6). The Nazarite vow could be for life—as in the case of Samson (see Judges 13:5, 7; 16:17) or Samuel (see 1 Samuel 1:11)—or for a shorter, defined period of time. (Compare Amos 2:11–12; see also Luke 1:15 concerning John the Baptist; and Acts 18:18 concerning Paul.)

The Israelites had been in bondage to the Philistines for four decades when an angel of the Lord came to the wife of Manoah, a member of the tribe of Dan, and pronounced an unexpected blessing upon her head:

> For, lo, thou shalt conceive, and bear a son; and no razor shall come on his head: for the child shall be a Nazarite unto God from the womb: and he shall begin to deliver Israel out of the hand of the Philistines. . . . And the woman bare a son, and called his name Samson [meaning "sun"]: and the child grew, and the LORD blessed him. (Judges 13:5, 24)

Most notable in the life of Samson was his fatal interaction with Delilah, who had been bribed by the Philistines to discover the secret of Samson's astounding strength. Ultimately, Samson, tiring of her persistence, shared the truth with her: "There hath not come a razor upon mine head; for I have been a Nazarite unto God from my mother's womb: if I be shaven, then my strength will go from me, and I shall become weak, and be like any other man" (Judges 16:17).

Delilah then caused the locks of his hair to be shaved off, leaving him powerless: "And he wist not that the LORD was departed from him" (Judges 16:20). Samson had let the locks of his covenant loyalty to the Lord be clipped away. The Philistines then put out Samson's eyes and imprisoned him at Gaza. Later—after Samson's hair had grown long again (see Judges 16:22)—the Philistines had assembled a vast throng of people to celebrate their victory and to make sport of Samson. It was then that he called one last time upon the Lord and pulled down the pillars of the house, destroying himself and all three thousand observers therein (see Judges 16:28–30).

Samson lives on as a symbol of a leader who failed to endure in full obedience to the higher cause. How does this symbol echo forth in other scriptural stories? Consider the following:

- *Look to the Lord and live*: Moses taught the people how to survive the bite of poisonous serpents in the wilderness. They were to look upon the brazen serpent elevated above them as a protecting force, a symbol of the Redeemer. Those who looked were saved; those who failed to look perished (see Numbers 21:8–9; John 3:14–15; 2 Nephi 25:20; Helaman 8:14–15).
- *Liahona leads by faith*: In their journey to the promised land, Lehi and his family were guided by a miraculous compass from the Lord. When viewed in faith, the compass, or Liahona, guided them to nourishment and

safety; when ignored out of disbelief and scorn (as with Laman and Lemuel), blessings were withheld (see 1 Nephi 16:10–11; 18:11–12, 21; Alma 37:38–47).

- *Listening to the Lord empowers one's gifts*: At the beginning of his mission to translate the Book of Mormon, Joseph Smith incurred the displeasure of the Lord when he allowed Martin Harris to borrow and then lose the first 116 pages of the manuscript. For a time, Joseph's gift of translation was taken away by the Lord and then later restored: "See that you are faithful and continue on unto the finishing of the remainder of the work of translation as you have begun. . . . Be diligent unto the end" (see D&C 10:3–4).

Pondering: How can we protect our "locks of faith" from being clipped away? How can we more fully honor our vows of loyalty and obedience before the Lord? How can we ensure that our gifts are used for the blessing and joy of others?

AGENDA FOR ACTION

The eternal Judge is watching over us in mercy and love. We can fulfill our destiny as sons and daughters of God by serving in friendship with our fellow Saints to help build the kingdom of Zion. We can follow the example of the Savior by learning how to serve more fully as "deliverers" to those in need. We can honor our covenants by enduring in faith and using our gifts from the Lord as a blessing to His children. We can express gratitude to the leaders and teachers in our ward and confirm our support and love for them as they fulfill their callings. In these and many other ways, we will find that the Lord's message to Gideon will also be His message to us: "Surely I will be with thee" (Judges 6:16).

LOOKING FORWARD: How have the gifts of eternal womanhood blessed your life?

CHAPTER TWENTY

GIFTS OF LOYALTY AND GRATITUDE

Gospel Doctrine Reading Assignment: Ruth; 1 Samuel 1

For whither thou goest, I will go; and where thou lodgest, I will lodge: thy people shall be my people, and thy God my God. (Ruth 1:16)

THE SOOTHING SPIRIT OF ETERNAL WOMANHOOD

WE LIVE IN AN AGE of conflict and contention, an age of deep yearning for more harmony, more reaching out in compassion and love toward one another. The story of Ruth and her mother-in-law, Naomi, preserved over millennia of time, kindles in the heart a renewed hope of unity and devotion in community and family relationships. Likewise, the story of Hannah is a tender reminder of how the Lord blesses women who live by hope and faith. It is the spirit of eternal womanhood that can lift souls above the shadows of sorrow and discord—in any age.

The book of Ruth and the account of Hannah date from the end of the period of the Judges and the commencement of the ministry of the prophet Samuel. Ruth, Naomi, and Hannah are central participants in the sacred sequence of women servants of God, beginning with Eve, continuing with Sarah, Rebekah, and Rachel, reaching forward to Elizabeth and Mary, then beyond to the heroines of the Restoration. President Joseph F. Smith saw this glowing congregation of womanhood in his vision of the work of the gospel in the spiritual realm: "And our glorious Mother Eve, with many of her faithful daughters who had lived through the ages and worshiped the true and living God" (D&C 138:39).

The spirit of eternal womanhood is a key element in spreading the gospel and sustaining harmony in the kingdom of God. In the Saturday morning session of the October 2012 General Conference, President Thomas S.

Monson made the announcement that the age for recommending able and worthy young people for missionary service was shifted from 19 to 18 for young men (who had graduated from high school or its equivalent) and from 21 to 19 for young women desiring to serve.[13] This welcome news was received with great rejoicing across the Church as it opened the gateway for earlier service in building the kingdom of God. Now, with the announcement by President Monson, the service of noble and gracious young women of faith is expanding and spreading across the world.

A TOUCH OF REALITY

The spirit of eternal womanhood can flow into all the shadows of discord and light a fire of harmony:

> The elevator was crowded with harried people anxious to get to their destinations. My wife and I were pressed against the back wall holding our two-year-old daughter. Then the car groaned to a stop on yet another floor en route to the lobby, and everyone sighed at the thought of taking on still another passenger. This time, it was a very large man in scruffy coveralls. He was covered with dirt and grease from head to toe. In his hand was a heavy tool kit; on his face was an ominous grimace. As he stepped into the elevator, it creaked and dipped slightly under the added weight. His scowl repelled everyone backward as they made ample space and retreated into an unspoken covenant of protection. Everyone fell silent, hoping the situation would be short-lived.

> Then a miracle occurred. Everyone saw and heard it at the same time. Our little baby girl in her pink outfit had taken the workman into her gaze. She looked intently at him; then, as only a two-year-old can, she leaned toward him smiling broadly and said, with utter sincerity and disarming warmth, "Hi!" The world was suddenly transformed. The victim of her charms was captivated. He broke out into a broad grin and returned the favor with his own "Hi!" A bond of friendship had been forged instantly between the biggest and smallest of the pack. There was nothing left to do but join in the celebration. People nodded in cheer. Others echoed the best greetings of the day. There was general tumult. Feet shuffled as the line of defense melted away. Somehow a group of strangers, brought together by chance, had been united in a union of loyalty and friendship—all because a little girl had demonstrated a simple truth: that everyone is worthy of our courtesy, respect, and kindness.

> Did Alma not say, "Little children do have words given unto them . . . which confound the wise and the learned" (Alma 32:23)? Here was a case where the tipping point was a single word of wisdom spoken by a child who already beamed the light of eternal womanhood.

WHAT LESSONS CAN WE LEARN FROM THE ACCOUNTS OF RUTH AND HANNAH?

1. Loyalty and humility are enduring qualities of eternal womanhood.

Ruth (meaning "friend or companion") is an exceptional example of a humble and loyal woman. As a Moabite who became the daughter-in-law of Naomi (meaning "pleasant"), she was a key progenitor in the lineage leading to Jesus Christ (see Ruth 4:17; Matthew 1:5). Compiled and written by an unnamed author, the book of Ruth covers events that likely took place in the middle of the twelfth century B.C., since Ruth was the great-grandmother of David (born around 1096 B.C.). The book of Ruth is a story of unsurpassed beauty and tenderness illustrating loyalty and devotion—especially in the context of the integration of a humble non-Israelite into the fold of Israel. The four chapters of the book cover the transition of Naomi's family to Moab during a time of famine, the marriages and deaths within the family, the return of Naomi and Ruth to Bethlehem, the touching courtship and marriage of Boaz and Ruth, and the birth of their son.

Ruth was a source of sunshine in the life of the sorrowing Naomi, who had lost her husband and both sons. The marriage of Ruth and Boaz replaced despair and longing with harmony and stability. As such, Ruth was an ideal model of womanhood (see Thomas S. Monson, "Models to Follow," *Ensign*, Nov. 2002, 60). A key theme of the story is this: In time, sorrows pass and circumstances improve. Moreover, the fruit of the new marriage was the birth of a son and the continuation of the covenant lineage leading to David and then to Christ himself.

Could the following have been some of Ruth's inner thoughts as she looked with joy upon her newborn son?

13   See "Welcome to Conference," *Ensign*, Nov. 2012, 6.

Who were the Moabites?

The Moabites were a tribe living east of Jordan when the Israelites returned from Egyptian bondage. Moab was the son of Lot's oldest daughter (see Genesis 19:37), and thus the Moabites were akin to the Israelites but represented a different way of life and religion. These two peoples were in conflict over the years, the most often cited episode being the campaign of Barak, king of the Moabites, to bring down a curse upon the Israelites through the influence of Balaam (see Numbers 22–24). Ruth represented the local Moabite culture at its best. Being a pure and virtuous woman with the highest aspirations and character, she embraced wholeheartedly the Israelite way of life—a reminder that converts from all kindreds, nations, tongues, and peoples are welcome to the kingdom of God.

With peace and contentment in her heart, Ruth looked over toward the child asleep in Naomi's arms. The young mother smiled in humble gratitude. A stream of memories flowed across her mind as she partook of this consoling view: how she had mourned over the loss of her young husband, son of Naomi, and how her mother-in-law had given her blessings of comfort and love in dire times, showering her with kindness so dear and so abundant that she had responded to Naomi with the words, "Entreat me not to leave thee, or to return from following after thee: for whither thou goest, I will go; and where thou lodgest, I will lodge: thy people shall be my people, and thy God my God" (Ruth 1:16).

Ruth remembered fondly her journey to Bethlehem. She had been amazed at the welcoming arms of hospitality extended to her by all. She could still hear the voices of friendship from kindly neighbors. She could still sense the fragrance of flowers and new growth as she labored in the fields of Boaz. With gladness she had received his affection and now whispered to herself once again his words of comfort leading to their marriage: "And now, my daughter, fear not; I will do to thee all that thou requirest: for all the city of my people doth know that thou art a virtuous woman" (Ruth 3:11).

The vision of her son asleep before her was a sublime reminder of God's eternal blessings. The women of the community had spoken well concerning the divine lineage unfolding before their eyes—that this child named Obed (meaning "serving, worshipping") would extend the reach of Israel over generations to the future Messiah of the world.

A tear of gladness rolled down her cheek as she said a prayer of thanksgiving and closed her eyes to peer into the future. She could see a light of glory rising above the horizon of time—the dawning of an era that promised redemption through the blessings of a merciful and compassionate God.

Pondering: How does the radiant example of Ruth enrich your life and lift your spirits? How does her story bring more hope and courage to those overcoming tribulations and challenges?

2. Prayerfulness and gratitude are enduring qualities of eternal womanhood.

Hannah (meaning "grace") was the wife of Elkanah, a devout Ephraimite who lived in the central mountain district of Israel (see 1 Samuel 1:1–2). Hannah mourned over her childless state and prayed one day, near the temple, for the special blessing of motherhood (see Samuel 1:10–11). When the priest Eli observed her struggles, he had compassion and promised her, "Go in peace: and the God of Israel grant thee thy petition that thou hast asked of him" (1 Samuel 1:17). Indeed, the Lord did remember Hannah with a blessing of fruitfulness: "Wherefore it came to pass, when the time was come about after Hannah had conceived, that she bare a son, and called his name Samuel, saying, Because I have asked him of the LORD" (1 Samuel 1:20).

Hannah fulfilled her promise and turned Samuel over to the Lord, leaving his care to the priests at the temple. Samuel (meaning "heard of God" or "God has heard") grew in stature as he "ministered before the Lord" (1 Samuel 2:18). His mother remembered him lovingly and "made him a little coat, and brought it to him from year to year, when she came up with her husband to offer the yearly sacrifice" (1 Samuel 2:19).

Soon Samuel took upon himself the stature of one of the Lord's greatest prophets. His life and ministry mirrored the love and grace of his mother, one of the choicest and most valiant women celebrated in the scriptures. Hannah was blessed thereafter with five more children, three sons and two daughters (1 Samuel 2:21).

The Saints who left Nauvoo in the wake of unending persecution were moved by a commitment to go where the Lord would have them go. A touching account of that devotion is the experience of Orson Spencer and his wife, Catharine Curtis, a girl from western Massachusetts who had been disowned by her parents for being baptized.

Before leaving Nauvoo, Orson had written to his wife's parents, pleading with them to permit their daughter to return, at least until the Saints found a place where they could rest in peace and security. One evening [eighteen days into their journey], Porter Rockwell rode into camp with the mail, and he handed Brother Spencer a letter. It was a letter from his wife's parents in which they reaffirmed their former position: Yes, they would appreciate having their daughter back—but not as a member of the Mormon Church. Orson Spencer took the letter to the covered wagon where his wife lay desperately ill. There, by the light of the lantern, he read this letter. And then, upon bended knees, with tears trickling down his cheeks, he pleaded with her to return under any circumstances. She looked up with a faint smile and said, "Orson, the Bible is there in the corner of the wagon; will you hand it to me?" He brought the Bible. She said, "Now turn to the first chapter of the book of Ruth and read the fifteenth and sixteenth verses."

Entreat me not to leave thee, or to return from following after thee. For whither thou goest, I will go; and thy people shall be my people and thy God, my God.

He ceased reading. He laid the Bible back in its place and turned to his wife. He saw a peculiar pallor creeping across her countenance. He saw her eyelids droop, and then they closed, never to open again in mortality. On the following morning, there by the side of the road, on that lonely prairie road, in a shallow grave, they laid to rest this wonderful woman to the music of lowing cattle. Within an hour the caravan was again on its way, and Orson Spencer sat alone with his five little kiddies driving westward, westward to his destiny. The eldest of those little kiddies took the place of the mother. And when that little girl grew up she [Aurelia Spencer Rogers] became the founder of the Primary Association of the Church [in 1878]. (From "Our Heritage," an address given by historian Nicholas G. Morgan, Sr., then president of the National Society of the Sons of Utah Pioneers, before the student body at Brigham Young University on October 27, 1953, p. 5–6.)

What might have been the stream of Hannah's inner thoughts after she had delivered her annual gift of a coat to young Samuel?

She turned and looked back peacefully toward the temple with a feeling of deep satisfaction. She had delivered another new coat to her son—an offering of motherly love. She smiled, knowing that the offering was, in truth, *her son*. She sighed—scarcely able to fathom her great blessing of motherhood from the Lord. She had gratefully given unto the Lord the greatest of all motherly offerings—her own dear child, to be an instrument of service.

Her mind soared back to the moment when she had pronounced her prayerful promise: "O Lord of hosts, if thou wilt indeed look on the affliction of thine handmaid, and remember me, and not forget thine handmaid, but wilt give unto thine handmaid a man child, then I will give him unto the Lord all the days of his life" (1 Samuel 1:11). Then, after the blessed child was delivered, she had uttered a thankful promise that still burned in her heart: "For this child I prayed; and the Lord hath given me my petition which I asked of him: Therefore also I have lent him to the Lord; as long as he liveth he shall be lent to the Lord" (1 Samuel 1:27–28). The memory of how she had thanked the Lord still blossomed within her soul: "My heart rejoiceth in the Lord, mine horn is exalted in the Lord: . . . There is none holy as the Lord: for there is none beside thee: neither is there any rock like our God" (1 Samuel 2:1–2).

At that moment, she felt a hand slip gently into her own. Her husband looked down into her eyes and smiled a silent confirmation of his love for her. They had been deeply blessed with this child. They knew that he was to become a great prophet, for his name meant "heard of God." Her husband whispered soft words into her ear: "Just as you have clothed our son each year with a coat of motherly protection, so the Lord is clothing him eternally in the fatherly mantle of prophetic authority." She nodded in agreement and lifted her eyes to heaven, remembering more of the words from the hymn of praise that she had uttered following her son's birth: "The LORD shall judge the ends of the earth; and he shall give strength unto his king, and exalt the horn of his anointed" (1 Samuel 2:10).

In her humility and sacred reverence before the Lord, Hannah did not yet realize that her inspired word "anointed" would one day be regarded as the earliest pronouncement of the equivalent of "Messiah." And so it was, hand in hand, the mother and father of the young prophet-to-be continued their walk back to their home, bathed in the light of joy and gratitude.

Pondering: How does the example Hannah's offering inspire you to offer more of your heart and service to the Lord? How can you express more words of praise and thanksgiving to the Lord—more "hymns of praise" for His eternal blessings?

AGENDA FOR ACTION

The purpose of the gospel is to bring to pass the eternal life of God's sons and daughters. We can learn line upon line, precept upon precept, how to bless our families and the kingdom of God. We can strive to cultivate loyalty, humility, gratitude, and love as exemplified in the lives of individuals like Ruth, Naomi, Boaz, and Hannah. We too, by the grace of God and the whisperings of the Spirit, can leave behind a legacy of obedience and honor (see D&C 42:61).

What specific deeds might we do during the current week to fulfill our commitment to be more loyal, humble, grateful, and loving? Could we write a note for a special woman in our lives and thank her for demonstrating a quality that has been a blessing in helping us cultivate that same quality? Could we have each of our family members choose a quality that they would like to work on during the week and then invite them the following week to share a report of their experience? Could we reach out to someone who seems to need encouragement and bring the light of hope into his or her life through our friendship and support? Could we spend time on our knees asking for guidance on how to improve our lives—and then listen for answers and improve day by day? There are rich and rewarding ways of improving our lives and showing charity to others.

LOOKING FORWARD: How can we know when the Lord is calling to us?

CHAPTER TWENTY-ONE

GOD WILL HONOR THOSE WHO HONOR HIM

GOSPEL DOCTRINE READING ASSIGNMENT: 1 SAMUEL 2–3, 8

Speak; for thy servant heareth. (1 Samuel 3:10)

THE ART OF LISTENING

FROM THE ACCOUNT OF SAMUEL and his contemporaries, we learn an important lesson about the importance of listening to the promptings of the Lord. Born of goodly parents, Samuel magnified his calling by listening to the Lord: "And the child Samuel grew on, and was in favour both with the LORD, and also with men" (1 Samuel 2:26). By contrast, Eli, high priest and judge of the day, remained aloof to the counsel of the Lord concerning the greed and immorality of his two sons, who were violating their priesthood callings, thus raising the concern of the people. Ignoring the word of God brings sorrow and destruction; listening to the word of God brings blessings of joy and favor. That lesson applies to God's children in all generations of time.

A TOUCH OF REALITY

Listening to the Lord empowers individuals, parents, and leaders to help build the kingdom of God. How does this principle work today?

As a stake presidency, we considered with humility the assignment of selecting a new bishop—a solemn and sacred task, one to be accomplished with much prayer and fasting. The several candidates were interviewed, one after the other—all good and noble men with great talent and capability, all men of God.

But the Spirit whispered clearly, not once but several times, "Not these, but him." The person identified was not on the short list at all. All three members of the stake presidency felt it. What a joy to discover that the same prompting had come to each and that the Lord had made the choice. We had but to listen and obey.

Subsequently, the brother selected served faithfully as a bishop in Zion. The Lord makes these calls. It is His Church. He looks upon the heart and reads the measure of talent and ability needed for a given mission. When the Lord extends the call, it is a divine call, attended with heavenly blessings of a very specific kind for His children. These modern miracles happen "through the knowledge of God, and of Jesus our Lord, According as his divine power hath given unto us all things that pertain unto life and godliness, through the knowledge of him that hath called us to glory and virtue" (2 Peter 1:2–3).

WHAT LESSONS CAN WE LEARN FROM THE EXPERIENCES OF SAMUEL?

1. When the Lord calls, listen and obey.

Having come under the care of the high priest Eli, Samuel retires to his bed one night and experiences a divine event that still touches our hearts and minds with its profound implications:

> The LORD called Samuel: and he answered, Here am I.
>
> And he ran unto Eli, and said, Here am I; for thou calledst me. And he said, I called not; lie down again. And he went and lay down.
>
> And the LORD called yet again, Samuel. And Samuel arose and went to Eli, and said, Here am I; for thou didst call me. And he answered, I called not, my son; lie down again.
>
> Now Samuel did not yet know the LORD, neither was the word of the LORD yet revealed unto him.
>
> And the LORD called Samuel again the third time. And he arose and went to Eli, and said, Here am I; for thou didst call me. And Eli perceived that the LORD had called the child.
>
> Therefore Eli said unto Samuel, Go, lie down: and it shall be, if he call thee, that thou shalt say, Speak, LORD; for thy servant heareth. So Samuel went and lay down in his place.
>
> And the LORD came, and stood, and called as at other times, Samuel, Samuel. Then Samuel answered, Speak; for thy servant heareth. (1 Samuel 3:4–10)

"Speak; for thy servant heareth"—eternal wisdom to bless our lives, today and forever. In the case of Eli, the word of the Lord was sad news concerning the impending judgment of God regarding the unrighteousness of Eli's sons (see 1 Samuel 3:1–14). But those who hear and obey the word of God are blessed with goodness and understanding: "And now, verily, verily, I say unto thee, put your trust in that Spirit which leadeth to do good—yea, to do justly, to walk humbly, to judge righteously; and this is my Spirit" (D&C 11:12).

Inspiration is the power that prompts us to rise productively as sons and daughters of God.

A delightful young family had just joined the Church and was telling us about their very first experience watching general conference on television. "We were all assembled downstairs in front of the TV waiting with great excitement," they reported. "All

What do modern prophets teach about listening to the Lord?

President Gordon B. Hinckley encouraged us to remember to call upon the Lord in faith, knowing with full assurance that our prayers will be answered. He reminded us that we need the help of the Lord in order to do our best in life, for we cannot succeed on our own. Thus we can ask the Lord personally to help us to realize our righteous ambitions, for He stands ready to bless our lives with all the things of importance. (See *Teachings of Gordon B. Hinckley* [Salt Lake City: Deseret Book, 1997], 468.)

except for our young son, who was still upstairs busy with his playthings. We kept calling up to him to remind him, but he didn't come. And then, when the broadcast started, we called once more, saying the Tabernacle Choir and General Authorities were coming on. In response, he called down, in all sincerity, saying: 'When God comes on, let me know.'"

Here was a young boy, wise before the age of wisdom. Even though he had not yet learned fully about the role of prophets, he was certainly putting his Father in Heaven at the top of his priority list, above everything else (even his toys). How marvelous it would be if all of us could have that kind of innocent focus and commitment—just as young Samuel displayed when he said, "Speak; for thy servant heareth" (1 Samuel 3:10).

The parents of Samuel—Hannah and Elkanah—were devout individuals who planted in his heart the seeds of listening and obeying. What power is it that nurtures such seeds through the ages of time, causing them to spring forth as a harvest of inspiration? If you would like an interesting study exercise, here is a quick summary of some key sources of inspiration:

- *The Almighty*: Job 32:8; Alma 37:47
- *The Holy Ghost*: 2 Nephi 32:5; Alma 5:46; D&C 11:12 ; 21:1–2, 7; Moses 6:5–6
- *The holy scriptures*: 2 Timothy 3:16–17; 2 Nephi 32:3; D&C 20:7–8, 11–12
- *The prophets of the Lord*: 3 Nephi 6:20; D&C 20:25–28
- *A desire for the welfare of your own soul*: 2 Nephi 32:9
- *The desire to serve others*: 2 Nephi 25:23, 26; 33:4; Alma 43:45–47

A memorable summary of these thoughts was preserved by Moroni from a speech given by his father Mormon: "But behold, that which is of God inviteth and enticeth to do good continually; wherefore, every thing which inviteth and enticeth to do good, and to love God, and to serve him, is inspired of God" (Moroni 7:13).

Pondering: In your own experience, what are the different ways the Lord has spoken to you? How can you help others to choose not only to hear the Lord, but to listen and obey?

2. One of the greatest lessons for parents to teach their children is to honor the Lord.

The Lord declared, "For them that honour me I will honour, and they that despise me shall be lightly esteemed" (1 Samuel 2:30). These words were quoted by a man of God sent to Eli with a divine warning concerning the actions of his two sons, Hophni and Phinehas. These two sons, both priests, were active in the house of the Lord when Hannah and her husband made their annual trip to offer sacrifices there, even prior to the birth of Samuel (see 1 Samuel 1:3). But the priestly service of Hophni and Phinehas was degraded by unrighteous behavior. Out of greed, they took advantage of the sacrificial offerings brought by the people (see 1 Samuel 2:12–16), causing the people to turn away from worshipping the Lord: "Wherefore the sin of the young men was very great before the LORD: for men abhorred the offering of the LORD" (1 Samuel 2:17). Moreover, the sons of Eli were guilty of immorality with the women who came before the tabernacle (see 1 Samuel 2:22). The scriptures give this summary of their character: "Now the sons of Eli were sons of Belial [i.e., worthlessness]; they knew not the LORD" (1 Samuel 2:12).

What was the response of Eli? He confronted his sons with reports about their "evil dealings" (1 Samuel 2:23), but his words were not sufficient to induce repentance "because his sons made themselves vile, and he restrained them not" (1 Samuel 3:13). So the judgment of the Lord took place. Hophni and Phinehas were slain in an attack on Israel by the Philistines (see 1 Samuel 4:11). Hearing the news, Eli, ninety-eight years old, fell backward in astonishment and lost his life (see 1 Samuel 4:18).

The voice of the Lord had pronounced a frightening verdict in the case of Eli: "Ye . . . honourest thy sons above me" (1 Samuel 2:29). By contrast,

What was the lineage of Eli?

Eli (meaning "ascending") was of the lineage of Ithamar, the youngest surviving son of Aaron (see Exodus 6:23; 28:1; Leviticus 10:12, 16; Numbers 3:2, 4; 26:60; 1 Chronicles 6:3; 24:1–3). The priestly office remained with the lineage of Ithamar and Eli's family until Abiathar, of that same lineage, was removed from office by Solomon because of his conflicting loyalty to Solomon's brother, Adonijah, who aspired to the throne (see 1 Kings 1:7; 2:26–27). At that point in time, the office was conveyed by Solomon to Zadok of the family of Eleazar, oldest surviving son of Aaron (see 1 Chronicles 6:3–8; 1 Kings 2:35).

Hannah and her husband joyfully embraced the divine calling of their son by fully sustaining him as he honored the Lord in righteousness. Thus, unlike the sons of Eli, Samuel was held in great favor by the people (see 1 Samuel 2:26).

In his very old age, Samuel learned that his own sons, Joel and Abiah, were turning away from the teachings of their father by accepting bribes as judges in Israel, thus strengthening the desire of the people for a king. The Lord told Samuel, "Hearken unto the voice of the people in all that they say unto thee: for they have not rejected thee, but they have rejected me, that I should not reign over them" (1 Samuel 8:7). Samuel warned the people that a king might well take from them much of their possessions (1 Samuel 8:13–17) and cause them to cry out in anguish to the Lord, "and the LORD will not hear you in that day" (1 Samuel 8:18). But the people demanded a king, and the Lord, knowing the lessons the people needed to learn, commanded Samuel to grant their request. Thus the era of the kings was about to begin.

How do the parenting experiences outlined above apply to our challenges today? There is no universal template for child rearing—beyond love and patience and the enduring principles of the gospel. Parents mark out the boundaries and specify the domain of acceptable behavior; then they look for the hidden windows of possibility in each child through which they can catch a glimpse of what a glorious individual this child is destined to become. Each is equipped by God with a different set of gifts that need to be unwrapped with care. Love and restraint, firmness and forgiveness, guidance and correction—all of these are part of the eternal recipe. Our Father in Heaven knows these children better than we, and we need to evoke His merciful guidance as we strive to be worthy parents in Zion. Parenting is a never-ending process suffused with both joy and sorrow, anxiety and satisfaction, worry and hope—but always guided by faith and confidence in the all-seeing wisdom of our Father in Heaven.

Pondering: How can we do a little more each week to help one another—especially our children and grandchildren—honor the Lord and listen to His promptings?

AGENDA FOR ACTION

The Lord has promised, "For them that honour me I will honour" (1 Samuel 2:30). We honor the Lord by keeping His commandments. We honor Him by teaching our children to follow in His footsteps. We honor Him by accepting the light of the gospel as a Liahona of guidance. We consecrate our time, talents, and resources to building up His kingdom. We teach allegiance to the Heavenly King rather than to worldly values. As parents in Zion, we make family home evenings a priority, sharing testimonies with one another and expressing love and encouragement with genuine warmth and sincerity. All of this brings glory to our Heavenly Father and blessings of light and truth into our family circles according to "the law of the celestial kingdom" (D&C 105:5).

LOOKING FORWARD: What is written in your heart?

CHAPTER TWENTY-TWO

GOODNESS OF HEART

GOSPEL DOCTRINE READING ASSIGNMENT: 1 SAMUEL 9–11, 13, 15–17

For man looketh on the outward appearance, but the Lord looketh on the heart. (1 Samuel 16:7)

THE LENS OF UNDERSTANDING

THE STORY OF THE RISE of King Saul and the subsequent calling of his successor, David, is a powerful reminder of three universal questions: What does God see and do? What do His prophets see and do? And what do His children see and do? The answers are given through a one-word lens of understanding: *heart*—a word that occurs eleven times in 1 Samuel and serves as an enduring ensign of light. When we peer through this lens, we learn the following truths:

- What does God see and do? He looks beyond the outward appearance into the *heart* of His children (16:7) to find those with a *heart* seeking after Him (13:14), a *heart* that He can touch and transform into one that is new and greater (10:9; 10:26).

- What do God's prophets see and do? They see into the *hearts* of God's children (9:19) and teach them to serve Him with all of their *heart* (12:20; 12:24).

- What do God's children and faithful servants see and do? God's children see in their leaders a good *heart* that inspires their support (two occurrences in 14:7), and God's chosen leaders see the coming victory of the Lord and serve as an example of how others can avoid doubt (17:28) and dispel fear within the *heart* (17:32).

That quick overview of eleven occurrences of the word *heart* might bring questions to your mind. What does the Lord see in *your* heart? How can He help you to change your heart to be more like His? How can you and your loved ones follow the counsel of the living prophets to bring about a change of heart?

Perhaps the hidden question is this: How large is the "goodness gap" between the heart the Lord wants us to have and the heart we have right now?

A TOUCH OF REALITY

Here is a true story recounted by a faculty member at a distinguished Eastern university:

> King Saul had a goodly beginning to his reign because "God gave him another heart" (1 Samuel 10:9), one that sought for things spiritual. But over time, his spiritual armor cracked. His outward show of spiritual nobility did not fully derive from a genuine and enduring inner faith. Harmony was lacking. There was a gap there. Several years after the

completion of the Washington D.C. Temple, I invited two good nonmember friends, also faculty members at the university where I was teaching, to drive down with me to the temple visitors' center for a tour. One was a Catholic priest who taught courses in comparative religion. Both listened and observed carefully.

After the tour, my Catholic friend made a significant statement that I recorded in my journal. He noted that, in general, many people seem to have two religions, one that they "carry in their pocket," and one that they present in public. "Often there is a considerable gap between the two," he said, inferring that they might be more outwardly religious than inwardly. "With the Mormons it is different," he observed. "The gap in their case seems to be rather small." With this compliment, he was sharing his own perspective that members of the Church typically live by their convictions, and since they seem to accomplish much practical good, they must, therefore, have a strong genuine faith.

Such is indeed the case with Latter-day Saints who abide by the teachings of the Master and strive to make their lives consistently centered on spiritual truth—both outwardly as well as inwardly. They belong to the good seed about which Jesus spoke: "But that on the good ground are they, which in an honest and good heart, having heard the word, keep it, and bring forth fruit with patience" (Luke 8:15).

WHAT LESSONS CAN WE LEARN FROM THE STORY OF SAUL AND DAVID?

1. The heart is a genuine measure of spiritual health and vitality.

The Lord directed Samuel to call Saul as king over the people, for, as He said, "they have rejected me, that I should not reign over them" (1 Samuel 8:7). Saul, of the tribe of Benjamin, was "a choice young man, and a goodly: and there was not among the children of Israel a goodlier person than he: from his shoulders and upward he was higher than any of the people" (1 Samuel 9:2). The Lord told Samuel, "Thou shalt anoint him to be captain over my people Israel, that he may save my people out of the hand of the Philistines: for I have looked upon my people, because their cry is come unto me" (1 Samuel 9:16). When Saul and his servant were at work with family duties, they sought after the prophet Samuel for counsel on how to locate some straying animals. That gave Samuel the opportunity to give Saul a promise: "I . . . will tell thee all that is in thine heart. . . . that I may shew thee the word of God" (1 Samuel 9:19, 27). Subsequently, he anointed Saul as leader over the people (see 1 Samuel 10:1) with the promise that "God is with thee" (1 Samuel 10:7). Thus "God gave him another heart: . . . And when they came thither to the hill, behold, a company

How can we close the "goodness gap"?

In the April 2011 General Conference, President Thomas S. Monson spoke of the widening gulf between eternal laws and modern social practices. Where the standards of society were, in the past, mostly compatible with the standards of the Church, there is now a growing chasm between the two as social practices continue to erode. President Monson provided an action plan for protecting ourselves from the growing evils around us: maintain a strong testimony, obey the commandments, pray and study the scriptures regularly, attend Church, repent sincerely, and build strong families. (See Thomas S. Monson, "Priesthood Power," *Ensign*, May 2011.)

of prophets met him; and the Spirit of God came upon him, and he prophesied among them" (1 Samuel 10:9–10). Thereafter Samuel informed the people of their new king: "And all the people shouted, and said, God save the king" (1 Samuel 10:24).

Saul's first act of leadership was to respond to the anguish of the people concerning threats from the Ammonites: "And the Spirit of God came upon Saul when he heard those tidings, and his anger was kindled greatly" (1 Samuel 11:6). He then took swift action to unify the people for a successful campaign against their enemies. Not boasting of himself, Saul declared, following the victory: "To day the LORD hath wrought salvation in Israel. . . . And all the people went to Gilgal; and there they made Saul king before the LORD in Gilgal; . . . and there Saul and all the men of Israel rejoiced greatly" (1 Samuel 11:13, 15).

But the rejoicing was not to last. Samuel warned the people: "I will teach you the good and the right way: Only fear the LORD, and serve him in truth with all your heart: for consider how great things he hath done for you. But if ye shall still do wickedly, ye shall be consumed, both ye and your king" (1 Samuel 12:23–25). In preparing for a conflict with the amassing Philistines, Saul took it upon himself, in the absence of Samuel, to offer up a peace offering unto the Lord—something that only the priesthood elect were authorized to do. Samuel arrived and declared that Saul's reign would end, for the Lord would now seek another leader, "a man after his own heart" (1 Samuel 13:14). The last straw in Saul's decline was his action following the defeat of the Amalekites. The Lord had commanded that the enemy and all their possessions should be fully destroyed, but Saul spared the king and the most precious of the animal stock, claiming that he was simply obeying the voice of the people so they could make sacrifices to the Lord:

"And Samuel said, Hath the LORD as great delight in burnt offerings and sacrifices, as in obeying the voice of the LORD? Behold, to obey is better than sacrifice, and to hearken than the fat of rams" (1 Samuel 15:22).

Saul had suffered a spiritual heart attack. What can we learn from him to help us avoid such an outcome? How can we take into our hearts the word of the Lord as an empowering force for good? Here is one example:

He was the meekest of the elders, a humble farm boy called as a servant of the Lord among a distant people. His speech was plain; his social skills basic; his only polish the weather-tanned skin of a man of the soil. But when he opened his mouth to bear fervent testimony of the truth of the gospel and the sacredness of the Book of Mormon, there was something special there, something that resonated with simple grandeur, for he spoke the words that were in his heart as conveyed by the Holy Spirit.

We, his missionary companions, noticed the light shining from his countenance. We learned from him. So did the families he taught. The lesson is simple: It is not the learning of the world or the elegance of cultural sophistication that brings about a "mighty change" in one's heart (Mosiah 5:2; Alma 5:13–14). Rather, it is the word of God, spoken by His humble servants and confirmed by the Spirit, that touches lives and opens the soul for gospel illumination. "Blessed are the meek, for they shall inherit the earth," was the promise of the Savior to His listeners in Jerusalem (Matthew 5:5) and in the New World (3 Nephi 12:5). This young elder, with a heart of noble goodness, was doubtless just the kind of Saint who shall indeed inherit the earth and partake of eternal glory.

Pondering: How is our own heart a measure of our spiritual health and vitality? If there is any "goodness gap" in our heart, how can we close that gap? How can we help others to do the same?

2. The Lord judges by the content of our heart.

The Lord sent Samuel to Jesse in Bethlehem: "For I have provided me a king among his sons. . . . and I will shew thee what thou shalt do: and thou shalt anoint unto me him whom I name unto thee" (1 Samuel 16:1, 3). When Samuel looked upon Eliab, the eldest of Jesse's sons, he supposed him to be the new king. But the Lord gave to him this memorable counsel: "Look not on his countenance, or on the height of his stature; because I have refused him: for the LORD seeth not as man seeth; for man looketh on the outward appearance, but the LORD looketh on the heart" (1 Samuel 16:7).

Six more of Jesse's sons were brought before Samuel, but he found none of them to be the chosen one. It was not until they sent for David, the eighth and youngest son, that Samuel knew the will of the Lord:

> Now he [David, meaning "beloved"] was ruddy, and withal of a beautiful countenance, and goodly to look to. And the Lord said, Arise, anoint him: for this is he.
>
> Then Samuel took the horn of oil, and anointed him in the midst of his brethren: and the Spirit of the Lord came upon David from that day forward." (1 Samuel 16:12–13)

At the same time, "the Spirit of the Lord departed from Saul" (1 Samuel 16:14), and he was troubled by an evil spirit "not of the Lord" (JST, 1 Samuel 16:14). It was only through the harp playing of David that Saul could find comfort, for he came to love David and appointed him as his armor bearer (see 1 Samuel 16:16–23). Thus was laid the foundation for the rise of David as the victor over the Philistine giant, Goliath.

The story is well known. The Israelite forces feared to confront the enemy champion until David stepped forward, saying boldly: "Let no man's heart fail because of him [Goliath]; thy servant will go and fight with this Philistine" (1 Samuel 17:32). When Saul hesitated to send a young man against a giant, David shared with the king his proven capability to protect his flock from attacking animals: "The Lord that delivered me out of the paw of the lion, and out of the paw of the bear, he will deliver me out of the hand of this Philistine. And Saul said unto David, Go, and the Lord be with thee" (1 Samuel 17:37).

Then ensued the astounding encounter between the future king and Goliath, who mocked and derided the young man. But the words of David resounded with power and authority:

> Thou comest to me with a sword, and with a spear, and with a shield: but I come to thee in the name of the Lord of hosts, the God of the armies of Israel, whom thou hast defied.
>
> This day will the Lord deliver thee into mine hand." (1 Samuel 17:45–46)

Goliath fell with the fatal stroke of a stone propelled from David's sling, and David rose to the stature of the future king of Israel (see 1 Samuel 17:49–50).

In our day as well, we rise to meet the challenges of life by serving, as the Lord says, "with all your heart, might, mind and strength" (D&C 4:2). Many stories of such heroic service abound, included the following true account:

> I recall a young elder who, with his companion, felt impressed to attend a lecture on the Mormons given by a minister in one of the large Protestant churches where they were serving. As the two missionaries sat in the back of the crowded cathedral listening, they became increasingly concerned with the untruths being promulgated about the restored Church. Finally, one of the young elders, according to his report, felt as though he were literally lifted up by unseen hands and transported down the central aisle of the cathedral to a position directly below the elevated pulpit where the minister was speaking. There, before a large congregation of awestruck listeners, he engaged the minister in a discussion in which he corrected the misinformation and bore fervent testimony about the truthfulness of the restored gospel and the mission of the Prophet Joseph Smith. The minister was rendered speechless.
>
> Afterward, the missionaries were able to distribute materials on the steps in front of the cathedral and found a more welcome entrance into the homes by virtue of their enhanced reputation. The young elder took no credit for the remarkable performance but instead gave credit to the Lord. It was a wonderful confirmation of the promise given in modern scripture: "Therefore, verily I say unto you, lift up your voices unto this people; speak the thoughts that I shall put into your hearts, and you shall not be confounded before men; For it shall be given you in the very hour, yea, in the very moment, what ye shall say" (D&C 100:5–6).

Pondering: What steps can we take to ensure that our hearts are more in harmony with the heart of the Lord—full of love, committed to obedience, and willing to serve with devotion? How does the example of David inspire us all to rise up together in the power of the Lord to overcome the Goliaths of our day?

AGENDA FOR ACTION

With a prayerful heart, we can come to understand better what the Lord sees and does, and what His prophets and faithful servants see and do in compliance with the laws of heaven. The Lord can work miracles if we have a willing heart and if we listen to the promptings of the Spirit. We can aspire to better understand the feelings and actions of those around us and view them as children of God without judging or finding fault. He reserves His choicest blessings of courage and strength for those who press forward after the Lord's "own heart" (1 Samuel 13:14) as did young David, who later sang the words, "Glory ye in his holy name: let the heart of them rejoice that seek the LORD" (Psalm 105:3).

LOOKING FORWARD: With whom do you have a covenant of eternal friendship?

CHAPTER TWENTY-THREE

"A COVENANT BEFORE THE LORD"

GOSPEL DOCTRINE READING ASSIGNMENT: 1 SAMUEL 18–20, 23–24

Behold, the LORD be between thee and me for ever. (1 Samuel 20:23)

UNITY ABOVE ENMITY

IN THIS TRANSITIONAL SCENE OF the majestic Old Testament drama, we view the tragic sunset of Saul and the hopeful sunrise of David. We view the binding covenant of fellowship between David and Jonathan, Saul's son. We view the compassion of Michal for her husband, David, and the honorable leadership of Abigail in preserving the destiny of the future king of Israel. This stream of intertwining threads of action forms a lively tapestry of conflicting values: greed and mercy, jealousy and forgiveness, hate and charity, love of self and love of God, blindness and vision. In the end, eternal values remain triumphant.

Does this same battle for the victory of eternal truth continue to rage in our day? The Prophet Joseph Smith was subjected to the most vicious and hateful persecution, ultimately giving his life as a martyr. Did mercy, forgiveness, charity, the love of God, and vision ever pale in his ministry? Consider the following:

A TOUCH OF REALITY

On Thursday, June 9, 1842, the Prophet Joseph Smith delivered an address on mercy to the sisters of the Female Relief Society of Nauvoo—one filled with spiritual nourishment. Here is a sampling of his wisdom: "Nothing is so much calculated to lead the people to forsake sin as to take them by the hand, and watch over them with tenderness. When persons manifest the least kindness and love to me, O what power it has over my mind, while the opposite course has a tendency to harrow up all the harsh feelings and depress the human mind" (*HC* 5:23–24). Furthermore, "The nearer we get to our Heavenly Father, the more we are disposed to look with compassion on perishing souls; we feel that we want to take them on our shoulders, and cast their sins behind our backs. . . . If you would have God have mercy on you, have mercy on one another. . . . How oft have wise men and women sought to dictate Brother Joseph by saying, 'O, if I were Brother Joseph, I would do this and that;' but if they were in Brother Joseph's shoes they would find that men or women could not be compelled into the kingdom of God, but must be dealt with in long-suffering, . . . till God shall bring such characters to justice. There should be no license for sin, but mercy should go hand in hand with reproof" (*HC* 5:24).

The Savior declared: "Blessed are the merciful: for they shall obtain mercy" (Matthew 5:7). We are to forgive and allow God to be the eternal judge. We are to honor our covenants with the Lord and with our fellow Saints. In the story of Joseph Smith, as well as in the stories about Saul and David and their contemporaries, we find inspiration to fulfill our mission in building the kingdom of God on the earth.

WHAT LESSONS CAN WE LEARN FROM THE EXPERIENCES OF DAVID, JONATHAN, AND SAUL?

1. When we honor our covenants with one another we honor our covenants with the Lord.

Saul had a promising beginning as a "choice young man" (1 Samuel 9:2) who was anointed by the prophet Samuel as a leader over the people (see 1 Samuel 10:1). From the Lord he received "another heart" by which he could prophesy and lead with clear vision (1 Samuel 10:9–10). But he soon found his heart poisoned with pride and greed because of David's conquests as commander of the king's armies. The saying went around the land: "Saul hath slain his thousands, and David his ten thousands" (1 Samuel 18:7). Thus Saul's jealousy nurtured seeds of hatred. He became obsessed with an all-consuming desire to kill young David by whatever means he could—whether by the thrust of a javelin (see 1 Samuel 18:10–11; 19:10), the secret acts of his royal servants (see 1 Samuel 19:1, 11–17), or by sending David into dangerous battlefield campaigns (see 1 Samuel 18:17, 20–21, 25). Bottom line: "And Saul became David's enemy continually" (1 Samuel 18:29).

But Saul's acts of attempted murder all failed because "David behaved himself wisely in all his ways; and the LORD was with him" (1 Samuel 18:14). In addition, David cultivated relationships with individuals willing to protect him. There was Michal, daughter of Saul, who "loved David" (1 Samuel 18:20) and saved him from being attacked by the king's messengers (see 1 Samuel 19:11–17). There was Samuel, who accompanied David on his exile before the senior prophet passed away (see 1 Samuel 19:18; 25:1). There were priests who provided food and supplies to David, though they were eventually executed by Saul for their kindness (see 1 Samuel 21; 22:18).

And there was Jonathan, son of Saul, who "delighted much in David" (1 Samuel 19:2), for his soul "was knit with the soul of David, and Jonathan loved him as his own soul" (1 Samuel 18:1, 3). David and Jonathan thus entered into a bonding covenant of mutual fellowship (see 1 Samuel 20:3–4, 16). Said Jonathan, "Behold, the LORD be between thee and me for ever" (1 Samuel 20:23). Bottom line: "And they two made a covenant before the LORD" (1 Samuel 23:18). Jonathan spared neither thought nor action to protect his friend from destruction.

In addition, another individual played a key role in preserving David during his exile in the wilderness. This individual is less frequently mentioned in scriptural discussions, so let us consider the following account of Abigail, a selfless and courageous woman "of good understanding, and of a beautiful countenance" (1 Samuel 25:3):

The breeze caressed her face in comforting strokes as she looked back toward her home nestled on the verdant pasturelands of Maon near Carmel. How she longed for peace at a time of looming danger. She turned again and looked toward the hilly landscape that lay ahead, squinting her eyes in search of clues of the approaching host. Nothing was to be seen. But she knew they were there, moving toward her with weapons of war. The silence was broken by the grunts of the donkeys around her loaded with bundles of corn and raisins and figs and all manner of provisions—including scented offerings that she prayed would bring peace in a world of contention.

"Are you all right, my lady?" asked one of her servants.

"Yes," she replied. "This is the shearing season, a time to extend goodness to all who are in need. It will work out."

But she still felt the rapid beating of her heart. The words of her servant rushed back into her mind. He had revealed how her husband, Nabal, had rudely refused the request of David's young men for provisions even though the warriors hidden in the hills had protected Nabal's sheepherders from any Philistine attacks. "They were a wall unto us both by night and day, all the while we were with them keeping the sheep," the servant had told her (see 1 Samuel 25:16). His fears were certain: "We feared that an attack of reprisal would come without delay." She immediately decided to take action on her own while her husband was busy reveling in the seasonal feast of harvest time. She knew that she had to save her community from destruction.

In that instant, she saw David riding over the crest of a distant hill, leading his hundreds toward her group. Her fear was dissolved instantly by the spirit of hope. This was the moment. She rode forward rapidly as her entourage came within view of his army. He drew closer. Soon she could read the features of his commanding face—a look of surprise and wonderment at what he saw: "Why is this woman coming up against my advance?"

She alighted from her donkey and fell on her face before David, bowing herself down at his

---

What do we learn from the source meanings of biblical names?

Note the origin of important names in the accounts from the Old Testament, such as: *The Unchangeable One* (Jehovah); *Father of a multitude* (Abraham); *Princess* (Sarah); *One who prevails with God, or let God prevail* (Israel—new name for Jacob); *Name of God,* or *God has heard* (Samuel); *Beloved* (David); *Asked* (Saul); *Gift of God* (Jonathan); *Who is like God?* (likely source meaning of Michal); and *Source of rejoicing* (Abigail).

See if you can decipher the following account that uses the meaning of the names of the principals involved:

Beloved, a descendant of the *Father of a multitude* and *Princess* through their grandson *Let God prevail*, faithfully worshipped *The Unchangeable One*. King *Asked* was jealous of *Beloved* and conspired to destroy him, but *Gift of God*, the son of King *Asked*, established with *Beloved* a covenant of loyalty and friendship and protected him from harm. The wife of *Beloved*, the princess *Who is like God?*, also helped save him from the wiles of her father King *Asked*, as did the prophet *God has heard*. The courageous woman *Source of rejoicing* persuaded *Beloved* to spare her family from harm and eventually became the wife of *Beloved*. When King *Asked* and his son *Gift of God* did not survive a battle with the Philistines, *Beloved* rose as the king of the land.

---

feet. The words she had prayerfully rehearsed flowed with sincerity from her mouth like streams of balm—words of pleading for peace, words of compassion concerning the supplies she was granting to his men, words of apology for the cold and mocking actions of her husband, and words of reminder and promise about the destiny of the future king before whom she was kneeling. She said to David, "And it shall come to pass, when the LORD shall have done to my lord according to all the good that he hath spoken concerning thee, and shall have appointed thee ruler over Israel; That this shall be no grief unto thee, nor offence of heart unto my lord, either that thou hast shed blood causeless, or that my lord hath avenged himself: but when the LORD shall have dealt well with my lord, then remember thine handmaid" (1 Samuel 25:30–31).

She beheld that David was deeply touched by her words. His face glowed with the light of a soul consumed by an inner change of heart: he knew that Saul had sought continually to kill him, but he had spared the king's life, leaving judgment to God. Now he would also spare Nabal and his men, knowing that the woman kneeling before him was speaking by the Spirit of the Lord. What he then said to her brought refreshing comfort to her soul: "And blessed be thy advice, and blessed be thou, which hast kept me this day from coming to shed blood, and from avenging myself with mine own hand. . . . Go up in peace to thine house; see, I have hearkened to thy voice, and have accepted thy person" (1 Samuel 25:33, 35).

Thus we see in the service of Abigail an example of exceptional leadership and humble devotion by a woman of God. She lived true to the meaning of her name—"the source of rejoicing." What she didn't know at the time was that her husband would the next day receive her report of deliverance with shock and that he would pass away ten days after that. She also did not know that David would later call upon her with a proposal of marriage and that she would become the wife of the future king.

The power of the redemption flows from the covenants we make with the Lord. But our happiness also depends on honoring mutual covenants made with those we love and support—covenants related to baptism, teacher and student relationships, the law of common consent in support of Church leaders, and sacred temple sealing ordinances. Said the Lord in our day, "Search diligently, pray always, and be believing, and all things shall work together for your good, if ye walk uprightly and remember the covenant wherewith ye have covenanted one with another" (D&C 90:24).

Pondering: How is our love for the Lord confirmed through our bonds of love and fellowship with His children? How can we improve in securing the spiritual and temporal well-being of our family members and other loved ones?

2. How we forgive others is a measure of our spiritual nobility before the Lord.

David was the ongoing target of Saul's murderous conspiracy. On one occasion, David came across Saul asleep in a cave and had the opportunity to silence the king's killer instinct forever—but David declined to harm him, saying, "The Lord forbid that I should do this thing unto my master, the Lord's anointed, to stretch forth mine hand against him, seeing he is the anointed of the Lord" (1 Samuel 24:6; see also 1 Samuel 24:12). On another occasion, David snuck into Saul's encampment and found the king asleep in a trench, but David again declined to harm him, leaving judgment to the Lord: "As the Lord liveth, the Lord shall smite him; or his day shall come to die; or he shall descend into battle, and perish" (1 Samuel 26:10). Saul later declared, "Blessed be thou, my son David: thou shalt both do great things, and also shalt still prevail" (1 Samuel 26:25). However, Saul did not prevail but soon thereafter lost his life in a battle against the Philistines, as did his sons (see 1 Samuel 31:4–6). David lamented deeply over these deaths: "The beauty of Israel is slain upon thy high places: how are the mighty fallen!" (2 Samuel 1:19).

The story of David's restraint concerning the murderous king is a glowing example of forgiveness. How can we learn better to forgive others and leave judgment to God? We might take to heart the following account:

> The middle-aged ward member came into my office, took a seat, and proceeded to outline in some detail certain failings of another ward member, counseling the bishop that it should be attended to. "That *is* a concern," I responded. "Wait just a minute. That member is still here. Let me go and have that person join us right now so we can get things cleared up." My visitor looked surprised, so I added, trying to repress the twinkle in my eye, "It's always best, when there's a concern, to get the parties together and talk things out."
>
> "Well," the member said, "I suppose things will work out." Then the person stood up and left my office, never to complain to me about anyone again. Perhaps the person went to review what the Savior said: "Therefore if thou bring thy gift to the altar, and there rememberest that thy brother hath ought against thee; Leave there thy gift before the altar, and go thy way; first be reconciled to thy brother, and then come and offer thy gift" (Matthew 5:23–24). Understanding and forgiveness are qualities of the divine nature.

Pondering: The Savior said while on the cross, "Father, forgive them; for they know not what they do" (Luke 23:34)? How can we follow His example of forgiveness—even when it might seem that others are intent on doing harm? How can we foster harmony and charity in the kingdom of God?

AGENDA FOR ACTION

Our covenant with the Lord includes a covenant to bless the lives of others and support them in their quest to be

What scriptures confirm the importance of mutual covenants in the gospel of Jesus Christ?

You may wish to search and ponder the key scriptures indicated:

- *Baptism*: Mosiah 18:9
- *Teacher and student relationships*: D&C 50:21–22; 88:132–133
- *Law of common consent in support of Church leaders*: D&C 26:2; 28:13
- *Sacred temple sealing ordinances*: D&C 132:19–20; also Malachi 4:5–6; D&C 2; 110:14–15

faithful sons and daughters of God. We can all join together in love to cultivate a spirit of humility and forgiveness. We can all strive to dispel any hint of jealousy and greed. Look into your "book of grudges" this week and make sure that all the pages are blank, that any lingering resentment has been resolved and that the light of mercy has dispelled the shadows of blame. Scan the pages of your "book of promises" and confirm that all the worthy pledges and assurances you have made to others have been fulfilled or are in the process of being fulfilled. We can all prayerfully strive to honor our infinite divine potential: "Yea, come unto Christ, and be perfected in him" (Moroni 10:32).

LOOKING FORWARD: How can we ensure that our hearts are clean before the Lord?

CHAPTER TWENTY-FOUR

ACCOUNTABILITY BEFORE THE LORD

GOSPEL DOCTRINE READING ASSIGNMENT: 2 SAMUEL 11–12; PSALM 51
Create in me a clean heart, O God; and renew a right spirit within me. (Psalm 51:10)

LET VIRTUE GARNISH THY THOUGHTS UNCEASINGLY

THE WORD OF THE LORD in our day confirms a universal principle:

> And let virtue garnish thy thoughts unceasingly; then shall thy confidence wax strong in the presence of God; and the doctrine of the priesthood shall distil upon thy soul as the dews from heaven.
>
> The Holy Ghost shall be thy constant companion, and thy scepter an unchanging scepter of righteousness and truth; and thy dominion shall be an everlasting dominion, and without compulsory means it shall flow unto thee forever and ever. (D&C 121:46)

This principle took root in David's heart from his earliest years and later unfolded within him as the Lord's emerging ruler in the Holy Land. He reigned as king over Judah for seven years and then as king over all of Israel for the next thirty-three years (see 2 Samuel 2:4; 5:3–5). "And David went on, and grew great, and the LORD God of hosts was with him" (2 Samuel 5:10). In his military undertakings, he sought and followed the counsel of the Lord, thus achieving astounding success (see 2 Samuel 5:19–25; 8:1–6; 10:15–19). When he offered to build a temple, he learned through the prophet Nathan that the Lord would have David's son build it (see 2 Samuel 7:12–13); nevertheless, the kingdom of David would endure, for his lineage would extend forward to the eternal King,

Jesus Christ: "And thine house and thy kingdom shall be established for ever before thee: thy throne shall be established for ever" (2 Samuel 7:16). Thus it was that "the LORD preserved David whithersoever he went. And David reigned over all Israel; and David executed judgment and justice unto all his people" (2 Samuel 8:14–15).

But then a chink in his spiritual armor was revealed; a widening crack in his spiritual shield appeared. David, the mighty king of Israel who secured and expanded the land of inheritance for the Lord's people, suddenly yielded the means to secure his own soul. The story is legendary. David happened to observe Bathsheba at a distance and was consumed by her beauty. Rather than following the example of Joseph of Egypt, who "fled, and got him out" when Potiphar's wife beckoned (Genesis 39:15), David yielded to his sinful desires by taking Bathsheba unto himself and later causing her husband to perish in battle (see 2 Samuel 11:14–17). Though David was triumphant against the enemies of Israel, he was tragically vanquished in the battle for his soul—

Who were Uriah and Bathsheba?

Uriah was a Hittite warrior and one of the chief officers in the army of King David. The Hittites were an ancient warlike people, descendants of Heth from the lineage of Ham, son of Noah (see Genesis 10:15). Uriah's wife, Bathsheba (meaning "daughter of the oath"), is characterized in the scriptures as "very beautiful to look upon" (2 Samuel 11:2). The word "beautiful" in holy writ is connected to only four other women: Rachel (see Genesis 29:17); Abigail (see 1 Samuel 25:3); Esther (see Esther 2:7); and Mary, mother of Jesus (see 1 Nephi 11:15). Bathsheba suffered because of the loss of her husband: "And when the wife of Uriah heard that Uriah her husband was dead, she mourned for her husband" (2 Samuel 11:26). She was loyal to her new husband, David, and fully committed to the rise and success of their son Solomon. She was also remembered in Matthew's statement about her place in the lineage of Jesus Christ: "And Jesse begat David the king; and David the king begat Solomon of her that had been the wife of Urias" (Matthew 1:6). Ruth and Mary are also referred to in this fourteen-generation review (see Matthew 1:5, 16).

for he failed to heed the warnings against sin and fell into the abyss of suffering brought on by disobeying the Lord's commandments.

David was a blend of two different personalities—on the one hand, a superb political leader who followed the Lord's guidance in unifying and securing the Israelite nation, and on the other hand, a tragic offender against moral righteousness. As king, he found favor with the Lord and the people; as a man, he knowingly went the wrong way and suffered intense remorse when the prophet Nathan was sent to reveal unto him the consequences.

A TOUCH OF REALITY

How can going the wrong way affect our lives today? Think about the following account about an emergency act of service performed by a courageous priesthood holder:

A number of years ago, a young man and his wife were driving along a stretch of interstate one day when he glanced across the median strip. Incredibly, there was a car on the other side of the median driving parallel to his car but moving directly *into* the line of traffic going in the opposite direction. The young man watched with horror as trucks and cars swerved to avoid a collision with the vehicle driving in the wrong direction in the lane closest to the median.

In a split second, he made a decision. He accelerated and looked for the next opportunity to cross over the median. Soon he came to a connecting road and maneuvered quickly toward the opposite lanes of traffic, coming to a screeching halt on the inner shoulder of the opposite lanes. Despite significant danger to himself, he ran toward the errant vehicle and flagged it down.

The elderly couple whom he forced to stop were at first indignant. What business did this stranger have interrupting their trip? Soon they realized, however, that he had surely saved their lives, and they were grateful for his Christian act of charity.

This true story is a modern-day parable about what happens when we ignore spiritual traffic laws and fail to heed the Lord's safety system of warnings. His chastening is anchored in love, as Samuel the Lamanite proclaimed to his wayward Nephite audience: "For behold, they have been a chosen people of the Lord; yea, the people of Nephi hath he loved, and also hath he chastened them; yea, in the days of their iniquities hath he chastened them because he loveth them" (Helaman 15:3). The Lord loved David and rejoiced over his leadership; but the Lord anguished over David's moral collapse. David, in his psalms (see especially Psalm 51), became a universal spokesperson for the urgent need to repent and help others to do the same.

WHAT LESSON CAN WE LEARN FROM THE STORY OF DAVID AND BATHSHEBA?

1. Joy flows from heeding the warning signals of the Lord; anguish flows from failing to do so.

What is the Lord's alarm system? How do we know when we are in danger of evil? What signals can we watch for and obey? Here are some possibilities:

A. Light from Heaven

- Light of Christ: The universal gift given to all mortals to help them make wise choices. It is this gift that allows mortals to detect goodness and separate it from evil, as Mormon confirmed: "For behold, the Spirit of Christ is given to every man, that he may know good from evil; wherefore, I show unto you the way to judge; for every thing which inviteth to do good, and to persuade to believe in Christ, is sent forth by the power and gift of Christ; wherefore ye may know with a perfect knowledge it is of God" (Moroni 7:16).

- Promptings of the Holy Ghost: The gift of the Holy Ghost is "the Spirit of truth" (John 15:26) that comforts and guides us along the pathway of righteousness. When the Spirit is withheld and ceases to strive with an individual or group, the alarm of pending destruction is sounded (see 2 Nephi 26:11; Ether 2:15): "And he that repents not, from him shall be taken even the light which he has received; for my Spirit shall not always strive with man, saith the Lord of Hosts" (D&C 1:33).

B. Words from Heaven

- Holy scriptures: The word of God provides a sure measure by which we can judge our thoughts and actions and choose the pathway of obedience. The Savior declared, "It is written, Man shall not live by bread alone, but by every word that proceedeth out of the mouth of God" (Matthew 4:4, referring to Deuteronomy 8:3). When we find that our manner of living strays from the course revealed in the scriptures, an alarm is sounded within our soul and we can take action to correct ourselves (see D&C 63:58).

- Counsel of the living prophets: The prophets of the Lord cry out anthems of joy for the righteous but sound the alarm for the disobedient. Ezekiel promised, "But he that taketh warning shall deliver his soul" (Ezekiel 33:5). Paul declared, "I write not these things to shame you, but as my beloved sons I warn you" (1 Corinthians 4:14; see also Colossians 1:28). In our day, the Lord confirmed that "the voice of warning shall be unto all people, by the mouths of my disciples, whom I have chosen in these last days" (D&C 1:4; see also D&C 112:5; 134:12; Jacob 4:6–7).

C. Words from Home

- Your own voice: Alma taught his son Corianton that mortals are equipped to sound their own alarms: "And thus they stand or fall; for behold, they are their own judges, whether to do good or do evil" (Alma 41:7; see also Deuteronomy 4:39–40; Isaiah 51:7). Nephi, despite his stature of honor, sounded the alarm about weaknesses that he had overcome: "Nevertheless, notwithstanding the great goodness of the Lord, in showing me his great and marvelous works, my heart exclaimeth: O wretched man that I am! Yea, my heart sorroweth because of my flesh; my soul grieveth because of mine iniquities" (2 Nephi 4:17; see also Mosiah 5:2). Amulek confessed that, until his coming together with Alma, he had repeatedly ignored the alarm sounded within his soul: "Nevertheless, I did harden my heart, for I was called many times and I would not hear; therefore I knew concerning these things, yet I would not know; therefore I went on rebelling against God, in the wickedness of my heart" (Alma 10:6). In our day, the Lord called attention to the alarm system within the hearts of those contacted by His missionaries: "And let those whom they have warned in their traveling call on the Lord, and ponder the warning in their hearts which they have received" (D&C 88:71; see also D&C 101:16; 112:10–11).

- Voices of loved ones and local Church leaders: It is the responsibility of the Saints to sound the alarm about the urgency to repent and build up the kingdom of God: "Behold, I sent you out to testify and warn the people, and it becometh every man who hath been warned to warn his neighbor. . . . He that seeketh me early shall find me, and shall not be forsaken" (D&C 88:81, 83; see also D&C 20:58–59). Moreover: "And let your preaching be the warning voice, every man to his neighbor, in mildness and in meekness. And go ye out from among the wicked. Save yourselves. Be ye clean that bear the vessels of the Lord" (D&C 38:41–42; see also D&C 63:37, 57–58).

The Lord's alarm system is summarized in the following chart.

If David, king of Israel, had heeded these warning alarms, he would surely have avoided plunging off the cliff of immorality and sinking into the abyss of sorrow and pain. The prophet Nathan, with the tenderness of a skilled surgeon, rehearsed the parable of the ewe lamb before David (see 2 Samuel 12:1–4) and opened up within the king a jolting realization of his guilt: "Thou art the man" (2 Samuel 12:7). Even though the Lord later assured Solomon, son of David, that his father had done grand things in building up the kingdom of Israel (see 1 Kings 9:4–5; 11:38; 2 Chronicles 7:17–20), there were eternal consequences to David's sin. In our day, these consequences were identified with precision:

David's wives and concubines were given unto him of me, by the hand of Nathan, my servant, and others of the prophets who had the keys of this power; and in none of these things did he sin against me save in the case of Uriah and his wife; and, therefore he hath fallen from his exaltation, and received his portion; and he shall not inherit them out of the world, for I gave them unto another, saith the Lord. (D&C 132:39)

How can we apply the case of David to our own lives? How can we help our loved ones and those we serve to avoid the sufferings and calamity that befell David? The following true story recounted by a former bishop opens a new perspective:

Here was a delightful young couple preparing for marriage—bright, faithful in church participation, eager to do the right thing. But there was a problem—a compromising of values and propriety. They were embarrassed and heartbroken as they sat across from me, wondering what to do. We counseled. We sorrowed together. We pondered the consequences. But we also took comfort in the process of repentance empowered by the Atonement. Yes, there needed to be change. There needed to be prayerful, godly sorrow and faithful commitment to do better. But they had caught themselves at the edge of the precipice, and they had recoiled under the strength of conscience and now wanted to do right before the Lord. They were good people with the desire for righteousness. The Lord loved them and wanted them to have the fulness of His blessings. There were some regular appointments for a few weeks, but things went very well, so we came up with a plan—a code between the bishop and these two. When we crossed paths at the meetings each week, it took only a nod of the head and a twinkle in the eye to indicate that all was well. You can't disguise the light of the gospel in the eye. It is a sure sign that the Spirit is at work. And it was at work for them. They prospered. They rebounded. They rose to new heights, and once more the age-old story of the gospel transforming lives was repeated. Thank heavens for the principles of the gospel. Thank heavens for the Atonement of Jesus Christ. "And how great is his joy in the soul that repenteth" (D&C 18:13).

Pondering: The story of David's accountability before the Lord is revealing. How does this story awaken a renewed determination to heed the Lord's alarm system and press forward faithfully on the pathway of salvation and exaltation? How can we help our loved ones to do the same?

AGENDA FOR ACTION

David concluded from his ordeal that "the sacrifices of God are a broken spirit: a broken and a contrite heart" (Psalm 51:17). We can learn from his experience a better way to tune into the alarm system of the Lord and allow the Light of Christ to burn more brightly within us. We can heed the promptings of the Spirit to avoid sin and "gather together, and stand in holy places" (D&C 101:22). We can search the scriptures and follow the counsel of the living prophets in order to ensure that our manner of living remains godlike and honorable. We can take to heart the principles of the gospel and receive in humility the counsel of our loved ones and the local leaders of the Church. How is this threefold alarm system working in your life and the lives of your family members? What responses will you give when corrections are called for? How can you help your loved ones to respond to warning signals in their own lives by heeding the Spirit, following the word of God, and accepting loving counsel from others? The gospel pathway leads to peace of soul, harmony of spirit, and confidence in the presence of the Lord.

LOOKING FORWARD: What makes the psalms of David so powerful and memorable?

CHAPTER TWENTY-FIVE

"MY SOUL DELIGHTETH IN THE SONG OF THE HEART"

GOSPEL DOCTRINE READING ASSIGNMENT: THE BOOK OF PSALMS

Who shall ascend into the hill of the Lord? or who shall stand in his holy place?
He that hath clean hands, and a pure heart. (Psalm 24:3–4)

THE POWER OF MUSIC AND POETRY IN THE GOSPEL

ALL SCRIPTURE CAN BE VIEWED as poetry of a heavenly nature. It is through the Holy Ghost that scripture is given and received. Scripture lifts and inspires, carrying us into the heights of understanding on eagle's wings (see Isaiah 40:31; D&C 124:18). In fact, much of our sacred canon—such as the book of Psalms—was written as poetry easily set to music.

When the Lord commissioned Emma Smith to prepare a new book of hymns for the Saints, He declared, "For my soul delighteth in the song of the heart; yea, the song of the righteous is a prayer unto me, and it shall be answered with a blessing upon their heads. Wherefore, lift up thy heart and rejoice, and cleave unto the covenants which thou hast made" (D&C 25:12–13).

Notice what happens when these magnificent words are arranged as poetic free verse:

> For my soul delighteth in the song of the heart;
> yea, the song of the righteous is a prayer unto me,
> and it shall be answered with a blessing upon their heads.
> Wherefore, lift up thy heart and rejoice,
> and cleave unto the covenants
> which thou hast made.

What do modern prophets say about religious music?

Brigham Young stated the following: "Sweet harmonious sounds give exquisite joy to human beings capable of appreciating music. I delight in hearing harmonious tones made by the human voice, by musical instruments, and by both combined. Every sweet musical sound that can be made belongs to the Saints and is for the Saints . . . and every sensation that gives to man joy and felicity are for the Saints who receive them from the Most High" (*Discourses of Brigham Young*, selected and arranged by John A. Widtsoe [Salt Lake City: Deseret Book, 1954], 242). In this context, Ezra Taft Benson confirmed that inspiring music has substantial consequences, such as filling our souls with heavenly thoughts, encouraging righteous action, and bringing peace into our lives (see *The Teachings of Ezra Taft Benson* [Salt Lake City: Bookcraft, 1988], 324).

Do we not gain an increased sense of the majesty of the Lord's words and how they lift us up as on eagle's wings? The blending together of music and the spoken word are expressions of thanks and praise unto the Lord. It is a gospel practice central to our worship. The scriptures are filled with references to music and song and hymns from the beginning of time. The premortal council in heaven was a time "when the morning stars sang together, and all the sons of God shouted for joy" (Job 38:7). The celestial era will be a time when the faithful shall "dwell in the presence of God in his kingdom, to sing ceaseless praises with the choirs above, unto the Father, and unto the Son, and unto the Holy Ghost, which are one God, in a state of happiness which hath no end" (Mormon 7:7; see also 1 Nephi 1:8; Mosiah 2:28; Alma 36:22). From the beginning to the end, anthems of praise and thanksgiving resound, whether in the liberation of the Saints from bondage, the building of temples, the birth and atoning sacrifice of the Savior, the latter-day gathering and redemption of God's people, or the glory of the Second Coming.

The book of Psalms, written by David and his successor composers, includes many of the most revered and admired expressions of spiritual poetry in all of world literature. David helped establish the music protocol for the tabernacle (see 1 Chronicles 6:31–32; 15:16) and authored some seventy-three of the psalms (the word *psalms* deriving from a Greek term for "a musical composition"). The 150 glorious pronouncements in the book of Psalms reflect three main themes: the Messiah as the Good Shepherd, the redemption of the repentant soul, and the building up the kingdom of God.

A TOUCH OF REALITY

The book of Psalms is the most well known volume of musical poetry in the Bible—even though the original melodies are no longer known. But what of modern-day scripture? Does the spirit of the psalms sprout and blossom in other formats? The following true account begins to answer this question:

Many years ago while serving as a young missionary in Germany, I spoke with an older woman concerning the Book of Mormon. She was highly educated and very familiar with a wide variety of subjects. It was encouraging when she agreed to read the Book of Mormon, especially since we had testified of its divine origin. Upon one of our return visits, I asked her to give us her impressions of the book. Her response was instructive. She said that she was very conversant with the Bible, especially with the poetic sections of the Old Testament, such as the Psalms. The Book of Mormon was interesting, she reported, but it contained

How wide is the reach of the book of Psalms in the sacred canon of scripture?

The psalms are cited frequently in the scriptures. For example, of the 283 direct citations of Old Testament material in the New Testament, 116 stem from the book of Psalms (see Bible Dictionary, "Psalms"). The psalms are memorialized in many of our current hymns, such as "The Lord Is My Shepherd" (*Hymns*, no. 108; Psalm 23), "The Lord Is My Light" (*Hymns*, no. 89; Psalm 27:1), "How Great Thou Art" (*Hymns*, no. 86; Psalm 8:3–9; 9:1–2), and "Praise to the Lord, the Almighty" (*Hymns*, no. 72; Psalm 23:6; 150). No fewer than 50 of the 150 psalms are quoted or referenced in 76 hymns in the LDS hymn book, making that source the second most frequently used (next to the Doctrine and Covenants).

none of the uplifting poetry she admired in the Bible. To this we could only respond by drawing her attention to the plain and precious truths contained in the Book of Mormon, often expressed with directness and clarity so that they could not be misunderstood. We encouraged her to continue reading, but we could discern in her that she was not looking at this material in the context of scripture but rather out of an aesthetic interest. She wanted to be lifted poetically rather than spiritually. We eventually moved on to others more open to the message of the restored gospel.

Over the years I have thought about this woman, wishing I had asked her to pay particular attention to certain passages from the Book of Mormon, especially 2 Nephi 4, which contains what is often called the "Psalm of Nephi" (2 Nephi 4:16–35). This magnificent outpouring of Nephi's personal witness is in the form of a poignant poetic testament to God's goodness.

In the final analysis, it is not the words, but rather the Word, that makes the difference. It is not through the beauty of language, per se, but by the confirmation of the Spirit of God that words of gospel truth can change lives for the better and draw people closer to the Master.

WHAT LESSONS CAN WE LEARN FROM THE PSALMS?
1. Jesus Christ is the Messiah and Redeemer of all mankind.
Key references of this theme from the book of Psalms:
- "My God, my God, why hast thou forsaken me?" (Psalm 22:1; a prophetic anticipation of the words of the Savior in Matthew 27:46)
- "The Lord is my shepherd; I shall not want. He maketh me to lie down in green pastures: he leadeth me beside the still waters. He restoreth my soul: he leadeth me in the paths of righteousness for his name's sake." (Psalm 23:1–3)
- "The Lord is my light and my salvation; whom shall I fear? the Lord is the strength of my life; of whom shall I be afraid?" (Psalm 27:1; a good example of the technique of parallelism used often in the Psalms)
- "I have said, Ye are gods; and all of you are children of the most High." (Psalm 82:6)
- "Also I will make him my firstborn, higher than the kings of the earth." (Psalm 89:27)
- "The stone which the builders refused is become the head stone of the corner." (Psalm 118:22)

How is this same theme reflected poetically in modern-day scripture? The Lord revealed the essence of His message of truth to His people in a revelation given through Joseph Smith the Prophet, at Kirtland, Ohio, May 1831. This revelation is expressed in poetic free verse as follows (see D&C 50:40–46):

40 Behold, ye are little children
and ye cannot bear all things now;
ye must grow in grace
and in the knowledge of the truth.
41 Fear not, little children,
for you are mine,
and I have overcome the world,
and you are of them
that my Father hath given me;
42 And none of them
that my Father hath given me shall be lost.
43 And the Father and I are one.
I am in the Father
and the Father in me;
and inasmuch as ye have received me,

ye are in me and I in you.
⁴⁴ Wherefore, I am in your midst,
and I am the good shepherd,
and the stone of Israel.
He that buildeth upon this rock
shall never fall.
⁴⁵ And the day cometh
that you shall hear my voice
and see me,
and know that I am.
⁴⁶ Watch, therefore,
that ye may be ready.
Even so.
Amen.

Pondering: How can we look upon the scriptures as wings of truth that can lift us upward toward greater joy and stronger faith? What are your own favorite examples of scriptures that teach how to become more like the Lord?

2. Through the blessings and grace of the Lord we can receive forgiveness and redemption.
Key references of this theme from the book of Psalms:
- "Who shall ascend into the hill of the Lord? or who shall stand in his holy place? He that hath clean hands, and a pure heart." (Psalm 24:3–4)
- "Create in me a clean heart, O God; and renew a right spirit within me." (Psalm 51:10)
- "For thou, Lord, art good, and ready to forgive; and plenteous in mercy unto all them that call upon thee." (Psalm 86:5)

How is this same theme reflected poetically in modern-day scripture? Alma counseled his son Helaman to learn how to apply the wisdom of obedience in order to receive miraculous blessings. His counsel is expressed in poetic free verse as follows (see Alma 37:35–37):

³⁵ O, remember, my son,
and learn wisdom in thy youth;
yea, learn in thy youth
to keep the commandments of God.
³⁶ Yea, and cry unto God
for all thy support;
yea, let all thy doings
be unto the Lord,
and whithersoever thou goest
let it be in the Lord;
yea, let all thy thoughts
be directed unto the Lord;
yea, let the affections of thy heart
be placed upon the Lord forever.
³⁷ Counsel with the Lord
in all thy doings,
and he will direct thee for good;
yea, when thou liest down at night

lie down unto the Lord,
that he may watch over you
in your sleep;
and when thou risest in the morning
let thy heart be full of thanks unto God;
and if ye do these things,
ye shall be lifted up
at the last day.

Pondering: How does seeing this passage in free verse affect your understanding of it? Do you more fully appreciate it? What are your own favorite examples of scriptures that help you to be more penitent and faithful?

3. Through the blessings and grace of the Lord we can help build the kingdom of God and stand in holy places.
Key references of this theme from the book of Psalms:
- "But as for me, I will come into thy house in the multitude of thy mercy: and in thy fear will I worship toward thy holy temple." (Psalm 5:7)
- "The Lord is my rock, and my fortress, and my deliverer; my God, my strength, in whom I will trust." (Psalm 18:2)
- "One thing have I desired of the LORD, that will I seek after; that I may dwell in the house of the LORD all the days of my life, to behold the beauty of the LORD, and to enquire in his temple." (Psalm 27:4)

How is this same theme reflected poetically in modern-day scripture? The Lord teaches us how we can work together in faith and harmony to establish a house of God. Consider the revelation on the priesthood given through Joseph Smith at Kirtland, Ohio—designated by the Prophet in the heading to section 88 of the Doctrine and Covenants as the "olive leaf . . . plucked from the Tree of Paradise, the Lord's message of peace to us." It is expressed in poetic free verse as follows (see D&C 88:118–120; also see the dedicatory prayer for the Kirtland Temple in D&C 109:7–9):

[118] And as all have not faith,
seek ye diligently
and teach one another
words of wisdom;
yea, seek ye out of the best books
words of wisdom;
seek learning,
even by study and also by faith.
[119] Organize yourselves;
prepare every needful thing;
and establish a house,
even a house of prayer,
a house of fasting,
a house of faith,
a house of learning,
a house of glory,
a house of order,
a house of God;
[120] That your incomings
may be in the name of the Lord;
that your outgoings

> may be in the name of the Lord;
> that all your salutations
> may be in the name of the Lord,
> with uplifted hands
> unto the Most High.

Pondering: How can we use the scriptures to increase our courage to help the Lord build His kingdom? What are your favorite examples from the scriptures concerning ways to stand in holy places and worship the Lord?

AGENDA FOR ACTION

The three grand themes sounded in the book of Psalms—the love and mercy of the Lord, the joy of repenting and living the gospel, and moving forward in faith to build the kingdom of God—remind us to sing praises unto the Lord for His protecting hand and merciful blessings. There are many ways to accomplish this: some express their praise through the medium of painting or sculpture; some through poetry or music; some in talks or personal journals; and some through quiet acts of selfless service when they "succor the weak, lift up the hands which hang down, and strengthen the feeble knees" (D&C 81:5). Each day we can look for new opportunities to praise the Lord and radiate our gratitude for His mercy and grace. When we immerse ourselves in the magnificent language of holy writ in the spirit of praise and thanksgiving, we come to feel a closeness to the Lord and His messengers. We sense more deeply our relationship with the Lord—as His sons and daughters, having a divine destiny to become more like our Father in Heaven and our Redeemer.

LOOKING FORWARD: How best can we gather together to stand in holy places?

CHAPTER TWENTY-SIX

HOW TO BE WISE—AS GOD IS WISE

GOSPEL DOCTRINE READING ASSIGNMENT: 1 KINGS 3, 5–11

Let your heart therefore be perfect with the LORD our God, to walk in his statutes, and to keep his commandments, as at this day. (1 Kings 8:61)

USING THE GIFTS OF GOD WITH WISDOM

WHEN WE LOOK AROUND US, we see many gifts, talents, and abilities. Often we are dazzled, even astounded, by what our fellow Saints are able to accomplish in blessing lives and building the kingdom of God. What is the source of these blessings? The scriptures make it clear: "And again, I exhort you, my brethren, that ye deny not the gifts of God, for they are many; and they come from the same God. And . . . they are given by the manifestations of the Spirit of God unto men, to profit them" (Moroni 10:8; see also D&C 46:26).

In the spirit of mercy and love, the Lord blesses each of His sons and daughters with heavenly gifts: "For all have not every gift given unto them; for there are many gifts, and to every man is given a gift by the Spirit of God. To some is given one, and to some is given another, that all may be profited thereby" (D&C 46:11–12).

Two of the gifts that flow from heaven are "knowledge" and "wisdom" (see 1 Corinthians 12:8; Moroni 10:9–10; and D&C 46:17–18). What is the difference between them? If knowledge is the understanding of truth as reflected in the gospel of Jesus Christ, then we can reasonably conclude that wisdom is the ability to apply this knowledge in such a way that lives are truly blessed with an abundant harvest of joy and spirituality.

Many of the Lord's servants are described in the scriptures as having wisdom, including Joseph (see Acts 7:9–10), Joshua (see Deuteronomy 34:9), Ezra (see Ezra 7:25), Daniel and his companions (see Daniel 1:3–4, 17;

2:14–23), seven men chosen to serve following the earthly ministry of Christ (see Acts 6:3), Stephen (see Acts 6:9–10), Paul (see 2 Peter 3:15), and Joseph Smith (see D&C 127:1).

The individual most often memorialized as one blessed with wisdom is David's son Solomon (meaning "peaceable"). His life unfolds in 1 Kings 1–11 as a fascinating pattern that shows how he gratefully received the gift of wisdom from the Lord at the beginning of his tenure as king of Israel: "And God gave Solomon wisdom and understanding exceeding much, and largeness of heart, even as the sand that is on the sea shore. . . . For he was wiser than all men" (1 Kings 4:29, 31; see also 1 Kings 10:23). But Solomon lost it over the years through wayward and unrighteous deeds. The king came to the precipice of temptation and plunged over the cliff into unwise practices of idolatry and immorality, thus losing the honor of the Lord (see 1 Kings 11:9).

We can learn valuable lessons by focusing on the details of Solomon's tenure as king of Israel. To set the stage, let's consider how the principle of wisdom still hangs on in the shaky world of modern relativistic values.

A TOUCH OF REALITY

It began as a routine statement about education but ended as a life-changing demonstration about wisdom. The presenter, a representative of a large publishing house, stood on the stage before a vast audience of educators and writers in Washington, D.C. Behind him was a gigantic banner that stretched from wall to wall, emblazoned with the words "Education Is the Acquisition of Knowledge." As he intoned his message about acquiring knowledge, it seemed that he was preaching to the choir, restating the age-old message about the need for expanding one's inventory of facts and figures. The audience was getting sleepy.

> **What do modern prophets say about wisdom?**
>
> David O. McKay taught that the key to having our souls grow in wisdom is to love others continually, always with the aspiration to become better ourselves as we seek to make the world a better place in which to live (see *Pathways to Happiness* [Salt Lake City: Bookcraft, 1957], 161).
>
> Bruce R. McConkie taught that the source for wisdom leading to salvation is revelation from the Lord and that when we seek righteousness with all of our hearts, we will receive guidance from the font of all truth and thus be blessed with all wisdom (see *Doctrinal New Testament Commentary*, 3 vols. [Salt Lake City: Bookcraft, 1965–1973], 3:246).

But then, just at the right moment, he raised the question about whether his thesis, in fact, was really true. That caught the crowd's attention. At the same time, he walked back to the banner and pointed out a fold midway in the material. With the help of several assistants, he caused this fold to be opened up, revealing the hidden text within. Now the expanded statement read: "Education is the acquisition of the art of the utilization of knowledge." The audience gasped at the implication. The statement, a quote from the British philosopher Alfred North Whitehead, was a clear reminder that education for its own sake, without application, was a shallow exercise. What truly counts is learning that can profitably be applied to good ends.

King Benjamin stated, "And behold, I tell you these things that ye may learn wisdom; that ye may learn that when ye are in the service of your fellow beings ye are only in the service of your God" (Mosiah 2:17). The greatest example of this kind of applied learning was the Savior Himself, whom Isaiah characterized in this manner: "And the Spirit of the Lord shall rest upon him, the spirit of wisdom and understanding, the spirit of counsel and might, the spirit of knowledge and of the fear of the Lord" (2 Nephi 21:2; compare Isaiah 11:2). It is this kind of service-centered learning that constitutes wisdom, concerning which Solomon assured us: "Happy is the man that findeth wisdom, and the man that getteth understanding" (Proverbs 3:13).

WHAT LESSONS CAN WE LEARN FROM THE STORY OF SOLOMON?

1. The Lord is the source of eternal wisdom.

What is the Lord's pattern for obtaining wisdom? There are 376 occurrences of the word *wisdom* in the scriptures. These scriptural passages suggest the following steps for gaining wisdom:

W—WORD OF THE LORD. Wisdom comes through the word of the Lord unto His children: "And now, it has hitherto been wisdom in God that these things [scriptures] should be preserved; for behold, they have enlarged the memory of this people, yea, and convinced many of the error of their ways, and brought them to the knowledge of their God unto the salvation of their souls. . . . for he doth counsel in wisdom over all his works, and his paths are straight, and his course is one eternal round" (Alma 37:8, 12; see also Colossians 3:16).

I—INQUIRE. Wisdom comes when we inquire of the Lord and invite His blessings, rather than seeking only worldly learning: "If any of you lack wisdom, let him ask of God, that giveth to all men liberally, and upbraideth not; and it shall be given him. But let him ask in faith, nothing wavering. For he that wavereth is like a wave of the sea driven with the wind and tossed" (James 1:5–6; see also D&C 6:7).

S—SPIRIT. Wisdom comes when we listen to the Spirit: "But the manifestation of the Spirit is given to every man to profit withal. For to one is given by the Spirit the word of wisdom; to another the word of knowledge by the same Spirit" (1 Corinthians 12:7–8; see also Moroni 10:9; D&C 46:17; 136:31–33).

D—DEPEND UPON THE LORD. Wisdom comes when we depend fully upon the Lord, the font of all wisdom: "Wherein he hath abounded toward us in all wisdom and prudence; . . . That the God of our Lord Jesus Christ, the Father of glory, may give unto you the spirit of wisdom and revelation in the knowledge of him" (Ephesians 1:8, 17; see also Jacob 4:10).

O—OBEDIENCE. Wisdom comes through our obedience to the Lord and His gospel plan: "O, remember, my son, and learn wisdom in thy youth; yea, learn in thy youth to keep the commandments of God" (Alma 37:35; see also 2 Nephi 28:30).

M—MEEKNESS. Wisdom comes when we endure in meekness and humility, always being receptive to the Lord's counsel: "Many . . . are truly humble and are seeking diligently to learn wisdom and to find truth. Verily, verily I say unto you, blessed are such, for they shall obtain; for I, the Lord, show mercy unto all the meek" (D&C 97:1–2).

These steps of W-I-S-D-O-M lead upward, repeating themselves over and over again as one magnifies this divine gift for the good of all.

In the case of Solomon, wisdom surely prevailed in his earlier years as king: "And all Israel heard of the judgment which the king had judged [to determine the true mother of the disputed child]; and they feared the king: for they saw that the wisdom of God was in him, to do judgment" (1 Kings 3:28). "And the LORD magnified Solomon exceedingly in the sight of all Israel, and bestowed upon him such royal majesty as had not been on any king before him in Israel" (1 Chronicles 29:25).

How did this come about? Looking back over his royal tenure, we see that Solomon embraced the *word of the Lord* conveyed to him by his father, David: "Only the LORD give thee wisdom and understanding, and give thee charge concerning Israel, that thou mayest keep the law of the LORD thy God" (1 Chronicles 22:12). Next, Solomon *inquired* of the Lord, asking for a blessing of wisdom, to which the Lord responded, "Behold, I have done according to thy words: lo, I have given thee a wise and an understanding heart; so that there was none like thee before thee, neither after thee shall any arise like unto thee" (1 Kings 3:12). Solomon then followed the *Spirit* to complete the temple of the Lord (1 Kings 6:14), convey the ark of the covenant into the central sanctuary (see 1 Kings 8:6), and dedicate the glorious edifice: "For the glory of the LORD had filled the house of the LORD" (1 Kings 8:11; see the remainder of chapter 8 for the dedicatory prayer).

Solomon then *depended* upon the Lord to grant him power to secure Israel and earn the respect and awe of its neighbors: "And when the queen of Sheba had seen all Solomon's wisdom, and the house that he had built . . . she said to the king . . . thy wisdom and prosperity exceedeth the fame which I heard. Happy are thy men, happy are these thy servants, which stand continually before thee, and that hear thy wisdom" (1 Kings 10:4, 6, 7–8). "So king Solomon exceeded all the kings of the earth for riches and for wisdom. And all the earth sought to Solomon, to hear his wisdom, which God had put in his heart" (1 Kings 10:23–24). Moreover, Solomon *obeyed* the Lord by teaching the people to obey the commandments: "Let your heart therefore be perfect with the LORD our God, to walk in his statutes, and to keep his commandments, as at this day" (1 Kings 8:61). He shared his wisdom with his people: "And he spake three thousand proverbs: and his songs were a thousand and five" (1 Kings 4:32). And from the very beginning, Solomon displayed genuine *meekness* in his calling: "And now, O LORD my God, thou hast made thy servant king instead of David my father: and I am but a little child: I know not how to go out or come in" (1 Kings 3:7).

Unfortunately, in his final years on the throne, Solomon rejected the warnings given him by the Lord (see 1 Kings 9:6–7) and abandoned the formula for wisdom that he had kept over the years. He turned to prideful pursuits and idol worship: "And the LORD was angry with Solomon, because his heart was turned from the LORD God of Israel, which had appeared unto him twice" (1 Kings 11:9). As a result, the kingdom was severed, with Jeroboam placed over the northern portion and Rehoboam (Solomon's son) placed over the southern portion (see 1 Kings 11:26–43). Thus the forty-year reign of Solomon came to an inglorious end with his wisdom vanishing into the sunset.

Pondering: How can we more fully follow the Lord's counsel for obtaining wisdom and thus increase our ability to serve and build His kingdom? How can we best use our gifts to bless the lives of others?

2. We can, in faith and humility, build a "temple" unto our God.

Solomon, in his wise years, built the first grand temple unto the Lord. How can we, in our wise years, do the same? The following true account provides a touching illustration:

> I recall my mission president, Theodore M. Burton, telling of his Grandfather Moyle, who had been a skilled craftsman. The gentleman had lost his leg in a farm accident in Alpine, Utah, and had great difficulty hobbling about. But he nevertheless traveled twenty-eight miles each week to reach the construction site of the Salt Lake Temple, where one of his appointed missions was to chisel in stone the phrase, "Holiness to the Lord." Those words are a form of praise unto the Lord that has inspired countless thousands who visit the temple and its sacred grounds. Genuine praise for God, in all of its forms, is a means to edify those giving thanks and magnify the joy of the gospel.

In what ways can we chisel the phrase "Holiness to the Lord" into the edifice of our personal lives? The temples of God are truly buildings of light and radiance. They are the architectural reminders that we too are temples of the Most High and places for the Spirit to abide. "Know ye not that ye are the temple of God, and that the Spirit of God dwelleth in you?" (1 Corinthians 3:16). Each one of us is the architect of his or her own life, and each has the opportunity to build that life and unfold it with a vision of the finished edifice being in the likeness of a temple of God, one reflecting the words "Holiness to the Lord."

Pondering: How best can we make the phrase "Holiness to the Lord" a fitting epithet for our own life, one dedicated to the service of God and His children?

AGENDA FOR ACTION

Wisdom is the essence of the light of the Godhead—Father, Son, and Holy Ghost—and the heart and soul of the gospel of redemption and Atonement. Wisdom is eternal truth and intelligence in action—fulfilling the work and glory of God "to bring to pass the immortality and eternal life of man" (Moses 1:39). As sons and daughters of the Almighty, we have the capacity to cultivate godly wisdom and attain to a fulness of light and understanding through obedience and valor (see D&C 93:20). Indeed, the "wellspring of wisdom" in our lives is likened by Solomon to "a flowing brook" (Proverbs 18:4)—one that we can experience as an endless stream of blessings from our Father in Heaven. Wisdom flows to the faithful as they follow the word of the Lord, inquire after His blessings, seek the Spirit, depend upon the Lord, obey His commandments, and endure in meekness and humility. "And their wisdom shall be great, and their understanding reach to heaven" (D&C 76:9).

Let us all strive to implement the W-I-S-D-O-M process in our lives on a continual basis. Let us elevate the words "Holiness to the Lord" in our homes, perhaps through placards, images of the temple, or through the example we set for one another.

LOOKING FORWARD: Where can we find righteous leadership in the world today?

CHAPTER TWENTY-SEVEN

THE LENS OF LEADERSHIP

Gospel Doctrine Reading Assignment: 1 Kings 12–14; 2 Chronicles 17, 20

Believe in the Lord your God, so shall ye be established; believe his prophets, so shall ye prosper. (2 Chronicles 20:20)

STAYING ON THE COVENANT PATHWAY

THE SCRIPTURAL ACCOUNTS OF THE kings of Israel following the reign of Solomon remind us about the urgency of remaining faithful. Jeroboam and Rehoboam had covenant appointments to the thrones of the Northern and Southern Kingdoms, respectively; however, they both polluted their potential as leaders by ignoring the commandments of the Lord. Of Jeroboam, the Lord declared, "But hast done evil above all that were before thee: for thou hast gone and made thee other gods, and molten images, to provoke me to anger, and hast cast me behind thy back" (1 Kings 14:9). Rehoboam journeyed down the side roads of evil as well, promoting the worship of false gods and acting contrary to the directives of the Lord: "And he made an house of high places, and made priests of the lowest of the people, which were not of the sons of Levi" (1 Kings 12:31; see also 1 Kings 14:22–23). By contrast, the reign of Jehoshaphat several generations later reflected the light of righteousness that was to prevail for twenty-five years, for he taught his people in the spirit of truth: "Believe in the Lord your God, so shall ye be established; believe his prophets, so shall ye prosper" (2 Chronicles 20:20).

How do the stories about the ancient kings of Israel have relevance in our lives today?

A TOUCH OF REALITY

Hi, Dad. Thank you for your letter. It was so thoughtful of you and Mom to send a little extra money. Comes in handy for a freshman student away from home! Guess what! My institute teacher has given us an assignment for next week—to answer a tough question. We are studying the Old Testament about ancient kings like (it's hard to remember the spelling) Jeroboam, Rehoboam, and Jehoshaphat. Anyway, the question is this: Why should we spend time studying these kings from so long ago? What does that have to do with our modern lives? I am a bit lost with that. Can you give me any help? (I know you can—you always do!) Love, your daughter.

Hi, sweet daughter! Glad the extra funds will help. Your question about the ancient kings is a good one. I asked myself that same question when I was your age. Seems like a hundred years ago! Time flies. Here's an idea. You might want to think of these stories like a lens—you know, like the lens of a microscope in your biology class or a lens of a telescope. You and Mom used to enjoy looking at the moon and stars with me in the summer. Think of these stories as a lens that helps you see things in a new light, causing things to show up that you might not otherwise see. Maybe you can call it the "Leadership Lens." Yes, those kings from years back are historical figures. They really lived. But why did the Lord save these scriptures for us? Could it be that these stories might help us look at our lives today in a new way—maybe help *us* be better leaders?

You're probably thinking, how do I set up this lens? Well, think of Jeroboam and Rehoboam. They took over after Solomon was finished with his reign, around 975 B.C. That wise old king had some problems in later years, as you know. The Lord gave his successors a chance to do better in the divided kingdom—Jeroboam in the north and Rehoboam in the south. The Lord told them to do right and follow His counsel—but they didn't measure up to their covenant duties and failed to lead their people in the way of the Lord. You could make that scary thought the first line of the manual for your new leadership lens: "Leadership based on covenants *broken* brings destruction and sorrow."

Then there was Jehoshaphat, the third king of Judah (the southern kingdom) after Rehoboam. By contrast, Jehoshaphat was a jewel. He learned good things from his father, Asa, who preceded him on the throne. He kept his covenant promises to the Lord and led his people along the pathway of goodness. He said, "Believe in the LORD your God, so shall ye be established; believe his prophets, so shall ye prosper" (2 Chronicles 20:20). And that's what happened. It confirmed the principle that "leadership based on covenants *honored* brings deliverance and joy." How about using that phrase as line number two of your leadership lens manual?

Now, dear daughter, with those two lines in mind, you can look through your leadership lens and start to see things with the eye of someone seeking new wisdom for today's world. What do you see? For example, look through your lens at the leadership of our country or the state or community. You can now vote. Have a peek through your lens. Does it appear to you that the leaders currently in office conduct their affairs with honor and dignity? After all, they have a covenant with us to act in support of our liberty and well-being. Are these leaders contributing to our deliverance and joy?

It reminds me of the counsel of the Lord in our day: "I, the Lord God, make you free, therefore ye are free indeed; and the law also maketh you free. Nevertheless, when the wicked rule the people mourn. Wherefore, honest men and wise men should be sought for diligently, and good men and wise men ye should observe to uphold; otherwise whatsoever is less than these cometh of evil" (D&C 98:8–10). Your leadership lens reminds you of the importance of putting decent people in office—people with qualities like those of Jehoshaphat or Hezekiah or Nephi or King Benjamin or Alma. We need those same qualities—today more than ever.

Then you can look through your leadership lens and see our Church leaders—from the living prophet down to local leaders. What a great reminder of line number two in your lens manual: "Leadership based on covenants honored brings deliverance and joy." What blessings our Church leaders bring into our lives as they honor their covenants. In return, we can do all in our power to support them in their callings.

Now guess what you can see through your leadership lens! It's a *mirror* you're looking at. And who shows up in that mirror? *You* do! Your leadership lens puts *you* in a new light—a reminder that you too are a leader with great potential. Your mom and I have kept a list of all the great things you have done already in your life, and serving others shows up again and again. Think of the inspiring words from your patriarchal blessing—

among your great covenant promises. You are a daughter of God with a great potential to serve the Lord and His children. You are our wonderful daughter. And yes, you can see *us* through your leadership lens as well. We hope that we show up through your lens as honorable parents and worthy leaders in our home. Nope. We're not perfect (surprise, huh?), but we strive to do better each day.

The gospel of Jesus Christ is true. He is our great Leader. He is our Redeemer. Through the scriptures we have the opportunity to partake of His word.

May the Lord bless you in using your new leadership lens—and all the other gifts and tools from heaven that flow as blessings in your blossoming life. We know that you will do a super job with your institute report next week. Hopefully the ideas I have shared will give you some ideas to build on—adding thoughts and encouragement from your own experience. We love you and always have you in our prayers. Your proud Dad.

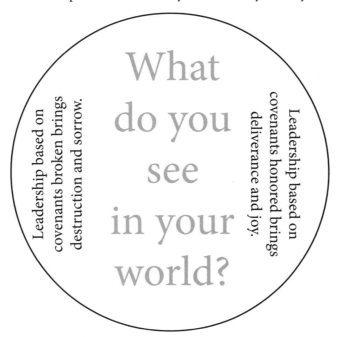

What do you see in your world?

Leadership based on covenants broken brings destruction and sorrow.

Leadership based on covenants honored brings deliverance and joy.

WHAT LESSON CAN WE LEARN FROM THE STORIES OF THE ANCIENT KINGS?

1. We are to hold to the gospel pathway—no matter what the cost.

The name Jeroboam means "whose people are many." Rehoboam means "enlarger of the people." Both names are reminders of the wide influence that leaders have on those they are called to serve. Jehoshaphat means "Jehovah judged"—an indication, in this case, that Jehoshaphat, great-grandson of Solomon (see 1 Chronicles 3:10), was approved of the Lord and served with consistent valor and dignity.

How can we apply the example of Jehoshaphat in our own lives? Here is a modern-day illustration:

I recall the training I went through as a young college student to qualify for summer work as a tour-bus driver in the Canadian Rockies. We were taken on dangerous switchbacks to learn the skills needed to maneuver a large vehicle safely in the mountains. One day, the trainer surprised us with an unexpected question: "Imagine you're driving a fully loaded bus on a mountain highway with a steep granite wall rising to your left and a deep precipice dropping to your right. Suddenly, you round a curve and find a car racing toward you in the middle of the road. What would you do?"

Naturally one's instinct is to veer out of the way—but that's the wrong answer. Any attempt to reposition the moving bus might take you too close to the edge and place your forty-five passengers in even greater danger—with the possibility of death. The answer our trainer was looking for was simply this: You stay in your lane and hit the oncoming car directly. Your enormous weight and size give you a powerful advantage in competition with the much smaller car—and the chances of maximizing your passengers' safety will thereby be secured. This strategy seemed drastic, but it soon sunk in as the only possible solution.

The collision of honor and principle with moral compromise presents a similar scenario. There are times in every person's life where a sudden and unexpected confrontation with evil and falsehood demands a head-on stand for what's right and true. At such times there can be no compromise. To leave the well-marked pathway and veer right or left will only make the crisis worse and lead to more tragic consequences.

When Moroni led his forces in a life-and-death battle against Amalickiah's power-hungry hordes, he demonstrated how to meet life's challenges head-on. His cause was the greater cause: "In memory of our God, our religion, and freedom, and our peace, our wives, and our children" (Alma 46:12). In countless variations every day, we experience similar occasions of greater or lesser scope, where we are called upon to meet the challenges of evil and temptation head-on, veering neither to the right nor to the left. Our model is the Lord Himself: "For God doth not walk in crooked paths, neither doth he turn to the right hand nor to the left, neither doth he vary from that which he hath said, therefore his paths are straight, and his course is one eternal round" (D&C 3:2).

Our commission in life is much like that of the bus driver. We journey along the highways of life with the responsibility to guide our families safely to the destination of sanctity and righteousness. There are many dangerous curves to maneuver. There are countless distractions to divert our vision. Our duty demands constant vigilance and the perpetual exercise of correct principles. When we come upon a sudden challenge in the road, we are then prepared to take a stand for the sake of our families, our peace, and our faith. We stay in tune with the Spirit and follow the promptings that come.

To overcome the perils of temptation and the threat of evil in this world, we need only emulate the example of the Lord and his faithful servant figures like Captain Moroni, of whom Mormon said, "Yea, verily, verily I say unto you, if all men had been, and were, and ever would be, like unto Moroni, behold, the very powers of hell would have been shaken forever; yea, the devil would never have power over the hearts of the children of men" (Alma 48:17).

Pondering: What steps do we need to take to ensure that we hold to the pathway of the gospel of Jesus Christ faithfully—no matter what obstacles might loom in our way? How can we help others to do the same?

AGENDA FOR ACTION

The Savior is our grand example of the perfect leader. His words ring true in our hearts: "And whatsoever thing persuadeth men to do good is of me; for good cometh of none save it be of me. I am the same that leadeth men to all good; . . . I am the light, and the life, and the truth of the world" (Ether 4:12). Let us follow our Savior each day as our standard for leadership. He cares about us and our happiness. He has preserved for our blessing a rich harvest of stories in the scriptures—ways we can gain greater understanding about how to avoid demeaning character traits and how to cultivate noble qualities. We can use that understanding day by day as a compass for enduring to the end.

As the Lord leads us to do good, we can rise up in the same spirit as worthy students of leadership with the desire to serve others. The best leadership reflects obedience to the will of God, adherence to divine principles, the ability to guide others by inspiration, and the gift to carry out wise planning and productive work. Our course of action is divinely appointed: "Wherefore, now let every man learn his duty, and to act in the office in which he is appointed, in all diligence" (D&C 107:99). Let us press forward with faith on the pathway of the gospel of Jesus Christ—no detours, no side roads, no wayward turns. Spiritual leadership generates harmony, peace, unity, increased faith, and good works. May the Lord bless us to magnify our callings with honor and joy.

LOOKING FORWARD: Where can we hear the still, small voice of the Lord?

CHAPTER TWENTY-EIGHT

"AND AFTER THE FIRE A STILL SMALL VOICE"

GOSPEL DOCTRINE READING ASSIGNMENT: 1 KINGS 17–19

Hear me, O LORD, hear me, that this people may know that thou art the LORD
God, and that thou hast turned their heart back again. (1 Kings 18:37)

THE POWER OF GOD TOWERS ABOVE WORLDLY EVIL

ELIJAH (MEANING "JEHOVAH IS MY God") is an imposing figure in the long sequence of the Lord's prophets. He is renowned for his divinely inspired overthrow of the evil forces of Baal during the reign of King Ahab in the northern kingdom. Elijah was later called forth on the Mount of Transfiguration to participate in the restoration of priesthood keys during the Lord's earthly ministry (see Matthew 17:1–13). It was Elijah whom the Lord sent once more on April 3, 1836, to the Kirtland Temple to restore the sealing power in the dispensation of the fulness of times (see D&C 110:13–16; compare also Malachi 4:5–6; 3 Nephi 25:5–6). Our lives are touched in many ways by this exceptional servant of the Lord.

Elijah's ministry is a witness of the how the Lord reaches out through His prophets to exert divine power for the good of the people. The highlights are familiar: On the Lord's errand, Elijah seals up the rain from the heavens in response to the unrelenting wickedness of the people and their ruler, Ahab, the most wicked of all the kings in a long line of succession:

> And he [Ahab] reared up an altar for Baal in the house of Baal, which he had built in Samaria.
> And Ahab made a grove; and Ahab did more to provoke the LORD God of Israel to anger than all the kings of Israel that were before him. (1 Kings 16:32–33; see also 1 Kings 21:25)

To escape the wrath of the king, Elijah is sent by the Lord into the wilderness, where he is sustained miraculously by ravens and later by a poor widow in the small Phoenician village of Zarephath near the coast. Her meager supply of meal and oil is miraculously multiplied. Her deceased son is restored to life (see 1 Kings 17:8–24). Elijah, who is ever unquestioning in his obedience, is able to prepare the way for the Lord's intervention in the idolatrous culture.

What is meant by *grove*?

Following the sinful practice of his predecessors (Solomon, Jeroboam, and Rehoboam) and the encouragement of his Phoenician wife, Jezebel, King Ahab set up a grove for idol worship (1 Kings 16:33). The word *grove* is used for the Hebrew word *asherah*, referring to a wooden image or pillar representing Ashtoreth (plural Ashtoroth), the principal female goddess of the Phoenicians, counterpart to the principal male figure, Baal (plural Baalim). Such idol worship was customarily set up in a grove of trees in high places (see 2 Kings 23:13; see also 1 Kings 15:13; 2 Kings 21:7; 23:4). Thus the word *grove* became a symbol for idolatry.

Elijah, moved by the Spirit, persuades Ahab's governor, Obadiah (who has secretly rescued one hundred righteous prophets from the hand of King Ahab), to set up an audience with the king. Elijah orders the king to assemble the prophets of Baal and challenges them to a contest, where, ultimately, the Lord displays His power by raining down a consuming fire upon the altar made by Elijah. Elijah then uses his priesthood powers to eliminate the prophets of Baal and cleanse the land of their iniquitous influence (see 1 Kings 18:37–40). He also invokes the blessing of the Lord to send rain once again to the people—and then goes into exile to avoid the murderous outreach of Queen Jezebel.

In the wilderness, he fasts for many days and hears the still, small voice of the Lord (see 1 Kings 19:12). The voice comforts him in his isolation and directs him to call Elisha as his successor and arrange for new royal leadership to emerge in the land.

The story of Elijah and his earthly ministry is proof that the power of the Lord prevails above the shallow weakness of worldliness. In fact, without the power of the Lord, mankind is left in a state of frail nothingness.

WHAT LESSONS CAN WE LEARN FROM THE STORY OF ELIJAH?

1. The power of the Lord prevails forever.

The line of demarcation between the forces of Baal and the power of the Lord was precise. On the one hand was arrayed a force of 450 priests of Baal, clad in their richly ornamented attire, staring down the isolated figure standing by himself across the way. But Elijah was not alone, for the power of the Lord rumbled within him:

> And Elijah came unto all the people, and said, How long halt ye between two opinions? if the LORD be God, follow him: but if Baal, then follow him. . . .
>
> And call ye on the name of your gods, and I will call on the name of the LORD: and the God that answereth by fire, let him be God. (1 Kings 18:21, 24)

The priests of Baal rose to the challenge and tirelessly pleaded from morning until evening for the response of their gods—but to no avail: "There was neither voice, nor any to answer, nor any that regarded" (1 Kings 18:29).

Then it was Elijah's turn. With his opponents looking on, he prepared his sacred altar of sacrifice, even soaking it in water three times before calling upon the Lord:

> LORD God of Abraham, Isaac, and of Israel, let it be known this day that thou art God in Israel, and that I am thy servant, and that I have done all these things at thy word.
>
> Hear me, O LORD, hear me, that this people may know that thou art the LORD God, and that thou hast turned their heart back again. (1 Kings 18:36–37)

The result was stunning: "Then the fire of the LORD fell, and consumed the burnt sacrifice, and the wood, and the stones, and the dust, and licked up the water that was in the trench. And when all the people saw it, they fell on their faces: and they said, The LORD, he is the God; the LORD, he is the God" (1 Kings 18:38–39). Subsequently, Elijah brought about the destruction of the hosts of Baal and invoked the blessings of the Lord to bring rain unto the drought-inflicted population.

How does this story apply to our lives today? Consider the following reasoning:

The miraculous drama of Elijah and the prophets of Baal plays itself out anew every day in the lives of individuals who are touched by the rejuvenating fire of the Spirit. Every time a young person says no to the influence of harmful drugs, there is a victory for God and a defeat for the forces of Baal. Every time a modern Joseph flees the enticements of immorality, there is a victory for God and a defeat for the forces of Baal. When the conscious decision is made to depose the forces of dishonesty, greed, envy, or unrighteous pride—in any of their countless guises or disguises—there is a victory for God and a defeat for the forces of Baal. It can be as simple as changing the television station or exiting an Internet site. Or it can be as transforming as abandoning one's spiritual emptiness in favor of membership in the kingdom of God, with all of its saving ordinances and service opportunities.

The drama of Elijah is universal. It is the miraculous transition from the natural man to the man of God (see Mosiah 3:19). It is the spiritual victory, as Joseph Smith described it: "Salvation is nothing more nor less than to triumph over all our enemies and put them under our feet. And when we have power to put all enemies under our feet in this world, and a knowledge to triumph over all evil spirits in the world to come, then we are saved."[14]

The story is told of the time Matthew Cowley felt impressed to call one of the more free-spirited Maori brethren to be a branch president. He walked up to this brother's home and found him there with cigar in hand. When the call was extended, the brother inquired, "You mean me *and* my cigar?" Elder Cowley replied, "Just you. We don't need your cigar," whereupon the brother immediately gave up his habit and took up his calling with full devotion.[15] Another victory for God. Another defeat for the forces of Baal. The Prophet Joseph Smith declared, "I made this my rule: *When the Lord commands, do it*" (*HC* 2:170). The prayer of Elijah is still at work for us today: "Hear me, O LORD, hear me, that this people may know that thou art the Lord God, and that thou hast turned their heart back again" (1 Kings 18:37).

> **What did President Gordon B. Hinckley teach about miracles?**
>
> President Hinckley identified as the greatest of all miracles the transformation that comes into the lives of those who accept and live the restored gospel of Jesus Christ. That Restoration, he confirmed, is the marvelous work and a wonder brought to pass by the Lord on behalf of all His sons and daughters in all generations of time (see *Teachings of Gordon B. Hinckley* [Salt Lake City: Deseret Book, 1997], 243).

Pondering: How can we follow the example of Elijah and purge the influences of evil trying to engulf our lives? How can we move forward in the strength of the Lord and guide our loved ones to follow in the Lord's pathway?

2. The gateway to personal revelation is humble fasting and prayer.

After Elijah had put an end to the work of the priests of Baal, Jezebel sought to take his life. He thus withdrew into the wilderness of Mount Horeb, where an angel gave him comfort and nurture before he commenced a period of fasting for forty days and forty nights. Lodging in a cave, Elijah was lonely and anguished over the waywardness of Israel. It was then that the word of the Lord came to him: "Go forth, and stand upon the mount before the LORD" (1 Kings 19:11). What then happened was an unforgettable lesson in personal revelation:

> And, behold, the LORD passed by, and a great and strong wind rent the mountains, and brake in pieces the rocks before the LORD; but the LORD was not in the wind: and after the wind an earthquake; but the LORD was not in the earthquake:
> And after the earthquake a fire; but the LORD was not in the fire: and after the fire a still small voice. (1 Kings 19:11–12)

---

14   *Teachings of the Prophet Joseph Smith* (Salt Lake City, Deseret Book, 1938), 297.
15   See Glen L. Rudd, "Keeping the Gospel Simple," *Ensign*, Jan. 1989.

Through the still, small voice, Elijah learned that he was not alone, for the Lord still had other followers among the people: "Yet I have left me seven thousand in Israel, all the knees which have not bowed unto Baal, and every mouth which hath not kissed him" (1 Kings 19:18). The Lord commanded Elijah to anoint Hazael to be king over Syria, Jehu to be king over Israel, and Elisha to be the successor prophet. According to the design of the Lord, mighty political forces were unleashed to destroy the wicked. Meanwhile, Elisha received the mantle of Elijah and commenced his mission with full devotion to the cause of the Lord.

The account of Elijah's humble way of approaching the Lord through fasting and prayer is exemplary for our own patterns of living. Great blessings flow to those who sincerely practice a prayerful fast. These blessings may come in the form of strength, healing, or an increase of understanding. Like Elijah, we can demonstrate our humility and devotion through fasting and prayer and thus prepare ourselves to receive the still, small voice of inspiration to ensure our safety and spiritual welfare.

Pondering: How have the blessings of fasting and prayer enriched your personal life? How have you helped loved ones reach out in humility to hear and follow the still, small voice?

AGENDA FOR ACTION

Just as Elijah purged the land of the evil influence of the priests of Baal, we too can purge our own lives of unrighteous influences and desires. We can fast and pray in seeking the guidance of the Lord during trying times. We can listen in our quiet moments for the still, small voice and apply that inspiration to our lives and the lives of our loved ones. In humility and faith, we can call down the powers of heaven to cleanse and purify ourselves and our families and ensure that we are building up an environment where the Spirit of the Lord can be made manifest in wondrous ways. We can grasp the truth of our own "nothingness" (Mosiah 4:5, 11), while learning at the same time that through faith and obedience we can accomplish great things—even miracles—in the strength of the Lord. Those miracles can render the pages of our personal journal a radiant witness of the love and grace of the Lord on our behalf. We can share our testimony of how the Lord empowers us to follow the action plan of the gospel—our own personal to-do list of light and truth. And we can reach out and help others to have the strength and courage to follow their own personal action plan toward salvation and exaltation.

Looking Forward: What is the nature of the "mantle" you are now wearing?

CHAPTER TWENTY-NINE

MANTLE OF A PROPHET

GOSPEL DOCTRINE READING ASSIGNMENT: 2 KINGS 2, 5–6

And the LORD opened the eyes of the young man; and he saw: and, behold, the mountain was full of horses and chariots of fire round about Elisha. (2 Kings 6:17)

THE NEW PROPHET

ELIJAH WAS A HARD ACT to follow. But Elisha, faithful and obedient, was lifted by the Lord to a station of honor and power in the service of Israel. With the mantle of the prophet upon him, Elisha (meaning "God shall save," or "God of salvation") proceeded to perform miracles as unfolded in 2 Kings 2–6. He parted the Jordan River and walked through on dry ground; the Israelites who met him on the other side knew that he was the prophet. He healed the stale waters of Jericho. He provided needed water in support of the forces of Israel, Judah, and Edom in their campaign to overcome the threat of the Moabites. He multiplied a poor woman's oil that she might pay her debts. He prophesied that an anxious couple would be able to have a son. Then, when the boy grew ill and died, Elisha called down the power of God to restore the child to life. He provided food for the people of Gilgal suffering from a famine. He healed Naaman the leper—the most frequently cited miracle of Elisha. These wondrous acts exemplified Elisha's righteousness and ensured a succession of leadership in the prophetic office.

A TOUCH OF REALITY

In his teachings, Spencer W. Kimball reminded us how the Lord magnifies a new leader when the mantle of the prophet is placed upon his shoulders. David O. McKay, for example, a noble counselor to two presidents, rose to new pinnacles of leadership as President of the Church, radiating inspiration that blessed many lives. President Kimball also recalled the day when the aging Joseph Fielding Smith became the successor to President McKay and, despite his senior years, exuded increased energy and liveliness and conveyed inspiring truths through sermons of power. Later, in July of 1972, when the mantle of the prophet fell upon Harold B. Lee, already a tried and true servant of the Lord, he too grew in stature and magnified his calling as a leader of the Lord's sons and daughters and the voice of the Good Shepherd.[16]

Soon thereafter, in December 1973, the mantle of prophet passed on to Spencer W. Kimball, and from him to the successor prophets down to the current day, empowering the Church to continue its destined expansion as "the only true and living church upon the face of the whole earth" (D&C 1:30).

This divine process of succession reminds us of the need to support and follow the voice of the living prophet of the Lord with all our heart, might, mind, and strength. We are also reminded that we can press forward with increased faith and devotion to fulfill our own callings for the cause of Zion.

WHAT LESSONS CAN WE LEARN FROM THE STORY OF ELISHA?

1. When we follow the counsel of living prophets, the Lord pours healing power into our lives.

Naaman was a nobleman in the royal court of Syria: "Now Naaman, captain of the host of the king of Syria, was a great man with his master, and honourable, because by him the LORD had given deliverance unto Syria: he was also a mighty man in valour, but he was a leper" (2 Kings 5:1). Naaman's wife had an Israelite maid who had been captured by the Syrians. This young girl was concerned about Naaman's disease and said to her mistress, "Would God my lord were with the prophet that is in Samaria! for he would recover him of his leprosy" (2 Kings 5:3). When the prophet heard that the Syrian king (Ben-hadad II) had sent a letter of request on behalf of Naaman, Elisha declared, "Let him come now to me, and he shall know that there is a prophet in Israel" (2 Kings 5:8). So Naaman and his company came before the house of Elisha, seeking a blessing:

And Elisha sent a messenger unto him, saying, Go and wash in Jordan seven times, and thy flesh shall come again to thee, and thou shalt be clean.

But Naaman was wroth, and went away, and said, Behold, I thought, He will surely come out to me, and stand, and call on the name of the LORD his God, and strike his hand over the place, and recover the leper. . . .

And his servants came near, and spake unto him, and said, My father, if the prophet had bid thee do some great thing, wouldest thou not have done it? how much rather then, when he saith to thee, Wash, and be clean?

Then went he down, and dipped himself seven times in Jordan, according to the saying of the man of God: and his flesh came again like unto the flesh of a little child, and he was clean. (2 Kings 5:10–11, 13–14)

Returning gratefully to the house of Elisha, Naaman declared: "Behold, now I know that there is no God in all the earth, but in Israel: now therefore, I pray thee, take a blessing

How did the Savior refer to the healing of Naaman?

The story of Naaman was recalled by Jesus on one occasion while He spoke in a synagogue at Nazareth: "And many lepers were in Israel in the time of Eliseus [i.e., Elisha] the prophet; and none of them was cleansed, saving Naaman the Syrian" (Luke 4:27). The Savior's listeners in Nazareth were incensed at this reference, since Naaman was a Syrian and not of the house of Israel, the implication being that Naaman had more faith and a higher degree of obedience than was to be found among the Israelites. Certainly the point was well put by Jesus in regard to the skeptical and distrusting leaders among His Jewish contemporaries.

of thy servant" (2 Kings 5:15). But Elisha refused compensation for his services, and Naaman departed in peace. Unfortunately, Gehazi, servant of Elisha, followed after Naaman in private to solicit gifts for himself, thus offending his master and bringing upon himself the very disease the Lord had lifted from Naaman (see 2 Kings 5:27).

16   For details on President Kimball's memories about the modern prophets, see *The Teachings of Spencer W. Kimball* (Salt Lake City: Bookcraft, 1982), 467.

Naaman was asked to do a small thing for a great result—wash himself in the Jordan to be healed of a major ailment. In a spiritual sense, it is often the performance of simple things that brings about life-changing blessings.

A modern-day illustration occurred when we were invited to the bridge of the massive ocean liner to observe the captain firsthand while he guided the ship into one of the destination harbors. His steering control consisted basically of a small platform lever only a few inches long that interacted with the complex steering system of the vessel and allowed him to complete his crucial task with a few simple motions of his hand. We watched in amazement as he skillfully performed his role. It struck us that sometimes a very small helm can achieve monumental results.

That reminded us of the words of Joseph Smith: "You know, brethren, that a very large ship is benefited very much by a very small helm in the time of a storm, by being kept workways with the wind and the waves" (D&C 123:16). He then gave prophetic counsel: "Therefore, dearly beloved brethren, let us cheerfully do all things that lie in our power; and then may we stand still, with the utmost assurance, to see the salvation of God, and for his arm to be revealed" (D&C 123:17; see also James 3:4).

The point is clear. Doing "all things that lie in our power" often includes performing small and simple acts of obedience—just as Naaman did. Centuries before, Moses instructed the Israelites, plagued by an infestation of poisonous snakes, to look upon the elevated brazen serpent and live (see Numbers 21:7–9; 2 Nephi 25:20). Look and live! What a simple thing to do. In all of the complexity of modern life, in all of the sophistication of modern society, we can often overlook the elegant simplicity of the gospel plan, the supremely straightforward and plain counsel of the prophets to direct our vision toward the Master. Nephi, son of Helaman, confirmed the infinite reward of small, righteous deeds: "And as many as should look upon that serpent should live, even so as many as should look upon the Son of God with faith, having a contrite spirit, might live, even unto that life which is eternal" (Helaman 8:15). All of us come to the bridge of decision every day of our journey on the seas of life. With the help of God, we can make the daily choice of fixing our gaze upon the Savior and steering our life toward our heavenly home. We can decide to do the simple deeds of righteousness, kindness, and obedience that lead to eternal life.

Pondering: Which small changes can we make in our daily lives in order to reap a grand harvest of the Lord's blessings?

2. Through the strength of the Lord, the lambs of His flock can rise as lions of truth.

Elisha gave wise counsel to the Israelite king on how to respond to assaults from Syrian forces. Thus the Syrians came to Dothan, home of Elisha, with the intent of destroying the prophet. When Elisha's servant viewed with fear the surrounding hordes of the enemy, Elisha counseled him:

> Fear not: for they that be with us are more than they that be with them.
> And the LORD opened the eyes of the young man; and he saw: and, behold, the mountain was full of horses and chariots of fire round about Elisha.
> And when they came down to him, Elisha prayed unto the LORD, and said, Smite this people, I pray thee, with blindness. And he smote them with blindness according to the word of Elisha. (2 Kings 6:16–18)

Thus Elisha was able to lead the sightless Syrians away and render them powerless. "So the bands of Syria came no more into the land of Israel" (2 Kings 6:23). The Lord used a single individual to bring about a colossal change in the affairs of His people.

We see from such an account that the Lord works with the lambs of His fold to enable them to rise as lions in support of the divine designs of heaven. In the strength of the Lord, His prophets—and all of His servants—can accomplish miracles.

So often the prophets in various dispensations had feelings of deep inadequacy when called into service. Before Elijah was translated upward on a "chariot of fire" (2 Kings 2:11), he asked Elisha what he might do to be of help to him. The humble successor, no doubt sensing his own weakness, asked for a generous inheritance—as if a birthright: "I pray thee, let a double portion of thy spirit be upon me" (2 Kings 2:9). He surely knew that he was about to join the ranks of the Lord's prophets who measured themselves as lambs while being called to the office of a lion.

Here is a chart of statements by seven prophets showing their humility relative to their calling. See if you can assign to each statement the name of the speaker: Elijah, Enoch, Isaiah, Jeremiah, Joel, Joseph Smith, Moses.

No.	Scripture	Speaker
1	"Why is it that I have found favor in thy sight, and am but a lad, and all the people hate me; for I am slow of speech; wherefore am I thy servant?"	
2	"O my Lord, I am not eloquent, neither heretofore, nor since thou hast spoken unto thy servant: but I am slow of speech, and of a slow tongue."	
3	"And I, even I only, am left; and they seek my life, to take it away."	
4	"Then said I, Woe is me! for I am undone; because I am a man of unclean lips."	
5	"Then said I, Ah, Lord GOD! behold, I cannot speak: for I am a child."	
6	"I was no prophet, neither was I a prophet's son; but I was an herdman, and a gatherer of sycomore fruit."	
7	"I am going like a lamb to the slaughter; but I am calm as a summer's morning."	

Answers: 1. Enoch (Moses 6:31; see also Moses 6:39). 2. Moses (Exodus 4:10; see also Numbers 12:3; Moses 1:6, 10). 3. Elijah (1 Kings 19:14; see also 1 Kings 19:12). 4. Isaiah (Isaiah 6:5; see also Isaiah 6:8). 5. Jeremiah (Jeremiah 1:6; see also Jeremiah 1:5, 7–8). 6. Amos (Amos 7:14; see also the famous statement in Amos 3:7). 7. Joseph Smith (D&C 135:4).

All of the Lord's prophets are lambs of humility. But they are likewise examples of how the Lord transforms lambs into lions of service. Just as the prophets are both lambs as well as lions, we too, in our humility and modesty, can embrace the call of the Lord to speak up and declare the truth to all mankind in the strength of the Lord. The Lord declared in His preface to the Doctrine and Covenants, "The weak things of the world shall come forth and break down the mighty and strong ones, that man should not counsel his fellow man, neither trust in the arm of flesh—But that every man might speak in the name of God the Lord, even the Savior of the world" (D&C 1:19–20).

Pondering: How can you apply the examples of the Lord's prophets as you humbly pray for the strength of the Lord in carrying out your covenant duties of service? How can you cultivate the humility of a lamb but serve with the strength of a lion?

AGENDA FOR ACTION

Elisha was clothed in the mantle of Elijah, the mantle of a prophet. We too can be clothed in the mantle of sacred callings assigned to us from above. We can each pray, "O Lord, wilt thou encircle me around in the robe of thy righteousness!" (2 Nephi 4:33). We can have the humility of lambs and the strength of lions. The Lord blesses us from time to time to catch a glimpse of His "chariots of fire" (2 Kings 6:17) surrounding us with the powers of heaven. Through faith, we can enjoy an inner vision of our destiny as children of God, lifted up by the Atonement of Jesus Christ. In the strength of the Lord, we can choose to abide by the simple and fundamental laws of the gospel and transform small daily acts of obedience into eternal blessings of life and joy. Let us continually look for the small and simple ways to improve our lives and come closer to the Lord hour by hour and day by day.

LOOKING FORWARD: When we seek in faith and purity, what do we discover in holy places?

CHAPTER THIRTY

GATHER TO HOLY PLACES

GOSPEL DOCTRINE READING ASSIGNMENT: 2 CHRONICLES 29–30, 32, 34
Sanctify now yourselves, and sanctify the house of the LORD God of your fathers. (2 Chronicles 29:5)

THE BEACON OF RIGHTEOUS LEADERSHIP

LET'S CATCH A VIEW OF the historical landscape for this and future chapters. Imagine looking down upon the stage of events and seeing the major actors gathered together. On one side are three non-Israelite villain kings: the Assyrians' Shalmaneser and Sennacherib, and the Babylonian Nebuchadnezzar. Then, in the center of the stage, you see a sequence of radiant prophets: Isaiah, Jeremiah, Ezekiel, and Lehi. Just offstage, you spy two noble kings of Judah: Hezekiah and his great-grandson Josiah awaiting their turn.

You hear a rousing overture announce the beginning of the drama—and then a century and a half of spellbinding history unfolds before your eyes. A watershed event takes place in 721 B.C. when King Shalmaneser carries away captive the ten tribes of Israel—thus putting to an end the Northern Kingdom, or Israel, after a long period of waywardness on the part of the Israelites. That world-shaking event occurs during the ministry of the prophet Isaiah (around 740 to 701 B.C.), who is serving in the Southern Kingdom, or Judah. During his later years, Isaiah functions as a counselor to King Hezekiah, who reigns in righteousness during the latter part of the eighth century B.C. and the beginning of the new century. Hezekiah brings about a thorough cleansing and purification of the temple in Jerusalem as well as the skillful bolstering of his people into a renewal of their covenant with the Lord. It is in answer to the prayer of Hezekiah that the Lord neutralizes the onslaught of the Assyrians under King Sennacherib around 701 B.C.

Engrossed, you watch the dramatic events continue. Following the reign of Hezekiah, the throne of Judah is occupied by unrighteous kings until the rise of Josiah, great-grandson of Hezekiah, who once again guides the people onto the pathway of obedience. Familiar names show up during the reign of Josiah and subsequent decades: Jeremiah, whose ministry lasts from around 626 B.C. to 586 B.C.; Ezekiel, who begins his ministry in 598 B.C.; and Lehi, whom the Lord guides away from Jerusalem around 600 B.C., prior to the capture of the city by the Babylonian king Nebuchadnezzar in 587 B.C.

Thus on the stage of history, we observe the ministry of a sequence of great prophets plus the service of two of the most righteous kings in the history of Judah: Hezekiah and Josiah. What was it that kindled the flame of honor in the lives of these two kings? What was it that brought about their monumental decision to take up the banner of the Lord and guide their people onto the pathway of faithfulness? How do we make our decisions today when we come to the great divides in our lives?

A TOUCH OF REALITY

A droplet of water flowing down this stream would face the prospect of going either toward the frozen expanse of the north or toward the more hospitable waters of the Pacific.

Where is this point of decision? A few miles west of the magnificent Lake Louise in Banff National Park, Canada, there is a stream flowing down the western slope of a mountain ridge and passing underneath the Trans-Canada Highway. It soon encounters an outcropping of rocks, where it divides into two tiny streamlets, each one barely a foot across. One of them flows northward into the Bow River, eventually following major waterways eastward into the Hudson Bay. The other flows southward into the Kicking Horse River, from thence into the Columbia River, and eventually into the Pacific Ocean.

As a young man, I used to drive a tour bus in that area. One of the most compelling sights for tourists was that stop near the large sign spanning the highway: "The Great Divide." Visitors would walk down a path along the small stream and peer with fascination at the spot where it divided into two. On one of the tours, I noticed a woman staring engrossed at the dividing stream for several minutes. "Why are you so interested in that stream?" I asked her.

"Because," she said quietly, "that's life." And so it was—and is. Life is a series of daily choices that define our ultimate directions. Out of the small choices of today will flow the mighty downstream rivers of tomorrow. In life, the small often defines the large; the seemingly insignificant frequently determines the big picture.

When Hezekiah and his great-grandson Josiah came to their own "Great Divide," they chose the way of the Lord—and countless followers made a covenant to do the same by embracing the pattern laid out by the Lord. We can follow their example as we come day-by-day to the great divides in our lives and choose to continue honoring our covenants with the Lord.

WHAT LESSONS CAN WE LEARN FROM HEZEKIAH AND JOSIAH?

1. The blessings of the Lord flow unto those who gather to holy places in righteousness.

Hezekiah (meaning "whom Jehovah has strengthened") was twenty-five years old when he commenced his twenty-nine-year reign upon the throne. Immediately upon becoming king, he focused his energy on the temple, causing the priesthood bearers to repair it and cleanse it after years of abuse by unrighteous kings. His directive was to "sanctify now yourselves, and sanctify the house of the LORD God of your fathers" (2 Chronicles 29:5). When the process of cleansing and restoration had been completed, the king gathered his people together to present offerings before the Lord and to worship Him amidst musical anthems of rejoicing and praise (see 2 Chronicles 29:30–36).

Next, Hezekiah organized a campaign to restore the ceremony of the Passover, which had been neglected for generations (see 2 Chronicles 30:8–9). He prayed for the people, saying, "The good LORD pardon every one that prepareth his heart to seek God, the LORD God of his fathers, though he be not cleansed according to the purification of the sanctuary. And the LORD hearkened to Hezekiah, and healed the people" (2 Chronicles 30:18–20). Many gathered

What is the nature of the two books of the Chronicles?

In a way, these two books (counted as one book in the Hebrew scriptures) comprise a mini-Old Testament within the greater Old Testament, covering the time from Adam to the decree of Cyrus authorizing the Jews to return to Palestine (537 B.C.). The first book of Chronicles covers events down to the death of David and the assumption of the throne by Solomon. The second book of Chronicles more specifically recounts the reign of Solomon—in particular the building of the temple—and the division of the kingdom into two parts—Judah and Israel. The book also covers the exemplary reigns of Hezekiah and Josiah, who are singled out as beacons of light amid the darkness of evil and idolatry rampant in the land. The authors and compilers of the Chronicles are unknown. Key events in the life of Hezekiah are also covered in 2 Kings 18–19 and Isaiah 37–38. Key events in the life of Josiah are also covered in 2 Kings 22–23.

from across the land to keep the feast of unleavened bread "with great gladness. . . . So there was great joy in Jerusalem: for since the time of Solomon the son of David king of Israel there was not the like in Jerusalem" (2 Chronicles 30:21, 26).

When Jerusalem was later besieged by the forces of Sennacherib, Hezekiah assured his people, "Be strong and courageous, be not afraid nor dismayed for the king of Assyria, nor for all the multitude that is with him: for there be more with us than with him: With him is an arm of flesh; but with us is the Lord our God to help us, and to fight our battles" (2 Chronicles 32:7–8). In response to the prayers of Hezekiah and Isaiah, an angel of the Lord cut off the threatening host and saved Jerusalem from the enemy (see 2 Chronicles 32:21–22).

From the account of the reign of Hezekiah, we see confirmed that the covenants we make with the Lord are eternal. When we honor our covenants by cleansing ourselves and gathering together to holy places of worship, we confirm our destiny as sons and daughters of God and receive blessings of glory and joy. Holy places endure continually as a protecting shield against the enemies of Zion. Here is an illustration:

Edward J. Wood, the first president of the Cardston Alberta Temple, was a leader of legendary vision. I recall, as a young person, hearing my father tell the story of the occasion when he and my mother were at the temple one day when she noticed a painting of Chief Mountain, a famous landmark in southern Alberta and northern Montana. She also observed that this same craggy granite peak is visible through one of the temple windows. President Wood happened to be passing by at the time, and she asked him her question, "Why would we have a painting of Chief Mountain hanging right here when we can look through the window and see it in reality?"

Without hesitation, President Wood responded, "Because this temple is going to be here longer than that mountain, and we want to remember what it looked like."

His point, taken in the spirit of faith and hope, is that the temple is evidence of the eternity of lives and the grand bonding that takes place among faithful families by virtue of the sealing power of the priesthood. Families under the new and everlasting covenant of eternal marriage are intended to endure forever, far beyond mortality. Mountains may come and go (see D&C 133:21–22), but the children of God and their covenant relationships are to be secured forever through the power of the gospel of Jesus Christ.

The Lord's holy house is a place of peace, safety, and love. It's a place where the Spirit resides. It's a place of instruction in the ways of the Lord. As in the case of King Hezekiah, our commission is to ensure that cleanliness abounds, that we honor our covenants, and that we remember the counsel of the Lord: "Behold, it is my will, that all they who call on my name, and worship me according to mine everlasting gospel, should gather together, and stand in holy places" (D&C 101:22).

Pondering: How can we be faithful "house cleaners" on the errand of the Lord? How can we be more devoted in honoring our covenants and guiding our loved ones to do the same? How does the protecting hand of the Lord manifest itself continually in our lives?

2. Abiding by the word of the Lord brings us joy and salvation.

Josiah (meaning "Jehovah will heal or support") ascended the throne in Jerusalem when he was but eight years of age. For thirty-one years he reigned over the people in nobility and goodness. "And he did that which was right in the sight of the LORD, and walked in the ways of David his father, and declined neither to the right hand, nor to the left" (2 Chronicles 34:2). Josiah purged away the poison of idol worship by destroying the graven images and altars of Baal that began again to infect the land after the death of Hezekiah, his great-grandfather. When Josiah set out to cleanse the house of the Lord, Hilkiah, the high priest, discovered "a book of the law of the LORD given by Moses" (2 Chronicles 34:14). When the book was read to Josiah, he was anguished, declaring, "for great is the wrath of the LORD that is poured out upon us, because our fathers have not kept the word of the LORD" (2 Chronicles 34:21).

The prophetess Huldah confirmed that the judgments of the Lord would descend upon the wicked who had ignored the revelations given through Moses—but she prophesied that Josiah, because of his humility and faithfulness, would be spared (see 2 Chronicles 34:23–28). Josiah, committed to cleansing his people and honoring God, took decisive action by making a covenant "to walk after the LORD, and to keep his commandments, and his testimonies, and his statutes, with all his heart, and with all his soul, to perform the words of the covenant which are written in this book" (2 Chronicles 34:31). He then caused all of his followers to do the same, "according to the covenant of God, the God of their fathers" (2 Chronicles 34:32).

How can we follow the example of Josiah by aspiring to cultivate holiness before the Lord and discovering anew the light and truth waiting for us in the scriptures? The following illustration shows how a mother helped her son to live by the scriptures:

> **What counsel did Joseph Smith give concerning the scriptures?**
>
> "Search the Scriptures—search the revelations which we publish, and ask your Heavenly Father, in the name of His Son Jesus Christ, to manifest the truth unto you, and if you do it with an eye single to His glory nothing doubting, He will answer you by the power of His Holy Spirit. You will then know for yourselves and not for another. You will not then be dependent on man for the knowledge of God; nor will there be any room for speculation. No; for when men receive their instruction from Him that made them, they know how he will save them. Then again we say: Search the Scriptures, search the Prophets, and learn what portion of them belongs to you" (*HC* 1:282).

On my shelf at home is a set of the four standard works bound in black leather. The pages are frayed and the bindings worn from over sixty years of continual use. These scriptures accompanied me on my mission as a young elder. They were again my companion over many decades of service with my family in many different cities. What's so special about this particular set of scriptures? This set was given to me by my mother. In fact, the triple combination bears a personal handwritten notation with the date corresponding to the very day she passed away giving birth to my younger brother. This set of scriptures was the last gift she gave me—the first being life itself.

Every time I pass by the shelf where these aging scriptures are stored, I have a new discovery of truth and gratitude. What greater gifts can a mother give than life itself, followed by gospel nurture opening up the pathway to life eternal? There is no more indispensable road map for life's journey than the scriptures.

When, on the watch of King Josiah, the missing law of the Lord was discovered, he read the ancient words to his people as a reminder of their covenant obligations to the Almighty. So too can we be reminded of our covenants as we study the words of the Lord.

Pondering: What lies hidden for us in the scriptures that we still need to discover? How can we search and ponder more faithfully in order to receive and apply the message the Lord intends us to have? How can we encourage others to do the same?

AGENDA FOR ACTION

Hezekiah and Josiah were noble servants of the Lord who repaired and cleansed the house of the Lord. We too can be cleansers—cleansers of our souls and of our environments. Like Josiah, we can search diligently for the word of God. When we cleanse and search, great blessings will follow. When we honor our covenants, we please the Lord and open a pathway of joy for ourselves and our loved ones. When we seek in faith and purity, we find divine truth in holy places—in our homes, our congregations, and the house of the Lord—just as we will find eternal life and everlasting joy in our heavenly home.

There are simple ways to aspire to these noble objectives. Through example and encouragement, we can plant in the hearts of our loved ones the vision of the temple. We can arrange for family walks on the temple grounds. We can display pictures of the house of the Lord and discuss how to prepare for temple service. We can focus on scripture study, not only by giving them personal copies of the scriptures but also by sharing our enduring testimony of the divine power of God's word. Simple acts of kindness and love bring about heavenly blessings. As Alma taught, "By small and simple things are great things brought to pass" (Alma 37:6).

LOOKING FORWARD: What favorite gems of truth reach out to you
personally in the books of Proverbs and Ecclesiastes?

CHAPTER THIRTY-ONE

BUDS OF WISDOM/HARVEST OF JOY

GOSPEL DOCTRINE READING ASSIGNMENT: PROVERBS AND ECCLESIASTES

Let us hear the conclusion of the whole matter: Fear God, and keep his commandments: for this is the whole duty of man. (Ecclesiastes 12:13)

THE GARDEN OF TRUTH

WHEN WE ENTER INTO THE books of Proverbs and Ecclesiastes, we step into a lush garden of truth. We see before our eyes the glory of countless flowers of all varieties. We smell the fragrance of nature's abundance. We feel the velvet smoothness of petals and leaves, and we hear the rustle of the wind whispering through the foliage. In these pages of wisdom, we discern the influence of the Lord in the lives of His children, budding forth as a harvest of short sayings and exhortations to guide our lives each day.

Proverbs and Ecclesiastes are two of the eleven books of the Old Testament belonging to the so-called Hagiographa ("sacred writings") of the Jewish canon, along with the books of Job, Psalms, Song of Solomon, Ruth, Lamentations, Daniel, Esther, Ezra-Nehemiah (counted as one book), and the Chronicles (also counted as one book).

From these words of Solomon and his successors, we find sayings of a spiritual and practical nature that echo in our minds because of imagery, comparisons, parallel construction, rhythmic flow, and lofty ideas. Are any of the following among your favorites?

* "For whom the LORD loveth he correcteth; even as a father the son in whom he delighteth" (Proverbs 3:12).
* "Wisdom is the principal thing; therefore get wisdom: and with all thy getting get understanding" (Proverbs 4:7).

- "He that is slow to anger is better than the mighty; and he that ruleth his spirit than he that taketh a city" (Proverbs 16:32).
- "Train up a child in the way he should go: and when he is old, he will not depart from it" (Proverbs 22:6).
- "For as he thinketh in his heart, so is he" (Proverbs 23:7).
- "Where there is no vision, the people perish: but he that keepeth the law, happy is he" (Proverbs 29:18).
- "To every thing there is a season, and a time to every purpose under the heaven" (Ecclesiastes 3:1).

> ### What do "Proverbs" and "Ecclesiastes" mean?
>
> The word *proverb* comes from the Latin term *proverbium*, meaning, "a common saying" or "words put forward"—from *pro* (forth) plus *verbum* (word). The word *ecclesiastes* is based on the Greek rendering of the Hebrew word *koheleth*, meaning "preacher."

How do the truths of the gospel, including sayings such as those in Proverbs and Ecclesiastes, echo in our lives? How do we cultivate our own proverbs of wisdom as we grow and advance in our development as sons and daughters of God?

WHAT LESSONS CAN WE LEARN FROM PROVERBS AND ECCLESIASTES?

1. Wisdom comes when we follow the Lord's pattern for learning and applying truth.

As we study the hundreds of sayings in these two books, we can gather them into many different patterns of application, according to our needs. For example, in chapter 26 of this book, we suggested a formula for how to acquire wisdom in our lives. Let's review the W-I-S-D-O-M formula using examples from Proverbs and Ecclesiastes:

THE LORD'S PATTERN OF WISDOM

W—*Word of the Lord*: Wisdom comes through the word of the Lord unto His children. "Every word of God is pure: he is a shield unto them that put their trust in him" (Proverbs 30:5; see also Proverbs 8:10).

I—*Inquire*: Wisdom comes when we inquire of the Lord and invite His blessings through prayer. "The LORD is far from the wicked: but he heareth the prayer of the righteous" (Proverbs 15:29; see also Proverbs 2:3, 5).

S—*Spirit*: Wisdom comes when we listen to the Spirit. "Turn you at my reproof: behold, I will pour out my spirit unto you, I will make known my words unto you" (Proverbs 1:23; see also Proverbs 8:4).

D—*Depend upon the Lord*: Wisdom comes when we depend fully upon the Lord, who is the font of all wisdom. "Trust in the Lord with all thine heart; and lean not unto thine own understanding. In all thy ways acknowledge him, and he shall direct thy paths" (Proverbs 3:5–6; see also Proverbs 16:20).

O—*Obedience*: Wisdom comes through our obedience to the Lord and His gospel plan. "Let us hear the conclusion of the whole matter: Fear God, and keep his commandments: for this is the whole duty of man" (Ecclesiastes 12:13; see also Proverbs 7:2).

M—*Meekness*: Wisdom comes when we endure in meekness and humility, avoiding pride, always being receptive to the Lord's counsel. "When pride cometh, then cometh shame: but with the lowly is wisdom" (Proverbs 11:2; see also Proverbs 16:18–19).

How are these truths active in our lives today? Let's take just one example from the final words of Ecclesiastes with the counsel to "fear God" (see Ecclesiastes 12:13). That famous saying confirms that we can see beyond the vanities of this world and peer into the future with "an eye single to the glory of God" (D&C 4:5). Contemplate the following words from a member of a branch presidency in the Provo Utah MTC:

> A few years ago, as part of an assignment at the Missionary Training Center, I was privileged to work with a number of new elders and sisters as they prepared to go out into their assigned fields of labor. Reflected in their attitudes was a range of emotions, from exhilaration and enthusiasm to apprehension and, yes, even fear.

We studied the subject of fear and learned that fear is not unfavorable to the errand of the Lord, especially if it reflects a deep respect and honor for the majesty, work, and glory of God. We saw that the expression "fear the Lord" occurs many times in the scriptures. We asked ourselves what the expression means as it is used by the prophets, and how we can know if someone fears the Lord.

By looking at the actions associated in the scriptures with fearing the Lord, we determined that the most frequently mentioned action was to *serve the Lord* (seventeen times, as in Joshua 24:14). *Keeping His commandments* is used thirteen times in parallel with fearing the Lord (as in Ecclesiastes 12:13). *Worshipping Him* is used seven times (as in 2 Kings 17:36), *praising Him* six times (as in Psalm 22:23), *trusting Him* six times (as in Psalm 115:11), and *heeding His words* six times (as in Deuteronomy 17:19). There is also frequent mention of such actions as *sanctifying Him* (four times), *keeping His statutes* (three times), *giving glory to Him* (three times), and various additional manifestations of obedience, including bearing testimony, paying tithing, acting in faith, rejoicing, and being unified. Thus, fearing the Lord is synonymous with serving Him and keeping His commandments in the spirit of worship, praise, and trust.

It is also interesting to note the blessings that are associated with fearing the Lord. The young elders and sisters came to realize that fearing the Lord in righteousness has profound rewards. Here are the most frequently mentioned ones: *wisdom* (mentioned twelve times in the scriptures, as in Proverbs 1:7); *knowledge* (nine times, again as in Proverbs 1:7); *salvation* (five times, as in Alma 34:37 and Mormon 9:27); *strength* (three times, as in 3 Nephi 4:10); *life* (three times, as in Proverbs 14:27); *freedom from want* (twice, as in Psalm 34:9); and a variety of additional blessings—learning the mysteries of the covenant, mercy, grace, glory, preservation, enduring forever, the protection of angels, confidence, refuge, prolonged days, and the comfort of the Holy Ghost. Thus, those who fear the Lord are endowed with eternal blessings of wisdom, knowledge, salvation, strength, life, and freedom from want.

Like those new missionaries, all of us have the opportunity in our own callings and activities to exemplify in our actions the spirit of fearing the Lord. We can experience in personal ways how the Lord enhances our wisdom, knowledge, and strength. Line upon line and precept upon precept, we can advance along the pathway of salvation and sense a budding increase in our confidence before the Lord as the doctrine of the priesthood distills upon our souls "as the dews from heaven" (D&C 121:45).

Pondering: How can we enhance our personal wisdom by following the pattern of spiritual growth outlined in the scriptures? How can we learn to fear the Lord through love and obedience, thus harvesting grand blessings from on high?

2. With the help of the Lord, we can cultivate our own family garden of divine inspiration and wisdom for life's journey.

The Washington D.C. Temple, located on a prominent wooded elevation just north of the nation's capital, was dedicated in November 1974. It has been an inspiring and beautiful addition to the landscape with its well-kept gardens and grounds to complement the whiteness of the imposing six-spired building. One day, as my wife and I were driving up the long road to the temple, we looked through the trees below the temple and caught site of a hidden garden a hundred feet or more off to the side of the road. It was a pleasant surprise. In a small clearing, someone had cultivated a magnificent little garden complete with a variety of beautiful flowers and shrubs. It was a secret jewel that delighted the eyes and lifted spirits.

As we talked about our discovery, we concluded that wisdom is like that. It opens up in the undergrowth of the mind a better vista, a sanctuary of thoughts and aspirations cultivated by faith and nurtured by hope. It is the essence of the righteous life. It is the mentor of spirituality and the guarantor of joy. It illuminates the pathway leading to the house of the Lord, the ultimate place of rest. One can delight in the wisdom of others, but only the wisdom cultivated in one's own life—through many years of listening, learning, doing, refining, building, and growing—can be the source of a spiritual harvest in the years to come. "Happy is the man that findeth wisdom, and the man that getteth understanding" (Proverbs 3:13).

How can we cultivate our own garden of truth and wisdom? How can the Lord's words unfold and be magnified within us? The following statement may serve to illuminate the process. After pondering the splendid portrait of a virtuous woman given in Proverbs 31:10–31, and after praying for inspiration from the Lord, a young man composed these words of love for his eternal wife:

> You are my eternal wife, a woman of perfect virtue and nobility, a treasure exceeding in value all the gold and diamonds of the world. Safely do I trust in the one who has been so good to me over the years. You have brought nurture to our home, day and night, with tireless and forgiving devotion. You are the one whose candle is never extinguished, who reaches out to all who need help, who brightens the lonely heart and strengthens the hope of the weak. Beauty follows in your footsteps, and comeliness radiates in your demeanor. You are the one who never looks back on sorrow but always looks ahead to joy. Peace and abundance flow through your hands into our home. Our children rise up and call you blessed. The praise of your husband is forever extended to you as his eternal companion. Your words are proverbs of kindness. Your fear of the Lord is confirmed through obedience and valor. Your hope is validated through radiant cheer. Your love is upheld through unceasing service. Many daughters of the Lord have risen in glory, but in my view you excel them all, for through you, the eternal woman draws us ever onward.

Pondering: How can we bring together our own words of gratitude and faith? How can we cultivate our own family garden of light and joy that will nurture us far into the future?

AGENDA FOR ACTION

Fearing the Lord—in the sense that we humbly trust in Him and obey His counsel—is the sustaining key of wisdom taught in Proverbs and Ecclesiastes. By listening to the whisperings of the Holy Spirit and following the advice of the prophets, we cultivate wisdom and facilitate the process described by Paul as coming "in the unity of the faith, and of the knowledge of the Son of God, unto a perfect man, unto the measure of the stature of the fulness of Christ" (Ephesians 4:13). By striving for spiritual enlightenment, we emulate the pattern established by the Savior: "And Jesus increased in wisdom and stature, and in favour with God and man" (Luke 2:52). When we dispel pride, envy, contention, and deceit, we assure that our existence will be free from the weeds of folly and iniquity, leaving room for the kind of wisdom that saves and exalts. Morsels of that kind of wisdom are available to us in the Proverbs, samples of which we can memorize or display in our homes as touching reminders of how we can do a little better each day to emulate the example of our Redeemer.

LOOKING FORWARD: What is the secret to rising above all tribulation and enduring to the end in faith?

What do the prophets say about obtaining wisdom?

Joseph Smith declared, "The best way to obtain truth and wisdom is not to ask it from books, but to go to God in prayer, and obtain divine teaching" (*HC* 4:425). In that same spirit, Howard W. Hunter proclaimed that the word of God, taught in purity and with conviction, will enable students to recognize that revelation has come into their hearts; such is the pathway for building faith and strengthening testimonies (see *The Teachings of Howard W. Hunter*, ed. Clyde J. Williams [Salt Lake City: Bookcraft, 1997], 185).

CHAPTER THIRTY-TWO

RISING ABOVE ADVERSITY

Gospel Doctrine Reading Assignment: Job 1–2, 13, 19, 27, 42

For I know that my redeemer liveth. (Job 19:25)

IN THE FOOTSTEPS OF A CHEERFUL SOUL

In today's world of tribulation and hardship, we can find a good friend in Job. His triumph over suffering, his invincible hope, his faith in the Lord—these qualities of endurance make Job a comforting friend and ally along the pathway of life. Job is identified in the scriptures as being a man who "was perfect and upright, and one that feared God, and eschewed evil" (Job 1:1). He was a man of considerable wealth—including the treasure of an impressive family and the abundance of flocks and herds. But in the mortal condition lurk the certainties of unexpected misfortune and unpredicted disaster—and Job learned this truth through sad experience. Over time, he lost all of his children, his estate, and his health. The only thing he retained was his most precious diadem—his faith and testimony, preserved despite the unspeakable suffering that carried him (as David expressed it) "through the valley of the shadow of death" (Psalm 23:4). But Job survived in honor at the highest level of perfection he could achieve. He trusted in the Lord. He confirmed his witness of the divine: "For I know that my redeemer liveth, and that he shall stand at the latter day upon the earth" (Job 19:25). And he also declared, "My righteousness I hold fast, and will not let it go: my heart shall not reproach me so long as I live" (Job 27:6).

Hold fast he did—and the Lord blessed him by renewing his prosperity and granting him more children. In the Lord's plan of salvation, joy will surpass sorrow, and eternal light will eclipse the darkness. The mercy and grace of the Lord transcend all adversity and suffering.

These truths resonate for us today, especially in the experiences of the Prophet Joseph Smith.

A TOUCH OF REALITY

Job steadfastly refused to extinguish the light of hope, even in the midst of the most trying adversity. His fervent testimony shone through the bleakness of the shadows of tragedy around him. The language of the Prophet Joseph Smith was also empowered by hope and cheer, despite tribulation. Writing from Liberty Jail in Missouri, he composed what would later serve as the basis for sections 121, 122, and 123 of the Doctrine and Covenants. The Prophet and several of his colleagues had been held prisoner under conditions of extraordinary deprivation for almost four months. In stark contrast to the squalid environment in which the men were confined, section 121 affords the most sublime language in holy writ concerning the blessings of honoring the priesthood. While suffering from monumental injustice, the prophet wrote to the Saints, "Let thy bowels also be full of charity towards all men, and to the household of faith, and let virtue garnish thy thoughts unceasingly; then shall thy confidence wax strong in the presence of God" (D&C 121:45). Section 122 is a source of unsurpassed inspiration in overcoming tribulation: "Know thou, my son, that all these things shall give thee experience, and shall be for thy good. The Son of Man hath descended below them all. Art thou greater than he? . . . Therefore, fear not what man can do, for God shall be with you forever and ever" (D&C 122:7–9).

The coming forth of these treasures of wisdom, revealed from the womb of adversity, is a lasting memorial to the process of how mercy flows from God: "For after much tribulation come the blessings" (D&C 58:4). In the language of soaring faith, the Prophet Joseph teaches us how to rise above adversity and tribulation with grace and thanksgiving.

Like Job, Joseph Smith was tenderly connected with his family. Consider the Prophet's words to his wife, Emma, during his confinement in Liberty Jail:

> My dear Emma, I very well know your toils and sympathize with you. If God will spare my life once more to have the privilege of taking care of you, I will ease your care and endeavor to comfort your heart. I want you to take the best care of the family you can, [and] I believe you will do all you can. I was sorry to learn that Frederick was sick, but I trust he is well again and that you are all well. I want you to try to gain time and write to me a long letter and tell me all you can and even if Old Major [their dog] is alive yet and what those little prattlers say that cling around your neck. Do you tell them I am in prison that their lives might be saved.[17]

Joseph, like many of the founding leaders of the restored Church, placed the will of God above personal will and comfort. The suffering occasioned by separation and the anxiety about longed-for relief were destined to last "but for a small moment" (D&C 122:4). The example of these devoted servants of the Lord is timeless and still reverberates in the hearts of the grateful heirs of their service. As Joseph Smith put it concerning the Saints of the Restoration, "Short though bitter was their pain, everlasting is their joy" (HC 3:330).

WHAT LESSONS CAN WE LEARN FROM JOB?

1. Overcoming adversity is a key part of the plan of salvation.

The account of the premortal council in heaven confirms one of the chief purposes for our earthly experience: "And we will prove them herewith, to see if they will do all things whatsoever the Lord their God shall command them" (Abraham 3:25). That test of obedience often comes as we struggle to gain passage through the ravines of adversity. Adversity is a reality of life. Without opposition, we could not understand or appreciate joy in contrast to sorrow; we could not know righteousness in contrast to wickedness. Enduring with patience and honor in the face of adversity is an eternal life-insurance policy. In our day, the Lord said, "Be patient in afflictions, for thou shalt have many; but endure them, for, lo, I am with thee, even unto the end of thy days" (D&C 24:8).

In the story of Job we perceive a hint of the premortal council, "When the morning stars sang together, and all the sons of God shouted for joy" (Job 38:7). That joyous anthem was sounded in response to the announcement of the Father's glorious plan of redemption. Only Lucifer and his followers were opposed to the plan, which was based

17   *The Personal Writings of Joseph Smith*, ed. Dean C. Jesse (Salt Lake City: Deseret Book, 1984), 408; spelling and syntax modernized.

on the agency of mankind and the mission of the Savior. In a similar context, the book of Job opens with references to a dialogue between the Lord and Satan: "And the LORD said unto Satan, Hast thou considered my servant Job, that there is none like him in the earth, a perfect and an upright man, one that feareth God, and escheweth evil?" (Job 1:8). When Satan suggests that Job would renounce his faith in the absence of the Lord's protecting hand, the Lord gives him permission to act against Job's possessions, "only upon himself put not forth thine hand" (Job 1:12). Satan then arranges to bring about the demise of Job's seven sons and daughters and the destruction of his estate. Job responds, "The LORD gave, and the LORD hath taken away; blessed be the name of the LORD" (Job 1:21). Next, the Lord permits Satan to strike Job with serious physical infirmities: "Behold, he is in thine hand; but save his life" (Job 2:6). Encumbered with threatening ailments, Job still remains faithful and proceeds through the rest of the account to conduct his life under the mantle of the Lord's mercy and love.

Does this remarkable resilience continue today? Consider the experience of Elder Neal A. Maxwell a few years ago:

> In the first of the worldwide priesthood training sessions conducted by satellite, Elder Neal A. Maxwell taught us a precious lesson in discipleship when recounting his challenges with leukemia. As he spoke on the subject of revelation and how our minds, hearts, feelings, and intellects are to be in tune with the Spirit, he shared how he had pleaded one day with the Lord concerning matters of serious health challenges as related to his continuing service in the kingdom. He shared the answer revealed unto him by the Lord—the Lord had given him the illness so that he could teach others with authenticity. What a transcendent expression concerning the nature of true discipleship and how each of us—despite the adversities of life—can rise in dignity to fulfill all of our opportunities for service in the spirit of humility and acceptance, always viewing things from a higher, more spiritual perspective.
>
> A number of years earlier, Elder Maxwell had explained that challenges in our mortal experience help us to develop the qualities that we lack. As in the case of Job, we learn that immunity from adversity is not in our best interest as sons and daughters of God, for "the Lord seeth fit to chasten his people; yea, he trieth their patience and their faith" (Mosiah 23:21).[18]

All of us, in our daily experiences, have similar opportunities to understand the role of adversity in bringing about a higher degree of "authenticity" and worthiness through the strength of the Lord. Through study and pondering, we can come to understand more fully that the role of adversity and opposition in all things is part of the Lord's plan for us to become even as He is. Adversity gives us the opportunity to overcome, to gain strength as we endure hardships, and to realize the goodness of our Savior—who did the will of the Father and descended below all things.

Pondering: How can we rise above adversity through the blessings of the Spirit? How can we use our own experience with tribulation in order come to a clearer understanding of the Lord's atoning sacrifice? How can we teach our loved ones the same precious lesson?

2. Faith in the mercy and support of the Lord brings comfort, cheer, and grand blessings.

Again, the ultimate witness of Job in the midst of life's challenges is precious: "For I know that my redeemer liveth, and that he shall stand at the latter day upon the earth: And though after my skin worms destroy this body, yet in my flesh shall I see God" (Job 19:25–26). Job's three friends, Eliphaz, Bildad, and Zophar, came to comfort him in his adversity but wound up rebuking him instead (see D&C 121:10). It was the Lord who was Job's friend, just as He reaches out to all of us in friendship and comfort:

> VERILY I say unto you my friends, fear not, let your hearts be comforted; yea, rejoice evermore, and in everything give thanks;

18   For details on Elder Maxwell's thoughts on this subject, see *Notwithstanding My Weakness* (Salt Lake City: Deseret Book, 1981), 20–21.

Waiting patiently on the Lord, for your prayers have entered into the ears of the Lord of Sabaoth, and are recorded with this seal and testament—the Lord hath sworn and decreed that they shall be granted. (D&C 98:1–2; see also D&C 88:3)

In the end of the story of Job, the Lord granted unto him abundant blessings—with twice the estate he had started with and seven new children in place of the ones he had lost (see Job 42:10–16). "So Job died, being old and full of days" (Job 42:17). But his story did not die. It remains as a monument to the cheer that flows from a life of patience, endurance, and faith.

The Savior often gives the counsel, "Be of good cheer." This phrase is used thirteen times in the holy scriptures, as in the following references concerning the challenging situations we face in life and the reasons why we can truly "be of good cheer" through the help of the Lord:

- When you feel weakness or illness, read Matthew 9:2–8. Key words: "Thy sins be forgiven thee; . . . Arise, and walk."
- When you are fearful because of conditions around you, read Matthew 14:24–27. Key words: "It is I; be not afraid."
- When you feel overcome with troubles, read John 16:32–33. Key words: "I have overcome the world."
- When you are persecuted for the sake of the gospel, read Acts 23:11. Key words: "Bear witness also."
- When you face danger on the Lord's errand, read Acts 27:22–25. Key words: "For I believe God."
- When you face a daunting challenge, read Alma 17:31. Key words: "Let us go" and do good.
- When your faith is tested, read 3 Nephi 1:12–13. Key words: "I will fulfill all that which I have caused to be spoken by the mouth of my holy prophets."
- When you face evil, read D&C 61:36–37. Key words: "I am in your midst."
- When you are called upon to bear testimony before the world, read D&C 68:3–6. Key words: "I the Lord am with you, and will stand by you."
- When you feel poor and without resources, read D&C 78:17–18. Key words: "The riches of eternity are yours."
- When you feel inadequate, read D&C 112:3–4, 10. Key words: "All thy sins are forgiven thee. . . . the Lord thy God shall lead thee by the hand, and give thee answer to thy prayers."

Why should we be cheerful?

Ezra Taft Benson assured us that God does not dwell in a gloomy or melancholy venue but rather in glory and light. Thus we should be cheerful, joyful, and happily enthusiastic (see *God, Family, Country: Our Three Great Loyalties* [Salt Lake City: Deseret Book, 1974], 4).

Pondering: How can we follow the counsel of the Lord to be of good cheer—despite all of life's challenges? How can we set a good example for our loved ones to do the same?

AGENDA FOR ACTION

Through the blessings of the Lord, we can cultivate qualities of spiritual resilience, steadfast loyalty, and unassailable faith in the face of whatever degree of adversity this mortal experience can place in our pathway. We can follow the counsel of King Benjamin and be "willing to submit to all things which the Lord seeth fit to inflict upon [us], even as a child doth submit to his father" (Mosiah 3:19). Patience, a firm testimony of the Lord's goodness and grace, and an enduring commitment to be of good cheer—these are the key elements for rising above tribulation and enjoying the harvest of eternal life through the gospel of Jesus Christ. No matter what befalls you in your mortal journey, you can love the Lord and say with Job, "Yet will I trust in him: . . . He also shall be my salvation" (Job 13:15–16).

Looking Forward: How can we accept callings from the Lord—no matter the circumstances?

CHAPTER THIRTY-THREE

THE INFINITE MERCY OF THE LORD

GOSPEL DOCTRINE READING ASSIGNMENT: JONAH 1–4; MICAH 2, 4–7

*And what doth the LORD require of thee, but to do justly, and to love
mercy, and to walk humbly with thy God?* (Micah 6:8)

THE GLORY OF GOD RESTS IN THE SALVATION OF HIS CHILDREN

THE BOOKS OF JONAH AND Micah radiate the same eternal message: the infinite mercy of the Lord will triumph in the end. The unnamed writer of the book of Jonah uses the experiences of the prophet to confirm the Lord's universal love for His children of all nationalities and origins—like the populace of Nineveh, the great Assyrian capital city. Just as Jonah had to grasp the all-embracing reach of the Lord's grace and loving kindness, so are we directed to practice obedience, tolerance, and brotherly kindness in sharing the gospel with everyone. In his writings, Micah echoes the recurrent theme of all the prophets: the Lord will bring judgment upon evildoers, while showing mercy and forgiveness to those who repent and follow His covenants. Goodness and truth—as evidenced in the coming forth of the Messiah to be born at Bethlehem (see the prophecy in Micah 5:2)—will eventually prevail over the forces of rebellion. The Lord's kingdom will rise in the latter days as a brilliant beacon of light, inviting all to come and partake of the blessings of heaven: "BUT in the last days it shall come to pass, that the mountain of the house of the LORD shall be established in the top of the mountains, and it shall be exalted above the hills; and people shall flow unto it" (Micah 4:1).

The following experience of a devoted Sunday School teacher helps to shed light on the everlasting theme of God's mercy and grace as unfolded in our day.

A TOUCH OF REALITY

When Lehi was teaching his son Jacob about the Atonement, he made a statement that engenders deep pondering: "And men are instructed sufficiently that they know good from evil. And the law is given unto men. And by the law no flesh is justified" (2 Nephi 2:5). The implication is inescapable: no mortal left to himself or herself can ever live the law of God perfectly. Some may be more faithful than others in keeping the commandments, but none can do it perfectly.

There will always be a gap that needs to be bridged if we are to be found worthy to return to our heavenly home some day. How can that gap be closed?

Over my years as a teacher, I have watched young students grapple with this paradox. Typically, I draw two horizontal lines on the chalkboard, labeling the lower one mortality and the upper one perfection. Then I will ask the students to join me in locating ourselves on the continuum stretching from the bottom

> **When did Jonah and Micah serve as prophets?**
>
> Jonah (meaning "dove") lived during the time of Jeroboam II of Israel (see 2 Kings 14:25), who reigned around the first half of the eighth century B.C. During this same period, the prophets Hosea and Amos were also active—preceding the ministry of Isaiah. Micah (meaning "Who is like God?") was a prophet of Judah during the reign of King Hezekiah (see Micah 1:1), who served on the throne from the latter part of the eighth century B.C. down to the beginning of the seventh century. Thus Micah was a contemporary of Isaiah, whose ministry extended from 740 B.C. to 701 B.C.

line to the top. "Where are we now in the process of perfection?" Our dots are placed at various points in the space between the two lines, but never will a dot be placed as high as the top line—perfection. There is always a gap between the highest dot and the top line. "So it appears that none of us can return to the presence of the Lord purely on the basis of being justified by total obedience to the law. Correct?" They always agree.

Then we read together the stirring testimony of Lehi concerning the Atonement:

> Wherefore, redemption cometh in and through the Holy Messiah; for he is full of grace and truth.
>
> Behold, he offereth himself a sacrifice for sin, to answer the ends of the law, unto all those who have a broken heart and a contrite spirit; and unto none else can the ends of the law be answered.
>
> Wherefore, how great the importance to make these things known unto the inhabitants of the earth, that they may know that there is no flesh that can dwell in the presence of God, save it be through the merits, and mercy, and grace of the Holy Messiah. (2 Nephi 2:6–8)

How magnificent are Lehi's words in defining how to bridge the gap through the "merits, and mercy, and grace of the Holy Messiah." How beautiful is this message of hope and salvation. We are, in effect, beneficiaries of the mercy and grace of the Savior, who closes the gap for each individual after all he or she can do through faith, repentance, and righteous compliance with all the principles and ordinances of the gospel (see 2 Nephi 25:23). What a grand opportunity we have to share this message of mercy and grace with others. As Micah wrote, "And what doth the Lord require of thee, but to do justly, and to love mercy, and to walk humbly with thy God?" (Micah 6:8).

WHAT LESSONS CAN WE LEARN FROM JONAH AND MICAH?

1. The love and mercy of the Lord are extended to all peoples.

The story of Jonah is among the most famous in the Old Testament, no doubt because of the unusual idea of taking up residence in a whale. But there are also deep lessons of a spiritual nature to be learned from this account.

The details are familiar: Jonah is called by the Lord to preach repentance to Nineveh. However, Jonah declines to participate and flees on a ship bound for Tarshish. In response, the Lord sends a fierce storm, and the crew finally casts Jonah into the sea for fear of capsizing. In the midst of the deep, Jonah is swallowed by a whale: "Now the Lord had prepared a great fish to swallow up Jonah. And Jonah was in the belly of the fish three days and three nights" (Jonah 1:17). Jonah repents of his wrong and prays for deliverance: "I am cast out of thy sight; yet I will look again toward thy holy temple. . . . Salvation is of the Lord" (Jonah 2:4, 9). The Lord accepts Jonah's change of heart and rescues him.

Jonah fulfills his prophetic call and warns the people they will be destroyed because of their wickedness. Much to his surprise, the king and his people respond to the call for repentance, and the Lord suspends the decreed judgments.

Jonah is displeased with the Lord sparing Nineveh out of mercy, so, as a lesson, the Lord prepares a gourd to shelter the vexed Jonah brooding on the outskirts of the massive city. Jonah is pleased with the gourd, but the Lord destroys the gourd the next day:

> Then said the LORD, Thou hast had pity on the gourd, for the which thou hast not laboured, neither madest it grow; which came up in a night, and perished in a night: And should not I spare Nineveh, that great city, wherein are more than sixscore thousand persons that cannot discern between their right hand and their left hand; and *also* much cattle? (Jonah 4:10–11).

In this way the Lord teaches a grand principle—that all people are the Lord's and that He will extend His invitation to all, that they might have a chance to repent and embrace the saving truths of the gospel.

When Jonah was called to do missionary work in Nineveh, he initially declined the assignment. How are we to respond to the calling of the Lord to preach the gospel to the whole world? The following illustration was shared by a member of a branch presidency at the MTC:

> A number of years ago, I had the honor of serving at the Missionary Training Center in Provo, Utah. It was in that capacity that I met a young elder who was on his way to his assigned mission field. He told me of a friend in his home stake who likewise had been called on a mission a year or two earlier. In that case, however, the calling had been to a mission in the western United States, whereas the friend had hoped for a foreign mission call. His feelings about it were so strong that the call was withdrawn for a time. Over the next year he was able to rethink his priorities, recover his spirit of missionary work, and seek once again the opportunity to serve a mission—wherever the Lord might send him.
>
> A calling was extended once more—to the same mission! This time he willingly responded. During his first days in the mission field, he and his companion came across a man who invited them enthusiastically into his home. The young man was stunned to hear the investigator state words to the effect, "I am so pleased that you have come to teach me the gospel. I had been praying to find the truth. A year ago I had a dream that young missionaries would call on me, but no one came—until now."

How important it is for all of us to respond willingly and forthrightly to the call to share our witness of the truthfulness of the gospel. We cannot realize how our efforts may gather specific individuals into the fold who are at present praying for guidance. We can only embark on the errand of the Lord with the faith that He will lead us to invest our talents and strength in ways that serve to contribute to His work and glory. As He said, "For there are many yet on the earth . . . who are only kept from the truth because they know not where to find it" (D&C 123:12). We are the ones who can point the way. If we act with devotion, our lives will be filled with more joy, more peace, more hope, and more faith. And we will be doing the will of the Lord in the spirit of thanksgiving.

Pondering: How can we serve as a beacon of the Lord, allowing our example and our spoken message to reflect the standards and

---

How does the story of Jonah foreshadow (or point toward) the Savior's Atonement?

When the scribes and Pharisees demanded of the Savior a sign of His divine calling, He responded with words that pointed toward His atoning sacrifice: "An evil and adulterous generation seeketh after a sign; and there shall no sign be given to it, but the sign of the prophet Jonas [i.e., Jonah]: For as Jonas was three days and three nights in the whale's belly; so shall the Son of man be three days and three nights in the heart of the earth. The men of Nineveh shall rise in judgment with this generation, and shall condemn it: because they repented at the preaching of Jonas; and, behold, a greater than Jonas is here" (Matthew 12:39–41; see also Matthew 16:4; Luke 11:29–30).

truths of the gospel? How can we reach out in love to all the sons and daughters of God—regardless of their backgrounds, origins, or circumstances—and invite them into the fold?

2. The Lord will gather His Saints to holy places of glory in the latter days.

The short book of Micah comprises three major divisions: prophecies of judgment and destruction because of idolatry and sinfulness (chapters 1–3), prophecies concerning the Restoration and the Messiah (chapters 4–5), and prophecies concerning the goodness of the Lord toward His covenant people (chapters 6–7). Four passages from Micah are especially memorable:

- *Temple of Zion in the last days*: "But in the last days it shall come to pass, that the mountain of the house of the Lord shall be established in the top of the mountains, and it shall be exalted above the hills; and people shall flow unto it. And many nations shall come, and say, Come, and let us go up to the mountain of the Lord, and to the house of the God of Jacob; and he will teach us of his ways, and we will walk in his paths: for the law shall go forth of Zion, and the word of the Lord from Jerusalem" (Micah 4:1–2; compare Isaiah 2:2–3; Ezekiel 20:40; 2 Nephi 12:2–3).
- *Bethlehem as the birthplace of Jesus Christ*: "But thou, Beth-lehem Ephratah, though thou be little among the thousands of Judah, yet out of thee shall he come forth unto me that is to be ruler in Israel; whose goings forth have been from of old, from everlasting" (Micah 5:2; the only Old Testament reference to the birthplace of the Redeemer).
- *Essence of the gospel*: "He hath shewed thee, O man, what *is* good; and what doth the Lord require of thee, but to do justly, and to love mercy, and to walk humbly with thy God?" (Micah 6:8).
- *Mercy of the Lord in the days of the Restoration*: "He delighteth in mercy. He will turn again, he will have compassion upon us; he will subdue our iniquities; and thou wilt cast all their sins into the depths of the sea. Thou wilt perform the truth to Jacob, and the mercy to Abraham, which thou hast sworn unto our fathers from the days of old" (Micah 7:18–20).

Such passages give us strength to serve with greater devotion in helping those in need and in building up the kingdom of God.

Pondering: How can we improve in our commitment to do justly, love mercy, and walk humbly with God? How can we show our gratitude for the blessing of being gathered with loved ones to holy places of security and light—the homes, stakes, and temples of Zion?

AGENDA FOR ACTION

Under the Abrahamic covenant (see Abraham 2:8–11), all of Israel is called into service to carry the gospel of salvation and the blessings of the priesthood throughout the world. The messages of General Authorities in our day frequently include inspiring and uplifting reports on how the gospel is transforming the lives of the Lord's children in all quarters of the earth. Such reports provide dynamic substance for our family home evening gatherings and serve to enrich our teaching moments and testimony bearing. In that same spirit, we can heed the promptings of the Holy Ghost to reach out in love to all who are seeking for the truth. We can serve in mercy and humility to spread the message of the gospel of Jesus Christ with boldness yet kindness. We can assist the Lord in gathering His faithful sons and daughters to the mountain of the Lord's house where eternal blessings of glory and light flow without end. Since the Lord loves all people, we can follow in His footsteps to serve them in kindness and love.

Looking Forward: How should we respond personally to the loving kindness of the Lord?

CHAPTER THIRTY-FOUR

THE LOVINGKINDNESS OF THE LORD

GOSPEL DOCTRINE READING ASSIGNMENT: HOSEA 1–3, 11, 13–14

For there is no saviour beside me. (Hosea 13:4)

HEAR THE WORDS OF THE PROPHET

Hosea (meaning "salvation") is the only prophet of the Northern Kingdom whose writings have been handed down to us as part of the canon. Hosea reflects the universal theme of all the prophets of God: that God is holy and supreme and that happiness and joy can flow to mankind only through obedience to His laws and commandments. Though the people trek through darkness and misery because of their iniquity, the Lord in His loving kindness and mercy will remember them in His own due time and guide them back onto the pathway toward redemption. In short, the theme of Hosea is love.

How do the words of Hosea relate to our personal lives? What thoughts and feelings might Hosea have experienced while on the errand of the Lord? How do these thoughts and feelings relate to our own ponderings and aspirations? Contemplate the following possibility, based on this prophet's own account in the book of Hosea:

A TOUCH OF REALITY

In the predawn coolness he made his way down the narrow pathway leading away from the city of Gilead. He carried heavy sadness within his heart. Once again the people had rejected his message. For days he had pleaded with them to give up their sinful ways and turn back to the Lord—they would hear none of it. He recalled the whisperings of the Spirit: "Gilead is a city of them that work iniquity, and is polluted with blood" (Hosea 6:8). He remembered seeking a morsel of bread from a baker who simply laughed at him, saying that the bread had all been consumed by the oven's fire during the night. Such is the fate of Israel, thought Hosea, "For they have made ready their heart like an oven, whiles they lie in wait: their baker sleepeth all the night; in the morning it burneth as a flaming fire" (7:6). He knew the design of the Lord: "My God will cast them away, because they did not hearken unto him: and they shall be wanderers among the nations" (9:17).

And I too shall continue to wander, he thought, thinking anxiously about his family waiting for him in the valley below. How he longed to see them again and find them well and secure after his long journey on the errand of the Lord. In that instant, he sensed a tingling in his nostrils, an aroma flowing to him from a grove of trees off in the distance. He shook his head in disgust when he recognized it—incense from a ceremony being carried out by the people of Gilead—worshippers of the cult god Baal (see 2:13). They've forgotten the Lord, he thought. "They sacrifice upon the tops of the mountains, and burn incense upon the hills, under oaks and poplars and elms, because the shadow thereof is good" (4:13), thus allowing them to hide in their immorality. He thought of the word of the Lord: "Woe unto them! for they have fled from me: destruction unto them! because they have transgressed against me: though I have redeemed them, yet they have spoken lies against me" (7:13; see also 8:12; 11:1–4).

He shook his head in sorrow. They will be scattered. He thought fondly of his older son, a choice lad to whom the Lord had given the symbolic name Jezreel (see 1:4), meaning "God will scatter." Yes, he thought, Jezreel is a reminder of the design of the Lord to teach His wayward people to return to the pathway of righteousness: "Though they bring up their children, yet will I bereave them, that there shall not be a man left: yea, woe also to them when I depart from them!" (9:12). How Hosea longed to take Jezreel into his arms and join with him and his other family members to worship the Lord in a spirit of joy and hope. I will see them soon, he thought.

Then he caught sight of an object partially hidden beneath the underbrush off to his left. He stopped and picked it up. It was a broken bow discarded by some unknown hunter. Hosea heard within his soul the warnings of the Lord: "And it shall come to pass at that day, that I will break the bow of Israel in the valley of Jezreel" (1:5). A lesson must needs be learned, he thought, knowing in his heart that a new era would someday commence in which Israel would be gathered together once again in righteousness, just as he would soon rejoin his family in the valley below.

He quickened his pace as he passed by a broken wall surrounded by thorns and thistles and covered with the moisture of the morning dew. The words of the Lord came to his mind: "Therefore, behold, I will hedge up thy way with thorns, and make a wall, that she shall not find her paths" (2:6).

Hosea felt the touch of the morning breeze blowing across his face as if to remind him of the prophecy sent forth by the Lord through his lips: "The wind hath bound her up in her wings, and they shall be ashamed because of their sacrifices" (4:19; see also 12:1), for "they have not known the LORD" (5:4). "Therefore they shall be as the morning cloud, and as the early dew that passeth away" (13:3; see also 6:4). But his gloom was dispelled as he feasted once again upon the glorious promise of a merciful Lord: "Yet I am the LORD thy God from the land of Egypt, and thou shalt know no god but me: for there is no saviour beside me" (13:4).

Better times will come, he reassured himself. Then, as he continued speedily down the pathway of the rocky terrain, his mind focused on his beautiful daughter. To her, the Lord had given a special name, Lo-ruhamah (see 1:6), which means "without love or pity." Yes, she was a wonderful girl, full of love and kind to everyone—but her symbolic name was a reminder that the people of Israel had abandoned the love and pity of the Lord through their unrighteousness: "For I will no more have mercy upon the house of Israel; but I will utterly take them away" (1:6). But as Hosea thought of his daughter, he smiled in remembrance of the Lord's promise: "Yet the number of the children of Israel shall be as the sand of the sea, which cannot be measured nor numbered; and it shall come to pass, that in the place where it was

When did Hosea serve?

He prophesied in the eighth century B.C., probably in the latter reign of Jeroboam II, down to the time of the ministry of Isaiah, who prophesied in the Southern Kingdom from 740 B.C. to 701 B.C. The ministry of Hosea preceded the scattering of Israel around 721 B.C.

said unto them, Ye are not my people, there it shall be said unto them, Ye are the sons [and daughters] of the living God. Then shall the children of Judah and the children of Israel be gathered together" (1:10–11).

As the sky began to brighten along the eastern horizon, he crossed a small stream flowing through a field where a few sheep were feeding on the vegetation—alone and without the guidance of a shepherd. The foam along the edge of the stream reminded Hosea of the fate of Israel: "As for Samaria, her king is cut off as the foam upon the water" (10:7). The flock of sheep also called to mind the sad condition of the Lord's people of that day: "They shall go with their flocks and with their herds to seek the Lord; but they shall not find him; he hath withdrawn himself from them" (5:6).

Farther down the slope, a farmer came into view as he worked the soil of his land in preparation for the planting. Hosea nodded silently as he recounted the wise counsel of the Lord: "Sow to yourselves in righteousness, reap in mercy; break up your fallow ground: for it is time to seek the Lord, till he come and rain righteousness upon you" (10:12).

Suddenly, a dove startled him, rising up on flapping wings without warning and disappearing into the trees. He remembered the whisperings of the Spirit: "Ephraim also is like a silly dove without heart: . . . I will spread my net upon them; I will bring them down as the fowls of the heaven; I will chastise them, as their congregation hath heard" (7:11–12). Moreover, "As for Ephraim, their glory shall fly away like a bird, from the birth, and from the womb, and from the conception" (9:11; see also 11:11).

As he looked into the sky, his eyes discovered in the far distance an eagle soaring in grand circles of majesty. His heart warmed as he thought about the glory of the Lord's eternal mission of merciful judgment: "Set the trumpet to thy mouth. He shall come as an eagle against the house of the Lord, because they have transgressed my covenant, and trespassed against my law" (8:1). Would the people respond and repent of their ways?

Hosea stopped and held out his hands before him, palms upward. He felt deep humility concerning his calling as a prophet. The Lord had told him, "I have also spoken by the prophets, and I have multiplied visions, and used similitudes, by the ministry of the prophets" (12:10). How Hosea yearned that his service would help to draw the wayward people back onto the chosen path so that they could once again become the Lord's people.

He thought of his younger son, Lo-ammi (see 1:9). How he missed him! The Lord had given the dear child that name—meaning "not my people"—as a symbolic reminder of the grand task to bring the people once again into the fold of righteousness. That glorious era would dawn in the future just as the sun was on this day about to rise. The warning of the prophets was being extended in boldness and power, "For I desired mercy, and not sacrifice; and the knowledge of God more than burnt offerings" (6:6).

At that moment, Hosea heard the roar of a wild animal off in the distance. He froze in place as a chill entered his heart. Then he lifted his head with a sensation of hope as he recalled the Lord's promise concerning the destiny of His people: "They shall walk after the Lord: he shall roar like a lion: when he shall roar, then the children shall tremble from the west" (11:10; see also 5:14–15; 13:7–8). What is the message of the lion? "O Israel, thou hast destroyed thyself; but in me is thine help. I will be thy king: where is any other that may save thee in all thy cities?" (13:9–10). The roar of the lion is the roar of redemption: "I will ransom them from the power of the grave; I will redeem them from death" (13:14).

As he looked down into the valley, Hosea saw the radiant rays of the rising sun beginning to flow warmly over the landscape below. His mind rehearsed the ultimate triumph of goodness and love through the blessings of the merciful Lord as husband to His faithful people: "And I will betroth thee unto me for ever; yea, I will betroth thee unto me in righteousness, and in judgment, and in lovingkindness, and in mercies. I will even betroth thee unto me in faithfulness: and thou shalt know the Lord. . . . and I will have mercy upon her that had not obtained mercy; and I will say to them which were not my people, Thou art my people; and they shall say, Thou art my God" (2:19–20, 23).

In brilliance, the sun then came into full view above the horizon. Hosea stopped briefly and lifted his arms in praise of the Creator and Redeemer. He joyfully remembered the words of the Lord: "Afterward shall the children of Israel return, and seek the Lord their God, and David their king; and shall fear the Lord and his goodness in the latter days" (3:5). "Come, and let us return unto the Lord: for he hath torn, and he will heal us; he hath smitten, and he will bind us up. . . . and we shall live in his sight. Then shall we know, if we follow on to know the Lord: his going forth is prepared as the morning; and he shall come unto us as the rain, as the latter and former rain unto the earth" (6:1–3).

Voices of gladness echoed in his ears. He looked down the pathway and saw in the distance three figures running toward him. His children were racing up to welcome him home! His wife waved from afar. He embraced his children and wept for joy to find them safe. The sunlight illuminated a stately olive tree and a handsome green fir rising nearby. Hosea was overjoyed and grateful to be far away from the groves of Gilead. Together, the four walked down the pathway toward the mother of the family, still waiting below. The mind of the prophet remembered the consoling words of the Lord:

> O Israel, return unto the Lord thy God; for thou hast fallen by thine iniquity. . . .
> I will heal their backsliding, I will love them freely: for mine anger is turned away from him. . . .
> His branches shall spread, and his beauty shall be as the olive tree, and his smell as Lebanon.
> They that dwell under his shadow shall return; . . .
> Ephraim shall say, What have I to do any more with idols? I have heard him, and observed him: I am like a green fir tree. From me is thy fruit found.
> Who is wise, and he shall understand these things? prudent, and he shall know them? for the ways of the Lord are right, and the just shall walk in them. (14:1, 4, 6–9; see also 12:5–6)

WHAT LESSON CAN WE LEARN FROM HOSEA?

1. The Lord corrects, reproves, and disciplines His children when they wander from the strait and narrow pathway—but in His infinite mercy and patience, He will gather them back into the fold through the healing influence of the gospel.

The words of Hosea capture with simplicity the essence of the Lord's message of love and healing: "Come, and let us return unto the Lord: for he hath torn, and he will heal us; he hath smitten, and he will bind us up" (Hosea 6:1).

A former bishop shared the following ideas on this theme:

> The final verse of "Did You Think to Pray?" asks the searching questions, "When sore trials came upon you, did you think to pray? When your soul was full of sorrow, Balm of Gilead did you borrow, at the gates of day?" I remember, as a young bishop many years ago, being approached by a new convert, a young father, who took me aside after a meeting and, in hushed tones, asked me to explain to him the meaning of the phrase "balm of Gilead." His reverential attitude and quiet humility seemed to suggest that he felt it was time to be introduced to yet another of the grand mysteries of the gospel. Smiling, I explained that balm of Gilead was simply a traditional natural remedy from the Holy Land that had healing effects and was widely used by the Israelites. As such, it is a symbol of the love of the Lord and the healing essence of the Atonement. He seemed almost relieved at the simplicity of the principle and went his way with a smile on his face.
>
> Since then, I have thought many times about his question concerning the balm of Gilead, for it is another way of asking, "What is the renewing essence of the gospel?" and, "What is the mystery of the Atonement that it should bring to mankind its miraculous healing influence?" When Joseph was betrayed by his jealous brothers, they sold him into the hands of itinerant Ishmaelite tradesmen who were en route from Gilead to Egypt with camels bearing "spicery and balm and myrrh" (Genesis 37:25). Gilead was a wooded highland region east of Jordan, with many bushes that produced the resin used to make the healing gum or balm known throughout the area. Later, when it was time for Jacob to persuade the Egyptian viceroy—his own missing son, Joseph—to provide food for his family in a time of dire famine, he facilitated the bargain by sending his other sons back to Egypt with gifts of nuts, myrrh, and native balm (see Genesis 43:11). Because forgiveness was the governing nature of Joseph, son of Israel, he took compassion on his family in a time of need and readily forgave his brothers their trespass.
>
> Similarly, because forgiveness is the essence of the divine nature, the Savior readily extends His loving kindness to all mankind. He rescues them from temporal death through the resurrection and from spiritual death through the gospel of repentance. Like the balm of Gilead in the temporal sphere, the balm of the

Atonement is the healing power of salvation proclaimed from the foundation of the earth as the answer to the spiritual quest of mankind. Through the Atonement of Jesus Christ there will be no remaining ailment, no enduring injury—for its renewing curative power is eternal, coming from the "Son of Righteousness" with "healing in his wings" (3 Nephi 25:2). The balm of the Atonement is extended to all—especially to those who slip for a time onto the side roads of worldliness and transgression and need to be gathered back into the fold of the Good Shepherd.

Pondering: How can we increase our faith and hope in the healing power of the gospel? How can we follow the example of the Savior in helping others to stay on the pathway of eternal life?

AGENDA FOR ACTION
When we embrace the eternal principles of the gospel of Jesus Christ and accept the compassionate invitation of the Lord to return home, we receive blessings of peace, harmony, and enduring vitality in our lives. "For there is no saviour beside me" is the unmistakable message of the Lord through his prophet Hosea (Hosea 13:4; see also 2 Nephi 31:21). The Savior often extends His reach of love to His children through the compassionate service of His faithful Saints. We should therefore open our eyes and hearts for more opportunities to become the "balm of Gilead" for those in need. Often small and tender deeds of caring will bring about a wonderful transformation in the lives of those struggling to rise above tribulation and partake of living bread and water.

LOOKING FORWARD: How are the mysteries of God revealed unto mankind?

CHAPTER THIRTY-FIVE

THE DAY OF THE LORD IS NIGH AT HAND

GOSPEL DOCTRINE READING ASSIGNMENT: AMOS 3, 7–9; JOEL 2–3

Seek the Lord, and ye shall live. (Amos 5:6)

WELCOME INTO THE CIRCLE OF THE PROPHETS

AMOS AND JOEL ARE TWO of the twelve prophets with short books in the Old Testament, along with Hosea, Obadiah, Jonah, Micah, Nahum, Habakkuk, Zephaniah, Haggai, Zechariah, and Malachi. Even though these twelve are often referred to as the "minor prophets," their message is not minor but grand and majestic, for they speak with the power of the Lord as ensigns of truth and light to all generations. Like their fellow prophets, Amos and Joel speak a message of contrast, one of darkness as well as light: darkness and warning because of persistent disobedience, and light and encouragement because of the ultimate triumph of the Lord's plan of exaltation. Though at times chastised and scattered because of iniquity, the Lord's people have the opportunity to follow His words and rise through faith and repentance as His destined sons and daughters.

How can we enter the circle of prophets like Amos and Joel and draw counsel and advice for our modern-day lives? The answer comes in the form of two related questions: Do we need the guidance of living prophets today? And what can we lay up in store to survive the effects of spiritual darkness or famine?

These answers come directly from the Lord. Amos proclaimed, "Surely the Lord GOD will do nothing, but he revealeth his secret unto his servants the prophets" (Amos 3:7). Joel prophesied of the coming flow of eternal nourishment: "And it shall come to pass afterward, that I will pour out my spirit upon all flesh; and your sons and your daughters shall prophesy, your old men shall dream dreams, your young men shall see visions: And also upon the servants and upon the handmaids in those days will I pour out my spirit" (Joel 2:28–29). These profound words of the prophets still resonate. Said the Lord, "Is not my word like as a fire?" (Jeremiah 23:29). Indeed it is, for His living words kindle the flame of spiritual vitality in all dispensations.

How does the prophetic flame of truth empower our lives today?

A TOUCH OF REALITY

One example of the need for living prophets is "The Family: A Proclamation to the World," read by President Gordon B. Hinckley at the general Relief Society meeting in 1995. Among the inspired words were the following:

> We, the First Presidency and the Council of the Twelve Apostles of The Church of Jesus Christ of Latter-day Saints, solemnly proclaim that marriage between a man and a woman is ordained of God and that the family is central to the Creator's plan for the eternal destiny of His children. . . . Happiness in family life is most likely to be achieved when founded upon the teachings of the Lord Jesus Christ. . . . Further, we warn that the disintegration of the family will bring upon individuals, communities, and nations the calamities foretold by ancient and modern prophets.

That stirring message of inspiration and warning spread as a flame of truth around the world, lighting within the souls of millions the spirit of improved family devotion. Similarly, the announcement about the younger age for new missionaries given by President Thomas S. Monson at general conference in October 2012 ignited the flame of inspiration and motivation in the hearts of thousands of young men and women around the world. Through the blessings of heaven, the Spirit of the Lord continues to direct the words of living prophets in the lives of Saints across the world.

WHAT LESSONS CAN WE LEARN FROM AMOS AND JOEL?

1. The Lord accomplishes His work and glory through the service of His chosen prophets in all dispensations.

Paul, a master of the history of the Lord's prophets over the ages, confirmed that "God hath chosen the weak things of the world to confound the things which are mighty" (1 Corinthians 1:27). Amos was one of those chosen "weak things," a humble man who said of his origins, "I was no prophet, neither was I a prophet's son; but I was an herdman, and a gatherer of sycomore fruit: And the LORD took me as I followed the flock, and the LORD said unto me, Go, prophesy unto my people Israel" (Amos 7:14–15).

Even though Amos lived in a community near Jerusalem, the Lord sent him to preach repentance to the people of the Northern Kingdom or Israel. Though the people had been continually blessed with deliverance and sustenance over generations, the message was piercing: "Yet have ye not returned unto me, saith the LORD" (Amos 4:6; repeated four more times in that chapter). Nevertheless, the promise of heaven could still brighten their lives:

> For thus saith the LORD unto the house of Israel, Seek ye me, and ye shall live; . . . Seek the LORD, and ye shall live; . . . Seek good, and not evil, that ye may live: and so the LORD, the God of hosts, shall be with you, as ye have spoken." (Amos 5:4, 6, 14)

However, the warning voice of the prophet still resounded against those who denied the Lord and placed their confidence in worldly influences. Said Amos, "WOE to them that are at ease in Zion" (Amos 6:1). Nephi would sound the same warning several generations later: "Therefore, wo

When did Amos and Joel serve?

Amos prophesied during the reigns of King Uzziah of Judah and King Jeroboam II of Israel, who both passed away around the middle of the eighth century B.C. Amos served prior to the ministry of Isaiah (740 to 701 B.C.).

The time span of Joel's writings is not known for certain—it could be as early as the ninth century B.C. or as late as the return from the Babylonian captivity following the decree of liberation issued by Cyrus in 537 B.C. Some believe Joel prophesied even later, around 400 B.C. Regardless of when he lived, his message is timeless.

be unto him that is at ease in Zion! . . . Yea, wo be unto him that hearkeneth unto the precepts of men, and denieth the power of God, and the gift of the Holy Ghost!" (2 Nephi 28:24, 26). Amos made crystal clear the consequences of ignoring covenant promises: "Israel shall surely be led away captive out of their own land" (Amos 7:11; see also verse 17). That is precisely what took place in 721 B.C. when the Assyrians captured and scattered the ten tribes of Israel.

The prophesies of Amos were to reach far beyond his time and extend to the latter days as well: "Behold, the days come, saith the Lord God, that I will send a famine in the land, not a famine of bread, nor a thirst for water, but of hearing the words of the Lord: And they shall wander from sea to sea, and from the north even to the east, they shall run to and fro to seek the word of the Lord, and shall not find it" (Amos 8:11–12). It was in that future time of spiritual famine that the dawning of the Restoration would bring new light and glory into the world, for the Lord had decreed that His people would again be gathered into His fold:

> And I will bring again the captivity of my people of Israel, and they shall build the waste cities, and inhabit them; and they shall plant vineyards, and drink the wine thereof; they shall also make gardens, and eat the fruit of them.
>
> And I will plant them upon their land, and they shall no more be pulled up out of their land which I have given them, saith the Lord thy God. (Amos 9:14–15)

That process of gathering commenced through the ministry of yet another one of the "weak things of the world," the young Prophet Joseph Smith, whose ministry served to bring about the Restoration in our day: "Verily, thus saith the Lord unto you, my servant Joseph Smith, I am well pleased with your offering and acknowledgments, which you have made; for unto this end have I raised you up, that I might show forth my wisdom through the weak things of the earth" (D&C 124:1; see also D&C 1:19–20; 35:13; 133:59).

We all belong to the "weak things" of the world who are nurtured and sustained by the blessings of heaven so that we can grow and be magnified by the Holy Spirit in realizing our eternal destiny. In gratitude, we can follow the words of the prophets of old as well as the prophets of our time, from Joseph Smith onward to living prophets of today.

To the world, it is a strange thing that the Lord has once again restored the prophetic office to the earth. How are prophets to be viewed and received in this modern-day culture of relative values and materialistic aspirations?

An interesting event in the life of the Prophet Joseph Smith illustrates the gulf that modern thinkers tend to erect between themselves and those who profess to be prophets. On Friday morning, November 6, 1835, Joseph was introduced to a man from the eastern part of the country. The man expressed surprise upon meeting the Prophet.

> After hearing my name, he remarked that I was nothing but a man, indicating by this expression, that he had supposed that a person to whom the Lord should see fit to reveal His will, must be something more than a man. He seemed to have forgotten the saying that fell from the lips of St. James, that Elias [i.e., Elijah] was a man subject to like passions as we are, yet he had such power with God, that He, in answer to his prayers, shut the heavens that they gave no rain for the space of three years and six months; and again, in answer to his prayer, the heavens gave forth rain, and the earth gave forth fruit [James 5:17–18; see also 1 Kings 17:1; 18:45]. Indeed, such is the darkness and ignorance of this generation, that they look upon it as incredible that a man should have any intercourse with his Maker. (*HC* 2:302)

To the Saints of God, it is no incredible thing that prophets speak again for the Lord. It is the most normal of all procedures to accept and honor the living oracles of the heavens. It is a privilege to ponder their words and to savor the wisdom they impart through inspiration—for we know that they reflect the truth of the gospel. As the Lord stated at the end of section 1 of the Doctrine and Covenants, "What I the Lord have spoken, I have spoken, and I excuse not myself; and though the heavens and the earth pass away, my word shall not pass away, but shall all be fulfilled, whether by mine own voice or by the voice of my servants, it is the same" (D&C 1:38). Again, the words of Amos, given in the Joseph Smith Translation, proclaim: "Surely the Lord God will do nothing, until he revealeth the secret unto his servants the prophets" (JST, Amos 3:7).

Pondering: How can we do better each day in following the counsel of the living prophets with faith and good cheer? How can we help our loved ones to do the same?

2. The message of the Lord's prophets is not only one of warning but also of the promise of glory for the faithful.
The prophet Joel revealed the pattern of life for us all to follow:

> Therefore also now, saith the Lord, turn ye even to me with all your heart, and with fasting, and with weeping, and with mourning: . . . and turn unto the Lord your God: for he is gracious and merciful, slow to anger, and of great kindness, and repenteth him of the evil. . . . Fear not, O land; be glad and rejoice: for the Lord will do great things. (Joel 2:12–13, 21)

During a period of serious drought in Judah, Joel reminded his listeners that a time would come in the future when a great spiritual drought would be relieved through the blessings of the Spirit of the Lord prior to the Second Coming:

> And it shall come to pass afterward, that I will pour out my spirit upon all flesh; and your sons and your daughters shall prophesy, your old men shall dream dreams, your young men shall see visions:
> And also upon the servants and upon the handmaids in those days will I pour out my spirit. . . .
> And it shall come to pass, that whosoever shall call on the name of the Lord shall be delivered: for in mount Zion and in Jerusalem shall be deliverance, as the Lord hath said, and in the remnant whom the Lord shall call. (Joel 2:28–29, 32)

Peter remembered Joel's encouraging words on the Day of Pentecost (see Acts 2:16–21), and Joseph Smith was reminded by the angel Moroni of the significance of these same ancient words: "He also quoted the second chapter of Joel, from the twenty-eighth verse to the last. He also said that this was not yet fulfilled, but was soon to be" (JS—H 1:41). Thus the message of Joel is the timeless message of the love of God and His everlasting kindness in endowing His children with exalting truth and the majesty of His Spirit. Truly, all who receive a testimony of the Savior through the Holy Spirit are endowed with the spirit of prophecy and revelation (see 1 Corinthians 12:3; Alma 17:2–3). In this sense, we can remember and understand the utterance of Moses to the young Joshua: "Would God that all the Lord's people were prophets, and that the Lord would put his spirit upon them!" (Numbers 11:29).

How can we make the enduring warmth of the gospel a central part of our lives? How can we maintain a cheerful heart when our assignments seem heavy and our burdens challenging? We can follow the example of an Apostle as preserved in the words of an LDS missionary many years ago:

> It was a cold winter when I was serving in the mission home as an assistant to the mission president. We looked forward to the coming visit of Marion G. Romney, then a member of the Quorum of the Twelve Apostles. There was among the staff the usual sense of nervousness concerning the presence of such a high-level servant of the Lord. On the day he arrived, we all gathered in the dining area to join him at dinnertime. Because of the winter season, the temperature in the room was rather cold, adding some shivering to the occasion. We all looked anxiously toward the Apostle sitting at the head of the table. He smiled and said, "Many are cold, but few are frozen." We all chuckled at his pleasant sense of humor—and his visit continued in good spirits as he encouraged and counseled us to carry on our service in the spirit of faithfulness and good cheer.

Pondering: How can we find light and glory shining through the shadows of our mortal experience? How can we demonstrate our worthiness to maintain a place in the circle of Saints upon whom the Lord is pouring out His Spirit? How can we reach out and help others draw closer to the Master?

AGENDA FOR ACTION
We can do as Amos counseled: "Seek the Lord, and ye shall live" (Amos 5:6). We can follow the words of Joel and "turn unto the Lord your God: for he is gracious and merciful, slow to anger, and of great kindness" (Joel 2:13). We can

be drawn forward by the light and warmth of the gospel of Jesus Christ and leave behind us forever the darkness of doubt and waywardness. To follow the prophets is the key to the gateway of eternal glory and peace. We can listen to the messages delivered by the living prophets at general conference. We can prayerfully review their speeches and apply those that have particular relevance for our circumstances. The advice of King Benjamin is particularly pertinent for us all: "And now, if you believe all these things see that ye do them" (Mosiah 4:10).

LOOKING FORWARD: Where can we find safety and protection from all worldly influences?

CHAPTER THIRTY-SIX

GREAT ARE THE WORDS OF ISAIAH

GOSPEL DOCTRINE READING ASSIGNMENT: ISAIAH 1–6

O house of Jacob, come ye, and let us walk in the light of the LORD. (Isaiah 2:5)

THE ARCHES OF TIME

ISAIAH PROPHESIED FROM 740 TO 701 B.C.—but his audience includes God's children in all dispensations. The resurrected Lord declared,

> Yea, a commandment I give unto you that ye search these things diligently; for great are the words of Isaiah.
>
> For surely he spake as touching all things concerning my people which are of the house of Israel; therefore it must needs be that he must speak also to the Gentiles.
>
> And all things that he spake have been and shall be, even according to the words which he spake. (3 Nephi 23:1–3)

Isaiah was blessed with a gift of conveying the word of the Lord with such power that his readers are able to "mount up with wings as eagles" (Isaiah 40:31) and soar to a higher perspective, where the full panorama of God's dealings with His children—from beginning to end—is brought clearly into view. In beautiful and symbolic imagery, Isaiah intermingles references to events of his own day, those of earlier times, and those that were to unfold in the future—thus enabling his readers to experience the breathtaking sweep of the arches of time—from the distant past to the distant future and back again, often within the same passage. As an example, ponder the following famous prophecy from Isaiah:

> And the LORD will create upon every dwelling place of mount Zion, and upon her assemblies, a cloud and smoke by day, and the shining of a flaming fire by night: for upon all the glory shall be a defence.
>
> And there shall be a tabernacle for a shadow in the daytime from the heat, and for a place of refuge, and for a covert from storm and from rain. (Isaiah 4:5–6; see also 2 Nephi 14:5–6)

Echoes of the distant past resound in these words as a reminder of the miracles of the Exodus—with the heavenly cloud, flaming fire, tabernacle, and deliverance at the hands of a merciful God. Isaiah's contemporaries—knowing the immediate dangers threatening—would surely have longed for the golden years, free from bondage and under divine guidance. Isaiah's view included the future, revealing how the same protective shield of glory would, in the last days, be poured out on dwellings, congregations, and tabernacles (temples) of the Lord. Ancient blessings would be restored anew. Defense and refuge, protection and shelter—these grand rewards of covenant worthiness blend together according to the eternal promise of a loving God. In grand and sweeping language, Isaiah takes us on a journey from centuries ago to the glory of the millennial era—in just two sentences!

How far into the future does this prophecy go? In 1874, Orson Pratt, one of the members of the original Quorum of the Twelve, discussed this prophecy in a speech in the Salt Lake Tabernacle: "I do not see any cloud covering this house, or the congregation that is before me. . . . But in the latter days there will be a people so pure in Mount Zion, with a house established upon the tops of the mountains, that God will manifest himself, not only in their temple and upon all their assemblies, with a visible cloud during the day, but when the night shall come, if they shall be assembled for worship, God will meet with them by his pillar of fire; and when they retire to their habitations, behold each habitation will be lighted up by the glory of God,—a pillar of flaming fire by night."[19]

Thus the words of Isaiah lift us across the arches of time to give us hope for a better future.

A TOUCH OF REALITY

How can students, teachers, and parents make it easier to apply Isaiah's lofty themes and poetic language to everyday living? The following thoughts might help to stimulate productive ideas:

What does a refrigerator have in common with Isaiah? When my children were very small, I used to enjoy placing them safely, one at a time, on top of our refrigerator, their little legs hanging down and their eyes wide open with anticipation. They seemed to enjoy for a short time a new vista across the full extent of the room and the lofty position of being above everyone else, including their father, waiting below as a guardian and protector against the daunting height. I would say, "When you have enough faith, jump down, and I promise I will catch you." Then, when they had built up enough courage, they would jump down into my waiting arms and enjoy a dizzying ride around and around before being gently dropped to their feet on the floor, where they would say, "Let's do it again!" This same practice has been continued with small grandchildren, who invariably insist that the ceremony be repeated over and over again as long as Grandpa's back can endure the challenge.

Life is an endless flow of opportunities to find new vistas that afford the privilege of seeing farther and farther into the distance—whether from the top of a fridge, the summit of a lofty mountain range, or the windows of an airplane as it rises into the higher reaches of the atmosphere, where the view of the earth below is always captivating. Moreover, now that space travel is a reality, we can even see, for the first time in history, the entire earth hanging in space as an exquisite jewel of vitality.

Many of us remember being glued to our television screens on July 20, 1969, watching spellbound as Neil Armstrong stepped from the Eagle lunar module and onto the surface of the moon, uttering the now historic phrase, "That's one small step for man, one giant leap for mankind." The spectacular color images of the earth captured on that Apollo 11 mission, and on subsequent space flights, allowed earthlings the first recorded glimpses of their magnificent

19   *Journal of Discourses*, 16:82.

blue-green, cloud-shrouded home as seen from a heavenly perspective. But these views of earth were not the first to be seen by mortals. As Moses was being instructed of the Lord a millennia before that, he "cast his eyes and beheld the earth, yea, even all of it; and there was not a particle of it which he did not behold, discerning it by the spirit of God" (Moses 1:27). Similarly, with a spiritual eye, Moroni saw his future readership: "Behold, I speak unto you as if ye were present, and yet ye are not. But behold, Jesus Christ hath shown you unto me, and I know your doing" (Mormon 8:35). It is reasonable to conclude that all of the Lord's prophets are blessed with this kind of visionary gift that enables them to lift their listeners from the confines of our mortal landscape and teach us saving truths from the Lord's perspective.

Said the Lord, "All things are present with me, for I know them all" (Moses 1:6). What is continually before the Lord is shared freely with His sons and daughters through His Spirit—at least "all things that are expedient for them" (D&C 75:10; compare 2 Nephi 3:19). Thus Isaiah was able to experience and share his magnificent panoramic vision of the unfolding of Israel's destiny, stretching in great arches from the beginning of time to the Second Coming and beyond, seeing all as if from a divine perspective. Isaiah's poetic pronouncements constitute, as it were, a visionary space flight more stunning and compelling than anything man's innovations could hope to imitate. No wonder Nephi said, "My soul delighteth in the words of Isaiah" (2 Nephi 25:5; see also 2 Nephi 11:2; 1 Nephi 19:23–24). No wonder the Savior commanded the Nephites to "search these things diligently, for great are the words of Isaiah" (3 Nephi 23:1).

Isaiah's extraordinary flight of soaring discourse takes us to the highest possible perspective—the perspective of God Himself—in order to teach Israel's remnants the refreshing and inspiring lessons of hope and redemption through the Atonement of the Savior.

Returning from an experience with Isaiah is analogous, in a way, to a homecoming from a hike through the high mountains, the safe landing of an aircraft after a long journey, or the return of a space vehicle to earth. If you will forgive an even more domestic comparison, just as the little grandchildren like to be lifted up and then repeatedly jump into the arms of the waiting grandfather below, we can, in like measure, "mount up with wings as eagles" (Isaiah 40:31) to the upper reaches of spiritual insight and discernment through the visions of Isaiah, and then return with greater confidence and understanding into the arms of the Savior, ready to say with faith and exuberance, "Let's do it again!"

WHAT LESSONS CAN WE LEARN FROM THE EARLY CHAPTERS OF ISAIAH?

1. Through the Atonement of Jesus Christ, we can receive forgiveness and redemption.

Isaiah ministered during the reign of several kings of Judah: Uzziah, Jotham, Ahaz, and Hezekiah (see Isaiah 1:1)—a period marked by the intense struggles of the people to return to a state of greater obedience before the Lord. Isaiah preached the gospel of repentance and redemption. He warned the people: "Woe unto them that call evil good, and good evil; that put darkness for light, and light for darkness; that put bitter for sweet, and sweet for bitter!" (Isaiah 5:20; also 2 Nephi 15:20). Even Isaiah, when he was called as prophet, felt humbly inadequate to the task: "Then said I, Woe is me! for I am undone; because I am a man of unclean lips, and I dwell in the midst of a people of unclean lips: for mine eyes have seen the King, the LORD of hosts" (Isaiah 6:5). But with the blessings of redemption and strength from heaven, Isaiah rose to the challenge, saying, "Here am I; send me" (Isaiah 6:8)—an echo of the very words the Savior said in the grand premortal council: "And the Lord said: Whom shall I send? And one answered like unto the Son of Man: Here am I, send me" (Abraham 3:27).

In the opening chapter of Isaiah, we find a precious gem of truth: "Come now, and let us reason together, saith the LORD: though your sins be as scarlet, they shall be as white as snow; though they be red like crimson, they shall be as wool. . . . Zion shall be redeemed with judgment, and her converts with righteousness" (Isaiah 1:18, 27). How can our scarlet sins be made white as snow and our crimson misdeeds be transformed into the lightness of wool? "Wash you, make you clean; put away the evil of your doings from before mine eyes; cease to do evil; Learn to do well; seek judgment, relieve the oppressed, judge the fatherless, plead for the widow" (Isaiah 1:16–17). Repentance, clean living, service to others—that is the pattern of covenant wisdom—and the lesson of the wisdom tooth as recounted by a former bishop:

For many years that impacted tooth had been dormant—a phantom object barely protruding from the gum. From time to time, various dentists had warned that it really should come out. But it had not offered any challenges—no pain, no discomfort. It had just continued its valueless existence as a kind of bothersome condition that one worries about under the surface of daily life. "This looks like it might be getting some decay," said yet another a year or so ago. No action—until, upon the most recent visit, the medical expert made it clear that this tooth was headed for trouble that could have far-reaching implications for health and well-being. Finally, action was taken, and within a half hour, the decades-old problem was history. It would have taken the same half hour decades ago. Procrastination doesn't help.

Spiritual wisdom teeth are very much like that. Sometimes there are spiritual conditions that call for review, correction, rejuvenation. Sometimes there is a history of transgression that calls for action. Sometimes the old impacted memories need to be brought forward so they can be subjected to spiritual correction: "For godly sorrow worketh repentance to salvation" (2 Corinthians 7:10). Rather than carrying an impacted burden for decades, we can find relief by taking immediate and decisive action, based on sincere, prayerful penitence. As needed, the guidance of loving ecclesiastical leaders can bring about a wondrous effect, leading to peace and solace.

That troublesome wisdom tooth decaying below the surface can be gone forever, opening up the channels of pure communication once more with our Father in Heaven. It's true that some conditions may take longer than others to heal, but action leading to that process of healing can be taken immediately. Amulek said, "Yea, I would that ye would come forth and harden not your hearts any longer; for behold, now is the time and the day of your salvation; and therefore, if ye will repent and harden not your hearts, immediately shall the great plan of redemption be brought about unto you" (Alma 34:31). May we all examine our spiritual condition and ensure that any troublesome wisdom teeth are removed—sooner rather than later.

Pondering: In what areas of our life can we step forward and do better in living the gospel and pleasing the Lord? In what ways can we say to the Lord with greater worthiness, "Here am I; send me"?

2. We experience today the fulfillment of Isaiah's prophecy about the Restoration of the fulness of the gospel of Jesus Christ. Isaiah declared these sublime words of prophecy:

> And it shall come to pass in the last days, that the mountain of the LORD's house shall be established in the top of the mountains, and shall be exalted above the hills; and all nations shall flow unto it.
>
> And many people shall go and say, Come ye, and let us go up to the mountain of the LORD, to the house of the God of Jacob; and he will teach us of his ways, and we will walk in his paths: for out of Zion shall go forth the law, and the word of the LORD from Jerusalem. (Isaiah 2:2–3; see also the similar words in Micah 4:1–2; 2 Nephi 12:2–3)

In these two verses are combined the essence of Israelite history, American history, the Restoration of the fulness of the gospel in the dispensation of the fulness of times, and the glory of temple work spreading over the earth in the last days. Isaiah's words thunder across the arches of time to confirm the reality of the Lord's ongoing work to "bring to pass the immortality and eternal life of man" (Moses 1:39).

How does this prophecy touch our lives today? A number of years ago, Harold B. Lee shared his thoughts concerning the phrase "for out of Zion shall go forth the law" (Isaiah 2:3). He was present at the dedication of the Idaho Falls temple in September 1945 and heard President George Albert Smith's inspired words explaining the meaning of Isaiah's phrase:

> We thank thee that thou hast revealed to us that those who gave us our constitutional form of government were men wise in thy sight and that thou didst raise them up for the very purpose of putting forth that sacred document [as revealed in Doctrine and Covenants section 101]. . . . We pray that kings and rulers and the

peoples of all nations under heaven may be persuaded of the blessings enjoyed by the people of this land by reason of their freedom and under thy guidance and be constrained to adopt similar governmental systems, thus to fulfill the ancient prophecy of Isaiah and Micah that . . . "out of Zion shall go forth the law and the word of the Lord from Jerusalem."[20]

Isaiah foresaw the day when a great Gentile nation would arise based on laws that were consonant with celestial principles—a seedbed for the Restoration and the establishment of Zion. Just as the everlasting influence of the Savior would emanate from His earthly ministry in Jerusalem, so would the glory of the Restoration emanate from "the mountain of the Lord's house" in the New Jerusalem as an ensign of light (see Isaiah 5:26–27)—and all nations would flow unto it.

Pondering: How can we show our eternal gratitude to the Lord for making available to us and our families the blessings of the Restoration and the establishment once again of sacred temple work?

AGENDA FOR ACTION

In all humility and devotion, we can follow the counsel of Isaiah to assist in building up Zion in these, the latter days. We can cultivate a "godly walk and conversation" (D&C 20:69) and "gather together, and stand in holy places" (D&C 101:22)—homes, congregations, and temples of the Lord—illuminated and protected by the light of the gospel of Jesus Christ. We can also add our own beam of righteous endeavor to the glory of God and thus declare, as Isaiah reported: "Holy, holy, holy, is the Lord of hosts: the whole earth is full of his glory" (Isaiah 6:3; see also Isaiah 4:2–3). With the inspiration of the Lord we can displace without delay any worldliness lingering within our system and replace such impediments with gems of pure gospel wisdom that will enrich and edify our lives in keeping with gospel principles.

LOOKING FORWARD: What is the nature of the "marvelous work and a wonder" foreseen by Isaiah (see Isaiah 29:14)?

---

20   *Improvement Era*, October 1945, 564; Donald W. Parry, Jay A. Parry, and Tina M. Peterson, *Understanding Isaiah* (Salt Lake City: Deseret Book, 1998), 27.

CHAPTER THIRTY-SEVEN

LOOK UNTO THE LORD

GOSPEL DOCTRINE READING ASSIGNMENT: ISAIAH 22, 24–26, 28–30

O LORD, thou art my God; I will exalt thee, I will praise thy name; for thou hast done wonderful things. (Isaiah 25:1)

UNDERSTANDING ISAIAH

THE WORDS OF ISAIAH BLEND into a radiant tapestry of profound historical insight, poetic symbolism, and prophetic majesty. The Lord said, "Search these things diligently; for great are the words of Isaiah" (3 Nephi 23:1). How can we come to understand these passages more fully and apply them to our lives?

Nephi, who commenced his ministry just a century after Isaiah's passing, has given us a plain and simple pattern to follow in order to understand Isaiah's messages. This approach consists of five steps: (1) focus centrally on the guiding theme: Jesus Christ as Redeemer; (2) follow the Spirit as you ponder and study; (3) learn line upon line and precept upon precept as you gradually increase in knowledge; (4) personalize the message by likening it unto yourself; and (5) act upon your increased understanding and share with others your witness of the truth of the things you're learning.

Let us consider Nephi's own words in relation to these five steps and show how they harmonize with the words of Isaiah:

- *Focus on Christ*: "And when the day cometh that the Only Begotten of the Father, yea, even the Father of heaven and of earth, shall manifest himself unto them in the flesh, behold, they will reject him, because of their iniquities, and the hardness of their hearts, and the stiffness of their necks. Behold, they will crucify him; and after he is laid in a sepulchre for the space of three days he shall rise from the dead, with healing in his wings; and all those who shall believe on his name shall be saved in the kingdom of God. Wherefore, my soul delighteth to prophesy concerning him, for I have seen his day, and my heart doth magnify his holy name" (2 Nephi 25:12–13). Moreover: "And the Lord will set his hand again the second time to restore his people from their lost and fallen state. Wherefore, he will proceed to do a marvelous work and a wonder among the children of men. Wherefore, he shall bring forth his words unto them, which words shall judge them at the last day, for they shall be given them for the purpose of convincing them of the true Messiah" (2 Nephi 25:17–18).

» Compare the words of Isaiah about focusing on Christ: "For unto us a child is born, unto us a son is given: and the government shall be upon his shoulder: and his name shall be called Wonderful, Counsellor, The mighty God, The everlasting Father, The Prince of Peace" (Isaiah 9:6). "For I am the LORD thy God, the Holy One of Israel, thy Saviour" (Isaiah 43:3; see also Isaiah 47:4).

- *Follow the Spirit*: "Wherefore, hearken, O my people, which are of the house of Israel, and give ear unto my words; for because the words of Isaiah are not plain unto you, nevertheless they are plain unto all those that are filled with the spirit of prophecy. But I give unto you a prophecy, according to the spirit which is in me; wherefore I shall prophesy according to the plainness which hath been with me from the time that I came out from Jerusalem with my father; for behold, my soul delighteth in plainness unto my people, that they may learn. Yea, and my soul delighteth in the words of Isaiah" (2 Nephi 25:4–5).

» Compare the words of Isaiah about following the Spirit: "I will pour my spirit upon thy seed, and my blessing upon thine offspring" (Isaiah 44:3; see also Isaiah 11:2; 26:9).

- *Learn line upon line*: "For behold, thus saith the Lord God: I will give unto the children of men line upon line, precept upon precept, here a little and there a little; and blessed are those who hearken unto my precepts, and lend an ear unto my counsel, for they shall learn wisdom; for unto him that receiveth I will give more; and from them that shall say, We have enough, from them shall be taken away even that which they have" (2 Nephi 28:30; see also Alma 12:10–11; D&C 50:24).

» Compare the words of Isaiah about learning line upon line: "For precept must be upon precept, precept upon precept; line upon line, line upon line; here a little, and there a little" (Isaiah 28:10; see also verse 13; see also Isaiah 34:16).

- *Liken it unto yourself*: "But that I might more fully persuade them to believe in the Lord their Redeemer I did read unto them that which was written by the prophet Isaiah; for I did liken all scriptures unto us, that it might be for our profit and learning. Wherefore I spake unto them, saying: . . . hear ye the words of the prophet, which were written unto all the house of Israel, and liken them unto yourselves, that ye may have hope as well as your brethren from whom ye have been broken off; for after this manner has the prophet written" (1 Nephi 19:23–24).

» Compare the words of Isaiah about likening it unto yourself: "And thine ears shall hear a word behind thee, saying, This is the way, walk ye in it, when ye turn to the right hand, and when ye turn to the left" (Isaiah 30:21).

- *Share your witness*: "And now I, Nephi, write more of the words of Isaiah, for my soul delighteth in his words. . . . and I will send them forth unto all my children, for he verily saw my Redeemer, even as I have seen him. And my brother, Jacob, also has seen him as I have seen him; wherefore, I will send their words forth unto my children to prove unto them that my words are true. Wherefore, by the words of three, God hath said, I will establish my word. Nevertheless, God sendeth more witnesses, and he proveth all his words" (2 Nephi 11:2–3).

» Compare the words of Isaiah about sharing your witness: "They shall lift up their voice, they shall sing for the majesty of the LORD, they shall cry aloud from the sea. Wherefore glorify ye the LORD" (Isaiah 24:14–15; see also Isaiah 25:9).

How does Nephi's pattern for understanding Isaiah blend with your own approach? The following chart summarizes the five steps and serves as a checklist:

Nephi's Pattern of Plainness for Understanding Isaiah

Follow the Spirit

Learn Line upon Line   Focus on **Christ**   Liken It unto Yourself

Share Your Witness

A TOUCH OF REALITY

She was an angel, a faithful daughter of God. As a full-time missionary, she blessed the lives of many who were seeking after the truth. She lived by the Spirit. She loved the scriptures and cherished the word of God with all her heart.

When her life was blessed with a sweet child, her very first daughter, she pondered how best to nourish this precious soul with spiritual light. She prayed about how to bring the Savior close to this new child as a guide and companion. She felt inspired to use her considerable artistic talent to paint a portrait of her daughter seated on the lap of the Savior. So line by line, and stroke by stroke, she converted her inner vision of this picture into a real-life representation of the warm personal companionship between the Son of God and one of His choice daughters.

Gradually, the picture emerged. The image of the daughter showed her glowing with joy to be so close to the Lord. The Lord held her tenderly with an outpouring of love and compassion. The mother had likened the eternal mercy of the Lord for His children to His personal relationship with her own daughter. When the gift was presented to the child, she was delighted, and her eyes revealed the light of understanding about how the Lord loved her and cared for her. The portrait became a testimony to the daughter—and to everyone in the family circle—of the truth of the gospel of Jesus Christ. Many have looked upon this portrait as an invitation to ponder how they too are sheltered and protected by the Redeemer of mankind. Is it not true that the word of God itself serves as a mirror in which we can discern a living portrait showing how each of us rests upon the lap of the Lord in humility and gratitude for His everlasting mercy and love?

WHAT LESSONS CAN WE LEARN FROM THE MIDDLE CHAPTERS OF ISAIAH?

1. Jesus Christ, the Holy One of Israel, is our Lord and Redeemer.

The words of Isaiah echo our own deep gratitude for the blessings of our Savior: "O Lord, thou art my God; I will exalt thee, I will praise thy name; for thou hast done wonderful things; thy counsels of old are faithfulness and truth" (Isaiah 25:1). The glory of the Lord in the latter days will melt away the darkness of worldly pride: "In that day shall the Lord of hosts be for a crown of glory, and for a diadem of beauty, unto the residue of his people" (Isaiah 28:5). In the dawning of the Restoration, the people will raise their voices of joy in praise of the Lord: "They shall sanctify my name, and sanctify the Holy One of Jacob, and shall fear the God of Israel" (Isaiah 29:23). Anthems of thanksgiving will resound around the world in gratitude for the blessings of the King of Peace (see Isaiah 24:14).

By the design of a loving Lord, blessings of strength and peace await the faithful: "Trust ye in the Lord for ever: for in the Lord Jehovah is everlasting strength: . . . Lord, thou wilt ordain peace for us: for thou also hast wrought all our works in us" (Isaiah 26:4, 12; see also Isaiah 30:18).

How does the Lord bring about these glorious blessings for mankind? A Sunday School teacher used the following approach to guide his youth class in a discussion about the words of Isaiah:

After the opening prayer, the teacher placed three objects on the table: a nail, a key, and a stone. Smiling, he said, "These are the symbols Isaiah used to help us focus on the mission of our Redeemer. Let's consider each one and read the passages from Isaiah."

- *Nail*: "And I will fasten him as a nail in a sure place; and he shall be for a glorious throne to his father's house. . . . In that day, saith the LORD of hosts, shall the nail that is fastened in the sure place be removed, and be cut down, and fall; and the burden that was upon it shall be cut off: for the LORD hath spoken it" (Isaiah 22:23, 25).

The teacher asked, "What do you think the nail refers to?" The class responded with the word *crucifixion*—the nail is a symbol for the atoning sacrifice of our Redeemer.

- *Key*: "And the key of the house of David will I lay upon his shoulder; so he shall open, and none shall shut; and he shall shut, and none shall open" (Isaiah 22:22). "To whom does this refer?" asked the teacher.

The class responded, "Jesus, our Lord."

"And what doors did Jesus open for us?" asked the teacher. They read the following verses:

He will swallow up death in victory; and the Lord GOD will wipe away tears from off all faces; and the rebuke of his people shall he take away from off all the earth: for the LORD hath spoken it. And it shall be said in that day, Lo, this is our God; we have waited for him, and he will save us: this is the LORD; we have waited for him, we will be glad and rejoice in his salvation. (Isaiah 25:8–9)

The class then shared their thoughts about the universal resurrection, after which the teacher asked: "What do you think Isaiah means when he talks about the tears that the Lord will wipe off from our faces?" The class then gave their thoughts about redemption and the forgiveness of sins, noting that all of God's children, even those in the spirit world, have access to this truth: "Open ye the gates, that the righteous nation which keepeth the truth may enter in" (Isaiah 26:2). "And they shall be gathered together, as prisoners are gathered in the pit, and shall be shut up in the prison, and after many days shall they be visited" (Isaiah 24:22).

- *Stone*: "Therefore thus saith the Lord GOD, Behold, I lay in Zion for a foundation a stone, a tried stone, a precious corner stone, a sure foundation: he that believeth shall not make haste" (Isaiah 28:16). "Who is this stone that Isaiah is referring to?" asked the teacher, and the class answered in unison. "Jesus Christ!" Then, the teacher read aloud these encouraging words from Isaiah: "For thou hast been a strength to the poor, a strength to the needy in his distress, a refuge from the storm, a shadow from the heat, when the blast of the terrible ones is as a storm against the wall" (Isaiah 25:4). The teacher bore witness of the truth of these principles and promised the class that if they would build their lives upon the foundation of Jesus Christ, this precious stone, they would be protected and happy, having "peace in this world, and eternal life in the world to come" (D&C 59:23).

Pondering: How can we follow our Savior with greater love and devotion? How can we help our family members and friends do the same?

2. The Restoration, including the coming forth of the Book of Mormon, brings untold blessings of joy and peace.

The coming forth of the Book of Mormon in our day as a voice from the dust was foreseen by Isaiah in astounding detail, showing that the Lord's design for blessing His people with the fulness of the gospel was prepared from the very beginning: "Therefore, behold, I will proceed to do a marvellous work among this people, even a marvellous work and a wonder: for the wisdom of their wise men shall perish, and the understanding of their prudent men shall be hid" (Isaiah 29:14; see also D&C 4:1; 6:1). The light of the Restoration burst upon a world languishing in the shadows of emptiness: "The earth also is defiled under the inhabitants thereof; because they have transgressed the laws,

STUDY COMMENTARY ON THE OLD TESTAMENT

changed the ordinance, broken the everlasting covenant" (Isaiah 24:5; see also JS—H 1:19). But the covenant was to be renewed; the earth was to be prepared for cleansing; the people were to be refreshed with truth: "And in that day shall the deaf hear the words of the book, and the eyes of the blind shall see out of obscurity, and out of darkness. . . . They also that erred in spirit shall come to understanding, and they that murmured shall learn doctrine" (Isaiah 29:18, 24).

The vision of the new and final dispensation revealed the gathering together of His people in the latter days: "And it shall come to pass that my people, which are of the house of Israel, shall be gathered home unto the lands of their possessions; and my word also shall be gathered in one" (2 Nephi 29:14). Multiple witnesses of the Lord's work were united with the coming together of the Bible and the Book of Mormon.

> **How many chapters of Isaiah are included in the Book of Mormon?**
>
> The Book of Mormon includes a total of twenty-one entire chapters of Isaiah, plus segments from others. Here's a summary: Isaiah 2–14 (2 Nephi 12–24); Isaiah 29 (2 Nephi 27); Isaiah 48–49 (1 Nephi 20–21); Isaiah 50–51 (2 Nephi 7–8); Isaiah 52 (3 Nephi 20; also portions in 2 Nephi 8 and Mosiah 15); Isaiah 53 (Mosiah 14); Isaiah 54 (3 Nephi 22). The New Testament also quotes extensively from Isaiah, with quotations from thirty-two chapters.

How was the prophecy of Isaiah concerning the Book of Mormon fulfilled? Consider the following story shared by an LDS college teacher:

I recall many decades ago attending a lecture on pre-Columbian trans-Atlantic migrations to America given by one of the faculty members at a well-known Eastern university. After the lecture, several students were questioning the professor about his theories, and one of them asked if he had ever heard of the Book of Mormon. He replied that he regularly received several copies of the Book of Mormon each year, always with certain pages marked for his reading guidance. His opinion of the book was that "any one could have put together such material in a short period of time." My mind immediately turned to the experience of Martin Harris in 1828, when he showed to Professor Charles Anthon of Columbia College (now Columbia University) in New York a transcript of the Book of Mormon and its translation. The professor had issued to Martin a certificate of authenticity concerning the characters but retracted it upon learning of the divine source of the material, saying, "I cannot read a sealed book" (*HC* 1:20; see also JS—H 1:63–65). He did not realize that he was fulfilling a prophecy of Isaiah concerning a future book that would speak "out of the ground" and "whisper out of the dust" (Isaiah 29:4). Said Isaiah: "And the vision of all is become unto you as the words of a book that is sealed, which men deliver to one that is learned, saying, Read this, I pray thee: and he saith, I cannot; for it is sealed" (Isaiah 29:11).

It was clear that the learned university professor who lectured to us on trans-Atlantic migrations had only scanty familiarity with the nature, merit, and divine mission of the Book of Mormon (see Ezekiel 37:15–19). To him, as well as to all others who seek knowledge by any means other than through spiritual light, the Book of Mormon remained sealed. How easily that seal can be broken to release the abundance of spiritual blessings awaiting the honest seeker after truth (see Matthew 7:7; Moroni 10:4–5).

Pondering: How can we show our gratitude to the Lord for the blessings of the Book of Mormon? How can we guide our loved ones to savor the lifting guidance of this sacred book?

AGENDA FOR ACTION

We can find greater joy and peace in life by focusing on the Savior and His priceless sacrifice. We can follow the Spirit, learn line upon line, liken the scriptures to ourselves, and share our witness of the truth with others. That pattern of living will bring us closer to the Lord and enable us to say, with our loved ones: "Lo, this is our God; we have waited for him, and he will save us: this is the LORD; we have waited for him, we will be glad and rejoice in his salvation" (Isaiah 25:9).

As we wait upon the Lord, we can be inspired and lifted by the emblems of truth conveyed in the writings of Isaiah: the *nail* reminding us of Christ's crucifixion to bring about the plan of salvation and exaltation on our behalf; the *key* of redeeming love that opens the door of eternal life for all of the Lord's faithful sons and daughters; and the *stone* of Zion, even Jesus Christ, the foundation upon which we can solidly build our lives and fulfill our destiny. We can uncover favorite passages in Isaiah and learn them by heart to recite them during family home evening gatherings. We can share favorite stories from the "marvellous work and a wonder" (Isaiah 29:14) foreseen by Isaiah, even the Book of Mormon, Another Testament of Jesus Christ. Waiting upon the Lord is not a passive undertaking but an active process through which we come closer to Him each day by aspiring to emulate His divine qualities.

LOOKING FORWARD: What is the key for increasing our faith day by day?

CHAPTER THIRTY-EIGHT

THE JOY OF BEING
THE LORD'S COVENANT PEOPLE

Gospel Doctrine Reading Assignment: Isaiah 40–49

I, even I, am the Lord; and beside me there is no saviour. (Isaiah 43:11)

ALL THINGS CONCERNING THE LORD'S PEOPLE

Isaiah is the mouthpiece of the Holy One of Israel, the Redeemer, who proclaimed, "For great are the words of Isaiah. For surely he spake as touching all things concerning my people" (3 Nephi 23:1–2). Could it be that the expression "all things" serves as a key to the greatness of the words of Isaiah? Could this expression confirm that Isaiah's message is *all-encompassing, all-revealing, all-embracing*? If so, then when we grasp and understand the words of Isaiah, we will find glowing within us a lamp of joy growing brighter and brighter as the Spirit unfolds a panoramic view of the origin and destiny of mankind according to the grand design and merciful promises of the Lord.

How we participate in the unfolding of this grand design depends on the choices we make. The counsel of the Lord guides us plainly: "Put me in remembrance" (Isaiah 43:26), for "I am the Lord thy God . . . which leadeth thee by the way that thou shouldest go" (Isaiah 48:17).

Isaiah, who prophesied over a century before Lehi left Jerusalem, provides a magnificent view of the principle of opposition throughout the dispensations of time. Those who are blind and deaf as to the things of the Lord choose the downward course leading to captivity and destruction. Those who look to the Lord in all things and follow His gospel plan choose the upward course leading to liberation and eternal life. The sacred key is to accept the outreaching hand of the Lord in faith: "Return unto me; for I have redeemed thee" (Isaiah 44:22). Moreover, "Look unto me, and be ye saved, all the ends of the earth: for I am God, and there is none else" (Isaiah 45:22).

A TOUCH OF REALITY

How does choosing the way of the Lord define our very existence? A young priesthood holder shared the following true account that focuses on this important theme:

> I recall hiking as a young boy with my family in a remote part of the Rocky Mountains. We had chosen as a destination for our day-long adventure—a small cluster of lakes that we had never before visited. Because of their location above a daunting granite cliff at the end of a box canyon, these lakes were among the least accessible in that area of the country. Not wanting to risk the climb up and along the cliff, we chose instead to reach these lakes by climbing over a mountain ridge from the other side. The problem was that we had underestimated the time it would take to follow the longer, indirect route, and it was already ominously late in the afternoon by the time we reached the lakes. Not having planned an overnight stay, we were faced with the unpleasant prospect of having to return to our car by traversing the cliff we had wanted to avoid. Facing our ordeal, we ventured over to the place where the trail led to the beginning of the granite cliff.
>
> The view was terrifying—perhaps over a thousand feet straight down. What was called a trail was nothing more than a series of ledges used by nimble mountain goats to cross over the cliff and go down into the lower valley. In some sections, the trail was only half a foot wide; in other parts, it was barely an inch, and it invariably curved downward—toward the abyss. There were no trees to hold on to. We were petrified. Even my father, no stranger to mountain adventures, seemed nervous. We looked down in silence as the evening sun disappeared behind the peaks.
>
> Then something unforgettable happened. We heard from somewhere in that isolated and lonely place the sound of happy whistling. We heard voices and laughter drawing nearer. Presently, two men appeared from nowhere, carrying their fishing gear and wearing broad smiles. They must have sensed our forlorn spirits, for they joked and teased us with their banter. I can still hear the one fellow named Slim saying in a kind of twang, "Anyone want a hard-boiled egg?" No one in our party really had much appetite at that moment—so he continued, "We can take you down the cliff. Come follow us. And don't look down."
>
> With that, Slim and his friend, whistling all the way, guided us painstakingly, step-by-step, across and down that cliff—one reach at a time—toward an enormous shale embankment located at what seemed like an endless distance away. I can still remember the fear of stepping from one goat ledge to another, sometimes reaching my foot gingerly around rock outcroppings to test the foothold on the other side, all the while clutching with sweaty fingers to the face of the cliff and trying not to look down. But we made it. And when we finally reached the shale embankment, it was an easier thing to make our way down the rest of the incline toward the valley floor far below. Those experienced mountain guides were heroes in our eyes.
>
> Since then, I have often thought of the words of those guides: "Come follow us." They knew the trail. They knew the dangers. They had cultivated the techniques—and the attitude of success. And they knew how to lead the inexperienced to safety. On the cliffs of life there are dangers lurking. There is an abyss of spiritual emptiness that yawns upward to the lonely traveler. But then the words echo: "Come, follow me" (Luke 18:22), and we know that the Shepherd is near and calls us toward pathways of safety and joy. He said, "My sheep hear my voice, and I know them, and they follow me" (John 10:27). The word of the Lord is the iron rod across the cliffs of life. It is the anchor to the fearful heart. It is the comfort to the weary, and the balance to the unsteady. It is like the consoling words of Isaiah, speaking for the Lord: "Fear thou not; for I am with thee" (Isaiah 41:10). Moreover, "And I will bring the blind by a way that they knew not; I will lead them in paths that they have not known: I will make darkness light before them, and crooked things straight. These things will I do unto them, and not forsake them" (Isaiah 42:16). We can thank our Heavenly Father for the word of truth to guide our journey in life and bring us safely home again.

WHAT LESSONS CAN WE LEARN FROM THE LATER CHAPTERS OF ISAIAH?

1. Beside the Lord there is no Savior.

The words of Isaiah contain compelling questions concerning our vital choices and preferences in life: "To whom then will ye liken God?" (Isaiah 40:18); "Is there a God beside me?" (Isaiah 44:8); "To whom will ye liken me, and make me equal, and compare me, that we may be like?" (Isaiah 46:5).

Such questions drill down through the shallow patterns of living savored by mortals who turn their backs on the Lord and choose to worship worldly gods and idols. The Lord warned of such folly in His preface to our latter-day revelations: "For they have strayed from mine ordinances, and have broken mine everlasting covenant; They seek not the Lord to establish his righteousness, but every man walketh in his own way, and after the image of his own god, whose image is in the likeness of the world, and whose substance is that of an idol, which waxeth old and shall perish" (D&C 1:15–16). Isaiah used the waywardness of Israel and her neighboring pagan cultures as a backdrop for teaching the principle that the Lord will ultimately prevail, that Zion will emerge righteous as an ensign of light and truth for the world, and that the Lord of salvation and exaltation is Jesus Christ, the Only Begotten of the Father, the only Savior of mankind: "I, even I, am the LORD; and beside me there is no saviour" (Isaiah 43:11).

How do the choices of our day reflect the stark contrast between walking after worldly gods and seeking the heavenly majesty of the Lord and Savior? We can tune into the thoughts of a husband and father in Zion as he drives home from work:

Another day at work, he thought. *Another opportunity to help support the family and contribute to our community.* As he pulled to a stop at a red light, his eyes wandered forward to the car ahead of him. A hand extended from the window of the driver's seat, the fingers nimbly fiddling with a cigarette. The observing father shook his head in sadness. He thought of modern choices—choices to escape into a state where people believed that certain substances could give them pleasure and fulfillment. Instead, they could so easily reach out to the bread of life and the living water of the gospel of Jesus Christ. His mind shifted to his own children, now adults. How he and his wife loved them and prayed for their well-being—every moment of every day.

As he passed by a field next to a school, he could see two teams of youth engaged in a late-afternoon practice. *Good choice,* he thought, *especially if they also seek spiritual fitness and well-being.* His mind shifted to a passage in Isaiah: "But they that wait upon the LORD shall renew their strength; they shall mount up with wings as eagles; they shall run, and not be weary; and they shall walk, and not faint" (Isaiah 40:31). He remembered a conversation he'd had years ago with Eli Herring, a former BYU offensive lineman who declined a potentially lucrative deal with the Oakland Raiders in 1995 because he chose not to play professional football on Sunday. Instead, he decided to become a high school coach and teacher and carry on his service to the Lord in other ways. What was the source of his strength to make such a far-reaching decision? He said it was four things: (1) his mother, (2) the word of God in the scriptures and in the counsel of modern prophets, (3) praying alongside his faithful wife, and (4) the example of other men in similar situations. A wonderful witness to wise choices in life.

The father passed by a large theater complex. The marquee displayed in dazzling lights the names of a dozen current films, many with an R rating. He was disheartened to think of how modern culture often elevated movie idols to a plane of adoration bordering on worship. He remembered that the word *idol* was used frequently in the scriptures in another context—an individual who had turned away from the Lord in favor of a worldly, man-made idol: "He falleth down unto it, and worshippeth it, and prayeth unto it, and saith, Deliver me; for thou art my god" (Isaiah 44:17). But the Lord warned such an individual, "Yea, one shall cry unto him [the idol], yet can he not answer, nor save him out of his trouble" (Isaiah 46:7), for "there is no peace, saith the LORD, unto the wicked" (Isaiah 48:22).

A feeling of relief came as the father remembered how his daughter and her husband had replaced commercial television in their home with a library of noble and uplifting films. Yes, modern technology can also bring great blessings of instruction and knowledge—if wise choices are made to look unto the Lord and make the home into a holy place where the children of God can gather.

He continued to ponder the consequences of choices in life—how an obsession with worldly wealth can detract from the quest for spiritual wealth, how immoral conduct can extinguish the whisperings of the Spirit, how prideful fixation on one's own strengths and talents can arrest the flow of blessings from on high. How could he help others make wise choices? At that moment he passed by a street that led toward a structure rising in majesty on the slope of a distant hill. He nodded and smiled. It was the temple of the Lord, radiant and white, with a statue of the angel Moroni atop the main steeple. Holiness to the Lord, he thought. He remembered with gratitude a line from the scriptures: "Look unto me, and be ye saved, all the ends of the earth: for I am God, and there is none else" (Isaiah 45:22). And he felt in his heart an assurance that his family would be a forever family "through the merits, and mercy, and grace of the Holy Messiah" (2 Nephi 2:8).

> **Knowing the Lord**
>
> President McKay characterized the Lord as being the one perfect Gentleman who ever lived, as the Anointed One and ideal Man of supreme character who is our Brother and Savior. President McKay entreated us to believe in the Lord with all our souls so that He will become real in our lives (see *Man May Know for Himself: Teachings of President David O. McKay* [Salt Lake City: Deseret Book, 1967], 423).

Soon the journey ended as he pulled into the driveway of his modest home. With peace and joy, he hurried through the doorway and embraced his loving and faithful wife, waiting for his return from another day of work. As he greeted her, his mind thought of the grand journey of life—the final return home with his family to the abode of the Father and Son, a place of eternal glory and everlasting happiness. And he was filled with peace.

The message is clear: there is no Savior beside the Lord, Jesus Christ:

- "Thus saith the LORD the King of Israel, and his redeemer the LORD of hosts; I am the first, and I am the last; and beside me there is no God" (Isaiah 44:6; see also Isaiah 45:5–6, 18).
- "There is no God else beside me; a just God and a Saviour; there is none beside me. Look unto me, and be ye saved, all the ends of the earth: for I am God, and there is none else" (Isaiah 45:21–22; see also Isaiah 46:9).

Pondering: How can we ensure that we focus our thoughts and actions on spiritual goals and look only to the Lord for life and salvation? How can we better guide our loved ones to do the same?

2. The faithful are gathered by the Lord to holy places of security and peace.

Though tribulations and challenges test and try our faith and resolve, we know that through the strength of the Lord we can come together to survive and flourish in the light of the gospel.

All of us find that the route of mortality passes through both rocky terrain as well as pleasant pastures, treacherous valleys as well as glorious summits. I recall a number of years ago facing a particularly challenging period requiring a great deal of faith and courage. The book of Isaiah—with its sublime passages about the Lord's promises of comfort and deliverance—became a particularly helpful companion, and I often found occasion to derive strength and spiritual sustenance from its pages. Certain passages began to stand out as particularly memorable formulas of transcendence and hope. I wrote these down in my journal and began to organize them into a pattern of phrases that I could rehearse again and again in moments of particular need. There was enormous strength and vitality in these quiet moments reviewing Isaiah's inspired formulations. I would often walk in the early hours before sunrise and in the late hours after sunset to ponder these comforting passages and seek guidance from the Spirit—guidance that would always come just when it was most needed. Here are several of the most memorable passages of hope and strength for me:

- *Lord will gather and nourish His flock*: "He shall feed his flock like a shepherd: he shall gather the lambs with his arm, and carry them in his bosom, and shall gently lead those that are with young" (Isaiah 40:11; see also Isaiah 41:8; 42:16).
- *Fear not, for the Lord will strengthen and uphold thee*: "Thou art my servant; I have chosen thee, and not cast thee away. Fear thou not; for I am with thee: be not dismayed; for I am thy God: I will strengthen thee; yea, I will help thee; yea, I will uphold thee with the right hand of my righteousness" (Isaiah 41:9–10; see also Isaiah 43:1–5).

- *Lord remembers our sins no more*: "I, even I, am he that blotteth out thy transgressions for mine own sake, and will not remember thy sins" (Isaiah 43:25; see also Isaiah 44:21–22; D&C 58:42).
- *In the furnace of affliction*: "Behold, I have refined thee, but not with silver; I have chosen thee in the furnace of affliction" (Isaiah 48:10).
- *Lord of salvation will deliver us*: "I will preserve thee, and give thee for a covenant of the people, to establish the earth, to cause to inherit the desolate heritages; That thou mayest say to the prisoners, Go forth" (Isaiah 49:8–9; thus even the faithful in the spirit world have hope of deliverance).
- *Rejoice that the Lord in His mercy will not forget us*: "Sing, O heavens; and be joyful, O earth; and break forth into singing, O mountains: for the LORD hath comforted his people, and will have mercy upon his afflicted. . . . yet will I not forget thee. Behold, I have graven thee upon the palms of my hands; thy walls are continually before me" (Isaiah 49:13, 15–16; see also Isaiah 49:2–3).

Pondering: How can we write the words of the Lord on the tables of our heart (see Proverbs 3:3; 7:3; Jeremiah 31:33; 2 Corinthians 3:3) and thus have the courage and strength to gather together to holy places and worship the Lord with faith and covenant obedience?

AGENDA FOR ACTION

We can shun worldly idols and false images and look to the Lord as our only Savior. We can live in faithful obedience and be guided to stand and worship in holy places—homes of peace, congregations of faith, and temples of purity (see D&C 101:22). We can serve as witnesses of the Lord's mercy and truth—and help every knee to bow and every tongue confess before the Lord (see Isaiah 45:23; Romans 14:11; Mosiah 27:31; D&C 76:110; 88:104). We can honor the Lord's eternal promise: "Look unto me, and be ye saved, all the ends of the earth: for I am God, and there is none else" (Isaiah 45:22).

These glorious aspirations can unfold in your life in simple ways. You can share your testimony of the Savior more often. You can write it down in your journal. You can invite your family members to list some of their favorite passages from Isaiah and have them explain how these words enrich their lives and bring them more hope and faith. You can reach out to less-active members and be a light by sharing your witness that the Lord loves them and welcomes them back. You can invite nonmembers to read the Book of Mormon and then ask the Lord to confirm its truth. In all of these things, you can rise to a higher level of service in the spirit of Isaiah, one of the Lord's great prophets.

LOOKING FORWARD: How can we know that the Lord's atoning sacrifice is a personal gift to each of us?

CHAPTER THIRTY-NINE

FOR THE LORD SHALL COMFORT ZION

GOSPEL DOCTRINE READING ASSIGNMENT: ISAIAH 50–53

He was wounded for our transgressions, he was bruised for our iniquities: the chastisement
of our peace was upon him; and with his stripes we are healed. (Isaiah 53:5)

WHO SHALL DECLARE THE GENERATION OF CHRIST?

ISAIAH PROPHESIED MORE THAN SEVEN centuries before the earthly ministry of Christ, but his vision of the future was so clear, so vivid, that he spoke as if he were present alongside his master Teacher, who said, "For all things are present before mine eyes" (D&C 38:2). As if he were sharing a place in the stable next to the shepherds, Isaiah declared, "For unto us a child is born, unto us a son is given" (Isaiah 9:6). In deep sadness, Isaiah observed that the Lord was viewed by His mortal peers as but a common man: "He hath no form nor comeliness; and when we shall see him, there is no beauty that we should desire him. He is despised and rejected of men; a man of sorrows, and acquainted with grief" (Isaiah 53:2–3). Isaiah shared the anguished sufferings of the Redeemer for the salvation of mankind: "Surely he hath borne our griefs, and carried our sorrows: yet we did esteem him stricken, smitten of God, and afflicted. But he was wounded for our transgressions, he was bruised for our iniquities: the chastisement of our peace was upon him; and with his stripes we are healed" (Isaiah 53:4–5). Thus Isaiah, as if a companion with the Redeemer on His journey, rejoiced at the ultimate triumph of the Son of God: "And the government shall be upon his shoulder: and his name shall be called Wonderful, Counsellor, The mighty God, The everlasting Father, The Prince of Peace" (Isaiah 9:6).

That phrase, "The everlasting Father," can be reformulated as a vital question posed by Isaiah: "And who shall declare his generation? for he was cut off out of the land of the living: for the transgression of my people was he stricken" (Isaiah 53:8). If the Savior was taken from the land of the living, how could He become "the everlasting Father"? Who would be His generation—His seed, His sons and daughters? For whom would He serve as Father? Isaiah gives us the answer: "Yet it pleased the Lord to bruise him; he hath put him to grief: when thou shalt make his soul an offering for sin, he shall see his seed, he shall prolong his days, and the pleasure of the Lord shall prosper in his hand" (Isaiah 53:10).

When we "make his soul an offering for sin," when we accept His Atonement and comply faithfully with the principles of the gospel, then "shall he see his seed." He will become our adoptive father, and we will become His adopted sons and daughters, "heirs of God, and joint-heirs with Christ; if so be that we suffer with him, that we may be also glorified together" (Romans 8:17).

Let us consider how Abinadi, a future prophet of the Lord, would shed further light on the miracle unfolded by Isaiah of how we can become the seed of Christ—His celestial generation—and how Alma, an observer of Abinadi in the court of wicked King Noah, went through the process of receiving a mighty change of heart as described in Mosiah 11–17.

A TOUCH OF REALITY

The young man nervously clutched the pure-gold outer rim of the vast, curved bench behind which he and his priestly associates were seated. A chill ran through his fingers, and he pulled back his hands in search of relief. The plush ornaments decorating the royal council chamber seemed like dead weights to him, his costly attire like a heavy burden. Standing below him on the floor of the royal council hall was a man of stately demeanor being held by the guards of the king. Two years earlier, this same man had come among the people to warn them with the voice of a prophet of God that disaster loomed if they did not repent of their wickedness. When they sought to slay him, he escaped and vanished into the shadows. But his message had touched the heart of the young priest now peering down at the prophet once more arrested after returning in disguise to proclaim even more boldly the coming judgments of God.

"He's a madman," whispered a fellow priest. But the young man ignored the words and listened with awe as the prophet repelled the king's threats and calmly responded, "Touch me not, for God shall smite you if ye lay your hands upon me, for I have not delivered the message which the Lord sent me to deliver" (Mosiah 13:3). With a countenance shining as bright as the sun, he proceeded to unfold the commandments of the Lord and the doctrines of salvation and Atonement. Quoting Isaiah, he challenged his captors to answer a question concerning the Messiah: "And who shall declare his generation? For he was cut off out of the land of the living; for the transgressions of my people was he stricken" (Mosiah 14:8; see also Isaiah 53:8). In response to their silence, he gave the answer: "When thou shalt make his soul an offering for sin he shall see his seed" (Mosiah 14:10; see also Isaiah 53:10).

The young man felt in his heart a swelling of peace. He knew that the prophet was speaking the truth. He asked within his soul the burning question, "Can I overcome my weaknesses and become the seed of the Lord?" As he looked on, the noble speaker turned in his direction and seemed to look directly into his eyes with a slight smile on his face. Then the young man heard the answer:

> Behold I say unto you, that whosoever has heard the words of the prophets, yea, all the holy prophets who have prophesied concerning the coming of the Lord—I say unto you, that all those who have hearkened unto their words, and believed that the Lord would redeem his people, and have looked forward to that day for a remission of their sins, I say unto you, that these are his seed, or they are the heirs of the kingdom of God.
>
> For these are they whose sins he has borne; these are they for whom he has died, to redeem them from their transgressions. And now, are they not his seed? (Mosiah 15:11–12)

"Yes, they are His seed," whispered the young man. "And who else might be included?"

The answer came from the prophet: "And again, how beautiful upon the mountains are the feet of those that are still publishing peace! And again, how beautiful upon the mountains are the feet of those who shall hereafter publish peace, yea, from this time henceforth and forever!" (Mosiah 15:16–17).

The young man gasped! He knew that he had a chance to rise in the strength of the Redeemer and publish peace to the world, for, as the continuing words confirmed, the Redeemer was "the founder of peace, yea, even the Lord, who has redeemed his people; yea, him who has granted salvation unto his people" (Mosiah 15:18).

At that moment, it was as though a heavenly force was lifting the young man upward. He stood with courage and shouted toward the king, pleading for the life of the prophet, begging "that he might depart in peace" (Mosiah 17:2). But when the king ordered his guards to seize the young man and slay him, he quickly fled and escaped into the darkness. For many days he remained in isolation to write down all the words of the prophet (see Mosiah 17:4).

Soon thereafter he returned in secret to observe the shocking scene of the prophet being led toward a pole illuminated by the fiery flames of burning faggots. The words of the prophet resounded around the courtyard: "Yea, and I will suffer even until death, and I will not recall my words, and they shall stand as a testimony against you" (Mosiah 17:10).

The young man, secluded in the background, felt a deep love for the prophet and for the Lord. He recalled the prophet's exact words about the Redeemer: "He is the light and the life of the world; yea, a light that is endless, that can never be darkened; yea, and also a life which is endless, that there can be no more death" (Mosiah 16:9).

He may well have heard the prophet speak the final words while fastened to the martyr's pole: "O God, receive my soul" (Mosiah 17:19). We know that the young man resolved, with an indomitable commitment, to gather together all the believers of the word of God in the land and guide them to a place of safety and security where they could worship the Lord and covenant to become His sons and daughters (see Mosiah 18).

How can we shed further light on the process of becoming the sons and daughters of the Lord? What follows is an account from an LDS missionary about how his experience in the mission field illuminated for him this process.

Elder Theodore M. Burton served as mission president in the West German Mission during my time there as a young missionary. One of the blessings that came with serving in the mission home during my final months was spending the first part of each morning in gospel study with all of the mission home staff, learning from President Burton, a consummate student of the scriptures. I shall never forget the day he offered his insightful commentary on those passages that dealt with Isaiah's compelling question concerning the Savior: "And who shall declare his generation?" (Isaiah 53:8; also Acts 8:33; Mosiah 14:8). President and Sister Burton had an adopted son who accompanied them on their mission. Because they were familiar with the complex legal process by which an adoption is consummated, it was natural for President Burton to relate his personal experiences to the doctrine of adoption into the kingdom of God, whereby we can become the sons and daughters of Jesus Christ (see Mosiah 5:7).

President Burton amplified this doctrine by explaining the exceptional transition for the adults adopting a child. They are required to appear before the court and answer the sobering question, in effect: "Are you willing to take upon yourself all responsibility for the welfare and well-being of this child, to nurture and care for the child under all circumstances just as if the child were your natural-born child?" To answer yes to this question and complete the legally binding covenants brings about an extraordinary change in the status of the adopting adults: the man becomes a father, and the woman becomes a mother.

Later, as a general authority, Elder Burton confirmed that when we are baptized we make a covenant with Heavenly Father to take upon ourselves the name of His Only Begotten Son. In this way, Jesus Christ becomes our covenant Father—and we become His covenant sons and daughters and members of His royal family.[21]

The message is life changing for all of us: Because Christ "became the author eternal salvation unto all them that obey him" (Hebrews 5:9), He magnified His role and became the adopting father of the faithful, just as the faithful become His adopted sons and daughters. In effect, the Savior took upon Himself the responsibility to be our eternal Caregiver and to assure that we, as His sons and daughters, enjoy everlasting vitality and nurture, being born again through a royal adoption into the family of Christ.

---

21   See Theodore M. Burton, "To Be Born Again," *Ensign*, Sept. 1985, 66ff.

WHAT LESSON CAN WE LEARN FROM THE LATER CHAPTERS OF ISAIAH?

1. Through His infinite love, the Savior brought about the Atonement for the good of mankind.

We cannot begin to grasp, with any degree of understanding, the infinite pain and suffering experienced by the Savior in bringing to pass the Atonement. He willingly descended below all things in order to lift mankind above all things relative to salvation and exaltation. Isaiah provides words that hint at the agony and torment involved: wounded, bruised, oppressed, afflicted, brought as a lamb to the slaughter, cut off, stricken, put to grief: "He was wounded for our transgressions, he was bruised for our iniquities: the chastisement of our peace was upon him; and with his stripes we are healed" (Isaiah 53:5; see also verses 6–10).

In our time, the Lord gave the most explicit revelation of all concerning His torturous sacrifice:

> Which suffering caused myself, even God, the greatest of all, to tremble because of pain, and to bleed at every pore, and to suffer both body and spirit—and would that I might not drink the bitter cup, and shrink— Nevertheless, glory be to the Father, and I partook and finished my preparations unto the children of men. (D&C 19:18–19)

Perhaps we have a slight inkling of the scope of His suffering when we experience the suffering for others as part of our given roles as parents and grandparents—and servants of the Lord. Perhaps we feel a hint of the degree of His merciful agony when we are called upon to sacrifice our time and resources, our comfort and personal interests for blessing others and for the cause of Zion.

We can follow in the footsteps of the Savior by doing all that He asks us to do and by giving all that He asks us to give. Joseph Smith taught, "Let us here observe, that a religion that does not require the sacrifice of all things never has power sufficient to produce the faith necessary unto life and salvation."[22] The Savior commanded: "And ye shall offer for a sacrifice unto me a broken heart and a contrite spirit" (3 Nephi 9:20). It is through covenant obedience, charitable service, and bearing sincere witness of the truth of the gospel that we can please the Lord and become worthy of His eternal blessings.

> ### What have modern prophets taught about the blessings of the Atonement?
>
> Joseph Smith declared, "How indescribably glorious are these things to mankind! Of a truth they may be considered tidings of great joy to all people; and tidings, too, that ought to fill the earth and cheer the hearts of every one when sounded in his ears" (*HC* 2:5).
>
> Howard W. Hunter confirmed that there would be no hope of eternal life without the Atonement of Jesus Christ—the most important aspect of the divine plan of salvation (see *The Teachings of Howard W. Hunter* [Salt Lake City: Bookcraft, 1997], 7).

Pondering: How can we best show our deep gratitude for the atoning sacrifice of the Lord? How can we help others accept the reality of the Atonement as the source of all blessings?

AGENDA FOR ACTION

Through the words of Isaiah, the Lord gives unto us a compass for following in His footsteps: "Trust in the name of the LORD" (Isaiah 50:10); "Hearken unto me, my people; and give ear unto me, O my nation" (Isaiah 51:4; see also verse 7); "Awake, awake, put on strength, O arm of the LORD" (Isaiah 51:9; see also Isaiah 52:1); "Be ye clean, that bear the vessels of the LORD" (Isaiah 52:11). Great blessings will follow: "Break forth into joy, sing together, . . . for the LORD hath comforted his people, he hath redeemed Jerusalem" (Isaiah 52:9; see also Isaiah 51:3). "Therefore the redeemed of the LORD shall return, and come with singing unto Zion; and everlasting joy shall be upon their head: they shall obtain gladness and joy; and sorrow and mourning shall flee away" (Isaiah 51:11). You can use these words as gateways of wisdom to inspire your study of the Atonement. You can include in your prayers night and day a request for increased understanding about the power and efficacy of the Atonement.

LOOKING FORWARD: How does the Lord nourish our souls?

---

22   *Lectures on Faith*, 6:7.

CHAPTER FORTY

WITH GREAT MERCIES WILL I GATHER THEE

GOSPEL DOCTRINE READING ASSIGNMENT: ISAIAH 54–56, 63–65

Enlarge the place of thy tent, and let them stretch forth the curtains of thine habitations:
spare not, lengthen thy cords, and strengthen thy stakes. (Isaiah 54:2)

THE JOY OF THE GATHERING

WE WELCOME ONCE AGAIN THE words of the Lord, confirming that the inspired message of Isaiah forms a majestic canopy of truth "as touching all things concerning my people . . . And all things that he spake have been and shall be, even according to the words which he spake" (3 Nephi 23:2–3). That canopy embraces the history of mankind from the beginning to the end, the endurance of the gospel plan from its inception until the Restoration and beyond, and the unbroken manifestation of the love and mercy of God throughout all dispensations. That canopy of truth forms a vast protective covering of light that dispels the darkness of doubt and pride and engenders in the hearts and minds of the Lord's children an everlasting spirit of hope and peace. Isaiah is surely one of the Lord's greatest presenters of the message of salvation and exaltation. Our lives are enriched and edified when we partake of the glory of this prophetic message in a day when moral values are eroding and spiritual commitments are weakening. The ultimate message of Isaiah is one of mercy and love, strength and deliverance:

I will mention the lovingkindnesses of the LORD, and the praises of the LORD, according to all that the LORD hath bestowed on us, and the great goodness toward the house of Israel, which he hath bestowed on them according to his mercies, and according to the multitude of his lovingkindnesses. (Isaiah 63:7)

Beneath the canopy of universal truth is another canopy, another covering for the Lord's people. It is the tent of Zion put forward by Isaiah as a metaphor for the protective covering provided by the gospel and the priesthood, the vast expanding pavilion of the Lord's Church that is to spread throughout the entire world as Saints gather to holy places in preparation for the return of the Lord and Redeemer of mankind.

The tent of Zion, with its securing stakes and reinforcing cords, is the picture-perfect image for the safe haven afforded by the hand of the Lord for His people. Just as the temple is symbolized by the immovable mountain of the Lord (see Isaiah 2:2–3), Zion, a tent, is shown as agile and growing, flexible and expanding, lithe and unfolding. The Saints can thus internalize both the fixed and unchanging character of eternal principles as well as the responsive and dynamic character of the expanding kingdom, whose saving and protecting influence extends into all quarters of the earth. The Lord's command is to enlarge this tent, lengthen its cords, and strengthen its stakes (see Isaiah 54:2).

How is the latter-day gathering of the Saints to the stakes and congregations of the Church a movement of joy and light?

A TOUCH OF REALITY

Wednesday, April 12, 1843. The steamer *Amaranth*—the first up the Mississippi River this season—arrives this day in Nauvoo about noon, at a time when a special three-day conference of the priesthood (including most of the Twelve) is being conducted. While the conference is busy ordaining elders and sending nearly ninety missionaries into the field (*HC* 5:347–352), the ship is delivering some 240 immigrant convert Saints from England, under the leadership of Lorenzo Snow. The Prophet Joseph Smith greets them in person with great joy. A few hours later, at 5:00 p.m., the steamer *Maid of Iowa* arrives with around two hundred more Saints from England under the leadership of Levi Richards and Parley P. Pratt (whose thirty-sixth birthday happens to fall on this day).

The Prophet notes in his journal, "I was present at the landing and the first on board the steamer, when I met Sister Mary Ann Pratt (who had been to England with Brother Parley) and her little daughter, only three or four days old. I could not refrain from shedding tears. So many friends and acquaintances arriving in one day . . . I was rejoiced to meet them in such good health and fine spirits; for they were equal to any that had ever come to Nauvoo" (*HC* 5:354).

Thus the fledgling Church sustains a beehive of activity spreading the gospel and gathering the Saints, as the Lord had commanded. These are the moments of truth that remind us to labor diligently to spread the "good news" so others might also obtain the blessings of the gospel.

> Remember the worth of souls is great in the sight of God; . . . And if it so be that you should labor all your days in crying repentance unto this people, and bring, save it be one soul unto me, how great shall be your joy with him in the kingdom of my Father! And now, if your joy will be great with one soul that you have brought unto me into the kingdom of my Father, how great will be your joy if you should bring many souls unto me! (D&C 18:10, 15–16)

WHAT LESSONS CAN WE LEARN FROM THE LAST CHAPTERS OF ISAIAH?

1. We can fulfill our callings to help the Lord gather His people to the holy places of Zion.

Under inspiration from the Lord, Isaiah promises that we will personally take part in the gathering of the Lord's sons and daughters in the latter days. The following excerpts suggest a series of five questions about how we can best help the Lord in

What is a "stake"?

"The expression 'stake of Zion,' first used in the revelation given in November 1831 (Sec. 68), is taken from the expression in Isaiah [see Isaiah 33:20; 54:2]. . . . Isaiah speaks of Zion as a tent, or tabernacle, having in mind the tabernacle which was built and carried in the wilderness in the days of Moses; the cords are the binding cables that extend from the tent, or tabernacle, to the stakes which are fastened in the ground. Now, the Lord revealed that Zion was to be built and surrounding her would be the stakes helping to bind and keep her in place. This figure of speech has almost been lost through the intervening years, but it retains its significance, or beauty" (*Church History and Modern Revelation*, 4 vols. [Salt Lake City: The Church of Jesus Christ of Latter-day Saints, 1946–1949], 2:88).

His design for the blessings of Zion. See how you might answer these questions by placing yourself in the context of Isaiah's words as the person being addressed or described:

- *How do you know what steps to take in fulfilling your role in the gathering?* "Ho, every one that thirsteth, come ye to the waters, and he that hath no money; come ye, buy, and eat; yea, come, buy wine and milk without money and without price. . . . Incline your ear, and come unto me: hear, and your soul shall live; and I will make an everlasting covenant with you, . . . Seek ye the Lord while he may be found, call ye upon him while he is near" (Isaiah 55:1, 3, 6).

- *How does your fasting prepare you to love and serve others?* "Is not this the fast that I have chosen? to loose the bands of wickedness, to undo the heavy burdens, and to let the oppressed go free, and that ye break every yoke? Is it not to deal thy bread to the hungry, and that thou bring the poor that are cast out to thy house? when thou seest the naked, that thou cover him . . . Then shall thy light break forth as the morning, and thine health shall spring forth speedily: and thy righteousness shall go before thee; the glory of the Lord shall be thy rearward" (Isaiah 58:6–8).

- *What will be your feelings as you fulfill your calling?* "For ye shall go out with joy, and be led forth with peace: the mountains and the hills shall break forth before you into singing, and all the trees of the field shall clap their hands" (Isaiah 55:12). "I will greatly rejoice in the Lord, my soul shall be joyful in my God; for he hath clothed me with the garments of salvation, he hath covered me with the robe of righteousness, . . . For as the earth bringeth forth her bud, and as the garden causeth the things that are sown in it to spring forth; so the Lord God will cause righteousness and praise to spring forth before all the nations" (Isaiah 61:10–11).

- *What is your agenda for action as you bless the lives of others?* "But he that putteth his trust in me shall possess the land, and shall inherit my holy mountain; And shall say, Cast ye up, cast ye up, prepare the way, take up the stumblingblock out of the way of my people" (Isaiah 57:13–14). "Go through, go through the gates; prepare ye the way of the people; cast up, cast up the highway; gather out the stones; lift up a standard for the people" (Isaiah 62:10).

- *How do you maintain courage and hope in your calling?* "For since the beginning of the world men have not heard, nor perceived by the ear, neither hath the eye seen, O God, beside thee, what he hath prepared for him that waiteth for him" (Isaiah 64:4; see also 1 Corinthians 2:10; D&C 76:10). "They shall not labour in vain, nor bring forth for trouble; for they are the seed of the blessed of the Lord, and their offspring with them. And it shall come to pass, that before they call, I will answer; and while they are yet speaking, I will hear" (Isaiah 65:23–24).

We can participate in the gathering with the spirit of love as servants of the Lord. The following true account shared by a youth leader illustrates this point:

A number of years ago, while serving in the Young Men organization of our ward, I had the privilege of developing a training retreat for the young men and women serving in leadership positions. One of the themes was to strengthen the wards and stakes by seeing the value of each person. As the youth leaders were assembling on the bus for the drive to the retreat site, they were reminded of the scripture from 1 Samuel 16:7: "Man looketh on the outward appearance, but the Lord looketh on the heart." They were asked to watch for opportunities that day to serve others without regard to outward appearance.

A mile or two away, we passed a homeless person walking along the road, disheveled, unkempt, and tattered. We asked the driver to pull over and stop about half a block beyond the vagabond. "Should we interrupt our retreat to help this person?" was the question posed to the young men and women. Clearly some were wondering if that would be the appropriate thing to do—after all, the whole day was already planned around a fun program.

After some discussion, however, the group was unanimous in the decision to stop and help. By then, he had caught up with the bus, and we opened the door and invited him to come in. With some difficulty, he mounted the steps of the vehicle and then stood there, somewhat embarrassed under the silent, watchful gazes of several dozen youth. He began to express his appreciation for their help, and it did not take the listeners long to discern that this person clothed in stained and torn rags was indeed a special person. In fact, it was the bishop of the ward himself—and his brief and loving remarks about seeing the value in every person cast a spiritual glow over the rest of the day.

The Apostle Paul asked, "Do ye look on things after the outward appearance? If any man trust to himself that he is Christ's, let him of himself think this again, that, as he is Christ's, even so are we Christ's" (2 Corinthians 10:7). What greater way to strengthen wards and stakes than to perceive within all members the seeds of greatness as sons and daughters of God? "For he said, Surely they are my people, . . . in his love and in his pity he redeemed them; and he bare them, and carried them all the days of old" (Isaiah 63:8–9).

Pondering: How can we rise with faith and courage to help the Lord gather His people to the holy places of Zion—her homes, stakes, and temples—in the spirit of love and compassion?

2. Our covenant with the Lord is to prepare ourselves and all the world for the Second Coming.

The flowing imagery of Isaiah concerning the Second Coming and the millennial era can be viewed by modern readers almost as if it were a high-definition cinematic stream of scenes focusing on the unfolding gospel of Jesus Christ:

- "With great mercies will I gather thee. . . . For the mountains shall depart, and the hills be removed; but my kindness shall not depart from thee, neither shall the covenant of my peace be removed, saith the Lord that hath mercy on thee" (Isaiah 54:7, 10).
- "And all thy children shall be taught of the Lord; and great shall be the peace of thy children" (Isaiah 54:13).
- "Who is this that cometh from Edom, with dyed garments from Bozrah? this that is glorious in his apparel, travelling in the greatness of his strength? I that speak in righteousness, mighty to save. Wherefore art thou red in thine apparel . . . I have trodden the winepress alone" (Isaiah 63:1–3; Edom and Bozrah serve as types of the enemies of God; see also Isaiah 59:20–21; D&C 133:48).
- "For thus saith the Lord, Behold, I will extend peace to her like a river, and the glory of the Gentiles like a flowing stream: . . . As one whom his mother comforteth, so will I comfort you; and ye shall be comforted in Jerusalem" (Isaiah 66:12–13; see also Isaiah 60:14–16).
- "The sun shall be no more thy light by day; neither for brightness shall the moon give light unto thee: but the Lord shall be unto thee an everlasting light, and thy God thy glory. . . . for the Lord shall be thine everlasting light, and the days of thy mourning shall be ended. Thy people also shall be all righteous . . . that I may be glorified" (Isaiah 60:19–21; see also Isaiah 62:12).
- "For, behold, I create new heavens and a new earth: and the former shall not be remembered, nor come into mind. . . . There shall be no more thence an infant of days, nor an old man that hath not filled his days: for the child shall die an hundred years old; . . . They shall not labour in vain, nor bring forth for trouble; for they are the seed of the blessed of the Lord, and their offspring with them. And it shall come to pass, that before they call, I will answer; and while they are yet speaking, I will hear. The wolf and the lamb shall feed together, . . . They shall not hurt nor destroy in all my holy mountain, saith the Lord" (Isaiah 65:17, 20, 23–25).

What glorious vistas are shared by Isaiah! How magnificent is his language! He strives with all his might to teach us lessons of preparation and readiness for the return of the Lord and the dawning of the Millennium. What follows is a short stroll into the light of gospel truth:

Who does not view with awe and gratitude the clouds that Mother Nature uses to give splendor and variety to the skies above us? Whether it is the wispy cloud streaks high in the sky or the all-encompassing cumulus clouds at times rolling down upon us; whether it is the delicate magenta clouds of a summer sunset or the heaven-covering clouds delivering moisture in any season—the miracle of the clouds lifts our vision to higher things.

The word of God also lifts our vision to higher things. The Savior spoke of His eventual return in the last days at a time when "the powers of heaven shall be shaken. And then shall they see the Son of man coming in a cloud with power and great glory" (Luke 21:26–27). The image of the cloud is used often in the scriptures as a reference for the presence and glory of the Lord. It is also used frequently to imply a vast number of individuals. Isaiah used the word *cloud* to describe the righteous gathering in the latter days for safety and deliverance: "Who are these that fly as a cloud, and as the doves to their windows?" (Isaiah 60:8). Paul speaks of "so great a cloud of witnesses" (Hebrews 12:1).

Many places in the scriptures speak about the faithful being caught up at the last day to meet the Savior—"gathered with the saints, to be caught up unto the church of the Firstborn, and received into the cloud" (D&C 76:102). Paul stated it thus, "Then we which are alive and remain shall be caught up together with them in the clouds, to meet the Lord in the air: and so shall we ever be with the Lord. Wherefore comfort one another with these words" (1 Thessalonians 4:17–18). Could it be that the clouds spoken of in association with the Second Coming are numberless concourses of righteous Saints caught up to meet the Redeemer? Joseph Smith rendered an early verse in the book of Revelation this way: "For behold, he cometh in the clouds with ten thousands of his saints in the kingdom, clothed with the glory of his Father" (JST, Revelation 1:7). Through the voice of His prophets, the Lord commands us to prepare ourselves for His Second Coming that we might be caught up in the "clouds of heaven" (D&C 45:16) on that glorious day: "And then they shall look for me, and, behold, I will come; and they shall see me in the clouds of heaven, clothed with power and great glory; with all the holy angels; and he that watched not for me shall be cut off" (D&C 45:44).

Pondering: How can we ensure that we are fully prepared for the Second Coming? How can we use Isaiah's inspired forecast of eternal peace and harmony to plant seeds of enduring righteousness and unity here and now?

AGENDA FOR ACTION

Through humble obedience to the Lord, we can prepare to meet Him in the clouds of heaven in the last days. The word of the Lord proclaimed by Isaiah and all the prophets provides our covenant agenda and opens the gateway to divine nurture and deliverance. We can purify ourselves through the blessings of redemption and guide our loved ones along the pathway of eternal life in the spirit of charity and devotion. We can reach out with compassion to strangers, regardless of their conditions and appearance, in order to "succor the weak, lift up the hands which hang down, and strengthen the feeble knees" (D&C 81:5; see also Isaiah 35:3). We can share the gospel message with others "who are only kept from the truth because they know not where to find it" (D&C 123:12)—and thus contribute to the gathering of Israel in preparation for the Second Coming. As sons and daughters of the Lord, we can strive to please Him with all our heart, might, mind, and strength.

LOOKING FORWARD: What is the key for overcoming all adversity?

CHAPTER FORTY-ONE

SPEAK THE WORDS OF THE LORD

Gospel Doctrine Reading Assignment: Jeremiah 1–2, 15, 20, 26, 36–38

But his word was in mine heart as a burning fire. (Jeremiah 20:9)

FEAR NOT, FOR THE LORD SHALL DELIVER

THE PROPHET JEREMIAH (MEANING "RAISED up by Jehovah") had keen and perfect vision—what we might call spiritual x-ray vision—for he could see through the impenetrable fog of wickedness rampant in his time and discern, beyond the impending day of judgment and scattering, a future day of glory and light for a repentant and reborn Zion. Jeremiah prophesied during a forty-year period, from around 626 B.C. to 585 B.C. His fellow prophets during those days were Lehi, Daniel, and Ezekiel. His themes still resound through the generations of time—that peace and happiness depend on honoring our covenants with the Lord; that the consequences of sin are destruction and war, dislocation and scattering, misery and woe; that the Lord will chasten His people until they learn to be virtuous and righteous; and that He will eventually establish a new covenant with His faithful children and gather them in from the four quarters of the earth.

The life of Jeremiah was flooded with tribulation and adversity. He was consigned to prison for speaking the warning of the Lord to the wayward people of Judah. His life was constantly under threat. Execution stalked after his every move. He languished for days without food or water in a subterranean dungeon simply because he refused to recant the words the Lord had commanded him to declare concerning the destruction of Jerusalem by the Babylonians. On one occasion when Jeremiah was overwhelmed by derision and mockery, he thought for a moment of holding back his prophecies. Yet he soon recovered his courage in the strength of the Lord, for "his word was in mine heart as a burning fire shut up in my bones, and I was weary with forbearing, and I could not stay [i.e., keep silent]" (Jeremiah 20:9). Thus, he went forth with unwavering devotion to complete his prophetic ministry. Adversity could not hold him back. Tribulation could not silence his lips. He remained the Lord's mouthpiece to the end of his life.

How does the example of Jeremiah serve to encourage us to overcome adversity and continue in our service to build the kingdom of God on earth? Nephi, a young contemporary of Jeremiah, would put it this way a few years later: "Wherefore, ye must press forward with a steadfastness in Christ, having a perfect brightness of hope, and a love of God and of all men. Wherefore, if ye shall press forward, feasting upon the word of Christ, and endure to the end, behold, thus saith the Father: Ye shall have eternal life" (see 2 Nephi 31:20).

A TOUCH OF REALITY

A modern-day example of how to overcome challenges and rise in the light of the gospel is presented in the following account:

It is often in the shadows of adversity that the light of the gospel shines with the greatest radiance. My wife often speaks about her vivid childhood memories of seeing her father seated in his chair, reading and pondering the scriptures. Life was not always easy in those days, and the family had to move from time to time to different cities in search of new career opportunities. But the light of the gospel was never extinguished. The image of her father faithfully striving to broaden his understanding and open up channels of truth through the word of God is an enduring source of inspiration and comfort to her. She remembers fondly the time when he noticed her watching, and called her to his side to read a passage from the Book of Mormon and offer his commentary and feelings about it. "Is that not beautiful?" he said with a tear in his eye. This interaction made a lasting and wholesome impression on his young daughter.

> ### Opportunities to Develop Faith
>
> Elder Dallin H. Oaks confirmed that our strength is forged through adversity and that our mortal challenges open up opportunities to develop faith in the future and power to achieve eternal blessings of great significance (see *Pure in Heart* [Salt Lake City: Bookcraft, 1988], 122).

In her own days of motherhood and homemaking, she also set an example of one who finds gospel light illuminating the pathway of the mortal journey. She often cites a favorite passage from Jeremiah: "Blessed is the man that trusteth in the LORD, and whose hope the LORD is. For he shall be as a tree planted by the waters, and that spreadeth out her roots by the river, and shall not see when heat cometh, but her leaf shall be green; and shall not be careful in the year of drought, neither shall cease from yielding fruit" (Jeremiah 17:7–8). The flourishing tree of life is an enduring symbol of the abundance of the blessings of the Lord always available to His faithful sons and daughters. When we rise to the occasion in faith, all of us can help to build the kingdom of God and light the candle of truth: "Out of Zion, the perfection of beauty, God hath shined" (Psalm 50:2).

WHAT LESSONS CAN WE LEARN FROM JEREMIAH?

1. As with the prophets, the Lord will also sustain and guide us until our mortal mission has been accomplished.

Do we ever feel inadequate for the duties and assignments given to us for the purpose of building the kingdom of God? When he was called to be a prophet, Jeremiah was certainly overcome by such feelings: "Then said I, Ah, Lord GOD! behold, I cannot speak: for I am a child" (Jeremiah 1:6). But the Lord assured him that his calling was foreordained—"Before thou camest forth out of the womb I sanctified thee, and I ordained thee a prophet unto the nations" (Jeremiah 1:5)—and comforted him with a covenant promise: "Whatsoever I command thee thou shalt speak. Be not afraid of their faces: for I am with thee to deliver thee, saith the LORD" (Jeremiah 1:7–8). Both Moses as well as Isaiah responded to their callings with the same feelings of humility and personal inadequacy (see Exodus 3:11–14; Isaiah 6:5). But the Lord blesses all of His chosen servants with strength and guidance to accomplish their missions.

To Jeremiah, the Lord said, "And they shall fight against thee; but they shall not prevail against thee; for I am with thee, saith the LORD, to deliver thee" (Jeremiah 1:19). Thus Jeremiah went forth to proclaim with power the message of the Lord:

- "Thou hast forsaken me, saith the LORD, thou art gone backward: therefore will I stretch out my hand against thee, and destroy thee; I am weary with repenting. . . . And I will make thee to pass with thine enemies into a land which thou knowest not: for a fire is kindled in mine anger, which shall burn upon you" (Jeremiah 15:6, 14).

- "I will give all Judah into the hand of the king of Babylon, and he shall carry them captive into Babylon, and shall slay them with the sword" (Jeremiah 20:4).

- "If ye will not hearken to me, to walk in my law, which I have set before you, To hearken to the words of my servants the prophets, whom I sent unto you, both rising up early, and sending them, but ye have not hearkened; Then will I make this house like Shiloh [where the ark was kept until it was seized by the Philistines], and will make this city a curse to all the nations of the earth" (Jeremiah 26:4–6).

Why did the people in Judah refuse to listen to Jeremiah's warning when they were fully aware that Israel (the Northern Kingdom) had been totally scattered just over a century earlier? Why did they ignore history and reject the word of the Lord concerning the coming onslaught of the Babylonians? It was a sad pattern of deafness and blindness, and they also rejected the warnings of Lehi, Jeremiah's contemporary (see 1 Nephi 1:18–20).

How did Jeremiah ensure that the word of the Lord would be brought forth? Not only did he proclaim his message boldly before the people (see Jeremiah 17:19–20), before the princes and priests of the land (see Jeremiah 20:3–6; 26:12–16), and in the court of the Lord's house (see Jeremiah 26:2), but he also worked with his scribe, Baruch, to write and deliver the words of the Lord:

> How is Jeremiah mentioned in the Book of Mormon?
>
> Jeremiah's writings, in part, were included in the brass plates of Laban (see 1 Nephi 5:10–13). Nephi also refers to Jeremiah in rebuking his rebellious brothers: "For behold, the Spirit of the Lord ceaseth soon to strive with them [the people of Jerusalem]; for behold, they have rejected the prophets, and Jeremiah have they cast into prison. And they have sought to take away the life of my father, insomuch that they have driven him out of the land" (1 Nephi 7:14). Many generations later, Nephi, the son of Helaman, invoked the name of Jeremiah, among many other prophets, to remind the people of the certainty of the coming of the Redeemer: "And now we know that Jerusalem was destroyed according to the words of Jeremiah. O then why not the Son of God come, according to his prophecy?" (Helaman 8:20).

> Take thee a roll of a book, and write therein all the words that I have spoken unto thee against Israel, and against Judah, and against all the nations, from the day I spake unto thee, from the days of Josiah, even unto this day.
>
> It may be that the house of Judah will hear all the evil which I purpose to do unto them; that they may return every man from his evil way; that I may forgive their iniquity and their sin. (Jeremiah 36:2–3)

When Jehoiakim, the king of Judah, heard these words read to him, he burned the document in his hearth (see Jeremiah 36:23). Then the Lord commanded Jeremiah to have the words written again—"and there were added besides unto them many like words" (Jeremiah 36:32). But these repeated words were also rejected. The king's successor, Zedekiah, likewise frowned on Jeremiah's counsel: "Then Zedekiah the king sent, and took him out [of the dungeon]: and the king asked him secretly in his house, and said, Is there any word from the LORD? And Jeremiah said, There is: for, said he, thou shalt be delivered into the hand of the king of Babylon" (Jeremiah 37:17). Jeremiah remained imprisoned until the Babylonian conquest in 587 B.C. Thereafter, he continued his prophecies and completed the book of Lamentations, in which he grieved over the pitiful state of the great fallen city of Jerusalem and bewailed the fate of her lost citizens—but he did so in the spirit of a prophetic messenger commissioned to cry repentance as well as confirm the love of a tender Lord: "Yet will he have compassion according to the multitude of his mercies" (Lamentations 3:32).

Pondering: How do stories about the courageous actions of the Lord's prophets encourage you to move forward in completing your callings despite tribulation or adversity? How can you help your loved ones to sustain their faith and to endure despite the trials of life?

2. When our testimony burns within us, we have a compelling desire to share it with others.

Jeremiah was commanded to bring forth the word of the Lord as given to him by the Lord. He could not be deterred. That word was seething in his heart "as a burning fire shut up in [his] bones" (Jeremiah 20:9). As such, he acted continually as "an iron pillar" of truth (Jeremiah 1:18) that his audience could not bring down or repel. In like measure, Nephi could not restrain himself from declaring the gospel to his rebellious older brothers, as his father Lehi confirmed: "And it must needs be that the power of God must be with him, even unto his commanding you that ye must obey. But behold, it was not he, but it was the Spirit of the Lord which was in him, which opened his mouth to utterance that he could not shut it" (2 Nephi 1:27). The same experience was had by Ether, the last of the Jaredite prophets, who "began to prophesy unto the people, for he could not be restrained because of the Spirit of the Lord which was in him" (Ether 12:2). Similarly, young Joseph Smith could not restrain himself from declaring his witness of the First Vision: "I have actually seen a vision; and who am I that I can withstand God, or why does the world think to make me deny what I have actually seen? For I had seen a vision; I knew it, and I knew that God knew it, and I could not deny it, neither dared I do it; at least I knew that by so doing I would offend God, and come under condemnation" (JS—H 1:25).

These same spiritual forces are active in our own lives—"a burning fire" of testimony that we cannot hold back, the influence of the Spirit that opens our mouth such that we "cannot shut it" nor be "restrained," our witness to the truth that is so certain we cannot "deny it" out of fear of offending the Lord.

How has this fulsome spiritual motivation been active in your life and in the lives of your loved ones? You might want to reflect on the following story recounted by an elder who had served as a missionary in a German city:

> He was somewhat older than the average missionary, but when he arrived at the mission home, it was immediately apparent that his enthusiasm to preach the gospel was vibrant and energetic. It was the custom in those days to take the new missionaries to a street meeting soon after their arrival in order to introduce them directly to proselyting work. So, without delay, we accompanied these new elders, none of whom could speak German, to our favorite place near a large cathedral located in the center of the city. There, on the sidewalk next to the wall of the church, we would hold our meetings for small gatherings of curious passers-by and pass out tracts about the Restored Church.
>
> Our practice was to have the new missionaries bear their testimony in English and have veteran missionaries translate for the German listeners, and that is what happened on this occasion. However, when it was this older missionary's turn to speak, he smiled with a particularly glowing countenance and said, "I won't need you to translate." Then he proceeded to bear his testimony in German, speaking very fluently and expressively, giving his witness to the truthfulness of the gospel and the Restored Church to an attentive audience. We were all amazed.
>
> Afterward, I asked him whether he had ever studied the German language, and he told me that he had heard some of his relatives speak a few words years ago. On this occasion, however, he felt inspired to speak to the people in their own language—so he did. It was a heartwarming display of the gifts of God at work in a faithful and humble servant of God.
>
> The Prophet Joseph Smith explained that the gift of tongues "was particularly instituted for the preaching of the gospel to other nations and languages" (*HC* 2:162)—a phenomenon in widespread evidence among the many tens of thousands of missionaries on the Lord's errand in countries where they need to teach in

foreign tongues. In a more general sense, this kind of gift might also be granted to any of us who feel lifted and encouraged by the Spirit to open our mouths and bear our testimony to those around us simply because we cannot be restrained or held back.

Pondering: How do stories about the irrepressible motivation of the prophets—even at the peril of their own lives—encourage you to share your testimony with increased fervor and valor? How can you help your loved ones to rise to the challenge of helping to spread the gospel more often?

AGENDA FOR ACTION

When we look about and observe adverse influences threatening us, we can take to heart the comforting promise of the Lord to Jeremiah: "And they shall fight against thee; but they shall not prevail against thee; for I am with thee, saith the Lord, to deliver thee" (Jeremiah 1:19). Because the Lord is always with us, we can renew our efforts to magnify our callings with increased courage every day of our lives. We can "feast upon the word of Christ" (2 Nephi 32:3) and follow the counsel of the Spirit continually. We can jubilantly raise our voices with "boldness, but not overbearance" (Alma 38:12) to bear witness of the truths of the gospel of Jesus Christ to our families, our neighbors, and to all the world. Then we can say with Jeremiah: "Thy words were found, and I did eat them; and thy word was unto me the joy and rejoicing of mine heart: for I am called by thy name, O Lord God of hosts" (Jeremiah 15:16).

Looking Forward: What sacred things do you have written on your heart?

CHAPTER FORTY-TWO

A NEW COVENANT

GOSPEL DOCTRINE READING ASSIGNMENT: JEREMIAH 16, 23, 29, 31

After those days, saith the LORD, I will put my law in their inward parts, and write it in their
hearts; and will be their God, and they shall be my people. (Jeremiah 31:33)

THE DAWNING OF A GLORIOUS DAY

WHAT DOES THE LORD YEARN for us to say as we cry unto Him? Through His prophet Jeremiah, He gave us the exact words: "My father, thou art the guide of my youth" (Jeremiah 3:4). From the beginning of our days, the Lord invites us to receive Him as our loving Guide, our merciful Teacher, our protecting Shepherd. How does He help us to do so? His prophets teach us the four-fold pattern: listen to the warning voice, choose the pathway of righteousness, avoid the devastating consequences of sin, and rejoice in the blessings of obedience.

For forty years, Jeremiah preached this same process to a wayward generation. His warning was clear: "Why then is this people of Jerusalem slidden back by a perpetual backsliding? they hold fast deceit, they refuse to return" (Jeremiah 8:5). They allow themselves to decline into a condition where they have to admit, "The harvest is past, the summer is ended, and we are not saved" (8:20). "They know not me, saith the LORD" (9:3). They "have walked after other gods, and have served them, and have worshipped them, and have forsaken me, and have not kept my law" (16:11; see also 23:36).

When the Lord called Jeremiah as prophet, He said, "Behold, I have put my words in thy mouth" (1:9). The Lord's words resounded in the ears of the people, giving them divine counsel: "O Jerusalem, wash thine heart from wickedness, that thou mayest be saved" (4:14). "Stand ye in . . . the good way, and walk therein, and ye shall find rest for your souls" (6:16). "Obey my voice, and I will be your God, and ye shall be my people: and walk ye in all the ways that I have commanded you, that it may be well unto you" (7:23; see also 13:15).

The price of failure to obey was made plain: "Therefore thus saith the LORD, Behold, I will lay stumblingblocks before this people, and the fathers and the sons together shall fall upon them; the neighbour and his friend shall perish" (6:21). "Behold, I will cause to cease out of this place in your eyes, and in your days, the voice of mirth, and the voice of gladness, the voice of the bridegroom, and the voice of the bride" (16:9). "Behold, I will give this city into the hand of the Chaldeans, and into the hand of Nebuchadrezzar king of Babylon, and he shall take it" (32:28; see also verse 36).

Yet there was a light shining in the distance. Through the heavy mist of rebellion and waywardness, Jeremiah was blessed to see and share a penetrating vision of better times: "I will bring you to Zion: And I will give you pastors according to mine heart, which shall feed you with knowledge and understanding" (3:14–15). "Behold, I will send for many fishers, saith the LORD, and they shall fish them; and after will I send for many hunters, and they shall hunt them from every mountain, and from every hill, and out of the holes of the rocks" (16:16). "And I will gather the remnant of my flock out of all countries whither I have driven them, and will bring them again to their folds; and they shall be fruitful and increase. And I will set up shepherds over them which shall feed them: and they shall fear no more, nor be dismayed, neither shall they be lacking, saith the LORD" (23:3–4). Beyond the era of captivity would arise an era of gathering and rejuvenation:

> For thus saith the LORD, That after seventy years be accomplished at Babylon I will visit you, and perform my good word toward you, in causing you to return to this place. . . .
> And ye shall seek me, and find me, when ye shall search for me with all your heart.
> And I will be found of you, saith the LORD: and I will turn away your captivity, and I will gather you from all the nations, and from all the places whither I have driven you, saith the LORD; and I will bring you again into the place whence I caused you to be carried away captive. (29:10, 13–14)

The promise of the Lord through Jeremiah echoed through the shadows of a suffering land with words of glory: "And ye shall be my people, and I will be your God" (30:22). That promise extends beyond the era of deliverance from Babylonian captivity and reaches forward to the time when the gospel would be carried to all quarters of the earth: "Hear the word of the LORD, O ye nations, and declare it in the isles afar off, and say, He that scattered Israel will gather him, and keep him, as a shepherd doth his flock. For the LORD hath redeemed Jacob, . . . Therefore they shall come and sing in the height of Zion, and shall flow together to the goodness of the LORD" (31:10–12).

In words of magnificence, Jeremiah declared the nature of the new covenant to arise in the latter days:

> Behold, the days come, saith the LORD, that I will make a new covenant with the house of Israel, and with the house of Judah:
> Not according to the covenant that I made with their fathers in the day that I took them by the hand to bring them out of the land of Egypt; which my covenant they brake, although I was an husband unto them, saith the LORD:
> But this shall be the covenant that I will make with the house of Israel; After those days, saith the LORD, I will put my law in their inward parts, and write it in their hearts; and will be their God, and they shall be my people.
> And they shall teach no more every man his neighbour, and every man his brother, saying, Know the LORD: for they shall all know me, from the least of them unto the greatest of them, saith the LORD: for I will forgive their iniquity, and I will remember their sin no more. (31:31–34)

Through the power of this covenant, there will come a blending of hearts: "And I will give them one heart, and one way, that they may fear me for ever, for the good of them, and of their children after them: And I will make an everlasting covenant with them, that I will not turn away from them, to do them good; but I will put my fear in their hearts, that they shall not depart from me. Yea, I will rejoice over them to do them good, and I will plant them in this land assuredly with my whole heart and with my whole soul" (32:39–41). Being forgiven of the Lord, the people will rejoice in anthems of thanksgiving: "The voice of joy, and the voice of gladness, the voice of the bridegroom, and the voice of the bride, the voice of them that shall say, Praise the LORD of hosts: for the LORD is good; for his mercy endureth for ever" (33:11).

The ultimate era of millennial glory will then begin to dawn on the horizon of time:

> Behold, the days come, saith the LORD, that I will raise unto David a righteous Branch [Christ], and a King shall reign and prosper, and shall execute judgment and justice in the earth. In his days Judah shall be saved, and Israel shall dwell safely: and this is his name whereby he shall be called, THE LORD OUR RIGHTEOUSNESS." (23:5–6; see also 33:15–16)

What is anchored in the heart of the prophet Jeremiah is trumpeted forth as the word of the Lord unto all mankind, celebrating the triumph over darkness and evil: "Is not my word like as a fire? saith the LORD; and like a hammer that breaketh the rock in pieces?" (23:29). What is certain is the victory of the plan of salvation; what is unstoppable is the rise of Zion as an eternal family of God.

A TOUCH OF REALITY

The voices of all the Lord's prophets reveal what is written in their hearts—the burning word of the Lord planted there as a majestic witness of His work and glory. When we bear our testimony of the gospel, we too impart what is written in our hearts. May I share my testimony with you:

I have been blessed to be the husband of a lovely wife for over a half a century. We experienced a miracle this week. In fact, we enjoy the same miracle every day as we read the scriptures together. We read them aloud because that helps the miracle come about. The miracle is the burning in our hearts when we are nourished by the word of God. I am so grateful for that. We came across a scripture recently that we had never focused on before. It comes from Jeremiah 23:29, where the Lord says in eight simple words, "Is not my word like as a fire?" That fire is the miracle that can happen every day of our lives. When we take into our heart the word of the Lord, it burns within us and then radiates outwardly as the glow of gospel truth. Jeremiah prophesied that in the last days the Lord would renew His covenant with His people: "I will put my law in their inward parts, and write it in their hearts; and will be their God, and they shall be my people" (Jeremiah 31:33).

Young Joseph Smith followed the counsel given in James 1:5 by going into the woods one spring morning in 1820 to pray for guidance in finding the truth. At first he was overpowered by an immobilizing force of "thick darkness" (JS—H 1:15). But soon thereafter, he was delivered through the power of a descending light "above the brightness of the sun" (JS—H 1:16). In that light he beheld two divine Personages, the Father and the Son, "whose brightness and glory defy all description" (JS—H 1:17). Does that sound like a fire? It was at that moment that the glory of the First Vision burst upon the world as the dawning of the Restoration. My wife and I found it very interesting that after Joseph had recovered his strength, he rose from off the ground and returned home, where he "leaned up to the fireplace" (JS—H 1:20). Sometimes the everyday warmth of a fire is a reminder of the spiritual fire of the gospel that comes through revelation. It reminded us again of what the Lord said in Jeremiah: "Is not my word like as a fire?"

The gospel of Jesus Christ brings light and warmth into our lives. The gospel is true. It burns as a fire of inspiration in our lives. How do we know when we're receiving personal revelation? The Lord says to pray about it, and if it's right, "I will cause that your bosom shall burn within you" (D&C 9:8), otherwise you'll have a "stupor of thought" (D&C 9:9) and know that you need to move on to better things. My wife and I love the miracle of that burning within us when we read the scriptures and pray together every day. Joseph Smith taught that those in the celestial kingdom would dwell in a place of "everlasting burnings" (King Follett discourse, April 7, 1844, *HC* 6:306). Isaiah said the same thing: "Who among us shall dwell with the devouring fire? who among us shall dwell with everlasting burnings? He that walketh righteously, and speaketh uprightly" (Isaiah 33:14–15).

I am grateful for the miracle that points to that future day of "everlasting burnings." I am grateful for the blessing of the comforting fire that comes through the Holy Ghost when we read the scriptures and follow the counsel of our living prophets. Through His Spirit, the Lord writes His covenant in our hearts, where it can burn with everlasting truth and glow with eternal comfort. The Church is true. The Father and Son live. The Holy Ghost is our Comforter and Companion. And the family is forever. Of this I testify in the name of Jesus Christ, Amen.

WHAT LESSON CAN WE LEARN FROM JEREMIAH?

1. The Lord reveals to us moment by moment, as needed, what He plants in our hearts as spiritual nourishment to sustain us along the pathway of life. This is accomplished through covenants.

The theme sounded again and again by Jeremiah is "covenant"—meaning the sacred relationship and formal bond between the Lord and His people. The Lord works by covenant. He draws people in by covenant. He teaches through covenant. Whenever a Zion people come together, it is by covenant. The word itself embodies the process, for covenant means, literally, "a coming together." Jeremiah foresaw a time when the holy covenant would be renewed. Like the Apostle Peter, he foresaw "the times of refreshing" that would come "from the presence of the Lord" (Acts 3:19). He perceived a time in the future when the Lord would make a new covenant leading to universal spiritual knowledge. That knowledge would be written in the hearts of the people as a fire of truth (see Jeremiah 31:33).

How do we know when a person has the law of the Lord written in his or her heart? The Savior gave a telling answer to this question when He sent His servants into the world in our day to proclaim the restored gospel: "Whoso receiveth you receiveth me; and the same will feed you, and clothe you, and give you money. . . . And he that doeth not these things is not my disciple; by this you may know my disciples" (D&C 84:89, 91). The divine directive to love and care for one another "both spiritually and temporally" (Mosiah 4:26) is the essence of the gospel plan and a manifestation of our love for God (see Matthew 22:36–40). Those who have the law of the Lord written in their hearts are blessed with the capacity to discern the needs of others and respond charitably through the promptings of the Spirit. Evidence of this kind of charity abounds as in the following true story about a faithful grandmother:

One day she had the strong impression to write to one of her grandsons—then serving as a missionary in a distant land—and provide some additional financial support. She knew that the missionaries receive funds regularly through the contributions of families and friends worldwide, but she could not shake off the feeling that something extra was needed. Without delay, she responded to the prompting and mailed off a letter containing a check.

Meanwhile, her grandson and his companion were ministering to the needs of investigator families in a remote part of their mission. Poverty was rampant. Many families had insufficient means for their daily needs. One family was destitute, so the missionary companions took everything they had—all of their reserve funds—and gave it to the family so that these poor people might have food for survival. The elders were acting on pure faith, for they did not know how they would be able to support themselves until the next regular mission payment would come many days hence.

> **What is the connection between obedience and knowledge?**
>
> Brigham Young said, "When we have faith to understand that He must dictate and that we must be perfectly submissive to Him, then we shall begin to rapidly collect the intelligence that is bestowed upon the nations, for all this intelligence belongs to Zion. All the knowledge, wisdom, power, and glory that have been bestowed upon the nations of the earth, from the days of Adam till now, must be gathered home to Zion" (*Journal of Discourses* 8:279, June 3, 1860).

When they arrived back home that day, they found the letter and check from the grandmother, and they gratefully thanked their Father in Heaven for His goodness and the faithfulness and responsiveness of the sweet woman. "And it shall come to pass, that before they call, I will answer; and while they are yet speaking, I will hear" (Isaiah 65:24). Such are the signs of the latter days when "I will put my law in their inward parts, and write it in their hearts; and will be their God, and they shall be my people" (Jeremiah 31:33; see also 2 Corinthians 3:3). At his missionary homecoming, the grandson made mention of this incident and bore witness about the love of God for His people. You can clearly identify those who have the law of the Lord written in their hearts because they walk the pathway of charity and respond to the promptings of the Spirit to minister to God's children.

Pondering: How can we look into our hearts and find nestled there the word of God as a guide for our lives? How can we apply His counsel in faith and hope, knowing that better times, even glorious times, lie ahead?

AGENDA FOR ACTION

We can respond in faith to the message of the Lord's prophets. Listen to the warning voice, choose the pathway of righteousness, avoid the devastating consequences of sin, and rejoice in the glorious blessings of covenant honor and obedience. We can reach out and help our loved ones and others to find the truth and enjoy the blessings of "peace in this world, and eternal life in the world to come" (D&C 59:23). We can pray to the Lord to give us a burning in our hearts as a confirmation of the truths of the gospel and the verity of the Atonement. We can open up our eyes as the Lord parts the curtains of heaven and reveals unto us unseen opportunities to "be anxiously engaged in a good cause, and do many things of [our] own free will, and bring to pass much righteousness" (D&C 58:27). To every receptive soul, the light of truth illuminates the pathway forward and kindles an increased assurance that the Lord is our eternal Redeemer.

LOOKING FORWARD: How can we find the true shepherds of Israel?

CHAPTER FORTY-THREE

SHEPHERDS OF ISRAEL

GOSPEL DOCTRINE READING ASSIGNMENT: EZEKIEL 18, 34, 37

*And I will set up one shepherd over them, and he shall feed them, even my servant David
[Christ]; he shall feed them, and he shall be their shepherd.* (Ezekiel 34:23)

THE MESSAGE OF THE RIGHTEOUS SHEPHERDS

EZEKIEL (MEANING "GOD WILL STRENGTHEN"), one of the Lord's great prophets of the Old Testament, was a priest of the lineage of Zadok and a younger contemporary of Lehi, Jeremiah, and Daniel. Like King Jehoiachin (son of King Jehoiachim), he was carried away captive to Babylon in 597 B.C., and he prophesied from 592 B.C. to 570 B.C. Ezekiel was granted extraordinary visions that proclaim principles of the gospel pertaining to the house of Israel, then as now. He taught that the consequences of apostasy and idolatry are destruction and scattering and that the consequences of repentance and remembering the covenants are peace, unity, and the blessing of being heirs with the Good Shepherd, to partake eternally of His everlasting glory. The forty-eight chapters of Ezekiel comprise three main sections: prophecies of God's judgment against Jerusalem and neighboring countries (chapters 1–24), prophecies concerning the gathering and Restoration (chapters 25–39), and visions of the future temple of the Lord (chapters 40–48).

A recurring theme in the book of Ezekiel is the role played by the shepherds of the people. The Lord condemned the shepherds for their obsession with their own well-being rather than loving the people they were to serve:

Woe be to the shepherds of Israel that do feed themselves! should not the shepherds feed the flocks? . . .
The diseased have ye not strengthened, neither have ye healed that which was sick, neither have ye bound

up that which was broken, neither have ye brought again that which was driven away, neither have ye sought that which was lost; but with force and with cruelty have ye ruled them. And they were scattered, because there is no shepherd. (Ezekiel 34:2, 4–5)

By contrast, the Lord will save His sheep:

As a shepherd seeketh out his flock in the day that he is among his sheep that are scattered; so will I seek out my sheep, and will deliver them out of all places where they have been scattered in the cloudy and dark day. And I will bring them out from the people, and gather them from the countries, and will bring them to their own land, and feed them upon the mountains of Israel by the rivers, and in all the inhabited places of the country. (Ezekiel 34:12–13; see also Psalm 23)

Ezekiel then proclaims the marvelous prophecy from the Lord concerning the coming of the Good Shepherd:

And I will set up one shepherd over them, and he shall feed them, even my servant David [Christ]; he shall feed them, and he shall be their shepherd. . . .
And I will make with them a covenant of peace, . . .
Thus shall they know that I the LORD their God am with them, and that they, even the house of Israel, are my people, saith the Lord GOD.
And ye my flock . . . and I am your God. (Ezekiel 34:23, 25, 30–31)

A TOUCH OF REALITY
Ezra Taft Benson magnified and illuminated the symbolism of the Good Shepherd as it applies to the Church today. Active and watchful shepherds working under the direction of the Lord are of vital importance. Elder Benson cited the Savior's words unto Peter: "Feed my lambs. . . . Feed my sheep. . . . Feed my sheep" (John 21:15–17). Priesthood watchcare and shepherding are essential elements of service. Charitable and loving service by the women of Zion is also of fundamental importance. The following are key questions for the shepherds of the Church: Are you watching over the families you are called to teach—including your own loved ones? Are you seeking after those who are lost? Are you solemnly honoring your covenants of service?[23]

WHAT LESSONS CAN WE LEARN FROM EZEKIEL?
1. By virtue of the Atonement of Jesus Christ, all will be blessed with immortality through the Resurrection, and the faithful will have eternal life.
The message of Ezekiel was about multiple gatherings: gathering the scattered people of the Lord to their covenant homeland, gathering the words of God into a great whole, gathering the Saints to the fold of the Good Shepherd at His Second Coming, and gathering spirit and body eternally through the resurrection. The vision afforded Ezekiel concerning the resurrection has endured through the ages as an icon of prophecy:

Again he said unto me, Prophesy upon these bones, and say unto them, O ye dry bones, hear the word of the LORD.
Thus saith the Lord GOD unto these bones; Behold, I will cause breath to enter into you, and ye shall live: . . .
And ye shall know that I am the LORD, when I have opened your graves, O my people, and brought you up out of your graves,
And shall put my spirit in you, and ye shall live, and I shall place you in your own land. (Ezekiel 37:4–5, 13–14; see also D&C 138:43)

---

23   For more details see Ezra Taft Benson, *Come unto Christ* (Salt Lake City: Deseret Book, 1983), 64–68.

What was Joseph Smith's view of the resurrection? Here are his words on one occasion:

Would you think it strange if I relate what I have seen in vision in relation to this interesting theme? Those who have died in Jesus Christ may expect to enter into all that fruition of joy when they come forth, which they possessed or anticipated here.

So plain was the vision that I actually saw men, before they had ascended from the tomb, as though they were getting up slowly. They took each other by the hand and said to each other, "My father, my son, my mother, my daughter, my brother, my sister." And when the voice calls for the dead to arise, suppose I am laid by the side of my father, what would be the first joy of my heart? To meet my father, my mother, my brother, my sister; and when they are by my side, I embrace them and they me.

It is my meditation all the day, and more than my meat and drink, to know how I shall make the Saints of God comprehend the visions that roll like an overflowing surge before my mind. . . . Hosanna, hosanna, hosanna to Almighty God, that rays of light begin to burst forth upon us even now. (HC 5:361–362)

The word *resurrection* derives from the Latin term *resurgere*, meaning "to rise again." The resurrection is the permanent reuniting of the body and the spirit following death in mortality (see Alma 11:45). Through the miracle of the resurrection we become immortal. The resurrection was made possible "through the merits, and mercy, and grace of the Holy Messiah" (2 Nephi 2:8). We will be resurrected whole, restored to our perfect frame (see Alma 40:23–24). We will take with us all the knowledge and intelligence we have learned through our experiences here upon the earth (see D&C 130:18–19).

In addition to the blessing of the resurrection (immortality), there is the magnificent blessing of eternal life and celestial exaltation that we can look forward to through our obedience to the commandments. Ezekiel proclaimed the word of the Lord: "Therefore I will judge you, O house of Israel, every one according to his ways, saith the Lord God. Repent, and turn yourselves from all your transgressions; . . . and make you a new heart and a new spirit: . . . Wherefore turn yourselves, and live ye" (Ezekiel 18:30–32; see also Alma 5:7–14; D&C 84:38).

How can we too cultivate our "meditation all the day" and try to comprehend the glory of the Atonement and its eternal blessings? Parents are some of the Lord's greatest shepherds, guiding their children along the gospel pathway home again. Consider how a mother might lovingly answer her young daughter's question about the resurrection:

Daughter: In my Sunday School class, we talked about the resurrection. It sounds like something way off in the future.

Mother (taking her twelve-year-old daughter by both hands): It can seem far away in the future. And it was a long time ago that the resurrection started.

Daughter: You mean with Jesus, right?

Mother: Right. He said, "I am the resurrection, and the life: he that believeth in me, though he were dead, yet shall he live" (John 11:25). Because of His love for us, He put into effect a process that overcomes death. Our spirit and our body will be united again forever through the resurrection.

Daughter: I remember how we all felt when Grandma passed away. We are so grateful to know that she's still alive. Whenever I look at the beautiful pair of gloves she made for me, I think of her, like when she smiled so much whenever we visited her.

Mother: Just think, when you put those gloves on and whisper thanks to your grandmother, you can make the resurrection a part of your life today. Imagine a family reunion with all our loved ones after the resurrection. I'm thinking we'll all be pretty healthy then.

Daughter: Even Grandma? She was so sick, so weak.

Mother: Even your grandmother. That's the blessing of the resurrection.

Daughter: Do you think Grandma was sad to pass away?

Mother: I remember what the bishop said at her funeral. He quoted a line from the Doctrine and Covenants: "And it shall come to pass that those that die in me shall not taste of death, for it shall be sweet unto them" (D&C 42:46). I think your grandmother passed on with a sweet feeling. She was such a good person, very faithful. She can look forward to the "glorious resurrection" (D&C 42:45) the bishop talked about.

Daughter: We're learning about the different kinds of resurrections in Sunday School.

Mother: The way I understand it, there's a different kind of resurrection for each of the three degrees of glory. We inherit a level of glory in keeping with our level of obedience and righteousness.

Daughter: Yes, the celestial resurrection is the highest kind, right? Our teacher said this kind of resurrection is reserved for the Lord's most faithful and obedient sons and daughters.

Mother (putting her arm around her daughter): And you're one of them! You're a great example for me and your father and your brothers and sisters.

Daughter: Mom! I'm just a regular person!

Mother: Remember what you did when your friend Julie got sick last month?

Daughter: I fixed some chicken soup and took it down to her. That's all.

Mother: Did you cheer her up and help her with her homework and take her dog for a walk while she had to say in bed?

Daughter: Yes. I guess I just felt sad that she was sick.

Mother (picking up a copy of the Book of Mormon): Can we read a passage about Alma at the Waters of Mormon? Let's look it up—Mosiah 18:9.

Daughter (opening up the book): Here's the place: "Yea, and are willing to mourn with those that mourn; yea, and comfort those that stand in need of comfort, and to stand as witnesses of God at all times and in all things, and in all places that ye may be in, even until death, that ye may be redeemed of God, and be numbered with those of the first resurrection, that ye may have eternal life."

Mother: Does that put the resurrection front and center in our daily life?

Daughter: Yes, it does, Mom. Thanks for helping me learn how serving others puts me on a list for the First Resurrection.

Mother: And for eternal life. What do you think it means "to stand as witnesses of God at all times . . . and in all places"?

Daughter: Hmmm. This coming Sunday is fast and testimony meeting. I think maybe I'll get up and bear my testimony. Maybe even mention the resurrection and the Atonement.

Mother (smiling): We'll all look forward to hearing you—and the Spirit will bless you in what you say. I love you, sweet daughter.

Daughter: Love you too, Mom. Well, I think I better go visit Julie. She said she needs some more help with her math assignment.

Mother: That reminds me what Joseph Smith taught: "Whatever principle of intelligence we attain unto in this life, it will rise with us in the resurrection" (D&C 130:18). All the good things we learn here we can take with us to the other side.

Daughter: Mother! Are you trying to make school a part of the resurrection? Even math?

Mother (laughing): It's all a matter of counting. Julie can count on you. We can count on you. And so can the Savior. Must be gospel math. Like 10 percent tithing, and forgiving others seventy times seven, and—

Daughter: And a kiss a day keeps every frown away! [Kisses her mother] See you soon!

Mother (touching the kissed cheek while she watches her daughter hurry down the walkway): Thank you, Heavenly Father. She'll be ours forever.

Pondering: How can we make immortality and eternal life the guiding theme of our daily journey? How can we help our loved ones to do the same?

2. In the latter days God's words to Joseph and Judah will be gathered together in one.

Ezekiel's vision of the blending of two sticks in the latter days is a striking prophecy about the Lord's gathering together His word as part of the Restoration:

> Moreover, thou son of man, take thee one stick, and write upon it, For Judah, and for the children of Israel his companions: then take another stick, and write upon it, For Joseph, the stick of Ephraim, and for all the house of Israel his companions:
>
> And join them one to another into one stick; and they shall become one in thine hand. (Ezekiel 37:16–17; see also verses 18–19)

The stick of Judah is the Bible, and the stick of Joseph is the Book of Mormon. "And it shall come to pass that my people, which are of the house of Israel, shall be gathered home unto the lands of their possessions; and my word also shall be gathered in one" (2 Nephi 29:14). The coming forth of the Book of Mormon in our day fulfills the design of the Lord to enlighten and lift the lives of His sons and daughters today. The Lord is likely very pleased with the following testimony a young sister shared recently:

> I tend to have a lot of moments when I find myself helplessly drawn to my knees in tears. I pray to my Heavenly Father and plead for help and most of all comfort. I get inspired to open my Book of Mormon to places I wouldn't think to read. And without fail in the middle of the page is my answer and a way for comfort. These hard times have given me a lifetime knowledge that the Book of Mormon is true and so is this gospel. Something that powerful could never be a lie.

What a beautiful confirmation of the word of the Lord about the Book of Mormon: "Proving to the world that the holy scriptures are true, and that God does inspire men [and women] and call them to his holy work in this age and generation, as well as in generations of old; Thereby showing that he is the same God yesterday, today, and forever. Amen" (D&C 20:11–12).

Pondering: How can we make the Book of Mormon the keystone of our faith? How can we best share our witness of the truth of the Book of Mormon with others as a blessing for their lives?

AGENDA FOR ACTION

In the spirit of humility and repentance, we can follow the counsel of the Lord: "Make you a new heart and a new spirit: . . . Turn yourselves, and live ye" (Ezekiel 18:31–32; see also Ezekiel 11:19–20; 36:26–28). We can follow in the footsteps of the Good Shepherd and serve others as faithful shepherds in Zion, rejoicing in the coming days of glory where "there shall be showers of blessing" and all "shall know that I am the LORD" (Ezekiel 34:26–27). We can feast upon the books of Joseph and Judah that the Lord has spread before us and find a secure path back to our heavenly home. Can we make it a practice to read from the Book of Mormon each day? Can we work to discover how the Book of Mormon blends with the Old Testament passages we are studying? If the Lord's word is to be "gathered in one" (2 Nephi 29:14) in the latter days, where shall this take place? In our hearts and minds! For that is where the truths of the gospel come to rest.

LOOKING FORWARD: Where can we partake of the living waters?

CHAPTER FORTY-FOUR

LIVING WATERS

GOSPEL DOCTRINE READING ASSIGNMENT: EZEKIEL 43–44, 47

*So the spirit took me up, and brought me into the inner court; and, behold, the
glory of the LORD filled the house.* (Ezekiel 43:5)

THE HOLY TEMPLE OF THE LORD

THE FINAL NINE CHAPTERS OF the book of Ezekiel constitute a visionary journey to a city of glory named "The Lord is there" (Ezekiel 48:35), where Ezekiel is granted entrance to the holy temple rising in the midst thereof. Nothing is withheld from the prophet's view, including the details of the building's construction, together with the sacred ordinances administered there:

Then brought he me the way of the north gate before the house: and I looked, and, behold, the glory
of the LORD filled the house of the LORD: and I fell upon my face.

And the LORD said unto me, Son of man, mark well, and behold with thine eyes, and hear with thine
ears all that I say unto thee concerning all the ordinances of the house of the LORD, and all the laws thereof;
and mark well the entering in of the house, with every going forth of the sanctuary. (Ezekiel 44:4–5)

Ezekiel is taught how the ministering priests are to conduct their service relative to the temple: "And they shall
teach my people the difference between the holy and profane, and cause them to discern between the unclean and
the clean" (Ezekiel 44:23). Ezekiel is also shown a current of water flowing from below the temple and expanding
in volume and depth as it continues eastward, bringing healing and life-sustaining influences to all the realm (see

Ezekiel 47:1–9). This surging river is a vibrant image of the flow of truth and light that enliven the souls of those seeking the Lord's endowment of eternal blessings through the work of the temple.

This vision of the temple lets us savor the eternal pattern of exaltation prepared by the Lord for His children. Just as Isaiah before him, Ezekiel surely had a clear view of how, in the last days, "the mountain of the LORD's house shall be established in the top of the mountains, and shall be exalted above the hills" (Isaiah 2:2). He knew with certainty of the impending devastation of the temple in Jerusalem, just as he was likely granted the comforting knowledge of its restoration to take place some seventy years later—as was Jeremiah (see Jeremiah 25:11–12; 29:10). He personally experienced the pains and trials of captivity under Babylonian conquest, but he was blessed with the reassuring hope that the temple would provide healing and saving powers for the Lord's faithful children in the latter days.

How can we participate with Ezekiel in the uplifting vision of temple work?

Important dates concerning the beginning of temple work in our day:

- March 27, 1836: Dedication of the Kirtland Temple and the beginning of initiatory ordinances.
- August 15, 1840: First proxy baptism performed in the Mississippi River; others were performed in the ensuing weeks in the river or in nearby streams while the Saints awaited the completion of the Nauvoo temple (see *Church History in the Fulness of Times*, rev. ed. [Salt Lake City: Corporation of the President of The Church of Jesus Christ of Latter-day Saints, 1993], 251; see also D&C 124:28–37).
- November 21, 1841: First baptisms for the dead are performed in the font in the basement of the Nauvoo Temple, then still under construction (see *HC* 4:454).
- May 4, 1842: First endowments for the living performed by Joseph Smith in the upper floor of the Red Brick Store; ninety more are performed over the next two years prior to his martyrdom (see *HC* 5:1; *Church History in the Fulness of Times*, 253–254).
- December 1845: Nauvoo temple sufficiently completed to perform endowment ordinances for the living (*Church History in the Fulness of Times*, 254).
- May 1, 1846: Nauvoo Temple dedicated by Orson Hyde. "In all, nearly 6,000 Latter-day Saints had received their temple ordinances in Nauvoo the previous winter" (William G. Hartley, "The Pioneer Trek: Nauvoo to Winter Quarters," *Ensign*, June 1997, 31).

A TOUCH OF REALITY

May 4, 1842, is a very special day in the history of the restored Church. It is a day to remind us that we have the opportunity to prepare to be endowed with the Lord's choicest blessings. Here's the background: In February 1831 in Kirtland, Ohio, the Lord made a promise to the Saints through the Prophet Joseph Smith: "And ye are to be taught from on high. Sanctify yourselves and ye shall be endowed with power, that ye may give even as I have spoken" (D&C 43:16). On March 27, 1836, the Kirtland Temple was dedicated and became the site for profoundly important heavenly visitations a few days later on April 3, including the appearance of the Savior and the restoration of essential priesthood keys through Moses, Elias, and Elijah for the unfolding and operation of the kingdom of God on the earth in the latter days, including temple work (see D&C 110).

A few years later in Nauvoo, on May 4, 1842, after the Saints had survived daunting dislocations and tribulations at the hands of their enemies, Joseph Smith introduced the particulars of the sacred temple endowment for the first time in this dispensation. Present at this meeting in the upper story of the Prophet's Red Brick Store were leaders such as Hyrum Smith, Newel K. Whitney, Brigham Young, Heber C. Kimball, and Willard Richards. The instruction from the Prophet included "all those plans and principles by which any one is enabled to secure the fulness of those blessings which have been prepared for the Church of the First Born, and come up and abide in the presence of the Eloheim in the eternal worlds. In this council was instituted the ancient order of things for the first time in these last days. And the communications I made to this council were of things spiritual, and to be received only by the spiritual minded: and there was nothing made known to these men but what will be made known to all the Saints of the last days, so soon as they are prepared to receive, and a proper place is prepared to communicate them, even to the weakest of the Saints; therefore let the Saints be diligent in building the Temple" (*HC* 5:1).

From this humble beginning, temple work has unfolded and expanded until it now reaches into all corners of the world. What Ezekiel foresaw in his vision of the Lord's house is now bringing healing and exalting powers to bear for all of the Lord's righteous sons and daughters.

WHAT LESSON CAN WE LEARN FROM EZEKIEL?

1. Through our obedience, we are blessed with the healing and exalting powers of the living waters of the Lord.

The image of the living waters of the gospel provides a beautiful symbol of the love of the Lord for His children and a comforting reminder of His eternal desire to nourish, strengthen, and lift them toward their heavenly home. Jeremiah spoke of "the fountain of living waters" that the Lord wanted all to receive (Jeremiah 2:13; 17:13). Zechariah prophesied of the "living waters" that would flow forth in the day when the Lord would reign as King over all the earth (Zechariah 14:8). Nephi shared the details of his glorious vision: "And it came to pass that I beheld that the rod of iron, which my father had seen, was the word of God, which led to the fountain of living waters, or to the tree of life; which waters are a representation of the love of God; and I also beheld that the tree of life was a representation of the love of God" (1 Nephi 11:25). Jesus used the same symbol to teach the Samaritan woman at the well about the power of His gospel to sanctify lives: "But whosoever drinketh of the water that I shall give him shall never thirst; but the water that I shall give him shall be in him a well of water springing up into everlasting life" (John 4:13–14).

Ezekiel was favored to view a similar vision of the healing powers of the waters of salvation:

AFTERWARD he brought me again unto the door of the house; and, behold, waters issued out from under the threshold of the house eastward: for the forefront of the house stood toward the east, and the waters came down from under from the right side of the house, at the south side of the altar.

Then brought he me out of the way of the gate northward, and led me about the way without unto the utter gate by the way that looketh eastward; and, behold, there ran out waters on the right side. . . .

Now when I had returned, behold, at the bank of the river were very many trees on the one side and on the other.

Then said he unto me, These waters issue out toward the east country, and go down into the desert, and go into the sea: which being brought forth into the sea, the waters shall be healed.

And it shall come to pass, that every thing that liveth, which moveth, whithersoever the rivers shall come, shall live: . . . and every thing shall live whither the river cometh. . . .

And by the river upon the bank thereof, on this side and on that side, shall grow all trees for meat, whose leaf shall not fade, neither shall the fruit thereof be consumed: it shall bring forth new fruit according to his months, because their waters they issued out of the sanctuary: and the fruit thereof shall be for meat, and the leaf thereof for medicine. (Ezekiel 47:1–2, 7–9, 12)

How is the process of sustaining life connected to the waters of the Lord? John the Revelator was shown the answer:

AND he shewed me a pure river of water of life, clear as crystal, proceeding out of the throne of God and of the Lamb. In the midst of the street of it, and on either side of the river, was there the tree of life, which bare twelve manner of fruits, and yielded her fruit every month: and the leaves of the tree were for the healing of the nations. (Revelation 22:1–2; see also Revelation 7:17)

The ordinance of the sacrament teaches the same lesson. The "bread of life" (John 6:35, 48) and the living water of the Atonement allow us to renew our baptismal covenant by showing our willingness to take upon ourselves the Savior's name and receive His Spirit to be with us always (see D&C 20:77, 79).

As an illustration of how the image of living water can touch our lives, consider the following account shared by a priesthood holder:

East of Lake Louise in Banff National Park lies Yoho National Park, just over the boundary between Alberta and British Columbia. One of the most spectacular sights in Yoho is Takakkaw Falls, where a free-flowing stream of water plunges in two stages more than a thousand feet downward into a forested Rocky Mountain canyon. As a young man, I used to drive a tour bus in that area, and both Lake Louise and Takakkaw were valued destinations. The former inspired feelings of eternal peace and calm; the latter inspired awe for the dynamic forces of nature. The word *Takakkaw* derives from a Cree word meaning "magnificent." According to a legend recounted to me by my trainers, the individual who first viewed this extraordinary waterfall saw it against a brilliant sky and had the impression that the river was flowing directly out of the sun, hence being "water from the sun." The tourists who accompanied me to this natural wonder would invariably stand transfixed as they viewed this amazing "water from the sun." Moreover, they could imagine in their mind's eye the invisible glacier, far above, that served as the source of the stream. Their hearts resonated with the wonders of nature.

John Taylor once used the image of a stream and its fountain to explain the essential nature of the infinite Atonement as central to the plan of salvation. "Why did it need an infinite atonement? For the simple reason that a stream can never rise higher than its fountain; . . . A man, as a man, could arrive at all the dignity that a man was capable of obtaining or receiving; but it needed a God to raise him to the dignity of a God" (*The Mediation and Atonement* [Salt Lake City: Deseret News Company, 1882], 145). The water that President Taylor referred to is the Son of God—the "fountain of living waters" (Jeremiah 2:13; 17:13; see also Ezekiel 47). It was He who was the source of the eternal water that would forever quench the thirst for spiritual vitality, being "a well of water springing up into everlasting life" (John 4:14).

Takakkaw Falls is accessed only by navigating fairly daunting switchbacks along the road. The roadway leading to the fountain of living waters is likewise marked by challenges and tribulations. Full access to the breathtaking view afforded by the plan of salvation can be gained only by faith, humility, and obedience. One must constantly hold to the iron rod that Lehi beheld in his dream (see 1 Nephi 8:19–20, 24, 30). On the journey toward the living waters and the tree of life (see 1 Nephi 11:25), we can keep our vision clear and open, "with an eye single to the glory of God" (D&C 4:5; 82:19). In this manner, the journey becomes joyful, regardless of the switchbacks and challenges. The outcome is worth it, for the reward that awaits the faithful traveler is to experience the blessings of salvation, the ultimate attainment of the source of the healing stream— the Son of God, the Redeemer, the Holy One of Israel. It is not water from the sun that truly matters—but water from the Son.

Pondering: How can we more fully bring the blessings of the temple into our lives and into the lives of our loved ones? How can we make partaking of the sacrament each week a more vibrant and life-changing event?

AGENDA FOR ACTION

In this world of evaporating values and moral decay, we can rise to our destiny and obey the Lord in honor. We should "gather together, and stand in holy places" (D&C 101:22)—the blessed homes and stakes and temples of Zion. We can join together with those who partake of the living waters, "for they shall be healed; and every thing shall live whither the river cometh" (Ezekiel 47:9). We can love the Lord and serve His sons and daughters. We can follow the admonition of the Lord in our day: "But unto him that keepeth my commandments I will give the mysteries of my kingdom, and the same shall be in him a well of living water, springing up unto everlasting life" (D&C 63:23).

That well of living water is accessed through simple acts of faith. We can teach our children to look to the temple as a beacon of heavenly glory. We can go with them for walks around the temple grounds, arrange for them to do baptisms for the dead, display the images of holy temples in prominent places around the home, make temple work an important part of family home evening discussions, participate together in family history work, and bear our testimonies about the nature of the eternal family and the sealing ordinances of the temple. We can share special scriptures concerning the living water, such as those cited in the previous paragraph or those taught by Jesus to the Samaritan woman by the well: "Whosoever drinketh of this water shall thirst again: But whosoever drinketh of the water that I shall give him shall never thirst; but the water that I shall give him shall be in him a well of water springing up into everlasting life" (John 4:13–14). We can partake of the sacrament, the bread and water of life, with a sincere commitment to renew our covenants. All such simple acts of faith lift our hearts in gratitude for the wonders of the holy places of Zion to which we gather. In simplicity, there is majesty; in quiet acts of worship, there is divine power.

LOOKING FORWARD: How can we have the courage to obey the Lord—even at the peril of our own lives?

CHAPTER FORTY-FIVE

THE GOD WHO DELIVERS

GOSPEL DOCTRINE READING ASSIGNMENT: DANIEL 1, 3, 6; ESTHER 3–5, 7–8
Thy God whom thou servest continually, he will deliver thee. (Daniel 6:16)

GIVING OUR ALL FOR THE LORD

SHORTLY BEFORE THE TURN OF the century leading to the destruction of Jerusalem in 587 B.C., young Daniel and three of his peers were captured and taken to the court of Nebuchadnezzar to be taught the Babylonian culture (see Daniel 1:4). The four young Hebrews immediately displayed their initiative by insisting on eating wholesome foods in place of the lush royal diet. As a result, their health and well-being flourished over those consuming the king's food and drink (see Daniel 1:8–15). The four then rose in magnificent courage by refusing to embrace the local idol worshiping—even when threatened with death. Daniel's three friends Hananiah, Mishael, and Azariah (renamed Shadrach, Meshach, and Abed-nego by the Babylonians) were thrown into a fiery furnace when they refused to worship the gods of the land. But an angel of the Lord preserved them (see Daniel 3:25), shocking Nebuchadnezzar into the realization that "there is no other God that can deliver after this sort" (Daniel 3:29). Similarly, Daniel (renamed Belteshazzar) was thrown into a den of lions for refusing to relinquish his worship of the Lord of Israel. Yet he was preserved by the hand of the Lord, for his mission was not yet fulfilled, causing Darius, then king, to make a decree throughout the land: "That in every dominion of my kingdom men tremble and fear before the God of Daniel: for he is the living God" (Daniel 6:26).

Well over a century after the experiences of Daniel and his brethren, Esther also displayed unyielding courage. When her captive Jewish people faced extermination at the hands of Haman, a leader in the court of Ahasuerus, king of Persia, Esther chose to risk her life in order to preserve their lives. She prevailed, and her people were blessed with "light, and gladness, and joy, and honour" (Esther 8:16).

Accounts of courage by such devoted children of God serve as a Liahona of guidance in our lives today. How can we join their circle of courage as we strive to give our all for the building of the kingdom of God in the latter days?

A TOUCH OF REALITY

Imagine that you are standing on the stage of life in association with people like Daniel and Esther. You watch as Daniel and his three peers step forward to form a circle. They hold hands in friendship; their faces radiate the light and joy of the gospel. Behind them you can see other figures waiting in the shadows. One of them steps forward and comes into view. It is Esther, glowing with joy and enlightened with the spirit of deliverance. She joins the circle of courage to hold hands with her friends. Then you see another figure step forward to enlarge the circle. You sense that this is Abinadi, who gave his life by refusing to recant his prophecies about the coming of our Lord, Jesus Christ. In turn, others join the circle: Joseph of Egypt and

What's in a name?

Why did the Babylonian royal officers change the names of the four captives of Jerusalem (see Daniel 1:7)? Daniel means "God is my judge" or "Judge of God"; Hananiah means "Jehovah has given" or "Jehovah has shown favor"; Mishael means "Who is like God is?"; and Azariah means "Jehovah has helped" or "Whom Jehovah helps"—all names that reflect allegiance to Jehovah, their sacred Lord and God. Their new names in Babylon suggest allegiance to idols: Belteshazzar to Bel (the supreme Babylonian god—see Daniel 4:8; 5:12; Isaiah 46:1), Shadrach and Meshach to Aku (moon god), and Abed-nego to Nego (also Nebo or Nabu—god of wisdom; see Isaiah 46:1). Could it be that the Babylonian captors were hoping Daniel and his friends would in time shift their allegiance to the local gods? If so, their hope was without foundation, as the four youth courageously maintained their faithfulness to Jehovah—even at the peril of their lives. Is the renaming tactic of Babylonia archaic? Or does modern Babylon seek to have us rename ourselves in honor of modern idols that direct us away from the Lord? In our day the Lord said, "Go ye out from Babylon. Be ye clean that bear the vessels of the Lord" (D&C 133:5). We are to take upon ourselves the name of the Lord, always remembering Him and keeping His commandments in order to be worthy of His Spirit (see D&C 20:77, 79).

Nephi, exemplars of covenant obedience, both of whom had brothers who threatened to take their lives out of jealousy and pride; Stephen, martyred for his undeviating devotion to the Lord; Joseph Smith and his brother Hyrum, who sacrificed their lives at Carthage for the cause of Zion; and many other righteous souls committed to giving their all for the blessing of God's children.

As the circle grows larger and the spirit of harmony and peace expands, you see a stately figure stepping forward from the shadows with the appearance of the Son of God—the very one who did the will of the Father and gave His life to bring about the Atonement. You see Him enter into the center of the circle, smiling at all who surround Him. Then He looks over toward you with kindness and quietly says the words, "Come, follow me" (Luke 18:22).

With humble devotion, you walk toward the circle, knowing that you are in the company of those who can teach you how to serve the Lord "with all your heart, might, mind and strength" and thus "stand blameless before God at the last day" (D&C 4:2). That is your reality. That is your opportunity. At the beckoning of the Lord, you are welcomed into the circle of courage as someone who has served the Lord with devotion and faithfulness. You are made to feel that you truly belong, that you are someone who is willing to give your all for the Lord. No, you may not be called upon to give your life as a martyr. But you have the ongoing mission to devote your life in love and service to the cause of the Lord, who is the Redeemer of the world. Therefore, quietly, with a broken heart and a contrite spirit, you join the enlarging circle to fulfill your own divine destiny through courage and sacrifice, knowing that in the strength of the Lord you can accomplish your mission with honor and joy.

Quietly and peacefully you remember in thanksgiving the Lord's word about a future sacrament meeting at which He will welcome all of His prophets as well as "all those whom my Father hath given me out of the world" (D&C 27:14). And you look forward in hope and faith for the opportunity to join in that sacred future occasion of glory and joy.

WHAT LESSONS CAN WE LEARN FROM DANIEL AND ESTHER?

1. We can survive the tests of life and serve the Lord with enduring faith and honor.

Daniel and his three friends were young people "in whom was no blemish, but well favoured, and skilful in all wisdom, and cunning in knowledge, and understanding science" (Daniel 1:4). Moreover, "God gave them knowledge and skill in all learning and wisdom: and Daniel had understanding in all visions and dreams" (Daniel 1:17). Endowed with gifts from heaven, they were prepared for the tribulation that awaited them when king Nebuchadnezzar sent forth a decree concerning the golden image that he had erected: "And whoso falleth not down and worshippeth shall the same hour be cast into the midst of a burning fiery furnace" (Daniel 3:6). When spies discovered that Shadrach, Meshach, and Abed-nego refused to worship the image, the king was furious and warned the young men, "If ye worship not, ye shall be cast the same hour into the midst of a burning fiery furnace; and who is that God that shall deliver you out of my hands?" (Daniel 3:15). In response, the young men confirmed their true colors—despite the peril that was placed upon their lives:

> If it be so, our God whom we serve is able to deliver us from the burning fiery furnace, and he will deliver us out of thine hand, O king.
>
> But if not, be it known unto thee, O king, that we will not serve thy gods, nor worship the golden image which thou hast set up. (Daniel 3:17–18)

That phrase "But if not" was a lucid and clear confirmation of the authentic faith of the three youth. They had a firm hope that the Lord would deliver them from the life-threatening peril. But their invincible faith in the Lord was doubly confirmed by their words "but if not"—for even martyrdom would not displace their commitment to remain steadfast in their honor and love for the Lord, no matter what.[24]

Immediately, the young men were bound and cast into a raging fire. But then a miracle ensued, causing the king to exclaim,

> Lo, I see four men loose, walking in the midst of the fire, and they have no hurt; and the form of the fourth is like the Son of God. . . . Blessed be the God of Shadrach, Meshach, and Abed-nego, who hath sent his angel, and delivered his servants that trusted in him, . . . and yielded their bodies, that they might not serve nor worship any god, except their own God. (Daniel 3:25, 28)

Thereafter, the king sent forth a decree of protection on behalf of the young men, "because there is no other God that can deliver after this sort" (Daniel 3:29). He then promoted the three within his realm.

A similar experience confirmed Daniel's obedience to the Lord. Darius, then king, set up an organization of 120 princes throughout his realm, with three of them serving as presidents, Daniel being the first, for he "was preferred above the presidents and princes, because an excellent spirit was in him; and the king thought to set him over the whole realm" (Daniel 6:3). Being jealous of Daniel and realizing that they could find no cause against him except "the law of his God" (Daniel 6:5), the other princes induced the king to issue a decree that "whosoever shall ask a petition of any God or man for thirty days, save of thee, O king, he shall be cast into the den of lions" (Daniel 6:7). But Daniel rejected the decree: "Now when Daniel knew that the writing was signed, he went into his house; and his windows being open in his chamber toward Jerusalem, he kneeled upon his knees three times a day, and prayed, and gave thanks before his God, as he did aforetime" (Daniel 6:10).

When this was made known unto the king, he was forced against his will to have Daniel cast into the den of lions but with a promise: "Thy God whom thou servest continually, he will deliver thee" (Daniel 6:16). The next morning Daniel reported to the anxious king: "My God hath sent his angel, and hath shut the lions' mouths, that they have not hurt me: forasmuch as before him innocency was found in me; and also before thee, O king, have I done no hurt" (Daniel 6:22). Relieved, the king then ordered Daniel released from the den, "and no manner of hurt was found upon him, because he believed in his God" (Daniel 6:23). The conspirators, however, did not experience such a happy

24   See Dennis E. Simmons,"But if Not . . .," *Ensign,* May, 2004.

outcome, for the king had them cast into the den of lions they had prepared for Daniel and sent forth a new decree: "That in every dominion of my kingdom men tremble and fear before the God of Daniel: for he is the living God, and steadfast for ever, and his kingdom that which shall not be destroyed, and his dominion shall be even unto the end" (Daniel 6:26). It was through the blessings of the Lord that "Daniel prospered in the reign of Darius, and in the reign of Cyrus the Persian" (Daniel 6:28).

These famous stories are unforgettable reminders that the Lord sustains and supports His faithful children until their mortal missions have been completed. Daniel and his three friends were spared to continue their service among their Hebrew people as the time approached for the decree in 537 B.C., issued by Cyrus, the Persian king, to allow the people to return from their Babylonian captivity to the land of their inheritance and rebuild the temple (see 2 Chronicles 36:22–23; Ezra 1; 3:7; Isaiah 44:28; 45:1).

All of us find along the mortal pathway many experiences where our covenant faithfulness is put to the test. In those times, we look to the example of the Lord's righteous prophets and leaders and seek the Lord's strength to overcome and endure in faith.

Pondering: How can we reach faithfully beyond the perils and challenges of life and confirm the Lord's promise to "go before your face. I will be on your right hand and on your left, and my Spirit shall be in your hearts, and mine angels round about you, to bear you up" (D&C 84:88)?

2. In the spirit of Esther, we can help bring deliverance and joy to our loved ones and to all those who seek the gospel of truth.

The story of Esther (meaning "star") is one of great courage and faith. The details of her memorable life are given in the book of Esther, one of the late historical books of the Old Testament (along with Ezra and Nehemiah). The events in the book of Esther occurred some half century following the return of many of the Jewish captives from Babylon, as authorized by the decree of Cyrus in 537 B.C.

Here is an overview of the key facts: Ahasuerus, king of Persia (usually identified with Xerxes, whose rule began around 486 B.C.), was seeking a new wife. Mordecai, a Jewish man who had not yet returned to Jerusalem, brought his adopted daughter Esther before the king: "And the king loved Esther above all the women, and she obtained grace and favour in his sight more than all the virgins; so that he set the royal crown upon her head, and made her queen" (Esther 2:17). Mordecai refused to pay homage to Haman, the king's chief officer, so Haman arranged a decree to slay him, together with all the Jewish people in the kingdom. Esther decided to go and plead before the king at considerable peril to herself—for such an uninvited appearance would, by law, result in death unless the king should "hold out the golden sceptre" (Esther 4:11) as a signal to preserve the life of the intruder. Thus Esther sent word to her people:

> Go, gather together all the Jews that are present in Shushan, and fast ye for me, and neither eat nor drink three days, night or day: I also and my maidens will fast likewise; and so will I go in unto the king, which *is* not according to the law: and if I perish, I perish. (Esther 4:16)

After the fast, Esther went forward in courage to secure the liberation of her people:

Her head high in keeping with the stately nobility of her mission, she offered a silent prayer to the Lord as she waited solemnly in the courtyard before the closed door leading to the throne room of her husband the king. To open the door unannounced and enter as an unscheduled visitor was considered sedition and could result in death. She perfectly understood the risk involved, but the preservation of her Jewish compatriots throughout the realm was at stake—their extermination having been ordered by the conspiracy of Haman, chief officer serving under the king. Thus she held the position of deliverer, the only one who might be able to intercede on behalf of every man, woman, and child of Jewish descent. She pondered silently what her cousin and adopted father had told her in recent days: "Who knoweth whether thou art come to the kingdom for such a time as this?" (Esther 4:14).

In a state of tranquility—despite the peril—she reached toward the handle of the door. "Am I not come into the kingdom for this very purpose?" she reasoned within herself. *If I turn back*, she thought, *thousands will disappear from the face of the earth under the hand of evil.* She pondered in her heart the faith of her people, who had fasted for three days and three nights on behalf of her mission of redemption. She sensed in her heart their sweet glow of hope. She took the handle in a firm grip. "If the king will listen with judgment and respond with wisdom, then my people will be saved with outpourings of joy and gratitude."

Slowly, with dedication and faith, she opened the door to reveal the view of the king seated on his palatial throne among the statesmen of the court. Becoming aware of the unscheduled visitor, the king turned directly toward her and stared into her countenance for what seemed an endless length of time without any change of his expression. Her heart began to increase in its vibrant rhythm as she awaited his response. Would he . . . ?

Then he smiled at her and held forth the golden scepter as a cordial and evocative gesture, directing her to advance and be received in dignity and acceptation. Immediately, a spirit of utter calmness and peace unfolded within her being, for she knew, in that instant, that her mission for the salvation of her people would succeed. The Lord had lifted her up as a scepter of faith and deliverance. At that moment, something whispered in her soul, "What is noble and right, what is brought forth by courage and honor, what is according to the eternal design of the Lord—that is what comes to pass in this life and in the eternities."

Esther caused the extermination decree to be reversed by the king, who ordered Haman hanged on the very gallows erected for hanging Mordecai. Mordecai was subsequently elevated into Haman's position at court, second only to Ahasuerus. The outcome was a blessing from heaven to be celebrated for generations to come: "The Jews had light, and gladness, and joy, and honour" (Esther 8:16).

Pondering: How can we follow the noble example of Esther by strengthening our faith and our resolve to lift and bless the lives of our loved ones and all those whom we are called to serve?

AGENDA FOR ACTION

In humility, we can join the circle of the Lord's righteous sons and daughters and fulfill our mortal mission to help build His kingdom. In humility, we can help the Lord preserve and deliver our loved ones as they embrace the gospel and move forward on the pathway toward their heavenly home. We can dedicate our lives for the cause of Zion—despite the perils and challenges that might arise—knowing that "in the strength of the Lord [we can] do all things" (Alma 20:4). We can, in humility, become examples of those who act in faith and hope, receiving with joy the protecting hand of the Deliverer. Let us aspire to focus our attention each day on how we can stand in courage as witnesses for the truth of the restored gospel—no matter what scorn, denigration, or evil threats might descend from adversaries and mockers. Let us conduct our lives with a firm conviction that "the truth abideth forever and ever" (D&C 1:39), and that we can likewise maintain our service to God "forever and ever" as His loyal and trusting sons and daughters.

LOOKING FORWARD: How are you part of the prophecy about the stone
cut from the mountain without hands that will fill the whole earth?

CHAPTER FORTY-SIX

THE STONE OF THE RESTORATION

GOSPEL DOCTRINE READING ASSIGNMENT: DANIEL 2

*And in the days of these kings shall the God of heaven set up a kingdom, which shall
never be destroyed: . . . and it shall stand for ever.* (Daniel 2:44)

THE GOSPEL WILL ROLL FORTH

DANIEL WAS GIFTED BY THE Lord with "understanding in all visions and dreams" (Daniel 1:17). He therefore spoke unto the dreamer Nebuchadnezzar a grand prophecy about a stone that was "cut out of the mountain without hands" (Daniel 2:45) to roll forth over all the worldly kingdoms until it "became a great mountain, and filled the whole earth" (Daniel 2:35). These words are some of the greatest in the Old Testament, for they symbolize in a striking and tangible way the coming forth of the kingdom of God across the generations of time to encompass the whole world in the latter days in preparation for the Second Coming of Christ.

What is the stone? Isaiah stated it well: "Therefore thus saith the Lord GOD, Behold, I lay in Zion for a foundation a stone, a tried stone, a precious corner stone, a sure foundation: he that believeth shall not make haste" (Isaiah 28:16). The stone is Jesus Christ, who said to His detractors, "Did ye never read in the scriptures, The stone which the builders rejected, the same is become the head of the corner [Psalm 118:22]: this is the Lord's doing, and it is marvellous in our eyes" (Matthew 21:42; see also Mark 12:10; Luke 20:17; Acts 4:11; Ephesians 2:20; 1 Peter 2:6–7).

Is was also marvelous in the eyes of young Daniel, for he was given a vision of how the work of the Lord would be accomplished despite the barriers and blockades set up by worldly kingdoms motivated by pride and greed.

Nebuchadnezzar had been given a taste of that truth in a dream that he had somehow forgotten—"The thing is gone from me" (Daniel 2:5). When his wise men and magicians could not recover the dream and give its interpretation, the king was determined to destroy them all. But Daniel knew how to proceed. He gathered his three peers together to seek the "mercies of the God of heaven concerning this secret" (Daniel 2:18). The Lord then blessed them:

> Then was the secret revealed unto Daniel in a night vision. Then Daniel blessed the God of heaven.
> Daniel answered and said, Blessed be the name of God for ever and ever: for wisdom and might are his:
> And he changeth the times and the seasons: he removeth kings, and setteth up kings: he giveth wisdom unto the wise, and knowledge to them that know understanding:
> He revealeth the deep and secret things: he knoweth what is in the darkness, and the light dwelleth with him.
> I thank thee, and praise thee, O thou God of my fathers, who hast given me wisdom and might, and hast made known unto me now what we desired of thee: for thou hast now made known unto us the king's matter. (Daniel 2:19–23)

How did the downfall of Nebuchadnezzar come about?

Despite the counsel of Daniel concerning his dream about the stone that became a great mountain, Nebuchadnezzar still refused to relinquish his idolatry. Then a second dream came to the king, depicting him as a great and mighty tree that was hewn down at the behest of "an holy one coming down from heaven" (Daniel 4:23). Daniel interpreted that dream as a foreshadowing of the king's impending demise and counseled him to "break off thy sins in righteousness, and thine iniquities by shewing mercy to the poor; if it may be a lengthening of thy tranquility" (4:27). But it was not to be: "The same hour was the thing fulfilled upon Nebuchadnezzar: and he was driven from men" (4:33). From his deposed perspective, it was an easy thing for the king, stripped now of his opulence, to confess: "I blessed the most High, and I praised and honoured him that liveth forever, whose dominion is an everlasting dominion, and his kingdom is from generation to generation: . . . and those that walk in pride he is able to abase" (4:34, 37).

The royal reveler Belshazzar, prince-regent in the wake of Nebuchadnezzar's reign, did not fare much better. Daniel interpreted the ominous writing on the wall of the prince-regent's chamber this way: "Thou art weighed in the balances, and art found wanting" (Daniel 5:27). That night Belshazzar was deposed by Darius the Mede, who elevated Daniel as a leader in the kingdom. Thus continued the unfolding of the prophesied fall of a succession of earthly kingdoms, one after the other until, ultimately, the Lord would restore a heavenly kingdom to the earth not made by the hand of man. The gold, silver, brass, and iron/clay of Nebuchadnezzar's dream could be interpreted, in turn, as the Assyrio-Babylonian monarchy, the Medo-Persian empire, the Greco-Macedonian kingdom, and the power of Rome (see the words of B. H. Roberts in the introduction to *HC* 1:xxxv). But the eternal celestial glory envisioned by Daniel and all of the Lord's prophets is the ultimate glory of the everlasting kingdom of the Father and the Son, which has been restored in the latter days.

Daniel then revealed unto Nebuchadnezzar the nature of his forgotten dream: "Thou, O king, sawest, and behold a great image. This great image, whose brightness was excellent, stood before thee; and the form thereof was terrible. This image's head was of fine gold, his breast and his arms of silver, his belly and his thighs of brass, His legs of iron, his feet part of iron and part of clay" (Daniel 2:31–33). Daniel then identified Nebuchadnezzar as the head of gold in the image, the mightiest in a sequence of great kings of the world in the midst of whom the great stone would roll forth: "And in the days of these kings shall the God of heaven set up a kingdom, which shall never be destroyed: and the kingdom shall not be left to other people, but it shall break in pieces and consume all these kingdoms, and it shall stand for ever" (Daniel 2:44). Nebuchadnezzar was delighted by Daniel's words, saying: "Of a truth it is, that your God is a God of gods, and a Lord of kings, and a revealer of secrets, seeing thou couldest reveal this secret" (Daniel 2:47). The king then promoted Daniel to be "ruler over the whole province of Babylon, and chief of the governors over all the wise men of Babylon" (Daniel 2:48)—and also approved Daniel's request to have his three Jewish companions elevated to positions of authority.

What Nebuchadnezzar did not grasp until later was that his dream predicted his certain downfall, for the kingdom of God would prevail over all the kingdoms of the earth until it filled the world as a great mountain.

A TOUCH OF REALITY

How does the dream about the stone cut from the mountain without hands factor into our lives today? In a revelation given through Joseph Smith, at Hiram, Ohio, October 1831, the Lord renewed the promise uttered by Daniel:

> HEARKEN, and lo, a voice as of one sent down from on high, who is mighty and powerful, whose going forth is unto the ends of the earth, yea, whose voice is unto men—Prepare ye the way of the Lord, make his paths straight.
>
> The keys of the kingdom of God are committed unto man on the earth, and from thence shall the gospel roll forth unto the ends of the earth, as the stone which is cut out of the mountain without hands shall roll forth, until it has filled the whole earth. (D&C 65:1–2)

The Restoration in our day opened the channels of priesthood power so that the gospel stone could roll forth in preparation for the ultimate return of the divine stone of glory, Jesus Christ. What is our covenant duty to help prepare the way?

> Pray unto the Lord, call upon his holy name, make known his wonderful works among the people. Call upon the Lord, that his kingdom may go forth upon the earth, that the inhabitants thereof may receive it, and be prepared for the days to come, in the which the Son of Man shall come down in heaven, clothed in the brightness of his glory, to meet the kingdom of God which is set up on the earth. (D&C 65:4–5; see also 2 Nephi 31:20–21)

In a news story released on June 25, 2007, President Gordon B. Hinckley was quoted as having declaring at the Provo MTC that, by reliable estimate, a million missionaries have served since the organization of the Church. Over a million missionaries sent forth from the Church organized on April 6, 1830, by a team of only six officials, including the Prophet Joseph Smith. The name Joseph means "increasing." The name of his wife Emma means "universal." That simple concept of "universal increase" expresses the essence of the rolling forth of the stone cut out of the mount without hands to fill the whole earth in the latter days. In keeping with the Lord's design, missionary work is expanding throughout the world.

The announcement given by President Thomas S. Monson at the October 2012 general conference concerning the lowering of the ages for missionary callings gave an electric boost to the global advancement of missionary work. More and more Saints are being gathered to Zion to worship in the growing expanse of stakes and temples of the Church throughout the world. We can all participate in this glorious work of the Restoration with greater devotion.

WHAT LESSON CAN WE LEARN FROM DANIEL?

1. Stone upon stone, we can help lay the foundation of the restored kingdom of God and help prepare the way for the Second Coming.

The book of Daniel confirms by prophetic pronouncements that the Lord is in charge of the destiny of humankind and that righteousness will ultimately prevail. Through obedience to the commandments of God, the faithful will receive magnificent blessings of wisdom and light and will inherit a place in the triumphant kingdom of the Lord, which will roll forth until it fills the entire world. Daniel is a prominent example of "apocalyptic" writing (from the Greek word meaning "revealed" or "uncovered"), as in the Apocalypse or Revelation of John, where similar great and symbolic visions of the ultimate consummation of God's work are presented. We can today follow the revelations given through chosen prophets, just as we can seek personal revelation to guide us in joining the hosts of the Lord engaged in building His kingdom in the last days.

Every time we partake of the sacrament to renew our sacred covenants, we can savor the promise of a future sacrament meeting where the Lord will join with us and His chosen prophets, from Adam to the present, in a glorious celebration of the victories won. To Joseph Smith, the Lord said, "Behold, this is wisdom in me; wherefore, marvel not, for the hour cometh that I will drink of the fruit of the vine with you on the earth, . . . And also with all those whom my Father hath given me out of the world" (D&C 27:5, 14). Daniel also perceived that such a conference would be convened at the time of the Second Coming:

> I saw in the night visions, and, behold, one like the Son of man came with the clouds of heaven, and came to the Ancient of days, and they brought him near before him.
>
> And there was given him dominion, and glory, and a kingdom, that all people, nations, and languages, should serve him: his dominion is an everlasting dominion, which shall not pass away, and his kingdom that which shall not be destroyed. . . .
>
> But the saints of the most High shall take the kingdom, and possess the kingdom for ever, even for ever and ever. (Daniel 7:13–14, 18)

In small ways, day by day, we can prepare for such a glorious blessing. How is it that small can become vast, and simple can become universal? Consider the following true account by a missionary of the Church:

> To experience the magnificent Church Conference Center north of Temple Square in Salt Lake City is to gain an inkling of the destiny of the stone cut out of the mountain without hands, rolling forth to fill the entire world. With translation capability for as many as 60 languages at a time, the 21,000-seat, 1.5 million-square-foot facility (about 40 times the size of the Tabernacle) has a worldwide reach that makes it truly a global enterprise in the service of spreading eternal truths.
>
> As I ponder this imposing edifice, my mind returns to a small garden house in a remote European city where my missionary companion and I once conducted Church services and taught the gospel. The garden house was really a tool shed perhaps six by ten feet in size with a small door and a few tiny windows. It was nestled in a beautiful orchard located behind the home of the only member-family in the city.
>
> Because the owner was also the proprietor of a small neighborhood grocery store, she was concerned that her business would suffer should it become known by her intolerant neighbors that she was hosting Church services in her home. Therefore, she suggested that we use the garden house for meetings on Sundays. Everyone came up through the back of the property from different directions through the trees in order to escape detection. And that's what we did. My companion and I would teach the gospel in the garden house to a handful of investigators (typically two or three), who would crowd into this humble facility to learn true principles. I recall one session where it rained so hard that the noise on the roof made it difficult to present the lesson on the Spirit. But the Spirit nevertheless touched our hearts in that lowly setting. Testimonies were cultivated. Lives were changed. It was all part of the motion of that stone cut from the mountain without hands. It was all part of the process by which the influence of restored truths was being felt once again—even by small and humble means in remote parts of the world.
>
> When the Prophet Joseph Smith conducted that historic meeting on April 6, 1830, at the Peter Whitmer farm house in Fayette, New York, at which the kingdom of God was once more organized on the earth, he very likely saw in his mind's eye the prophetic view of the divine destiny of that kingdom—and how a small stone "became a great mountain, and filled the whole earth" (Daniel 2:35). The Great Architect knows the final design: "Wherefore, be not weary in well-doing, for ye are laying the foundation of a great work. And out of small things proceedeth that which is great" (D&C 64:33).

Pondering: How can we faithfully contribute a little more each day to help expand the kingdom of God on the earth and bring joy and salvation to more of God's children?

AGENDA FOR ACTION

We can do the will of the Father according to the covenants and promises given to us through the gospel of Jesus Christ. Christ is the grand stone of the gospel, the chief cornerstone of our foundation of salvation and exaltation. May we follow Him in humble obedience and thus, with our families, harvest joy and eternal life.

These noble aspirations can be realized through regular acts of service. What can you do this week to lay another stone on the brickwork of the kingdom of God? Perhaps it is within your own "temple" of personal character that the foundation of righteousness can be strengthened and as you don the "armour of God" (Ephesians 6:13; see also D&C 27:15). Perhaps you can contribute to the forward motion of the stone cut from the mountain without hands by writing letters of encouragement to missionaries, arranging for missionary referrals, or contributing more generously to the missionary funds of the ward and the Church. Perhaps you can do more to encourage members of your family to think of their challenges and tribulations as part of the pathway of becoming joint-heirs with Christ, "the head stone of the corner" (Psalm 118:22). Through all such contributions, you can add to the momentum of Zion's growth as it becomes "a great mountain, and [fills] the whole earth" (Daniel 2:35; see also D&C 65:2).

Looking Forward: How can we personally help "build" temples in our day?

CHAPTER FORTY-SEVEN

GATHER TOGETHER IN JOY

GOSPEL DOCTRINE READING ASSIGNMENT: EZRA 1–8; NEHEMIAH 1–2, 4, 6, 8

And they said, Let us rise up and build. So they strengthened their hands for this good work. (Nehemiah 2:18)

THE LORD IS YOUR STRENGTH

THE BOOKS OF EZRA AND Nehemiah (originally one book in the Hebrew canon) cover a dramatic milestone in the history of Israel—the return of the Jewish people from seventy years of Babylonian captivity (see Jeremiah 25:12; 29:10) and the rebuilding of a devastated city and temple. The principles reflected in these writings are repentance and reform, recovery and rebuilding, rejoicing and reunion. The account celebrates the loving kindness of the Lord in remembering His covenant people as they transcend the adversities and challenges of life and return to His pathways with faith and joy. The individuals who play starring roles in this unfolding drama of courage and devotion include the following:

- *Cyrus the Great of Persia*—who issued his decree in 537 B.C. allowing the captive Jewish people to return to Jerusalem and rebuild the temple.
- *Zerubbabel* (meaning "born in Babylon")—grandson of King Jehoiachin of Judah and the one appointed governor over Judaea by the Persian authorities to oversee the return of the first wave of Jewish captives and the rebuilding of the temple (finished in 515 B.C.); Zerubbabel was also called by the Persian name "Sheshbazzar, prince of Judah."
- *Ezra* (meaning "help")—a noted priest and scribe who accompanied the second wave of the liberated Jewish people around 458 B.C. for resettlement in Jerusalem.

- *Nehemiah* (meaning "consolation of the Lord")—Jewish official appointed in 444 B.C. as governor over Judaea to help rebuild the walls of Jerusalem and continue instituting reforms among the people.
- *Sequence of Persian kings after Cyrus*—leaders who supported the return of the Jewish people to Judaea and the rebuilding of Jerusalem and its temple: Darius I, Xerxes I, and Artaxerxes I.

A TOUCH OF REALITY

How do the words of Ezra, Nehemiah, and their associates whisper to us today with truths that we can apply to our daily lives? Like these leaders of old, we too are engaged in the process of gathering souls, renewing covenants, and helping build up Zion through the blessings of the Lord. As you read the following choice selections, see how they might apply to your life in guiding your loved ones so that they might "gather together, and stand in holy places" (D&C 101:22):

- *Worship the Lord through song.* "And they sang together by course in praising and giving thanks unto the LORD; because he is good, for his mercy endureth for ever toward Israel. And all the people shouted with a great shout, when they praised the LORD, because the foundation of the house of the LORD was laid" (Ezra 3:11).
- *Follow the words of the living prophets in order to build Zion.* "And the elders of the Jews builded, and they prospered through the prophesying of Haggai the prophet and Zechariah the son of Iddo. And they builded, and finished it, according to the commandment of the God of Israel, . . . for the LORD had made them joyful, and turned the heart of the king of Assyria unto them, to strengthen their hands in the work of the house of God, the God of Israel" (Ezra 6:14, 22).
- *Prepare ourselves to teach the gospel by word and deed.* "For Ezra had prepared his heart to seek the law of the LORD, and to do it, and to teach in Israel statutes and judgments" (Ezra 7:10).
- *Discern the grace and mercy of the Lord.* "And now for a little space grace hath been shewed from the LORD our God, to leave us a remnant to escape, and to give us a nail in his holy place, that our God may lighten our eyes, and give us a little reviving in our bondage. For we were bondmen; yet our God hath not forsaken us in our bondage, but hath extended mercy unto us in the sight of the kings of Persia, to give us a reviving, to set up the house of our God, and to repair the desolations thereof, and to give us a wall in Judah and in Jerusalem" (Ezra 9:8–9).
- *Inspire others to rise up in strength to build Zion.* "Then I [Nehemiah] told them of the hand of my God which was good upon me; as also the king's words that he had spoken unto me. And they said, Let us rise up and build. So they strengthened their hands for this good work" (Nehemiah 2:18).
- *Spread the word of the Lord with joy and inspiration.* "And Ezra opened the book [law of Moses] in the sight of all the people; (for he was above all the people;) and when he opened it, all the people stood up: And Ezra blessed the LORD, the great God. And all the people answered, Amen, Amen, with lifting up their hands: and they bowed their heads, and worshipped the LORD with their faces to the ground. . . . So they [the priests] read in the book in the law of God distinctly, and gave the sense, and caused them to understand the reading. And Nehemiah, which is the Tirshatha [Persian administrative title for a governor], and Ezra the priest the scribe, and the Levites that taught the people, said unto all the people, This day is holy unto the LORD your God; mourn not, nor weep. . . . neither be ye sorry; for the joy of the LORD is your strength" (Nehemiah 8:5–6, 8–10).
- *Give continual thanks to our loving God.* "But thou art a God ready to pardon, gracious and merciful, slow to anger, and of great kindness" (Nehemiah 9:17; see the entire chapter for a panorama of such divine qualities).

WHAT LESSON CAN WE LEARN FROM THE BOOKS OF EZRA AND NEHEMIAH?

1. Through the strength of the Lord we can help build up Zion and advance the work of the holy temples.

The rebuilding of the temple in Jerusalem was a major undertaking—one that did not proceed without daunting threats and challenges from the enemies of Zion, including the Samaritans living nearby. The Samaritans were descendants of colonists placed in the mountainous region of Palestine by the Assyrian conquerors who scattered the Israelites of the Northern Kingdom of Israel around 721 B.C. These descendants desired to assist in the rebuilding of

What are the important historical dates in the accounts of Ezra and Nehemiah?

The following are approximate dates:

- *Reigns of the Persian kings*: Cyrus the Great (559–530 B.C.), Darius 1 (522–486 B.C.), Xerxes I and his wife Esther (486–465 B.C.), Artaxerxes I (465–424 B.C.)
- *Milestones in the return from Babylonian captivity*: edict of Cyrus the Great (537 B.C.); return of the first wave of Jewish captives (starting in 537 B.C.); temple completed (515 B.C.), return of the second wave of Jewish captives accompanied by Ezra (458 B.C.); ministry of Ezra (458–440 B.C.); Nehemiah appointed governor over Judaea (444 B.C.); ministry of Nehemiah as governor (444–432 B.C.); Nehemiah returns to Jerusalem for a second visit (432 B.C.)

the temple at Jerusalem—a privilege denied them by the Jewish leaders who feared the influence of their cultural practices. Said Zerubbabel and his chiefs, "Ye have nothing to do with us to build an house unto our God; but we ourselves together will build unto the LORD God of Israel, as king Cyrus the king of Persia hath commanded us" (Ezra 4:3). The Samaritans raised objections before the Persian authorities and threatened violence against their returning neighbors: "Then the people of the land weakened the hands of the people of Judah, and troubled them in building" (Ezra 4:4). However, upon appeal from the Jewish leaders, the Persian authorities confirmed the edict of Cyrus and authorized the construction of the temple to go forward (see Ezra 6:1–12). The temple was completed in 515 B.C. "And the children of Israel, the priests, and the Levites, and the rest of the children of the captivity, kept the dedication of this house of God with joy" (Ezra 6:16).

But the troubles were not over. When Ezra and his company of the second wave joined the expatriates in Jerusalem, he found that many of the men had intermarried with non-Israelite women from nearby communities (see Ezra 2:61–62). This was a covenant-breaking practice that needed to be corrected through repentance so that the names of the faithful would be recorded in "the book of the law" (D&C 85:11–12, a reference to Ezra) and thus return to the pathway of the Lord (see Ezra 9–10). Furthermore, when Nehemiah set about to rebuild the walls of Jerusalem, the Samaritans threatened to attack and destroy the workers. But Nehemiah was firm in his resolve: "And I looked, and rose up, and said unto the nobles, and to the rulers, and to the rest of the people, Be not ye afraid of them: remember the Lord, which is great and terrible, and fight for your brethren, your sons, and your daughters, your wives, and your houses" (Nehemiah 4:14; compare the words of Captain Moroni concerning the title of liberty—Alma 46:12–13). What happened then was unforgettable:

> And it came to pass from that time forth, that the half of my servants wrought in the work, and the other half of them held both the spears, the shields, and the bows, and the habergeons; and the rulers were behind all the house of Judah.
>
> They which builded on the wall, and they that bare burdens, with those that laded, every one with one of his hands wrought in the work, and with the other hand held a weapon.
>
> For the builders, every one had his sword girded by his side, and so builded. And he that sounded the trumpet was by me.
>
> And I said unto the nobles, and to the rulers, and to the rest of the people, The work is great and large, and we are separated upon the wall, one far from another.
>
> In what place therefore ye hear the sound of the trumpet, resort ye thither unto us: our God shall fight for us. (Nehemiah 4:16–20)

Thus, the walls of the city were finally completed and the enemies retreated into the shadows, "for they perceived that this work was wrought of our God" (Nehemiah 6:16).

In like manner, the work of the Lord in the latter days continues unabated. Missionary work advances at ever higher levels of progress. More new temples dot the earth each year. How can we use the same spirit of resolve and industry shown by our forebears—Zerubbabel, Ezra, Nehemiah, and many others—to assist in building the "walls" of Zion and erecting the "temples" of the Lord all around us?

The story of Nehemiah's leadership is a reminder of an incident from Church history that occurred on Wednesday, January 8, 1834, in Kirtland, Ohio. On that day, guards were placed to protect the Kirtland temple as a result of persecution by detractors and the threat of violence at the hands of the gathering mob. Some workmen were seen with a hammer in one hand and a rifle in the other. Joseph Smith recorded in his journal: "On the morning of the 8th of January, about 1 o'clock, the inhabitants of Kirtland were alarmed by the firing of about thirteen rounds of cannon, by the mob, on the hill about half a mile northwest of the village" (*HC* 2:2). However, with the coming of dawn, it was determined that the temple was not damaged. Of this period, Heber C. Kimball wrote in the *Times and Seasons*: "And we had to guard ourselves night after night, and for weeks were not permitted to take off our clothes, and were obliged to lay with our fire locks [rifles] in our arms" (*HC* 2:2; footnote).

> **What was the nature of the rebuilt temple?**
>
> Scholar Sydney B. Sperry reports, "The plan of Solomon's temple was followed in general, but due to the poverty of the people, not on such a lavish scale. Many of the vessels used in the former temple were restored (see Ezra 1:7–11). The Holy of Holies was empty, for the ark of the covenant disappeared when Nebuchadnezzar's forces invaded Palestine. This temple, called after Zerubbabel, and sometimes known as the Second Temple, was completed in the sixth year of Darius, 515 B.C. (see Ezra 3:8; Ezra 6:15)." ("Ancient Temples and Their Functions," *Ensign*, Jan. 1972, 67)

Do we ponder often enough upon the sacrifices and trials of our forebears—including our ancient brothers and sisters in Old Testament times—and upon their vigilance and endurance in securing for us the blessings that we enjoy so abundantly today? Are we prepared to stand up for righteous principles and guard the things of God with our lives as they did?

In the days of Nehemiah, as in the days of the Kirtland Saints, the righteous were constrained to carry on their labors with a tool in one hand and a weapon in the other. And so it is today—and at all times during the mortal journey. The prudent and wise never venture forth in their pursuits without first protecting themselves with divine armor. As Paul stated it, "Wherefore take unto you the whole armour of God, that ye may be able to withstand in the evil day, and having done all, to stand" (Ephesians 6:13; see also verses 14–18). In our own day, the Lord has repeated that counsel (see D&C 27:15–18). When we venture into the world to complete our labors, we wisely leave no part of our being exposed to worldly onslaughts and temptations but instead fight our battles like the stripling warriors, "as if with the strength of God" (Alma 56:56). We can all don the whole armor of God and triumph over every assault against the cause of Zion. We can apply with wisdom the gifts of productivity with which the Lord has blessed us, and we can thwart all enemies—including our own weaknesses and fears—by putting into operation the weapons of victory from heaven: truth, faith, hope, courage, unity, and revelation through the Holy Spirit. With a tool in one hand and a weapon in the other, we can become "fellowcitizens with the saints, and of the household of God" (Ephesians 2:19). Then, as Nehemiah said, "The God of heaven, he will prosper us; therefore we his servants will arise and build" (Nehemiah 2:20).

Pondering: How can we apply our tools of service more effectively and deploy our spiritual armor more victoriously in order to advance the cause of Zion with greater progress each day? How do we guide our loved ones to do the same? How can we use the scriptures as a spiritual compass to guide our forward motion through this mortal experience?

AGENDA FOR ACTION

We can listen faithfully to the Spirit of the Lord as it guides us in the ongoing work of building—building families of joy, building temples, building a Zion society, building the kingdom of God. When we work in faithful obedience to secure the well-being of our families and our communities, the Lord will fight our battles for us by opening new windows of opportunity and softening the hearts of those with influence over us (as he did in the case of the ancient kings). We can fast and pray for guidance in passing through the shadows of adversity. We can "build" temples through our tithes, family history work, and ongoing attendance in the house of the Lord. Like the Saints at the time of Ezra and Nehemiah, we can don the whole armor of God and take comfort in the hope of Israel: "For the joy of the Lord is your strength" (Nehemiah 8:10).

As you ponder this wide-ranging agenda of enduring service—characterized by the Doctrine and Covenants as "a godly walk and conversation" (D&C 20:69)—what specific actions of charitable leadership come into your mind that you can implement without delay? Who among your loved ones needs extra help and encouragement? How can you magnify your callings in the Church with great commitment? How can you pray with greater humility and openness to the promptings of the Spirit?

LOOKING FORWARD: How can we become fully prepared for the Second Coming?

Even the lesser-known portions of the Old Testament can provide uplifting passages to light up our personal lives and strengthen our testimonies. A report from a home teacher confirms this truth:

We completed our monthly lesson and asked the members of the family if they had additional comments. A light went on in the eyes of the wife and mother. She spoke up with enthusiasm about being a participant in a study group of neighborhood women who were teaching one another more about the Old Testament. She was inspired to learn in a recent session about how a certain chapter in the book of Nehemiah was an amazing source of truth concerning the nature of the Lord and His many divine qualities. "It is chapter 9," she said eagerly, going on then to mention some of the many aspects of the divine nature given in that chapter. She bore witness to those words with such inspiration that I took the time the next day to return to that chapter of Nehemiah and study more intently the flow of words concerning how the Lord blessed the lives of the ancient Israelites.

There I found a sublime panorama of the qualities of the divine nature, including the following:
- "But thou art a God ready to pardon, gracious and merciful, slow to anger, and of great kindness, and forsookest them not" (9:17).
- "Thou gavest also thy good spirit to instruct them, and withheldest not thy manna from their mouth, and gavest them water for their thirst" (9:20).
- "And in the time of their trouble, when they cried unto thee, thou heardest them from heaven; and according to thy manifold mercies thou gavest them saviours, who saved them out of the hand of their enemies" (9:27).
- "For thou art a gracious and merciful God" (9:31), "And because of all this we make a sure covenant, and write it" (9:38).

The words of that chapter in Nehemiah were uplifting and encouraging. But it was the sincere witness of the good sister concerning those passages that taught a memorable lesson about how the word of God enriches lives and ennobles His children in righteousness. Would we not all benefit by following her example—and that of many other devoted Saints of Zion—as we write and share our own book of remembrance concerning our life's journey toward our eternal home?

CHAPTER FORTY-EIGHT

PREPARING FOR THE COMING OF THE LORD

GOSPEL DOCTRINE READING ASSIGNMENT: ZECHARIAH 10–14; MALACHI

But who may abide the day of his coming? and who shall stand when he appeareth? . . .
And he shall purify the sons of Levi, and purge them as gold and silver, that they may
offer unto the LORD an offering in righteousness. (Malachi 3:2–3)

LIFTED BY THE WORDS OF THE PROPHETS

PROPHESYING IN THE MID–EIGHTH CENTURY B.C., the prophet Amos declared, "Surely the Lord GOD will do nothing, but he revealeth his secret unto his servants the prophets" (Amos 3:7). Both Zechariah and Malachi continued with this divine pattern of communication by giving unto us in glorious language the secrets of how to prepare for the coming of the Lord. Zechariah spoke of the travails and future redemption of the covenant peoples of God against the backdrop of the Savior in the meridian of time and His ultimate appearance in glory at the dawning of the millennial era. Malachi closes the Old Testament canon by entreating the priests and all their followers to set their houses in order, submit themselves to the refining process of covenant obedience, and look forward to the grand unifying blessings of heavenly glory in the last days.

Zechariah (meaning "God has remembered") gives us precious prophecies about the Messiah: His triumphal entry into Jerusalem during His earthly ministry (see Zechariah 9:9; Matthew 21:1–11); His betrayal for the price of "thirty pieces of silver" (Zechariah 11:12; see also Matthew 26:15); and His atoning sacrifice that would be recognized by His slayers at the time of the Second Coming: "And one shall say unto him, What are these wounds in thine hands? Then he shall answer, Those with which I was wounded in the house of my friends" (Zechariah 13:6; see also D&C 45:51–53). Zechariah concludes his sayings with a prophecy about the Second Coming: that the Lord will fight for the beleaguered Israel and prevail in a final victory over evil: "And the LORD shall be king over all the earth: in that day shall there be one LORD, and his name one" (Zechariah 14:9).

Malachi (meaning "my messenger") gave the people of his day—and ours—a broad spectrum of reminders: that we should honor God (see Malachi 1:5–6), bring a "pure offering" before Him in righteousness (Malachi 1:11; see also Malachi 3:3), give glory to Him (see Malachi 2:2), walk with Him "in peace and equity" (Malachi 2:6), remain faithful within the covenant bonds of marriage (see Malachi 2:11), care for the poor and needy (see Malachi 3:5), return unto God in righteousness (see Malachi 3:7), pay our tithes (see Malachi 3:10), fear God and always keep Him in our thoughts (see Malachi 3:16), avoid pride (see Malachi 4:1), and—through the sealing power of the priesthood to be restored by Elijah—enjoy oneness of heart within family relationships over the generations (see Malachi 4:5–6; see also D&C 2; 110:14–16). Such a pattern of obedience will result in grand blessings: "And all nations shall call you blessed: for ye shall be a delightsome land, saith the LORD of hosts" (Malachi 3:12).

A TOUCH OF REALITY

We are not told in the scriptures about the family of Malachi, the last of the Old Testament prophets. However, like the other prophets of the Lord, he was most likely blessed with a loving wife and children. The scriptures are rich in the accounts of loving parental guidance as demonstrated in the lives of Adam and Eve, Noah and his family, Abraham and Sarah, Isaac and Rebekah, Jacob and Rachel, Lehi and Sariah, as well as King Benjamin, Alma, Mormon, and many others. Let us suppose that on one spring morning Malachi was accompanying two of his children—let's call them Joshua and Rachel—for a walk near the reconstructed temple in Jerusalem to teach them about the mercies and grace of the Lord.

Let us imagine how this dialogue might have unfolded—using quotes from the holy scriptures. Perhaps a creative scene of this kind might encourage parents and teachers to develop new ways to teach young people the principles of the gospel—much in the spirit of the Church's new innovative program for youth learning, "Come, Follow Me."

The sun had just risen over the eastern horizon, and the rays of light were stroking the stately walls of the temple like fingers from heaven. Malachi slowed and paused, his arms tenderly around two of his children, one on each side. They all felt the warmth of the morning sun pushing away the coolness hovering over the landscape. "What are your feelings when you look over at the temple?" Malachi asked.

After a moment, Rachel replied softly, "It's beautiful. It's tall."

Joshua added, "It makes me thankful. It's a gift from God."

Their father smiled. "You're both right. It has been here for not yet a hundred years. We can thank the Lord for giving us back this beautiful temple with the help of our leaders who returned from captivity in Babylon."

Just then a dove rustled upwards from a nearby olive tree and flew toward the temple grounds. The three watched the bird disappear into the distance. "That reminds me of the words of Isaiah," said Malachi. "But they that wait upon the LORD shall renew their strength; they shall mount up with wings as eagles; they shall run, and not be weary; and they shall walk, and not faint" (Isaiah 40:31).

"Father, that wasn't an eagle," said Rachel with a hint of teasing in her voice.

Malachi smiled and gave her a squeeze. "You are right, dear daughter. But we can start with a dove and go from there. We go forward one step at a time, 'line upon line; here a little, and there a little' (Isaiah 28:10). You have an eagle waiting inside you to fly upwards and rise higher and higher."

"Higher than the temple?" she asked.

"Yes, Rachel. Higher than the temple—as high as heaven, where the Father and Son live."

"When will the Son come to us?" she asked.

The father motioned to his children to join him in sitting down along a rocky ridge softened by patches of grass swaying in the morning breeze. "Over there, near the temple, is where the Lord will visit during His earthly ministry—only a few generations in the future. Do you remember when our governor Nehemiah returned to Jerusalem for the second time?"

"Yes," responded Joshua. "Everyone was lined up along the streets to greet him. We were there too with Mother and our younger brothers and sisters."

Rachel joined in with enthusiasm, "And we were all singing and cheering."

"It was a joy," agreed Malachi. "Many years ago the prophet Zechariah prophesied about the coming of the Lord to Jerusalem. He said: 'Rejoice greatly, O daughter of Zion; shout, O daughter of Jerusalem: behold, thy King cometh unto thee: he is just, and having salvation; lowly, and riding upon . . . a colt'" (Zechariah 9:9).

"The people will be so happy when the Lord comes," said Rachel.

"Yes," replied her father. "But the priests and other leaders will be jealous of Him. They will sell him, as Zechariah prophesied, for a price of 'thirty pieces of silver' (Zechariah 11:12). He will give His life for us and take it up once again that we might all have life after death, and, through our obedience to His commandments, return again to be with Him and our Father in Heaven some day."

"Would not Father in Heaven protect Him from that suffering?" asked Rachel.

Her father turned to her and looked upon her beautiful countenance, saying, "Isaiah explained why the Father would allow this to happen: 'He hath put him [the Son] to grief: when thou shalt make his soul an offering for sin, he shall see his seed, he shall prolong his days' (Isaiah 53:10). Rachel, when you accept the suffering of the Son in faith, He will receive you as His daughter and your life will be eternal. The same blessing awaits all of us as the sons and daughters of the Lord. That's what the Father wants, and that's what the Son has accomplished through His suffering. Zechariah spoke of the good news that lies ahead for our people: 'Sing and rejoice, O daughter of Zion: for, lo, I come, and I will dwell in the midst of thee, saith the Lord' (Zechariah 2:10)."

For a moment, all three remained silent and kept their gaze focused on the temple, now fully bathed in the spreading light of the sun. Then Joshua spoke up. "Father, have you seen in vision the same things that Zechariah saw?"

> **When did Zechariah and Malachi prophesy?**
>
> Zechariah prophesied around 520 B.C., shortly after the first wave of the Jewish people had returned from Babylonian captivity under authority of the liberating edict of Cyrus the Great in 537 B.C. (See Ezra 5:1—"THEN the prophets, Haggai the prophet, and Zechariah the son of Iddo, prophesied unto the Jews that were in Judah and Jerusalem in the name of the God of Israel, even unto them"; see also Ezra 6:14). The temple was rebuilt during the ministry of Zechariah and was completed around 515 B.C.
>
> Malachi prophesied almost a century later, perhaps around 432–430 B.C., concurrent with the second visit to Jerusalem by Nehemiah, governor of Judaea, in 432 B.C. Zechariah thus prophesied during the reign of the Persian king Darius 1 (522–486 B.C.), and Malachi during the reign of the Persian king Artaxerxes I (465–424 B.C.). The Greek philosopher Plato was born shortly after the time when Malachi prophesied.

The father took his son's hand in his and opened it up by extending the fingers. "See this hand," said Malachi. "Like this hand, the Lord extends His hand out to all of us to know the truth. When the prophets receive the word of the Lord, just as I have done, it is their joy to pass this word along to His people. Remember the words of Isaiah that we speak about so often? He said, 'For unto us a child is born, unto us a son is given: and the government shall be upon his shoulder: and his name shall be called Wonderful, Counsellor, The mighty God, The everlasting Father, The Prince of Peace' (Isaiah 9:6)."

They pondered that for a moment before Malachi continued. "The Lord has shown me in vision how the way will be prepared for His ministry among the people. Here is what I heard and saw, what I have declared to the people in this land: 'Behold, I will send my messenger, and he shall prepare the way before me: and the Lord, whom ye seek, shall suddenly come to his temple, even the messenger of the covenant, whom ye delight in: behold, he shall come, saith the Lord of hosts' (Malachi 3:1; also Matthew 11:10–11; 3 Nephi 24:1)."

"Who's the messenger?" asked Joshua.

His father smiled and replied, "It will be a special individual anointed for that calling—one who will grow up at the same time the Lord will grow up near Jerusalem, one who will prepare the way for people to listen to the Lord. His name will be John, and he will also be the Lord's messenger again in the last days."

At that moment, a sheepherder passed below them on the hill, guiding a small flock of sheep after him. "See that shepherd?" began Malachi. "The Lord guides us in the same way. He calls us by name, and we recognize His voice. We follow Him like these lambs so that we can find food and drink. Are you getting hungry this morning?" The children nodded. "Well, let us stand up and start back toward our home. I can see that the workers are coming to continue the task of maintaining the temple."

"I wonder how they're supported in their work," said Joshua.

"That's a good question," replied his father. "They are supported from the tithes and offerings of the people. That's why the Lord needs our help in building His kingdom. We are blessed when we give. That is why I spoke before the people about tithing recently. Not all are participating as they should."

Joshua spoke up as if a light had turned on within him. "Is that why you said, 'Will a man rob God' (Malachi 3:8)?"

Malachi nodded: "Yes, the words of the Lord came to me. 'Bring ye all the tithes into the storehouse, that there may be meat in mine house, and prove me now herewith, saith the Lord of hosts, if I will not open you the windows of heaven, and pour you out a blessing, that there shall not be room enough to receive it' (Malachi 3:10). When we joyfully give a tenth part of our increase, then the Lord blesses us with the fruits of the earth and with grand opportunities to build up His kingdom so that it can reach out to all parts of the earth."

"The whole world?" asked Joshua as the three of them walked briskly along the pathway. "When will that happen?"

"The final return of the Lord will come in a day when there are troubling signs given. Zechariah warned of a day when the enemies of Israel would rise up against the Lord's people to destroy them. He said, 'Behold, the day of the Lord cometh, and thy spoil shall be divided in the midst of thee. For I will gather all nations against Jerusalem to battle' (Zechariah 14:1–2)."

"Oh, that makes me shiver!" exclaimed Rachel.

"Do not fear, daughter," said her father, "for the Lord will fight our battles for us. He said, 'Behold, I will save my people . . . and they shall be my people, and I will be their God, in truth and in righteousness' (Zechariah 8:7–8)." Pointing toward the Mount of Olives, Malachi continued, "Zechariah reported what the Lord would do at that very spot in the last days: 'Then shall the Lord go forth, and fight against those nations, . . . And his feet shall stand in that day upon the mount of Olives, which is before Jerusalem on the east, and the mount of Olives shall cleave in the midst thereof toward the east and toward the west, and there shall be a very great valley; and half of the mountain shall remove toward the north, and half of it toward the south. And ye shall flee to the valley of the mountains; . . . And the Lord shall be king over all the earth: in that day shall there be one Lord, and his name one' (Zechariah 14:3–5, 9). How does that make you feel?"

"The Lord as King," said Rachel. "I like that. I am looking forward to that time."

Malachi replied, "Just like your brother and your mother, you are a humble follower of the Lord. You know His name, and He knows your name. You will be safe—just like all the righteous."

Rachel smiled and put her arm around her older brother. "We're going to make it," she said.

"Yes," said Joshua. "We'll make it."

"We will all make it," agreed their father. "For we are blessed of the Lord to follow humbly in His footsteps and avoid evil. It's just as I was inspired to prophesy: the proud and wicked "shall be stubble. . . . But unto you that fear my name shall the Sun of righteousness arise with healing in his wings' (Malachi 4:1–2). My dear children, when we saw the dove earlier this morning, we spoke about mounting up on wings. The Lord gives us that opportunity, for He has healing in His wings, and we can follow Him."

"Will our family be together in heaven?" asked Rachel.

"Yes," said her father, "for that is the Lord's plan. He will have our hearts blended together forever. It is as He commanded me to proclaim in recent days: 'Behold, I will send you Elijah the prophet before the coming of the great and dreadful day of the Lord: And he shall turn the heart of the fathers to the children, and the heart of the children to their fathers, lest I come and smite the earth with a curse' (Malachi 4:5–6)."

"When will Elijah come?" asked Joshua.

His father replied, "Both at the time of the Lord's work upon the earth, as well as again in the latter days when the gospel is restored in preparation for the return of the Lord in glory. I have seen that day in my visions, and I know that it will come."

As the three continued along the pathway leading down into their neighborhood, they saw several figures waving in the distance. Soon they could see clearly who was approaching them on the pathway ahead. It was Malachi's wife and the other children of the family. When the two groups met, they embraced one another with joy. They sensed deeply the truth of the gospel plan: families are to be united; families are to stay together on the pathway of truth; families are the sons and daughters of God, meant to be together for the eternities through the power of the gospel of salvation.

WHAT LESSON CAN WE LEARN FROM ZECHARIAH AND MALACHI?

1. We can all follow the Spirit in getting our houses in order as we prepare for the Second Coming.

Through His infinite sacrifice, the Lord achieved victory over death for all mortals and salvation and exaltation for the faithful (see 3 Nephi 15:24; D&C 27:14; 50:41–42; 84:63). A grand focus of our preparation for the Second Coming of the Lord centers in our willingness to follow His example of sacrifice. We bring unto Him a sacrifice of a "broken heart and a contrite spirit" (3 Nephi 9:20; D&C 59:8). We sacrifice our time and gifts in the service of our loved ones and our fellow Saints. And, as Malachi stressed, we remember to pay our tithes, for which sacrifice the Lord has promised to open "the windows of heaven, and pour you out a blessing, that there shall not be room enough to receive it" (Malachi 3:10). That promise is certainly reflected in the following story:

> There have been so many opportunities in the Church for my wife and me to interact with people having remarkably saintly dispositions. While we were living in the eastern part of the country a number of years ago, we invited a young woman over to our home one day to talk about the gospel. She had been referred to us by a previous stake president as one having considerable interest in learning more about the Church. My journal entry of this experience gives the details:

> "If anyone was a converted person, she was. She spent several hours with us, and toward the end of her stay she asked whether it was not so that Mormons paid tithing. I said yes, and asked what her understanding of that might be. She replied that it was her understanding that this meant one-third of one's income. Somewhat surprised, I asked her whether she would be willing to pay this much to the Lord. 'Certainly,' was her response, and she had the most sincere and warm spirit about her. I then explained what the law of tithing meant—paying 'one-tenth of [our] interest annually' (D&C 119:4)—and complimented her on her humble devotion and generous willingness to do whatever the Lord asked of her."

This young woman soon joined the Church and rendered much service in the spirit of humility and obedience. She was blessed by the Lord, who opened the "windows of heaven" (Malachi 3:10) and poured out upon her a great spiritual harvest. To this day my wife and I remain impressed with her angelic faith and acceptance of the will of the Lord. She so well exemplified the principle taught by the Lord: "Verily I say unto you, all among them who know their hearts are honest, and are broken, and their spirits contrite, and are willing to observe their covenants by sacrifice—yea, every sacrifice which I, the Lord, shall command—they are accepted of me" (D&C 97:8).

What are the words of Joseph Smith about preparing for the Second Coming?

"When I contemplate the rapidity with which the great and glorious day of the coming of the Son of Man advances, when He shall come to receive His Saints unto Himself, where they shall dwell in His presence, and be crowned with glory and immortality; when I consider that soon the heavens are to be shaken, and the earth tremble and reel to and fro; and that the heavens are to be unfolded as a scroll when it is rolled up; and that every mountain and island are to flee away, I cry out in my heart, What manner of persons ought we to be in all holy conversation and godliness!" (*HC* 1:442)

Pondering: How can we weigh our thoughts and actions with authentic faith by committing to do a little better each day to prepare ourselves more fully for the coming of the Lord? How can we bless the lives of our loved ones by helping them to do the same?

AGENDA FOR ACTION

Let us all prepare for the Second Coming by doing what the Lord asks of us. The following is an alphabetical checklist of recommended actions based on the scriptures that refer specifically to the Second Coming. You may wish to select one or two items each week as reminders of how to do better in living the gospel of Jesus Christ:

- Abound in love toward all (1 Thessalonians 3:12–13).
- Be cheerful and fear not, for the Lord is with you (D&C 68:6).
- Be diligent, without spot, and blameless, steadfast and growing in grace and the knowledge of the Lord (2 Peter 3:9–18—a statement by Peter on how to prepare for the Second Coming).
- Be faithful, just, and wise (D&C 51:19–20).
- Be not troubled (Matthew 24:6; JS—Matthew 1:23; see also D&C 45:35).
- Be pure and free of sin (D&C 88:86).
- Be steadfast and not deceived; look forward to the day; repent; pray (D&C 49:23–28).
- Be wise and watchful, having your lamp trimmed and full of oil (Matthew 25:1–13; see also D&C 45:56–57).
- Be wise, receive the truth, and take the Holy Spirit for your guide (D&C 45:56–57).
- Believe in the Lord and cry repentance to the world through the power of the Holy Ghost (D&C 34:4–12).
- Care for the life of the soul and seek the face of the Lord in patience (D&C 101:36–38).
- Covenant with the Lord through sacrifice (Psalm 50:3–6).
- Disassociate from those who abide in wickedness (1 Corinthians 5:4–13).
- Exercise the gifts bestowed by Christ (1 Corinthians 1:4–8).
- Fear the name of the Lord; be righteous; keep the commandments (Malachi 4:1–4; see also 3 Nephi 25:1–4).
- Gather to Zion and then preach the gospel unto the world (D&C 133:8–19).
- Gather together and seek the Lord in meekness and righteousness (Zephaniah 2:1–3).
- Gather together with the Saints and stand in holy places (D&C 101:16–24).
- Gird up your loins, i.e., prepare with faith and courage (D&C 36:8; 75:19–22; 106:4–5; Moses 7:62; see also D&C 27:15; 38:9; 43:19; 61:38).
- Know Christ now (John 4:25–26).
- Prove all things and hold fast to the good (1 Thessalonians 5:21–23).
- Receive the truth and take the Holy Spirit as your guide (D&C 45:56–57).
- Rejoice, be pure, and do temple work (D&C 128:23–25; see also D&C 2; 110:14–16).
- Repent and go forth while receiving the guidance of the Lord (D&C 49:26–28).
- Sanctify yourself and receive an endowment of power; call on the nations to repent; be sober and keep all the commandments (D&C 43:16–35—a statement by the Lord on how to prepare).
- Seek good and not evil (Amos 5:14–20).
- Stand in holy places and be not moved (D&C 45:32; 87:8).
- Take the scriptures as your guide and follow the Spirit, praying in faith, and having your lamp trimmed and burning, with a supply of oil with you (D&C 33:16–18).
- Treasure up the word of the Lord and be not deceived (JS—Matthew 1:37).
- Turn to the Lord with all your heart; gather together and let the ministers of the Lord pray for you; receive the Spirit; call upon the Lord (Joel 2:12–13, 15–18, 28–32—one of the classic summaries of how to prepare; see also Acts 2:17–21, quoting Joel 2:28–32).
- Warn your neighbor and remain clean (D&C 88:81–86).

- Watch and be sober, cultivating qualities of faith, love, hope of salvation, peace, support for others, joy, prayer, and following the Spirit (1 Thessalonians 5:1–23—Paul's checklist of qualities to cultivate; see also Luke 21:34–36).

> Looking Forward: What will be your feelings when the hour of the Second Coming finally arrives? How can you ensure that you will be welcomed at that hour among the Lord's elect sons and daughters to sing anthems of comfort and joy?

EPILOGUE

THE ETERNAL COVENANT

ASSIGNMENT: YOUR OWN CONTINUING PERSONAL AND FAMILY JOURNAL

And he humbled thee, . . . that he might make thee know that man doth not live by bread only, but by every word that proceedeth out of the mouth of the LORD doth man live. (Deuteronomy 8:3)

THE FIRST TESTAMENT

WE HAVE CONSIDERED A VARIETY of new and easy ways to learn from the Old Testament. Paul referred to the doctrinal basis of the Old Testament as the "first testament" (Hebrews 9:15, 18). Indeed, the Old Testament constitutes the beginning statement of gospel truths that are eternal, never ending. The New Testament and the testaments of modern revelation (the Book of Mormon, the Doctrine and Covenants, the Pearl of Great Price, and the words of living prophets) constitute the ongoing and unfolding guide for understanding and applying the eternal truths of the gospel in our lives.

The word *testament* means "covenant." The power of the gospel derives from the Atonement of Jesus Christ— according to the covenant terms of His own "will and testament" from the Father. Because of this sublime act, all mortals will have life after death (immortality), and the faithful and righteous will inherit eternal life and exaltation by honoring their covenant vows.

How do we honor our covenant vows? By living "by every word that proceedeth out of the mouth of the LORD" (Deuteronomy 8:3; see also Matthew 4:4; D&C 84:44). Our spiritual feast is made up of the full array of stories and admonitions included in the gospel canon—beginning with the "first testament" and continuing onward through an endless stream of truth flowing from heaven to sustain and nurture our progress. All of that constitutes the eternal covenant of God with His children.

A TOUCH OF REALITY

There are four standard works in the grand spiritual feast of truth. But there is also a fifth standard work—the life of each individual with the word of God written upon his or her heart. That word blossoms forth as a tree of everlasting life for the blessing of self, family, and community. In the present volume, we have provided many real-life illustrations about how the word of God changes lives. We have also included a variety of creative scenes about how Old Testament personalities and their modern counterparts might have thought, reasoned, and acted in accordance with the truths of the gospel laid before them. Why have we used this approach? So that you as a reader might continue to ponder and organize your own personal stories and illustrations that confirm the everlasting truths of the gospel of Jesus Christ.

The fifth standard work is one's own inspired journal—recorded for the blessing of loved ones and any seekers after truth who welcome encouragement along the way. How does this fifth standard work take root and emerge as a vibrant, living entity? It does so when those nourished by the sacred canon come upon ideas and truths that ignite spiritual energy and inspire them to share their witness of hope and cheer with others seeking the eternal blessings of the gospel of redemption and atonement.

We all have our favorites among the writings of the prophets. Rejoice over the following passages, and see how these might open up for you the gates of inspiration to stimulate the ongoing unfolding of your own fifth standard work as a testament of truth and as a commitment to fulfill your covenant duties:

- "For behold, this is my work and my glory—to bring to pass the immortality and eternal life of man" (Moses 1:39).
- "And in thy seed after thee . . . shall all the families of the earth be blessed, even with the blessings of the Gospel, which are the blessings of salvation, even of life eternal" (Abraham 2:11).
- "Choose you this day whom ye will serve; . . . but as for me and my house, we will serve the Lord" (Joshua 24:15).
- "Entreat me not to leave thee, or to return from following after thee: for whither thou goest, I will go; and where thou lodgest, I will lodge: thy people shall be my people, and thy God my God" (Ruth 1:16).
- "For I know that my redeemer liveth, and that he shall stand at the latter day upon the earth" (Job 19:25).
- "Who shall ascend into the hill of the Lord? or who shall stand in his holy place? He that hath clean hands, and a pure heart" (Psalm 24:3–4).
- "And it shall come to pass in the last days, that the mountain of the Lord's house shall be established in the top of the mountains, and shall be exalted above the hills; and all nations shall flow unto it" (Isaiah 2:2).
- "For unto us a child is born, unto us a son is given: and the government shall be upon his shoulder: and his name shall be called Wonderful, Counsellor, The mighty God, The everlasting Father, The Prince of Peace" (Isaiah 9:6).
- "But this shall be the covenant that I will make with the house of Israel; After those days, saith the Lord, I will put my law in their inward parts, and write it in their hearts; and will be their God, and they shall be my people" (Jeremiah 31:33).

> **What did Brigham Young say about the nature of God's word to us in the sacred canon?**
>
> "On reading carefully the Old and New Testaments we can discover that the majority of the revelations given to mankind anciently were in regard to their daily duties; we follow in the same path. The revelations contained in the Bible and the Book of Mormon are examples to us, and the book of Doctrine and Covenants contains direct revelation to this Church; they are a guide to us, and we do not wish to do them away; we do not want them to become obsolete and to set them aside. We wish to continue in the revelations of the Lord Jesus Christ day by day, and to have his Spirit with us continually. If we can do this, we shall no more walk in darkness but we shall walk in the light of life" (*Discourses of Brigham Young* [Salt Lake City: Deseret Book, 1971], 12).

- "Surely the Lord God will do nothing, but he revealeth his secret unto his servants the prophets" (Amos 3:7).
- "He hath shewed thee, O man, what is good; and what doth the Lord require of thee, but to do justly, and to love mercy, and to walk humbly with thy God?" (Micah 6:8).
- "Behold, I will send you Elijah the prophet before the coming of the great and dreadful day of the Lord: And he shall turn the heart of the fathers to the children, and the heart of the children to their fathers, lest I come and smite the earth with a curse" (Malachi 4:5–6).

Perhaps one or more of the passages just quoted might serve as a means to help you "mount up with wings as eagles" (Isaiah 40:31) and be a more expressive messenger of truth eternal, using your own experiences and wisdom in guiding others. Very likely there are many other special passages in the Old Testament that inspire you to fulfill your covenant obligations with added courage and with an increase of faith and hope.

Let us all be grateful for the Old Testament as the first installment of covenant truth eternal given by the Lord unto His sons and daughters for strength, encouragement, and guidance on the pathway of life. May we all continue to act in faith, applying the counsel given in the father's blessing referred to in the introduction to this book: "And now my beloved son as you journey forth into the uncertain world, reach up your hands to the lap of God. And if you will do this He will lead you, He will guide you, save and exalt you in the eternal worlds."

INDEX

ABOUT THE AUTHOR

RICHARD J. ALLEN IS A husband, father, grandfather, teacher, and writer. He has served on several high councils, in several stake presidencies, and as a bishop. Richard's teaching assignments in the Church have included service as a full-time missionary, instructor in various priesthood quorums, and Gospel Doctrine teacher for adults and youth. He and his wife Carol Lynn have served together as stake institute instructors and stake missionary preparation instructors. Richard has a PhD from The Johns Hopkins University, where he served on the faculty and in the senior administration for a number of years. He was also a faculty member at Brigham Young University. He has served on a number of national educational boards and has authored and coauthored many articles, manuals, and books—including over thirty books with Covenant Communications. He and his wife have four children and five grandchildren.